Acclaim for *Overcoming Autism*

"An excellent guide that comes at a much needed time. There are few clinical resources out there for autism and PDD spectrum children and their families. *Overcoming Autism* fills this gap and provides solid information and a practical head start toward understanding children's needs and managing their behavior effectively and to productive ends. I will be recommending it to student, colleagues, and parents."

> —Bruce J.Masek, Ph.D., ABPP, Clinical Director, Child and Adolescent
> Psychiatry at Massachusetts General Hospital and associate professor
> of psychology at Harvard Medical School

"I just finished reading your book. I honestly believe it is the best and most practical book I have ever read in the area of autism. The content has great technical and scientific integrity, yet it is presented in friendly language in a straightforward, common sense kind of manner. I will be promoting the book in every talk and workshop I give in the coming months and years."

> —Glen Dunlap, Ph.D., Executive Director, Center for Autism and
> Related Disabilities, University of South Florida

"*Overcoming Autism* is brilliant. It is written in a very different voice from anything else in the field, and is accessible in a way that we all wish our research could be. This is a real contribution, and you are to be commended. You have blended solid research, impressive writing, and a credible vision for families."

> —Rob Horner, Ph.D., professor of special education, University of Oregon

"BRAVO! This book will be wonderful for our families. Thanks for a valuable contribution!"   —Joyce Mauk, M.D., developmental pediatrician

"As a parent of a child with autism, I can certainly relate to Lynn and Claire's statement that 'everything you do will make a difference.' I found their book *Overcoming Autism* to be an invaluable guide to many of those 'everythings.'"

> —Joe Mantegna, actor

PENGUIN BOOKS

OVERCOMING AUTISM

LYNN KERN KOEGEL is one of the world's foremost experts on the treatment of autism. She and her husband founded the renowned Koegel Autism Center at the Graduate School of Education at the University of California, Santa Barbara, where she is currently the clinical director. She holds a Ph.D. in educational psychology and an M.A. in speech and hearing sciences. She lectures frequently at universities, conferences, and school and parent organizations. She has won numerous awards for her work on behalf of children with autism, including the first annual Sesame Street Award for "Brightening the Lives of Children" and the Autism Speaks Award for Excellence in Science. She has also appeared on numerous television shows, including *Supernanny*, where she worked with a child with autism, and on the Discovery Channel series *Ingenious Minds*, discussing the strengths of individuals with autism.

CLAIRE LAZEBNIK has written five novels for adults, including *Same As It Never Was* (which was made into the ABC Family movie *Hello Sister, Goodbye Life*), *The Smart One and the Pretty One*, and *Families and Other Nonreturnable Gifts*. Her young adult novels include *Epic Fail* and *The Trouble with Flirting*. She has contributed to *GQ, Self Magazine*, the *New York Times*, and the *Wall Street Journal*, among other publications, and to the anthology play *Motherhood Out Loud*. A graduate of Harvard University, she lives with her TV writer husband and four children in Pacific Palisades, California.

OVERCOMING
AUTISM

Finding the Answers, Strategies, and Hope
That Can Transform a Child's Life

Revised Edition

LYNN KERN KOEGEL, Ph.D.,
and
CLAIRE LaZEBNIK

PENGUIN BOOKS

PENGUIN BOOKS
Published by the Penguin Group
Penguin Group (USA) LLC
375 Hudson Street
New York, New York 10014

USA | Canada | UK | Ireland | Australia | New Zealand | India | South Africa | China
penguin.com
A Penguin Random House Company

First published in the United States of America by Viking Penguin, a member of
Penguin Group (USA) Inc. 2004
Published in Penguin Books 2005
This revised edition published 2014

LIBRARY OF CONGRESS CATALOGING-IN-PUBLICATION DATA
Koegel, Lynn Kern.
    Overcoming autism : finding the answers, strategies, and hope that can transform a child's life / Lynn Kern Koegel, Ph.D., and Claire LaZebnik.—Revised edition.
        pages cm
    Includes index.
    ISBN 978-0-14-312654-6
    1. Autism in children.   2. Child rearing.   3. Autistic children—Care.   4. Parents of autistic children.   I. LaZebnik, Claire Scovell.   II. Title.
    RJ506.A9K636 2014
    618.92'85882—dc23
    2013046676

Printed in the United States of America
10 9 8 7 6 5 4 3 2 1

Set in Horley Old Style
Designed by Spring Hoteling

For Andrew, who brought our families together,
and who tackles every challenge with courage,
good humor, and enthusiasm

CONTENTS

FOREWORD
TEN YEARS LATER

BACK in 2003, the two of us—clinician Lynn Kern Koegel, Ph.D., and author Claire LaZebnik—decided to join forces and write a book that would combine an autism expert's extensive knowledge of research-based interventions with a parent's firsthand experiences.

Since its publication, we've both received countless e-mails from people literally around the world, telling us that the accessible, well-researched advice in our book has taught, trained, reassured, and inspired them.

The interventions in these pages are still as valid as they were ten years ago: time has only tested and proven their worth, and recent research only confirmed that a thoughtful, individualized behavioral approach is the best way to help children with autism. The interventions we recommend and describe in this book are just as useful and valid today as they were when the book was first published.

So Why Come Out with a New, Updated Edition?

Dr. Koegel and her husband, Dr. Robert Koegel, have continued to do groundbreaking research at their clinic in Santa Barbara, California, and each new study has added to the information and knowledge that they've been gathering steadily for decades. This newer research builds upon what's already in the book, elucidating some areas, adding more detail to others, and strengthening the advice overall.

We also wanted a chance to incorporate and reflect the changing national dialogue about autism: over the last decade there's been an enormous shift in the way both professionals and nonprofessionals think about and approach people on the autism spectrum.

Research has shown that, for both professionals and family members, focusing on the strengths of individuals with autism leads to clearer goals, greater success, and reduced stress, so we've added sections explaining how parents can capitalize on their children's skills and talents and how professionals can discuss their clients' programs and progress in positive ways that encourage and energize their families.

In recent years, the autism advocacy movement has grown and gained attention, changing the national dialogue with its insistence that our goal not be a negative one (eliminating autism) but rather a positive one: creating the best possible future for children and adults who live with symptoms of autism spectrum disorder, both by supporting them and by educating our society on how to understand and celebrate differences and unconventional strengths.

We feel strongly that the unique perspectives of individuals on the autism spectrum add to any conversation; some of our most original thinkers are and have been on the spectrum. Our message has always been upbeat and supportive, but in this revision, we would like to acknowledge the strides made by autism advocates in recent years and to encourage our readers to celebrate the strengths, talents, and ideas of our children on the spectrum.

We also want to make it clear that our society needs to be supportive of families with children who have special needs. We all lose when a child is shunned for being different or his parents condemned for including him in their activities. We would like to see communities draw together in supporting all their members, not just those who fit into someone's preset and narrow idea of acceptability.

Finally, the general public's awareness of autism has increased dramatically in recent years, and families who are dealing with it firsthand have far more access to information than they once did. Back when we wrote the first edition of this book, we felt we needed to keep things as basic and explanatory as possible. While clarity is still the goal, we feel we can now include more sophisticated discussions of the options available to families and their therapists and more detailed explanations of both what Pivotal Response Treatment means and why sticking to evidence-based interventions is important.

Ten Years Later

The last decade has changed us both in personal and professional ways that have also had an impact on this revision.

The clinic that Drs. Lynn and Robert Koegel have run for decades at the University of California, Santa Barbara, has now officially been renamed the

Koegel Autism Center. The Koegels and their associates and students continue to be at the forefront of behavioral research and treatment in this country.

On a more personal note, Lynn's nephew was diagnosed with autism in recent years, so her involvement and interest are now deeply personal as well as professional, and she brings the added insight of seeing things from both perspectives to this new edition.

Claire's son Andrew—who was just entering sixth grade when we finished writing the original edition of *Overcoming Autism*—is now a (gulp) twenty-one-year-old college junior. The stories that she first told in this book are starting to feel like ancient history, and as she looks back, she has a clearer sense of how many of the choices her family made were right—and also a need to think deeply about the few she now questions.

We're Here to Tell the Tale

We're old pioneers at this point. Together, we have over fifty years of involvement in the autism world, and we've seen a lot of movements come and go. Don't get us started on the miracle cures that weren't or the celebrity rants that hurt more than they helped. We'll just say that it's extremely gratifying to be able to stand here, ten years after we published *Overcoming Autism*, and tell you that time and research have backed up everything we recommended in that first edition, that what was right before is just as right now, and that we've pinpointed some areas to improve what was already pretty good before.

ACKNOWLEDGMENTS

WE would both like to thank our first editor, Janet Goldstein, whose intelligent and insightful notes helped enormously to shape and refine this book, and Emily Murdock Baker, who allowed us to breathe new life into it. We owe its existence to Kim Witherspoon and Alexis Hurley. Our husbands, Robert Koegel and Rob LaZebnik, were valiant and helpful readers, as were Colin Summers, Lee Kern, Becky Mode, and Jeff Wood. Finally, we would like to thank Catherine Johnson and Ed Berenson, who have done so much for children with autism, and who introduced us many years ago.

LYNN'S ACKNOWLEDGMENTS

For Bob—my husband, partner, coworker, and a brilliant researcher—my biggest critic and biggest supporter. Thanks for bringing me into the world of autism and teaching me that with a lot of blood, sweat, and tears (and good experimental design) we can make a difference for children with autism and their families. I remember when we first met at Camarillo State Mental Hospital, and I expressed an interest in volunteering. He said, "You don't want to volunteer here. It's depressing. I only have a lab here to try and wipe this place out!" Well, now it has been torn down, and in its place is a state college!

I also would like to express my appreciation to my daughters, Ashley Kern Koegel, M.D., and Brittany Lynn Koegel, Ph.D., who have let me share their personal stories of their childhood—some that were flattering and some that were not so flattering—for the altruistic purpose of helping others. They have both dedicated their lives to helping children and their families, and for that I am truly grateful. They have both worked so hard to get where they are today and their discipline, perseverance, and commitment to helping improve the physical, emotional, and behavioral health of children is what makes the world a better place—and at the end of the day making others' lives better is what it's all about. I am the luckiest mom to have them.

This book would not have been possible without the efforts of our graduate students and clinicians who helped work with the children whose examples are presented in the book and who are, quite simply, the best.

I would also like to express my sincere gratitude to the children and their families described in this book, whose names and identifying characteristics have been altered to preserve their privacy. The kids have had to work overtime, as have their parents, and are greatly appreciated for their efforts. You parents deserve the Parent of the Year Award, and you kids deserve the Child of the Year Award. There is no parallel for this dedicated and hardworking group of individuals.

Next, I express my sincere appreciation to the researchers around the country with whom I have had the pleasure of interacting, who have dedicated their lives to finding answers, through science, to improve the quality of life for individuals with disabilities and their families, and who have helped shape my own research. In addition to being great friends, the Broad family, Nori Brown, the Douglas family, Scott Hedrick, Mer James, the Kellys, Lou Vismara, the Openden family, Norm Waitt, the Towbes family, and Margaret Baker have been so supportive of our work. I'm sincerely indebted. They've made such a difference. Also, I am so fortunate to have such a wonderful family that has always been a source of support and encouragement over the years—Mom, Sam, Dad, Rita, Lexi, Ron, Jack, Lee, Scott, Tyler, Mia, Alex, Monica, Tina, Dar, and Alexa Lin. I am so fortunate to have all of them for relatives.

The clinical examples and procedures described in this book are based in part upon research funded by the U.S. Public Health Service, the National Institute of Mental Health, the U.S. Department of Education, the California State Department of Developmental Disabilities, the Department of Rehabilitation, and the University of California, Santa Barbara, Graduate School of Education's Koegel Autism Center's Gift account. Thank you to all you parents and others who have donated.

And most important, Claire. Every minute I work with her is a blast. Her enthusiasm, intelligence, complete honesty, and great personality make writing seem like a vacation.

Thanks for being who you are, Claire, and making Andrew who he is. You have a super amazing family!

A MOTHER'S ACKNOWLEDGMENTS

You meet a better class of people when your kid is diagnosed with special needs.

In addition to being an absolutely brilliant clinician, Lynn Koegel has been the most generous, gracious, and insightful writing partner anyone could ask for, and I'm honored that she invited me to join her on this project. I'm grateful to her for the experience, which has been unqualifiedly wonderful, and even more grateful to her for the enormous role she played in helping my son blossom into a fine young man. When we decided to do this update of *Overcoming Autism*, I was delighted, not just because it was a worthwhile project, but because it meant I'd get to see Lynn more often—we live in separate cities, and I miss her when we're not constantly e-mailing back and forth! Her husband, Bob, has been a crucial adviser to and proponent of this book over the years. I feel very lucky to have them both in our lives.

Lynn was one of a team of extraordinary people who worked with Andrew over the years and helped to transform him from a silent, withdrawn toddler into a social, kind, and interesting young man. I can't ever thank any of these people enough—how do you sufficiently thank someone for rescuing your child?—but my gratitude, affection, and admiration go to Dawn Davenport, Wayne Tashjian, B. J. Freeman, Pete Candela, Sandra Arntzen, Roberta Fields Poster, Christine Stanton, Cynthia Ferber, Allison Zevallos, and Suzy Getty. I'm also grateful to my brother, Ted Scovell, for teaching me to demand scientific proof and not believe everything I read. Everything I've learned about autism over the past two decades has reinforced the lesson he taught me, that a real scientist doing valid work *welcomes* peer review and allows the research to guide his conclusions and not the other way around.

I'm so grateful to my wonderful friends, who meet me for lunch, coffee, and walks, and who patiently remind me over and over again to trust in my kids and not inflict my anxieties on them. I'm not going to list names here, because I'm terrified of leaving someone out, and because they already know who they are and (I hope) how much I love them.

My biggest thanks go to my family for letting me place them and our lives under a microscope. I've chosen not to use my children's real names, not because I feel there's anything shameful about these anecdotes but because the choice should be theirs to claim these stories as their own.

Every triumph that my kids have known is because of Rob, the most loving, supportive, active, and involved father in the world. He never stops fighting for them and taking care of us all.

INTRODUCTION

QUESTION: My son was just diagnosed with autism. The developmental specialist gave me a list of therapists, but I don't know where to start. I'm overwhelmed and deeply depressed. What if I make the wrong decisions and my son doesn't get better? What kind of future does he have?

QUESTION: We've been struggling to understand what's wrong with our son. In many ways his development has been normal, but he doesn't play the way other kids do, and there's definitely something different about him. Nothing is adding up. Now we're hearing the term "autism spectrum disorder" and don't know what to make of it. What do we do with this diagnosis? Where do we go from here?

THERE are few things in life scarier than having a child diagnosed with any kind of special need, and autism is one of the scariest disabilities, because the diagnosis tells you nothing about a child's prognosis. No one can honestly say to you, "We know exactly what your child will be like when he's twenty."

People will, however, feel free to comment on the diagnosis in every way, most of them unhelpful. You'll hear things like "They're crazy, he's just a late talker," "My cousin's brother's kid had autism, and they changed his diet and he was cured," and "How sad—he'll probably never go to college." You'll start reading articles and combing the Internet for helpful information, and you'll find that there are a lot of conflicting opinions out there—some people swear by certain approaches, others by completely different ones, and some even believe a kid with autism should just be left alone, since "he'll be whatever he's going to be, and nothing you do will make any difference."

Now, that's where they're wrong. So wrong it's mind-boggling. Everything you do will make a difference.

There's a lot you can do for your child, more than you may be aware of right now. That's why we wrote this book—to show you how intelligent, well-planned early interventions based on years of field research *can* improve the symptoms of autism enormously, often to the point where many or all of the symptoms might be said to have been "overcome." Some children with autism become indistinguishable from their peers.

Does that sound miraculous to you? It's not. There are no miracles. It would be nice if a nonverbal kid suddenly started talking in sentences, if a self-injurious girl suddenly decided she preferred playing the piano to hitting herself in the head, if a withdrawn boy suddenly realized that it's fun to play with other kids. But none of that's simply going to happen. Well, not *suddenly*, anyway.

The good news, though, is that if you remove "suddenly" from the previous paragraph, it's a completely different story, because we have seen all these things happen. They just didn't happen *suddenly* or out of the blue—they were the result of hard work, a well-planned schedule of interventions, and a consistency of approach stretching from the family to the school to all therapies and clinical work.

It Takes Hard Work

There are no miracle cures in autism, just a lot of blood, sweat, and tears. As of yet, there are no pills, shots, diets, or any other "quick fixes" that cure autism completely and across the board. To date, there are no medications that can make broad and widespread improvements in children with autism. Further, many medications can have serious and harmful long-term effects on young children. However, there *are* well-researched, time-proven procedures that can make a difference—excellent behavioral interventions that allow families and professionals systematically to reduce or eliminate each undesirable symptom and improve each area of need.

Your child has a huge job, too, and some big challenges ahead of her. Unfortunately, the goals may not be as clear to her as they are to you: she's always known life the way it is and may not be eager to change things. It's not like she was talking and socializing and then suddenly "lost" all that and now is highly motivated to work hard to get back those missed skills. No, talking and communicating will feel like hard, unnecessary work at first, and your child will most likely resort to behaviors that have worked in the past to get her what she wanted, like crying and tantrums. This will, of course, be tremendously frustrating to both of you: you want to get past the tantrums and your child wants the tantrums to work like they used to. You're at cross-purposes, united only in your frustration.

Right now it may seem like the only thing your child is motivated to do is to get out of having to use communication, but if you follow our suggestions, your child *will* learn how much more efficient and effective it is to use social communication. It won't happen instantly, and it will be a lot of work for both of you—but it will happen, and it will change your lives.

So, now back to you. . . . We know it's tough right now. If your child was just diagnosed, you might need some time to get used to the idea. (See chapter 1, "Diagnosis.") Take a few days. Cry, moan, scream, bitch, blame your spouse's family—do whatever you need to for a little while. A very little while. Then roll up your sleeves and get to work. Your child needs you to help her get better.

HOW TO USE THIS BOOK

We wrote this book because we wanted to get the message across that with the right interventions, you can improve a child's prognosis enormously.

In these pages, we offer both a general understanding of how to tackle the symptoms of autism in someone you know and a description of the specific interventions you'll need to do so. It's a starting point and a way of unifying your approach across the board. It is *not* a replacement for finding talented and dedicated clinicians and therapists in your area to aid you in your journey, but we *will* offer advice on how to find those professionals if you're a parent, or how to better serve your patients if you're already in the field.

Separating Out Symptoms

If you glance through the table of contents, you'll see that by and large we've organized the book by symptoms—the various ways that the disability of autism tends to make itself known. You may be used to child-rearing advice books that are organized by the child's age or by his temperament, and that offer a wide range of advice that may or may not be applicable to your child at that point in time. Ours is different.

We chose to focus on one symptom at a time for a very simple reason: every child with autism is different and needs a different intervention plan. This plan needs to be based on that specific child's needs and the symptoms being exhibited, *not* on some general idea of how a kid with autism behaves.

There can't be one intervention plan for all children with autism, because autism is just a name for a cluster of symptoms that can (but don't always) include repetitive motions, aggression, a lack of speech development, and an inability to interact socially. By taking each symptom your child expresses and systematically addressing it with a comprehensive intervention plan (which we'll show you how to do), you will see gradual, steady improvement in your child or client.

Our approach has grown out of years of research and positive outcomes and is based on what's known as "behavior interventions" or "applied behavior analysis"—in other words, if a child is exhibiting problematic behaviors, we can intervene, decreasing the negative behaviors by introducing and reinforcing positive behaviors to take their place.

We'll also help you put it all together through Pivotal Response Treatment (PRT). PRT focuses on finding and teaching key target areas that are "pivotal" in terms of creating widespread improvements. We're in a race against time: your child needs to catch up to his peers, and we don't have the luxury of working with him on each and every individual behavior; that's why we focus on these pivotal ones. You'll find specifics in chapter 10 on the pivotal behaviors that research has shown bring about the kind of improvement across the board that we're all hoping to see.

Remember, just a few short decades ago, children with autism were given up as hopeless cases, incapable of learning, and often stuck in institutions for the rest of their lives. Now we know not only that these kids can learn, but also that the brain's ability to lay down new neural pathways is astounding. It's important to be aware of this history, because there are still people out there who believe children with autism cannot be taught, that their futures are written at birth. These people are clinging to archaic beliefs that have long been proven inaccurate, so don't allow anyone to discourage you from teaching your child.

Different Levels, Different Needs

We're aware that children with autism fall in very different places along the spectrum of the disability. Because our approach is geared toward an individual child's needs, it's appropriate for use with children of all different levels and skills. It's not one-size-fits-all, but instead allows you to tailor any and all information to the child you're concerned about. The single diagnosis of autism, or autism spectrum disorder, can cover a very wide range of strengths and weaknesses.

When you first read this book, you may choose to focus on the behaviors that are most problematic in your child. Does he hum and flap his arms? You'll definitely want to read the chapter on self-stimulatory behaviors. Is she aggressive toward other children? Take notes on chapter 3, "Tears, Meltdowns, Aggression, and Self-Injury." Not talking even though he's over three? Chapter 2,

"Ending the Long Silence," covers our approach to teaching verbal skills. And so on. If you find that one of these topics is not a problem area for your child, you might want to read the chapter about it anyway, but focus first on the areas that are causing the most stress to your family and the most difficulties for your child. Ironically, we address these challenging areas by drawing on the child's strengths.

These "focused interventions"—that is, interventions that focus on areas that are causing difficulties for your child—are not a replacement for a multi-component plan that helps your child learn to communicate, socialize, and behave well in mainstream, everyday settings. You still need to be sure that your child's comprehensive needs are being met with systematic, effective, and caring interventions, but the focused interventions will help you address specific areas in an efficient way, so that you see the most change in the least amount of time, and these changes can help improve your family life and allow your child to participate in more community activities.

Other chapters in this book will help you ensure that your child is a motivated, enthusiastic learner and prevent future problems from cropping up.

A Literary Support Group: Reading for Empathy

This book is a description of interventions that will help your child overcome the most severe symptoms of autism. But it's also the story of one family's life with autism, from diagnosis to better days, aided by those same interventions. We want every parent of a child with autism—or any clinician who works with one—to know that she isn't alone in her frustration, fears, hopes, anxieties, and occasional despair.

This book is written by two women. Lynn Kern Koegel, Ph.D., is the clinical director of the Koegel Autism Center at the University of California, Santa Barbara, which she runs with her husband, Robert Koegel, Ph.D. The interventions used at the center, one of the oldest research and clinical programs in the country, are data-based applied behavior analysis (ABA) procedures that have been shown to improve the symptoms of children with autism. The clinic's aim is to develop and teach the children "pivotal responses," a method of focusing interventions on specific areas whose improvement has been shown to lead to widespread positive improvements in many other symptoms of autism. Research has shown that focusing on certain behaviors results in greater gains in less time and more positive long-term outcomes.

Too many treatments developed in the past were so unpleasant that the child had to be dragged into the clinic sessions kicking and screaming, and then long periods of time would elapse while the child's disruptive behavior was ignored—or, even worse, punished. In contrast, the approaches described in this book are individualized, family centered, and child friendly. In fact, the goal is for the child to have fun while learning—so much fun she doesn't even know she's doing "work."

The Koegels' work with children has been nationally recognized and acclaimed, and they were recipients of the Children's Television Network's Sesame Street Award for "brightening the lives of children." The interventions that Dr. Koegel recommends in this book are humane, cutting-edge, developed and tested in the field, and generally fun for the whole family.

Dr. Koegel's coauthor, Claire LaZebnik, did not set out to become any kind of expert on autism. She's a novelist and the mother of four children, the oldest of whom was diagnosed with autism at the age of two. Necessity compelled her to become a full-time (with lots of overtime) organizer, implementer, and coordinator of behavior-based interventions for her son's autism. Throughout this book, Claire describes her own thoughts and experiences as the mother of a child with autism and explores how her family dealt with each specific symptom.

Dr. Koegel gives advice and describes interventions; Claire talks about trying to make interventions work in real life, amid all the distractions, stresses, and needs of a busy family.

Stories of Hope

This is a book about hope. We're optimistic, but not irrationally so. We'd like you to see for yourself how much children with autism can and do improve when a well-thought-out intervention plan is formulated and consistently followed. Toward that end, Dr. Koegel has included several different families' stories, starting with where they were when they first sought her help, and ending with where the child is today. We hope these true stories will inspire you. In virtually every one, the child had behaviors or delays that were so overwhelmingly disruptive, the family could hardly cope. And yet, with the right help and interventions, these children have all grown into happy, contributing teenagers and adults.

If you're feeling discouraged, it will do you good to read these stories. They're proof that even the most difficult child will improve under the right circumstances. And we're going to give you the tools to create those right circumstances.

Taking Care of Business and Yourself

When you have a child with a disability, it affects every area of your life. So we've included some chapters that aren't about symptoms and interventions but are more generally about how to deal with various aspects of living with autism—how to process the original diagnosis, how to keep your family life intact, and how to deal with your child's schooling needs. Once again, the one-two punch of both a professional and a mother allows you to see the subject at hand from every angle. Chances are, if you have a child with autism or are working with one, you've had to deal with many of the issues we discuss in these chapters.

Why This Book?

Currently there's an epidemic in the number of children being diagnosed with an autism spectrum disorder. Almost every major periodical has devoted a cover story to the disability, and just about every major network station has aired a story or even a series on autism. Virtually everyone knows someone who's dealing in some way with the specter of autism.

This book describes specific, concrete interventions, tested in the field and designed to fit into a family's daily interaction, and which, if correctly pursued, will immediately begin improving the symptoms of a child with autism, while at the same time offering the emotional support and understanding a parent needs during what may well be the toughest period of his or her life.

Dr. Koegel has worked extensively with children of all different levels and skills. Claire knows what it's like to be the mother of a kid with special needs. We want our readers to feel both understood and empowered.

You may feel like the work is hard and the road long. It is, but with the help of this book, you're not going to slog through it alone or ignorant.

A MOTHER LOOKS AT STARTING THE PROCESS

When your child is first diagnosed with autism, you're about as vulnerable as a parent can be. All you want is to make things better for this little person you love. You're terrified that this mysterious disability will ruin your child's life forever, that he'll never know romantic love or what it's like to go to college or—your worst nightmare—maybe even how to talk. You cast about, desperate for someone to come along to make everything okay again. That's when you have to be most careful.

Sorting Through the Choices

All that vulnerability makes you a nice plump target for anyone who can promise you instant success. But don't buy into that. There are no miracle cures, no overnight successes, in autism—at least not that I've seen, and I've been looking hard for about twenty years. There are, however, good, effective interventions, documented by years of research and rigorous scientific study. Do those.

The very first therapist we saw was a speech pathologist recommended by our pediatrician when our son Andrew was two and a half years old. Andrew was completely nonverbal. I think he may have been able to make a couple of animal sounds, but that was it. At some point after Roberta had been working with Andrew for a while and we had, on her advice, taken him to the Neuropsychiatric Institute of UCLA, where he was officially diagnosed with autism, she sat down with us and said, "I think he'll learn to talk. But it's not going to be an easy or a fast process. Be prepared for a lot of hard work and for it to take a very long time."

Great.

Back in those days, I had a recurring dream where I'd be with Andrew and he'd suddenly turn to me and say something—not just a word or two, but a perfect, full sentence. And I'd feel this incredible sense of relief, like the world had been put right. Until I woke up again. And then it was awful to lie there and know that it wasn't true, that Andrew still couldn't even say "Mommy."

People were always telling me stories about kids who didn't seem to be able to talk at all but who were just biding their time and, when they did speak, spoke perfectly. I was still nursing a tiny hope that Andrew would be one of the kids who would do that. I had thought that by taking him to see a speech pathologist, I'd be jump-starting the whole language acquisition thing, and within weeks of starting to see her, he'd "get" how to talk. So it was pretty tough to sit there and hear a professional tell us that nothing was going to happen quickly.

I think that if another therapist had miraculously appeared just then and said, "Are you kidding? I can have this kid speaking in full sentences by the end of the month," I would have followed that second person anywhere or paid her anything. Since that didn't happen, though, I stuck with Roberta, who was one hundred percent right about Andrew. His language acquisition was a slow process and required years and years of speech therapy. Even after he started saying words, he was still almost entirely echolalic for a long time (he repeated parts of our sentences but was unable to construct his own).

That's the bad news. The good news? Roberta was also absolutely right when she said Andrew *would* start talking eventually. His language did come. Slowly, painfully, at times maddeningly—but it came. Today, as a young adult, he speaks more or less like others his age—maybe slightly more haltingly, and there are some oddities that I'll discuss in later chapters, but nothing anyone would notice from just chatting with him casually.

Roberta was always honest with us, even when she was telling us something we didn't want to hear. She was open and communicative, sharing the frustrations and the breakthroughs, making it clear we were a team and would face each step together. She became and remains a dear friend, and we learned to replace unreal dreams of a miracle with joy in the actual progress our son was making.

"Trust Me. I'll Make Miracles Happen."

Now contrast our experience with a conversation I had a number of years ago with a friend of a friend, who had called me for some advice. She had recently hired a therapist whose m.o. was to whisk her screaming kid off and drill him for long periods in a separate room, no parents allowed, and not much parent-therapist communication taking place after, either. This mom said neither she nor her child was comfortable with this arrangement, but when she tried to talk to the therapist about her concerns, he said, "You want results? I can tell you right now—the only way your child will improve is if he continues to see me. If you stop the therapy, you'll be harming your child and destroying any progress he might have made."

So she was terrified and as distressed as a parent could be—her instinct told her the guy was no good, but she was scared that firing him would harm her son's progress. And her entire life was centered on helping her child make progress.

So I told her what I thought: A therapist who plays on your fears to keep you bound to him isn't a good person or a good therapist. Neither is one who makes extravagant promises about how well your child will do with his help and *only* with his help. A good therapist shares his work and knows he's part of a team.

The Interventions in This Book

What you'll see, as you read this book, is that the most effective interventions aren't miraculous or dependent on any one specific therapist. In fact, what's so great about the methods in this book is that they're logical and straightforward and user-friendly. Which isn't to say you shouldn't have professionals working with your child. It takes a team of professionals and family members, working together, to create a plan and to keep a steady flow of teaching and reinforcement going at all times. But anyone who's smart, dedicated, and willing to learn can certainly contribute.

Knowledge should always be shared. If an intervention is successful for your child, *everyone* who comes in contact with him should know it. And the same goes for an unsuccessful approach—people should know to avoid it. Consistency is key.

Trust Yourself

All of this is to say, trust your guts a little bit when it comes to the people who work with your child. Recognize that there aren't miracles, but there should be steady progress, and the good guys acknowledge both these things. Stay away from anyone who plays on your fears and insecurities, who says he knows your child better than you do, who doesn't let you in the room when he's working with your child (or at least tell you in detail what he's doing in there), who promises miracles, who demands your trust without earning it.

You want to put your trust in someone? Trust your kid. He's the one who's going to be doing all the hard work, and odds are, he'll succeed. Trust that he'll try his best to overcome the worst of this disability. My brother used to call Andrew the hardest-working kid in L.A., and I still think Andrew works harder on any given day than anyone else we know, since he has to learn and memorize so much of what comes naturally to the rest of us. The motivation is there, though—you can see his pride and relief at every gain he makes.

You Don't Have to Be Extraordinary

One last thought: You know those mothers in those other autism books, the personal-memoir type? The mothers who are tough and strong and do scientific research on their own and never take a break from working with and fighting for their child?

I'm not like that at all. I am *so* not a tiger mother. I'm fairly shy, I'd rather go out to lunch with my kid than sit in a room and drill him, I'll do anything to avoid confrontation, and I know absolutely nothing about the science of autism except that someone somewhere is trying to locate the genes for it, which would be helpful information, I guess.

I'm totally in awe of the kinds of mothers I've read about in those other books, the ones who knock down doors to get their kids what they need, who contact every expert they hear of, who question authority and read any bit of information they can get their hands on. They deserve their child's success, and I hope every one of them finds it. But I'm not like that, and if it's not in your nature, either, I don't think you need to be to help your child.

You just have to take the right steps and be willing to do some work.

Start by reading this book.

OVERCOMING
AUTISM

Chapter One
Diagnosis: Surviving the Worst News You'll Ever Get

QUESTION: I saw my pediatrician yesterday, and she asked me if my two-year-old child was talking. I said he doesn't say a word yet. Then she asked if he played with other children. I said he doesn't take much of an interest in other children, and sometimes he seems like he's in his own little world. Then she pulled out a brochure on autism. Just like that. I was shocked. Is it possible that a child this young could have autism? And, if so, what do I do now?

QUESTION: My child is four. When she was three, she could recite nursery rhymes and count to ten. She also knew most of the alphabet. We thought she was a genius. But in the last year she hasn't seemed interested in talking with us much. At the park she pushes the other children away and just seems to want to sift sand through her fingers. My sister asked me if I've considered the possibility that she has autism, but she likes to cuddle with me and doesn't seem to mind being touched. That doesn't sound like autism, does it?

AUTISM is one of the most alarming diagnoses a parent can hear. Every parent has hopes and dreams for her child, and often these can be shattered when the child gets diagnosed with autism. Most other diagnoses dictate a clear course of action and lead to an undisputed likely outcome, but every child with autism is different and will progress differently. There is no known cause and no known cure. Not only is it a serious disability—it's also a bewildering one.

I love my job. In fact, I am one of the few people in the world who can honestly say that each day I get up, I feel fortunate to be able to do something I love. But delivering the news that a child has autism is the one part of my job that I hate. Fortunately, most people who bring their children to see us already have a diagnosis or at least a suspicion that their child has autism—after all, they *are* coming to an autism center. But when I do have to be the one to tell a family that their child has autism, it's difficult. In fact, it's especially difficult because—as we'll discuss below—our society hasn't come together yet to really appreciate the many gifts of children with autism. Nor has our society come together to give the families the support they need and deserve. But, from a clinician's point of view, the one ray of hope I can give parents is that with good intervention their child is likely to improve, and that even though I can't read the future, many children do improve enormously. At this point in time, at least 20 percent will lose the diagnosis completely and almost half will be pretty close to their typical peers with only some minor areas that need to be addressed, and *all* will improve immensely if the right interventions are implemented. And as the intervention research improves, the outcomes get better and better.

But you *will* need to stay on top of things. You'll need to make sure that you're providing the best interventions and that anyone else who works with your child—at school, in home programs, during after-school programs, and so on—are also using the same methods and that everyone is being consistent. It will take effort, but it will be well worth it in the end.

What Is "Autism" Anyway?

To understand what autism is today, a little history is helpful. Relatively speaking, the field of autism is young. In 1943 the term "autism" was first used by Leo Kanner, who wrote a paper entitled "Autistic Disturbances of Affective Contact." *Autistic* literally means "alone," and that's what Kanner observed—a tendency in these children to want to be alone. In this paper, published in the *Nervous Child* (a journal that no longer exists), Dr. Kanner described eleven children between two and eight years old who had similar symptoms, which included difficulties communicating with others, difficulties interacting with others, and unusual interests. Prior to this article, children with these symptoms were usually labeled schizophrenic.

Although the symptoms of autism have been refined, these general areas still continue to provide the basis of the symptoms of the spectrum. To be diagnosed with autism, children must have difficulties with social communication. Prior to 2013, there were three separate symptom areas—social, communication, and restricted interests. But many people felt that the social and communication couldn't really be isolated from each other, so these have now been grouped together. They must also show restricted interests to qualify for a diagnosis of autism. This sounds pretty straightforward, but it's complicated by the fact that although most agree that the disability is neurological, no biological marker has been found. That means that there is no blood or chromosomal test that can tell you if a child has autism. The diagnosis is simply based on observation of the behavioral symptom areas, and the expression of these symptom areas can vary considerably. For example, a child who socializes fine with adults but has no interest in children his own age would qualify, as would a child who has absolutely no interest in either adults or other children. A child who echoes everything another person says, a child who can make short sentences but cannot maintain a conversation, and a child who says nothing whatsoever would all qualify under the impaired-social-communication category. And finally, the child who spends all day riding her rocking horse, the child who spends hours each day lining up his mom and dad's shoes in a certain specific order, and the child who only plays with one toy repeatedly would all be a "yes" on the restricted-interests category, as would the child who spends all day on the computer developing a better operating system.

To make things even more confusing, most children express some of these symptoms, so it's not even a simple "Do they have this symptom?" but the more complicated question of "To what extent do they have this symptom?" that determines where they fall on the continuum. In other words, does each symptom area fall within or outside the typical range?

If your child has difficulties in the symptom areas (social communication and restricted interests) that are outside of what would be expected from a typical child, she may meet the diagnostic criteria for autism. I'm going to complicate things even more for you: there are other disabilities that now fall into the autism spectrum category.

For example, another change that took place in 2013 is that the American Psychiatric Association has not found significant data to differentiate a diagnosis of Asperger's syndrome, PDD-NOS, and "high-functioning" autism, so they'll be grouped under the general category of autism spectrum disorder (ASD).

Previously, Asperger's syndrome was diagnosed when the child didn't really have any delays in language per se but did have difficulties in social interaction. These children tended to have special interests and difficulty making conversation. For example, we work with one little boy who only wants to talk about lavatories in airplanes. Another only wants to talk about Rolex watches.

Kids who became experts on topics that were of little or no interest to others, while they themselves showed little interest in what occupied their peers, would often be diagnosed with Asperger's syndrome.

Then there was PDD-NOS (pervasive developmental disorder, not otherwise specified), also called "atypical" autism. Children were labeled with this when they had only two of the three categories. That is, they tended to have difficulties with social interaction and either communication difficulties or restricted interests, but not both.

So, as you can see, over time, in an attempt to make the diagnosis more homogeneous, more subcategories of autism spectrum disorder were defined. Now they will all be grouped together.

The new diagnostic approach is to assign a number on a scale from 1 to 3 in each of the two symptom areas, depending on how significantly the deficits effect everyday functioning and how much support the person needs. So if the child requires substantial support because the social communication deficit is "severe," she has restricted interests and distracting repetitive behaviors, and she's hard to redirect and easily frustrated, she'll likely be given a 3.

In contrast, if the child has noticeable difficulties with social communication and has restricted interests in some contexts and is only somewhat difficult to redirect and may only need some support, he will be given a 1.

So what does this mean? Some people are concerned that individuals previously diagnosed with PDD-NOS or Asperger's syndrome may not qualify for the diagnosis any longer, although the recommendation is *not* to remove a diagnosis once it's been made (which makes it even more complicated, because two people with identical symptoms may have different diagnoses based on the year they were diagnosed).

Other people are concerned that grouping symptoms will result in less specificity.

But time will tell and no doubt there will be more changes in the future. The most important thing for families to remember is that if your child needs support, you must make sure he gets it. If your child no longer qualifies for services because he doesn't have enough symptoms, but he's still having social problems, the school absolutely needs to provide social programs for your child. As we'll discuss throughout the book, if your child isn't interacting socially and peer relationships are challenging, every effort you make now to help with his conversation and social interaction abilities will make a big difference for the rest of his life.

The Cause

We still don't know what causes autism. Researchers have been working hard to figure it out, but even the best in the world have started referring to "the autisms" to indicate that there isn't just one single cause—there are many. And this isn't totally surprising, given the wide variability in the expression of the symptoms of autism.

We do know a few things. Because almost five times as many boys are affected as girls, and because the odds are high that a child will have autism if his identical twin does, we know that there is some underlying genetic/neurological cause. We also know that autism is slightly more likely to be evident in siblings. But even these facts are complicated. Sometimes only one identical twin will have autism, which means that in these cases, something other than the DNA must have triggered it. Sometimes only one child in the family will have autism, and no others in the entire family history are known to have autism. It's definitely complicated and not a whole lot is understood.

However, there have been a few studies suggesting that mothers over thirty-five and fathers over forty have an increased likelihood of having a child with autism. Other studies have suggested that autism is rare in children whose mothers were under twenty years old when they gave birth. So there may be some correlation with parental age or some environmental factor that kicks into action when parents are older.

Quite likely, autism stems from a combination of genetic and environmental factors, but the bottom line is that after spending more than a billion dollars on research, we still don't know exactly what causes it. We may not be able to pinpoint the causes of autism in our lifetimes, but we *are* discovering lots of ways to help children with autism reach their full potential, and that's what's most important for you as a parent to focus on.

Hard News to Get

I saw one family not long ago with a nineteen-month-old son—cute as could be. But Caleb didn't say one single word, he wasn't interested in anyone, and he spent the full two hours we were with him spinning in circles. He didn't play with any of the toys in the room and didn't respond to his name. He had such clearly pronounced symptoms of autism that there wasn't even any question in my mind what his diagnosis should be.

The parents had a book on autism with them and had brought Caleb to our center because the child's cousin had autism. I assumed they understood what we were dealing with and told them that we would be able to work with him. But then they asked if he had to have autism to participate in our center. At that moment, I realized that they hadn't yet accepted that any diagnosis had been made. So, as gently as I could, I said that Caleb appeared to have the symptom areas associated with autism. To my surprise, they said they were hoping I would say that nothing was wrong with him. *Nothing.* That word was piercing, and I got that weird feeling like the blood is rushing out of your head.

I pointed out Caleb's specific symptom areas—that he wasn't talking yet (notice I said *yet*); that his social areas appeared to be a little delayed, which could happen if he wasn't talking; and that while he didn't interact much, he did seem to enjoy cuddling with his parents, which was a great starting point. I told them that there were good treatments available and that we would just take one symptom at a time and work on each one, and I was confident we would make progress.

The dad, who was quite well read and informed, said that although he agreed that his son didn't talk and wasn't interested in others, he really didn't see any restricted interests in his behavior. Very gently, I pointed out that a typically developing child of Caleb's age would be playing with toys and getting into things, but he was spending most of his time spinning, which would be considered a repetitive stereotyped behavior. The dad looked shocked. And I felt horrible. Maybe people who work at diagnostic centers and break the news several times a day get used to it, but I still haven't.

The father stopped talking and looked down, his shock turning to depression. Interestingly, the mother began to open up—she almost seemed relieved to air all the concerns she'd had about her son. Once again I reminded them that autism is just a group of symptoms, that there are good interventions available, and that the most productive way to proceed would be by addressing the symptoms one by one. We would begin with teaching Caleb words using motivational procedures (see chapter 2), which would be likely to help his socialization and decrease the spinning.

I knew that all the helpful advice and hopeful suggestions I gave them still wouldn't make it any easier for them to get that diagnosis. (We have worked with Caleb for about two months, and he's now saying about seventy-five words, has a bunch of social activities he loves, and only spins when he's not engaged in one of these activities.)

My Own Experience

Although I can't pretend to know what it's like to be the parent of a child diagnosed with autism, I have experienced what it's like to know there's something wrong with your child and not know what the outcome will be.

When I was pregnant with my second child, I had placenta previa. That's when the placenta covers the opening of the uterus, making it impossible for the baby to come out. The first sign of a problem was some blood spots during my third month of pregnancy. Distressed, I called my doctor, and his response was shocking. He didn't invite me to his office, he didn't counsel me, he simply and abruptly said, "You're probably going to have a miscarriage. I've gotta run, I have a patient in my office. Don't worry about it." This was my first experience of what it was like to be at the mercy of an unsympathetic doctor.

I changed doctors after that and, psychologically, everything was better with the new obstetrician, but I continued to have bleeding, and when I was five months pregnant, I was put on bed rest and then hospitalized.

When my daughter was finally delivered, I immediately knew something was wrong. They didn't hand her to me as they had my first child. Instead, they rushed her into neonatal intensive care. When the pediatrician came to see me some time later, he said, "She's got an eighty percent chance of survival." I cried out, "You mean she has a twenty percent chance of dying?" He seemed surprised by my outburst and completely unaware of what it means to a parent to be told that her child's outcome is uncertain and possibly tragic. To him, the odds were still in our favor, and that was what he lived by—odds. But all I could see was that 20 percent possibility my baby could die. My husband told me later that the whole experience had been just as bad, if not worse, for him, as they were taking him aside and giving him these statistics all the way through. (She's a healthy, happy young woman now, I'm glad to say—I wish I'd known that then.)

And since the first edition of *Overcoming Autism* was published, my nephew has been diagnosed with autism. Except for a few random echolalic words, he was virtually nonverbal at the age of two and a half, when most children are social and producing short sentences. His restricted interest consisted of throwing items: anyone who entered his house was at risk of being hit by a flying toy. His communication was almost exclusively limited to screaming and tantrums, and he would risk life and limb to do things for himself rather than get an adult to help him.

When we attempted to elicit speech, through play, he'd usually get upset and throw a toy. He had a favorite toy, which we used a lot, and it had about fifteen pieces. It was one of those tunnel and ramp things that you roll balls down. He loved that toy, but whenever we prompted him to say "ball" he'd get angry and frustrated and pick up the ramp toy and throw it. Of course, the toy was pretty useless to him when it was in a million pieces, so he'd put it back together at lightning speed. It would have taken me at least several minutes to repair it, and I'd probably have needed a manual—but he could get it up and working within seconds. So remember what I said about strengths? I knew he was really, really smart to be able to put that toy together so quickly, which meant that—despite the fact that he didn't talk yet—we had a lot to work with.

Of course, this didn't take the stress away. I remember one assessment when a state worker came by the house and glared at him like he was a little terror after he'd hurled a couple of toys in her direction. I tried to explain that throwing things was his restricted interest, but she wasn't interested and didn't try to engage him at all—just got out of there as quickly as possible. And that felt completely wrong. He was my adorable little nephew, and when it's a family member, getting the right help isn't an academic issue: it's life or death, and we'll fight tooth and nail for our kids.

So I can empathize with the feeling of finding out that something isn't right with your child and the fears that an uncertain prognosis can lead to. Over the years, I've talked with thousands of parents of children with autism, and I can tell you that getting the news is horrific, terrifying, stressful, and depressing, and I know how many nights' sleep I lost worrying about my nephew. Parents react in different ways: They cry, they get mad, they deny that their child has autism. Sometimes they even accept it resignedly—but it's never easy.

No Way to Prepare Yourself

There are no known prenatal tests that can alert or prepare a parent for the shocking diagnosis of autism. Even after a child with autism is born, there may be signs early on that she's not developing typically, but most new parents don't recognize or know to look for these signs. Therefore the family often assumes, for the first year or two of life, that everything is fine, especially because most of the motor milestones—sitting up, crawling, walking, and so on—seem to happen like clockwork.

For most parents, it's not until their child is eighteen months or older and still not talking that they start to worry and ask questions. Even then, they're likely to be told by friends and pediatricians that language develops at different times for different kids, and not to worry about it. They can lose precious time because of this.

There are some earlier signs (before words are expected) that can help you recognize possible symptoms of autism, if you know what to look for. For example, the child may not enjoy playing little games like peek-a-boo and may not point to items, preferring instead to take her parent's hand and place it on the desired object, such as the doorknob when she wants to go out. The child with autism may not respond to her name when called, or she may play with the same toy over and over again. Some parents even report that their child never cried for them when left in her crib but seemed content alone for long periods of time.

Of course, parents tend to remember these things *after* their child has already been diagnosed, but the truth is that most parents don't usually become very concerned until they notice that their child isn't starting to talk.

Can Professionals Make Mistakes When They Give a Diagnosis?

Sometimes a diagnosis is wrong. But that's rare. Most children with autism can be reliably diagnosed well before they're three, if the person who diagnoses them has experience and expertise in the area of autism. We're even doing some research now to try to understand and treat the early social symptoms in infancy. (See "Resources" at the end of this book for centers specializing in autism.) However, there are a few reasons why a rare mistake can happen.

The most common mistake is failing to diagnose a child whose symptoms of autism are so mild that they're overlooked. In addition, sometimes children develop difficulties with communication and socialization before they begin to show repetitive behaviors or restricted interests, so they aren't initially diagnosed as having autism but get the diagnosis later. Some have even hypothesized that the restricted interests and repetitive behaviors of autism are *caused* by the lack of social communication, but whatever the reason, if something isn't right with your child's development, even if it's just communication and social skills, it needs to be addressed immediately.

Finally, sometimes people will suggest that your child has been misdiagnosed even if he hasn't been. This usually happens when a child is showing considerable improvement. That is, some children who receive intervention at a very young age can get over some of the symptoms early on, so they may appear to look more like they have a communication delay, atypical autism, or Asperger's syndrome. Which is still another reason to get intervention as early as possible—children can improve tremendously when they're little.

Could It Be Something Else?

The doctor who diagnoses your child will first need to rule out other possible underlying problems. How do we differentiate autism spectrum disorder from other childhood disabilities that don't have a genetic cause? It can be tricky. For example, children with hearing impairments can exhibit symptoms similar to autism. My daughter did when she had severe and chronic middle ear infections. She didn't socialize, didn't respond, and spent the bulk of her time engaging in self-stimulatory behaviors. I've seen others like that, too—it's rare, but it does happen. But many children with autism will respond to some sounds, like a candy wrapper opening or a favorite video, whereas children with hearing impairments won't respond to anything below their threshold of impairment. A good audiologist or ear, nose, and throat specialist will be able to help you rule out hearing difficulties as a possibility.

Another possibility is a language delay. If a child has a language delay, he will most likely have some difficulty interacting socially at the same level as his peers, but usually he won't *avoid* social interaction, like a child with autism. In addition, a child with a language delay doesn't generally have the limited interests we see in children with autism.

A lot of parents ask me whether their children may just be "late talkers," as Einstein was supposed to have been. Well, it is true that some children do learn to talk a little late, but it's rare that a child who has a significant language delay (even if it isn't autism) will overcome it without intervention. This only happens with a very, very small subgroup, and we really don't know what variables account for children who catch up without intervention. I wouldn't leave it up to chance. The right intervention won't hurt, and it will help, so waiting and hoping for another Einstein may be a waste of time and result in your child's falling further behind.

Finally, there are many other types of developmental delays. Usually children with developmental delays have somewhat flat functioning across the board. Children with autism tend to have strengths in nonverbal areas. They may be good at puzzles and nonverbal activities and may even line up items in some order.

What Does the Diagnosis Really Mean?

The short answer is, unfortunately, that no one really knows. "Autism" is a name given to the cluster of symptoms I've discussed above. But every child expresses these symptoms differently. Don't try to compare your child to other children with autism. Each child is an individual. While one may have a lot of difficulty controlling his self-stimulatory behaviors, like rocking and spinning, another will find language hard to master and, at the age of four, may still be nonverbal or echo everything you say. One may rage and hit; another may be calm and passive. One may dislike the feeling of being held tightly; another may cling to his parents constantly. You have to get to know your own child and what his strengths and weaknesses are before you jump to any conclusions about who he is and what he needs.

At this point in time, no one can predict what a child with autism will be like as an adult—and don't believe anyone who says he can. One family we worked with had a three-year-old who would lie on the floor with all of his muscles stiff and straight, screaming nonstop. His parents were told, by professionals, that he would never have friends, that he would never marry, and that he probably would never talk. We started him on a program of interventions, and by kindergarten he didn't have any symptoms of autism whatsoever.

You never can tell. No one can.

But you *can* make a difference in the outcome.

How to Interact with Your Newly Diagnosed Child

When parents get the news that their child has a serious disability, they tend to question their own ability to parent that child and wonder if they have to treat him differently than they might have otherwise—more gently or more severely, more like a therapist, less like a buddy, and so on.

Here's the golden rule: When in doubt, treat your child just as you would treat him if he didn't have a disability.

All parents want to make their children's lives easier, and parents of children with autism are no exception. We all want to avoid situations or demands that are likely to cause tantrums or to upset our children. That's understandable, but if you're finding yourself in a place where you're constantly lowering your standards of good behavior and making excuses for your child because he has a disability, you need to stop and find a new approach. If you were expecting good manners and good behavior from your child before you knew he had autism, or if you expect a certain type of behavior from your other children, continue to insist on those things.

If you had goals for your child, stick to them. Don't assume there's anything he can't master in time. He may never have said a word, but don't let anyone jump to the conclusion that he never will. If someone says to you, "He's not learning such-and-such," assume it's the method of teaching that's failing and not the child. Researchers have studied every symptom of autism and know there are many ways to work on everything, from learning first words to keeping a conversation going. Keep trying different teaching methods until you find the one that works for your child.

Above all, don't lower your expectations: expect your child to overcome the symptoms of autism and lead a rich and fulfilling life. Your continuing perseverance is your child's biggest asset. If you give up, your child will never make it.

What Do You Tell Your Child?

Many, many parents of children with autism, especially children who are able to engage in social conversation, ask me whether they should tell their child that he or she has (or had) autism. I'm not really sure what the answer to this question is, but I do have some general thoughts on the matter, having observed some situations where this issue has arisen.

First, discussing a child's disability is an individual family's decision and often relates to just how much the child wants to know. My general feeling (and I must say that this is only a feeling, not based on any data) is that since we really don't know what autism is at this point, I think we may want to focus on symptoms and discuss areas of weakness and strength with our children, rather than impose any labels on them.

Let me give you some examples. Mia's mother reported that Mia sometimes came home saying that she just didn't feel like she was part of the social clique at school. Her mother asked whether this would be a good time to tell her that she'd had autism as a child and still continues to demonstrate some minor symptoms. I suggested that since Mia was so mildly affected, her mother just discuss her strengths and weaknesses. A few weeks later, when I was driving Mia in the car, we were discussing her little brother, and she said, "Avery learned to talk early, and I learned to talk late, but I learned how to read really early." These were the facts, and she seemed very comfortable with them. Presenting Mia with the information by discussing not only her challenges but also her strengths and pointing out that every child has strong and weak areas did not exacerbate her feelings of isolation and being different.

In contrast, we had a brilliant graduate student in our clinical psychology program who had received intervention in our center when she was in preschool and during the elementary school years. Although she excelled in college and graduate school, had a large group of friends, and was one of the nicest people you could ever know, her parents told her she had autism as a child, and she always worried about what was wrong with her brain. In fact, she was so stressed about it that she couldn't work with anyone who had autism.

However, not every child has difficulty with the diagnosis. We worked with one adolescent girl who had been in counseling all her life and had a whole slew of psychological labels applied to her by various doctors for almost a decade. Finally, when she was fourteen, a psychiatrist suggested that she had Asperger's syndrome, and that's how I ended up seeing her. One night I was talking to her mom on the phone, and the girl picked up the extension and listened in from the other room. She confronted her mother, who decided to show her my report. The report had very specific areas she needed to work on, such as responding empathetically to others, improving eye contact, decreasing inappropriate body posturing during conversations, and so on. But the important thing was that each area had effective interventions. This particular child was actually relieved to understand what her disability was, and she was also extremely motivated to learn specific ways to interact with others, to engage in interesting conversations, and to address each symptom head-on. So, for her, it was quite helpful to know specifically what the disability was.

I guess what I'm saying is, there isn't really a best way to approach telling your child he has or had symptoms of autism. The fact that we don't really know what autism is makes it even more difficult. Telling someone that he has "something," but no one knows exactly what that means, may be more difficult than simply talking to him about his strengths and weaknesses. On the other hand, some children may feel a sense of relief to know what exactly is going on, that there are interventions, and that there are a whole lot of other people who have the same challenges. So there are still questions as to how best to address this issue. As more children receive improved interventions so that they can reach a level where they can discuss their past symptoms, more research should help us determine the best ways to discuss the disability with children. Again, try to remember that each child has strengths, too. All of us have strengths and weaknesses, and it can often be a waste of time to dwell on weaknesses.

Good Treatments Are Available. Use Them.

With the right intervention, almost all children diagnosed with autism improve. There has been and continues to be much progress in treatments. Researchers around the country are making new findings daily. This book will help you start down the path of appropriate and worthwhile interventions and allow you to see how steady and knowledgeable efforts really can turn things around.

Similarly, remember that *without treatment, your child will very likely get worse.* Your child will not simply "outgrow" the symptoms of autism. Few children even outgrow language delays without intervention. You need to start a treatment plan of specialized interventions as soon as possible.

Even if your child is very young and has mild symptoms, and you're not sure if she has autism, you still need to deal with those mild symptoms she's displaying—remember, labels don't matter, but symptoms do, and symptoms can and must be dealt with. You don't need a diagnosis to develop an intervention plan—helping your child with each and every symptom is what's important.

I can't stress strongly enough the importance of diving into action immediately. Every expert in the field agrees that early intervention is essential and critical. The "wait and see" approach is detrimental to your child. Children with autism tend to avoid things that are difficult, and communication is difficult for them, so they avoid situations where they might be expected to communicate. As a result, they become more isolated and withdrawn. So it's critical that you get a program started right away. This book will help you do that.

Strengths, Talents, and Abilities

Most autism professionals' training is deficit based. We're taught to zero in on every area in which a child needs help, to define those areas, and to intervene with them. We make up goals and target behaviors based on these weaknesses. It's not surprising: funding agencies often only provide services—or provide *more* services—if a child can be shown to have significant deficits, so we're forced to focus on those to get the aid.

Unfortunately, that model isn't a very reassuring one for parents who love their children; nor is it necessarily the most effective way to guide us toward intervention goals.

Let's take, for example, a sample description of a child with autism: "Three-year-old Jason is severely language impaired and only says six expressive words." Now reconsider how this could be rephrased to emphasize his strengths: "Three-year-old Jason is able to say six expressive words: 'juice,' 'cookie,' 'iPad,' 'video,' 'ride,' and 'up.' Since Jason has learned to use these expressive words to request the items he wants and the activities he enjoys, it is recommended that these be expanded upon to increase his vocabulary." Doesn't that just make you feel a lot better? A lot more hopeful and eager to get to work? And the information is exactly the same—it's just presented in a different way. A more positive way.

Studies show that parents constantly feel as if professionals focus on their child's weaknesses. This needs to change. We need to rethink and relearn the ways we do our assessments so we are *always* focusing on a child's strengths.

The same goes for interventions. Professionals need to focus on the areas in which the child is doing well and the ways that he's succeeding—and then they need to figure out why, so this success can be broadened into other areas. Many parents have told me that their child's teacher or school staff member will only call and report to them when there's a problem. Not only is this discouraging for the parents, it's probably not helping the child progress. You need to know not just that your child is having tantrums during circle time (which the teacher is likely to report), but also that he or she has perfect behavior during *music* time (which you're less likely to hear about). Once you have the full picture, you can start to investigate why music time is more successful for your child than circle time: maybe the material being presented during circle time is too challenging or the seating requirement too restrictive. Knowing your child can sit quietly when the conditions are right will allow you to figure out how to increase and generalize that positive behavior.

While focusing on strengths, remember that a child with a diagnosis of an autism spectrum disorder is likely to be stronger in visual areas than in language-based areas. Learning letters, numbers, and anything else highly visual may be quite easy for your child. You wouldn't believe how many preschoolers I've taught to read long before kindergarten. In fact, by kindergarten many of my children with autism are reading books to the rest of the class (which makes them a valued member among the peer group and can make the other parents very envious!).

If we spend time looking for the strengths, we can then use them to our child's advantage, but if we spend all of our time focusing on the deficits, we'll lose that edge. So make sure anyone and everyone who works with your child approaches her with a positive attitude that includes a primary focus on her strengths, talents, and abilities.

KEEPING CONTROL OF YOUR EMOTIONAL LIFE

Because our society has not yet learned to accept disabilities gracefully, parents are distraught when they're told that their child has one. We've tried and tried to help parents deal with the stress of discovering their child has autism and then the stress of coping with the demands the disability places on their time and money, but even with support, parents inevitably go through some tough times.

Here are some common feelings parents have after first learning that their child has autism, and some suggestions for coping with them.

Denial

Parents know when their child has a disability. In fact, most of my parents know it before their pediatricians do. But pediatricians are trained to calm worried new parents. And the truth is that we parents *want* to hear that our children are fine. So if the pediatrician tells a parent of a child with autism something like "Don't worry, he's not talking because he's got an older sister who talks for him," or a well-meaning relative says, "His dad didn't talk until he was five," the parent may seize on those excuses and cling to the hope that nothing is wrong.

One mother even told me that she was pretty sure something was wrong with her child but never aired those concerns to the pediatrician and always just told him that things were fine. She was relieved after each well-baby visit that the doctor didn't "find" anything wrong. Of course, the doctor only saw the child for fifteen or twenty minutes a few times a year, and without the mother's prompting, he didn't even think to look for signs of a disability. She lost a lot of time not wanting to admit what she was seeing with her own eyes.

In the past, doctors didn't always ask questions that focused on potential developmental disabilities, but these days, especially with the rise in autism, they're much more likely to do exactly that.

Even after a child is diagnosed with autism, some parents will continue to hope that a mistake has been made and nothing is wrong at all. They'll insist that their child is merely a late talker and the diagnosis is way overboard. Others may try to make excuses for their child's behavior, such as saying, "All two-year-olds tantrum." Others will bring their child to three or four experts, hoping to find a dissenting opinion, before finally accepting the diagnosis— and the necessity of taking action.

Sometimes one parent stays in this stage of denial for months or even years, long after the other parent has already accepted the need to start taking the necessary steps toward helping their child. Unfortunately, a spouse's unwillingness to come on board can put a huge strain on a marriage.

It's very difficult to find out that the child you love so much has a disability, and it's very natural and understandable to hope against hope that the people who have diagnosed him are in error. (Although, as I discussed earlier in the chapter, errors in diagnosis are rare when done by a competent professional.) But don't let your uncertainty about the diagnosis get in the way of taking action. I've said it before, and I'll say it again: the label doesn't matter nearly so much as the symptoms your child is displaying. Deny the autism if you must, but don't deny what your child is doing, and most of all, don't deny him the help he needs to overcome any symptoms he's expressing.

Guilt

Most parents feel overwhelmed with guilt when they discover that their child has autism. They wonder if they did something during the pregnancy or shortly after their child was born that may have affected him. I even had one parent ask me if her child could have autism because she and her husband had lots of arguments when the child was a newborn and they weren't getting much sleep! Another mother asked me if her son could have autism because he wasn't breast-fed.

Feelings of guilt have been compounded by early unsubstantiated psychoanalytic theories that suggested that cold, unloving mothers were the cause of autism. Since then, scientific research has shown that mothers of children with autism are no different from mothers of children without autism, but not until after a lot of heartsick women had already been condemned as bad mothers.

As parents, we feel guilty about every little thing that isn't perfect about our offspring. It's human nature to worry, blame ourselves, and wonder if we could or should have done something differently.

Parents of children with autism are especially susceptible to this kind of self-doubt, partially because their kids hit early motor milestones spot on in the typical range, so it's a huge shock when they start showing signs of social and communicative delays. The parents may feel like they haven't said or done the right things to encourage their little ones to develop correctly, that it's their fault things have stopped progressing on track. And if the parents rush to blame these delays on bad parenting, they may not be so quick to get the professional help the family needs, which can lead to much bigger problems down the road: what start off as minor problems with kids on the spectrum can turn into much bigger ones as they get older. So it's important not to blame parenting when a child isn't showing the same social development as his peers, but to look instead for ways to help him.

It's natural to wonder if you could have prevented your child's autism, but you need to remember that guilt doesn't help your child. There is no evidence to suggest that poor parenting is a cause of autism, and while there may be some type of environmental factor to blame, that's not yet known. And it's highly unlikely that you simply weren't as good at teaching your child to talk as everyone around you! Don't waste your time torturing yourself with vague fears when you could be swinging into action.

Blame

There are increasing numbers of multiple children with autism in the same family, and it's logical to try to think where the genetic mix-up could have been, but too often family research turns into family blame. I can't tell you how often I've sat in my office and had one parent tell me that the other parent has symptoms of autism—I've even had *both* parents tell me, confidentially, that their spouse has symptoms of autism!

You know what? We all have symptoms of autism—each symptom falls on a continuum, and somewhere on that continuum it turns from typical to a disability. A husband who bites his fingernails or doesn't particularly enjoy socializing isn't necessarily genetically responsible for producing a child who rocks back and forth constantly. And a mother who has trouble expressing her emotions and likes to sit in a rocking chair isn't necessarily genetically responsible for a child who fixates on spinning fans.

I would guess that almost every family has some member with mental disabilities in its lineage. While assessing these issues may be helpful in genetic planning, playing the blame game doesn't help your child get the help he needs—nor does it help your marriage in any way. The last thing your spouse needs is to feel like he or she has done something wrong in mating with you. You had children together because you loved each other.

Having a child is always a gamble. Sometimes a child is born with a disability.

That's the harsh reality. Passing around blame is an emotionally harmful game that serves no useful function.

Anger

Some parents feel angry when their child is diagnosed with autism. I met with one family whose four-year-old son had just been diagnosed with mild autism, and the dad sat in the corner, arms crossed, glaring at me throughout our first session. Not long after, he realized that I was doing my best to help his son, but at that point he just felt angry, and I was the nearest target.

Anger isn't always a waste of time. A friend of mine once pointed out that people who get angry under adverse situations and who *channel that angry energy toward appropriate and useful action* will often succeed where others fail. I'm all in favor of the kind of anger that makes you say, "We're going to lick this thing!" But anger that just makes you sullen and resentful toward people who are trying to help you is working against you and your child.

Isolation

When a child is diagnosed with a disability, you would expect society to rush in and help. But that doesn't happen. Parents are usually left alone, without support or guidance, to figure the whole thing out. Children with disabilities are excluded from community schools, activities, and social events on a regular basis. In fact, I've been told by some parents that their children are even excluded from family gatherings.

It's not surprising, then, that many parents feel alone and isolated when their child gets a diagnosis of autism. Not only can there be very real social exclusion, but there's an emotional isolation as well. Parents feel alone in their grief. They have spent the last few years going on outings and interacting with friends whose children are developing typically, and now they're devastated by the fact that their own child has significant disabilities in a variety of areas.

Rather than continue to socialize as normally as possible, some parents will go out of their way to avoid having to compare their child to their friends' children, frequently declining invitations to parties and outings. But the fewer invitations they accept, the fewer their chances to connect with friends and realize they can still enjoy themselves.

Similarly, many parents allow their fears of how their child might act out in public to prevent them from leaving the house. This starts a bad cycle: the child is isolated socially and therefore doesn't learn to behave in social situations; as his behavior in social situations deteriorates, the parents feel even more compelled to stay at home. And so on. Meanwhile, the parents are losing touch with their friends and relatives, and their feelings of emotional isolation increase until they feel truly abandoned.

If your child has behaviors that make it difficult to go out in public, read chapter 3, on disruptive behaviors, and start getting control of the problem behaviors. Try to create as many positive social opportunities as you can, so your child can learn and grow. Meanwhile, find someone to help you out now and then, so you and your spouse can still go out together.

If the greater problem is that it's emotionally difficult for you to see other children who are developing typically, that's something you're going to have to come to terms with. I would recommend trying to find a good friend, a family member, a psychologist, a support group, or even your child's therapist to talk to about these feelings. Many parents also report that online chat groups can provide a good form of emotional support. In fact, one mother of a child with Asperger's syndrome met another mother online whose child was very similar, and not only did they offer support for each other, but they also shared ideas for working through challenges. You need to be able to talk with someone who'll listen and sympathize. Remember that your friends are probably full of admiration for you right now because you're showing strength in dealing with something you've all had little experience in. Enjoy their company and be honest with them, and you'll find yourself grateful to have friends who'll rally around you.

Sometimes strangers rush to judgment and that can be difficult for any of us to deal with. The rest of the world isn't always compassionate or understanding about neurological and emotional differences. For some reason, people will show sympathy toward visible, physical disabilities; a perfect example is my height. I'm so short that I can't reach the top shelf in a grocery store and constantly have to beg the help of a tall person to retrieve something from a high shelf. The same people who are gracious about this because they can see I have a height deficit might not be so helpful when a child with autism is throwing a tantrum or crying, since they can't *see* the neurological difference.

Every parent knows what it's like to be out in public with a misbehaving child and to get that painful stare, that disgusted look, or even that lecture about the parenting skills you apparently lack. For parents of kids with autism, these moments may be frustratingly frequent.

Ignore other people's criticism—what do they know?—and remind your-self that research has proven that parents are *not* the cause of their children's autism but *are* part of the solution. Research also shows that most parents in-stinctively respond to their child at a level that's appropriate for the child's comprehension—so if someone else is accusing you of babying your child or of not being authoritative enough, remind yourself that you know how to talk to your child so he'll understand much better than any stranger does.

The most important thing to remember when people volunteer unsolic-ited and unwelcome criticism is that you can't waste energy arguing with or emotionally defending yourself against advice that isn't helpful. You need to surround yourself with helpful and supportive people so that you can focus your energy and talents on helping your child reach his full potential. So when a stranger or acquaintance feels the need to tell you you're not parenting cor-rectly, beg to differ . . . and then walk away.

Depression

Not surprisingly, depression is common in parents of children with autism. Sometimes it lasts a long time and sometimes just a little while. I've known some parents who experienced such depression after their child was diagnosed with autism that their doctor prescribed antidepressants. Once again, I recom-mend finding someone you can talk to who will help you work through your feelings of sadness. It's natural to be depressed upon hearing that your child has a disability, but if that depression leads to inactivity and withdrawal from society, it will damage you, your marriage, and your children. Sometimes your child's interventionist is a good source of emotional support; anyone working in the field has a good feel for what parents are going through. There are also organizations that put parents of similar kids in touch with one another. Some parents find support groups helpful and others don't—you might want to try one and see what you think. A friend, family member, interventionist, thera-pist, or any other person who understands what you're going through may be helpful in providing the support you need to stay positive. A happy parent is usually able to provide much more help to his or her child than a deeply de-pressed parent, so take care of your own emotional needs, and take action if you need a little extra psychological assistance and comfort.

One thing that parents have said to me over and over again is that their initial feelings of depression and hopelessness lifted once they plunged into actively seeking interventions for their child. *Nothing* is more depressing than uncertainty and inactivity. When you start taking the necessary steps to improve your child's symptoms, you'll feel energized and hopeful again. Raising children is always a roller-coaster ride, but a sense of competence and optimism will see you through a lot of the harder times.

STRESS: DEALING WITH THE EMOTIONAL, PHYSICAL, AND FINANCIAL BURDEN OF AUTISM

Of all the questions that parents have during the first few months—or years—after their child has been diagnosed with autism, the one they may wonder about the most but ask the least is probably "Will I ever sleep soundly again?" The stress of having a child with a disability is unfathomable: you don't know what the future holds, you don't know whether you're making the right choices, you don't know if you can continue to handle the craziness of your days, and you often don't know how you're going to pay for all the special services your child now needs. Add to that the exhaustion of those sleepless nights, and you've got people who are under an overwhelming amount of stress.

Interestingly, mothers and fathers of kids with special needs tend to have different areas of stress—moms feel more stress related to caring for their children and worrying about their progress, while dads often feel more stress related to finances and the burden of paying for special services. They also often deal with their stress differently—women find some release in talking about it, but men tend to find relief in action. For example, say a clerk in a store asks a family to leave because their child is having a tantrum and it's disturbing the other customers. The mom would probably want to spend an evening talking to a good friend or relative about how embarrassed she was—just talking about it serves as a release for her. But the dad is more likely to feel like he has to take action—he may well insist on making a phone call to chew out the store manager. Because of this basic difference in approach, spouses can lose patience with each other, so you can add marital stress to an already long list of problem areas.

No matter what kinds of support families find, it's difficult to alleviate all parental stress when a child has a disability. And I don't mean the stress that any parent has. I mean clinical levels of stress that can actually lead to ill health—parents of children with autism report more health problems than other parents their age. And without getting help and taking action for their child, many can feel less energetic, and some can even lose interest in sex.

Below, I describe the areas of stress most likely to affect parents of children with autism and make some suggestions for coping with them. Remember, my advice in no way replaces good psychological support from a professional, a close friend, a family member, or a parent group, so please seek this out if you're feeling overwhelmed and frightened.

The Stress of Wondering About the Future

Of all the fears that keep a parent awake at night, concern about his or her child's future—how well the child will ultimately be able to function in the real world—is probably the biggest one.

Many children with autism don't perform well on standardized tests, and many professionals, especially in the schools, base much of their analysis on the results of these tests, so the picture that parents get of their child's cognitive abilities is often bleaker than it needs to be.

A helpful thing to focus on when thinking about cognitive levels is the brain's plasticity. Many children who have suffered from a stroke, gunshot wound, or other severe brain trauma are able to fully recover by developing neural pathways around the damaged areas. Our goal is to help children with autism do the exact same thing. We haven't yet met a child with autism who couldn't learn with good, sound interventions.

Of course, while you're working with your child to lay down those new pathways, you're going to have some long days ahead. Children with autism are more dependent on their parents, especially in the early years. They often need more help with dressing, hygiene, and toileting skills than typical children. Because their language is delayed, parents may need to help them communicate. All of these demands on a parent's time and energy can feel overwhelming, and it can sometimes feel like there's no relief in sight.

Just remember that the early years are tough with all children, and while you may have a longer row to hoe than most, better times do lie ahead. Most children with autism do learn basic self-help skills, and the day will come when your child won't need you to do everything for her.

Alleviate the Stress by Actively Pursuing the Right Interventions

It's scary to have to question your own child's potential, but the best way to relieve your fears is to take action with productive interventions.

The first step is to be informed. Talk to people you trust—parents who've been there, experts in the field, doctors you have a relationship with, and so on. There are a lot of fly-by-night practitioners who prey on distraught parents who'll do anything for their child. Make sure that the interventions you're using are scientifically sound and well documented. Make sure they've been tested with many children with autism and that they've been replicated by other experts and clinics. Also, make sure you understand their limitations—some interventions only work on a small number of symptoms or on a small subgroup of children with autism. If you're going to spend time and money for interventions, be informed about the degree and extent of the change they may bring about.

When to Be Wary

There's plenty of evidence showing that children with autism do better when parents are actively involved in the intervention and when programs are coordinated. Find programs that encourage you to be involved—you should be learning all the procedures and coordinating your child's program across every environment. You can't do that if you're being shut out. If a treatment provider tells you that you can't watch the sessions or that your child does better when you're not there, *this is a red flag*. It may be reasonable for a therapist to request a few sessions alone to bond with the child, but more than that just doesn't make sense, and the therapist needs to communicate fully with you so that you know exactly what's going on at all times.

If a clinician tells you that she's not documenting any types of changes, be concerned—the only way to evaluate whether a treatment program is working is to analyze the changes your child is making. Also be wary of any therapist who says that he's working on the "parent-child bond," and that fixing *your* relationship with your child will improve her behavior.

In other words, if your therapist is excluding you, blaming you, or using techniques that don't have measurable outcomes, you should consider looking for another therapist or agency.

The Stress of Feeling Emotionally Cut Off from Your Own Child

Most children with autism don't seek adult attention and don't share things they enjoy or are interested in. Children with autism don't usually get pleasure out of simple little social games like peek-a-boo, and they probably won't come running when you call out to them that you see something interesting out the window. These simple and meaningful little interactions bring out the best in parents, whose very attention usually acts as a positive reinforcement for their children's responsiveness, but unfortunately they don't often happen when a child has autism. For this reason, parents of children with autism need to master a whole new set of parenting skills, which adds even more stress to their emotional lives.

Sadly, many wonderful parents feel that they lack competence in dealing with their child with autism. It can be strange, alienating, and depressing to feel like your instincts are wrong when it comes to interacting with your own child. People frequently go too far in the opposite direction and stop having any natural parent/child interactions, worrying that if they relax and just fool around or talk nonsensically with their child, they'll lose precious moments of intervention time.

There are interventions that *increase* parents' stress by requiring unusual and difficult-to-engineer interactions between them and their child, and there are equally effective interventions—like those described in this book—that can be implemented in the context of natural activities. Don't feel like you have to sit down and spend hours drilling your child—you'll end up feeling guilty either because you don't spend as much time drilling him or her as you think you should or because you're taking time away from other important people in your life to do so.

Your child will learn more if you weave interventions into the context of daily activities, and your family life will be stronger for it.

Find Ways to Appreciate Your Child: Focus on His Strengths and Celebrate His Progress

Your child may have areas that need intervention, but every child also has special areas of strength. Don't just focus on the problem areas. Areas of strength can be used to improve areas of weakness. Focus on these areas of strength. Expand these areas.

For example, we worked with one preschooler who liked books but never engaged in any other kind of play, not interactive play, not pretend play, nothing. Rather than force him to play with toys he didn't like, we started using the books for imaginary play, pretending we were doing what the characters were doing. We were also able to use the books to work on turn taking, social conversation, and academic skills. Over time, he learned to pretend, to share, and to make comments about the stories. And by the time he got into kindergarten, he had learned to read and was able to read out loud to the class. This greatly impressed his classmates, who sought him out to read to them during unstructured class times.

It's also important that you celebrate improvements, no matter how small. It's easy to keep thinking about how far behind your child is, but if you focus on the improvements he's made, you'll realize how far he's come. And be sure to share your joy in his progress with the people who love him and you.

Last, don't forget that your child is still your child and that every child wants to feel loved by his parents. Any activity that the two of you enjoy together is precious, whether it's spending a half hour curled up on the sofa watching a favorite television show or going out for ice cream. While it's necessary to alter some of your ways of interacting with your child to facilitate his learning, it's equally necessary to maintain the basic loving relationship of parent and child, and if you're only thinking of yourself as his therapist, then you need to find your way back to being a parent again.

The Stress of Maintaining a Regular Family Life

Having a child with autism can change the family dynamics. Many parents—especially moms—can get so involved with the child with autism that they practically forget they have a spouse and other children. That's why it's important to use the interventions that are in the context of natural activities the whole family can enjoy. If you have other children, teach them how to interact with their sibling in positive, enriching ways. They can be great helpers. Research suggests that siblings of children with autism do not experience the high levels of stress that their parents do and aren't excessively worried, so don't feel you have to "protect them" from the disability. And, as adults, siblings of children with autism have a unique understanding of what goes on in day-to-day life and can be especially compassionate professionals. I've seen many siblings go into the field of disabilities as a result of their childhood experiences.

Again, remember that interventions have to work for the whole family system. If a program is requiring you to do things that interfere with your family's routines, or if the program is teaching a child to use a behavior that does not fit with your personal or cultural values, you must tell the person who's designing the program.

Make sure you and your spouse spend time alone together and that you get breaks from your job as caretaker and therapist. Don't be afraid to ask for help from relatives, friends, and others. If some times of day are especially difficult for you, hire a helper or find a volunteer from your local youth group, high school, or college. You'll be a much better parent if you have help, and you'll be a much better spouse if you have some free time. A good marriage and a happy family life will do wonders for every member of your family, including the one with special needs.

For more advice and thoughts on family life, see chapter 8.

Financial Stress

Dads, especially, feel stress in the area of finances.

Intervention for a child with autism can be very costly, and dads bear most of the financial burden in a lot of families. While no one will admit it, the truth is that agencies that are designed to help people in need—schools, insurance companies, centers for individuals with disabilities—are often reluctant to use their resources to help a child who will most likely need intensive intervention for many years. So not only do you have the stress of dealing with your child's severe disability, but the treatment you need to overcome it is expensive, and no one wants to pay for it.

If you can't afford the intervention, look into other sources of support. Schools usually will cover the costs of an established intervention program. Many states have regional centers that assist with the costs. Insurance companies often cover costs. Universities often have gift funds or grants that can help. And many universities and high schools have volunteer programs that might provide you with help for free. Keep looking. There *are* agencies that will help you financially.

FAQ

QUESTION: The developmental psychologist we saw told me that my child has autism and intellectual disabilities. This was a double whammy and extremely distressing to my family. Can children have both?

Generally, diagnosticians will try to find a primary diagnosis, then a secondary, if one exists. Children who have intellectual disabilities tend to have verbal and nonverbal areas that are delayed fairly equally, while children with autism usually have some relatively higher abilities, most often in the nonverbal areas, such as putting together puzzles, figuring out how the DVD player works, and so on. In addition, children with autism often meet most of their developmental milestones in the motor areas, such as sitting up, walking, and so on, on time, whereas children who have other types of disabilities may not.

It's possible that because your child is delayed socially and verbally, he's not scoring well on tests, which may give the impression that he has an intellectual disability. Keep in mind that it's very difficult to test children with autism, as these children are usually uninterested in and unmotivated by the tests. Many children score better under non-standardized conditions. You can often tell by observing the child if the nonverbal areas are higher than the verbal areas. Does your child play with toys and/or figure out tasks such as opening a latch to get a treat or fitting a key in a door? I'll never forget the dad who told me that he was watching his son take a vocabulary test: when the son was told to point to the bed, he pointed to the oven. The dad said that every night he told his son to jump into bed, and he always went straight to bed—not once had he ever jumped into the oven! Context makes a big difference in how children with autism perform.

Again, remember that settling on a diagnostic label is less important than teasing apart, one by one, the symptoms your child is expressing and developing an individualized intervention plan to specifically address those areas.

QUESTION: My child's teacher says that my child has both autism and hyperactivity. Is this possible?

Many children with autism have activity levels that are either higher or lower than that of their peers (hyper- or hypoactivity). This may be because the children aren't learning socially appropriate ways to interact, because they're not getting environmental stimulation in a typical way, or because learning is difficult, so they "tune out" and appear lethargic. Their active avoidance of activities may also make them appear more active than their peers. As the children begin to learn how to interact in socially appropriate ways, and as their communication improves, the activity levels often stabilize.

Hyperactivity can also be associated with self-stimulation (in other words, they have an excessively high activity level in the form of repetitive behavior)—the children may need a certain level of stimulation, and they're not getting it in a typical way. Whatever the reason, you can change the activity level of your child through good intervention programs.

> **QUESTION:** Because my husband works during the day, I'm the one driving my son to all his therapies and talking to all the clinicians who work with him. So when we need to work with him at home or when he's being disruptive and needs intervention, my husband always says, "You're the one who knows what to do." I'm tired of being the only expert in the family, but I have to admit it's hard trying to explain in detail what we're supposed to do. How can I make this more equal?

Often the parent who's around more will acquire more strategies for dealing with the child with autism, which can set up a cycle—the more she learns, the more she's called upon to do; the more expert she becomes, the more she continues to do. Your husband may genuinely feel like he's not as knowledgeable or capable as you when it comes to dealing with your child, but that doesn't mean he should excuse himself—it means he should catch up.

Schedule some one-on-one time for him with a therapist you both like on the weekend or in the evening, so he can learn successful strategies for dealing with your child. Then make sure he spends some time with your child each week as well, doing activities that are fun for both of them. We worked with one family whose son needed to develop socially. When we planned indoor activities, the father always got "tied up at work," but when we tried planning outdoor activities—a visit to the park or a hike—he never missed a single one.

Remember that it's often difficult for one parent to "teach" the other all the strategies that come along, and, depending on your relationship, it may strain the marriage to have one always dictating to the other. It's far better for you both if you're equally capable of interacting successfully with your child.

> **QUESTION:** I've accepted the fact that my daughter has autism and am ready to get started helping her, but my husband is furious that anyone would slap a label on a two-year-old child. He says she's just delayed and will catch up. What am I supposed to do?

You don't need to get your husband to accept a diagnosis, but you do need him to recognize that your child needs intervention to help with her symptoms. If he's uncomfortable with the term "autism," don't feel you need to use it. He has already acknowledged that she has delays, so point out that it can't *hurt* to address those delays in a thoughtful manner and it *will* definitely help. Together, you can identify the symptoms that are worrisome and ask the experts you've been seeing to recommend strategies that will help her overcome them.

If you both stay focused on the symptoms, you'll get the right results in the end, without having to stress about labels.

A MOTHER LOOKS AT DIAGNOSIS

There was no one moment when we found out that Andrew had autism. Maybe if we had been more in denial, there would have been some shock at the moment when the psychologist said to us, "I don't think he has autism . . . I *know* it," but, honestly, it wasn't entirely a surprise. It was painful news, and we didn't want to hear it, but we saw it coming.

Andrew was two and a half when we got the official diagnosis. We'd known for a while that he was different from other kids. He didn't talk, and he was socially withdrawn. At first—and for a long time—I just thought I was a bad mother. I wondered what I was doing that made my kid so much weepier and clingier than the other kids, so insistent on staying in my lap, so unwilling to play with the others. He was beautiful and healthy and had crawled, sat up, and walked exactly when he was supposed to. He knew his letters and could do challenging puzzles. That meant that his oddness and his nervousness were the result of bad parenting, right? What was I doing wrong? Did I coddle him too much, hold him too much, let him watch TV too much? He was my firstborn—at that point still my only child—and being a mother was a new and bewildering experience.

But the language thing—surely that couldn't be my fault? I talked to him all the time, repeated back his babbling sounds, did everything parents are supposed to do to encourage language development. And still he wasn't talking.

Was I a bad mother, or was there something seriously wrong with him? I wasn't crazy about either option. I just wished he'd start acting normal.

The Pediatrician Gets Involved

I remember Andrew's two-year checkup, because it was the first time his delayed language came up as an issue. Early in the appointment, I had accidentally dropped something that rolled under the chair, and Andrew leaned over to see where the object had gone. The pediatrician said at the end of the appointment that he was concerned Andrew still wasn't talking, given how "verbal" his parents were (i.e., we talked a lot), but then he said that he was reassured by the "appropriateness" of Andrew's interest in the dropped object. The doctor said he just wasn't sure whether there was a problem or not, so he left the decision of whether to see a speech pathologist up to us.

I was wildly relieved to hear someone I liked and trusted say that he didn't see anything obviously wrong with Andrew, apart from a minor speech delay—so relieved that I ignored the little voice in my head that was saying, "But I *know* he's different from other kids." The pediatrician was an expert, right? And he wasn't particularly worried? Great. I wanted so badly to believe that there wasn't anything really wrong with Andrew that I didn't acknowledge the fact that I spent a lot more time with him than the doctor was able to, and I just ran out of there as fast as I could. But six months later, at the next checkup, the pediatrician admitted he was now concerned about Andrew's lack of speech and recommended we take him to a speech therapist named Roberta Poster.

So we did. We watched Roberta get to know Andrew and hoped she'd tell us that we were being silly, that he was perfectly normal, that we should just go home and enjoy him and he'd be fine.

She didn't say anything like that, just set a regular weekly appointment for Andrew and suggested we play some games with him to heighten his social interaction.

At a subsequent session, when Roberta said to us, "Do you have any guesses about what's going on here?" I actually muttered something about how maybe it could be autism—hoping, I guess, that she would adamantly disagree with me. I mean, it wasn't like it hadn't crossed my mind.

And she said, carefully, "I'm not a diagnostician, but his behaviors do suggest that that could be a possibility. You might want to have him evaluated."

If step one was our sneaking little fear that something was seriously wrong with our child, then step two was hearing a professional say that maybe there was something to our sneaking little fear. We decided we needed to know for sure and took Andrew to see Dr. B. J. Freeman at UCLA, and she said her thing about being certain he had autism.

And that was step three: Utter and Complete Confirmation of Our Worst Fear.

Talk to Each Other

I come from an unemotional family. People don't cry or say "I love you," and they downplay big moments. So I thought I had to be cool about this. Act like it was no huge deal. Do the research, call some experts, fix my kid. Breaking down would just waste everyone's time. That first day, Rob and I were both very calm. We asked B. J. some questions, then went home and vowed to go to the bookstore the next day to buy some books on autism. We discussed it all fairly dispassionately.

But that night, I rocked our younger son to sleep and, alone with the sleeping baby in the dark, finally allowed myself to sob. My beautiful little boy had autism. His future was dark and awful. I loved him, but I couldn't save him from this. In my whole sheltered, charmed life, nothing had ever hurt this much.

Months later, I found out Rob had done the same thing—snuck off somewhere by himself to cry. I don't know why we didn't cry together. We should have. It took us almost a year to recover from the news, a year that almost destroyed our marriage, because we both chose to hide our misery instead of share it.

When I talk to people now who've just had a child diagnosed with any kind of special need, one of the first things I say is, "Talk to each other about how sad you are." You may think you need to be brave for your spouse's sake, but putting on a false front doesn't help anyone. You both need to mourn, and you need to mourn together. You're the only two people in the world who are feeling the same thing at that moment. You've just had a rough bit of news—at least let it pull you closer together instead of push you apart.

And don't forget what being brave actually means: it doesn't mean not being scared; it means taking action and facing the truth *even though* you're scared. So don't feel like you need to be stoic and impassive: go ahead and let yourself feel the emotions as they come, but let them be the spur that gets you to plunge into the work you need to do to help your child learn.

Telling People

You should, you know. Tell people. You don't have to walk up to strangers on the street or anything, but confide in the people who love you. That was one thing we did right: we told our families and our friends right away. First we called them, and then we copied a good, comprehensive article someone had written about autism and annotated it with specifics about Andrew, and we mailed it to everyone we knew. (You could do the same thing with sections from this book, by the way.)

None of our good friends pulled away from us because our kid had autism. Just the opposite—our friends and families rallied around us in amazing ways and have continued to cheer Andrew's progress on year after year.

In all honesty, telling people what we were going through only made our lives easier. Before then, we worried that Andrew's occasionally aberrant behavior was off-putting. But once he had a formal diagnosis, everyone cut us a lot of slack, and instead of wondering what the hell was wrong with us as parents, most people we knew admitted to a newfound respect for us for dealing with so much.

Real friends don't love you more for being successful or less for having problems. If anything, it works the opposite way—we're all so busy that sometimes we forget to stay in touch with friends when everything's fine for them, but we rush forward when they need us. Now is the time to take advantage of that. Talk your friends' ears off, complain, bitch and moan to them about how miserable you are, and if they should offer to help out, *let them*. You're dealing with a huge challenge—take advantage of every minor plus it has to offer.

What People Say

I know I said I was glad I told people, but I have to admit that I was horrible about judging everything said to me in response back then. I was hurting all over, and however calm and rational I may have sounded, inside I was quivering with the expectation of being hurt more. Let me give you some examples of the innocuous things people said and how I overreacted to them.

There were the people who jumped a little too eagerly at the news, in my opinion—"Oh, well, *that* explains it. I mean, it was clear something was going on. . . ." That reaction always pissed me off. Are you telling me my kid looked and acted weird to you? You never said anything to me, but now you're telling me you were sitting there *judging* us all the time?

(Remember, I wasn't being rational—I was being emotional. Also remember I didn't say any of this out loud. Thank goodness.)

Another group went for reassurance. "Oh, really? Well, I'm sure in a few years he'll be fine." Yeah? How do you know that? The experts we're consulting don't know what lies in Andrew's future, but you're so incredibly clairvoyant *you* do? Give me a break.

Sometimes people would try to act like it was no big deal, that they themselves went through something similar with their totally normal kids and came out the other side. "The early years are hard for all kids," they'd say. "We were so worried when our kid was three and didn't play catch, and now look—he's captain of the softball team!" Wait a second—was your kid diagnosed with autism? Excuse me, but was your kid diagnosed with autism? *Was he diagnosed with autism?* Because, if he wasn't, I don't really want to hear about your experiences.

I knew that those who expressed sympathy meant well—"Oh, how awful! I'm so sorry for you. You must be overwhelmed," etc. The problem was that, at that emotional point in my life, they only made me feel worse. My son—my gorgeous, bright, loving little boy—had apparently turned into something so awful that people *pitied* me for having him. That sucked.

Worst of all were the people who questioned the diagnosis without any medical or neurological information to back up their challenge: "Are they sure? Because he looks fine to me. Sometimes doctors just *say* these things because it's what they like to say. I just don't believe it." You don't, huh? Did it ever occur to you that we didn't particularly want to believe it, either? That we ran home to read everything we could about autism only to discover, with a sick stomach and heart, that Andrew had pretty much *every single symptom* of your basic classic autism? Self-stimulation? Check. Social delays? Check. Language delays? Check. Inability to make eye contact? Check. Inability to point to something he wants? Check. Inability to follow simple directions? Check. And so on. We're telling you our kid has autism because we've done the research and know it's true. So please don't start second-guessing us or the experts we trust.

The Point of All This

I realize I've gone on kind of at length about how easily I slipped into feeling offended at that time, but it's for a reason: I want to make it clear how incredibly fragile and wounded the diagnosis had left me.

The truth was, of course, that every friend and relative I spoke to was kind and sympathetic. They all offered help and support. I just couldn't see it because I was one raw, gaping wound, an exposed nerve, a total wreck.

You are, you know, when you get that diagnosis. You're a wreck.

There's this huge *thing* in your life that wasn't there before. It sits there looking at you, and you try not to spend all your time thinking about it, but it just takes up too much space. You can't *not* think about it all the time.

The worst is in the middle of the night, when you lie awake wondering what the future holds for your kid. You want to be positive, but you just keep coming back to Dustin Hoffman in *Rain Man*, with his institutionalization and staccato speech and no social life and just this awful bleak nothing of a future.

Was that going to be my son? I'd never seen an adult with autism in real life. Was that because they all ended up in institutions? I honestly didn't know. Say Andrew did have to be institutionalized one day. Would we ever be able to save up enough money to keep him in a *good* institution for the rest of his life? Or would he end up in a snake pit, beaten and tortured and starved into some sort of brain-dead submission? What about his little newborn brother—would he have to work hard his whole life to support his brother in an institution?

Which led, of course, to a far worse thought—what if his baby brother had autism, too? Could I ever survive two diagnoses?

Middle-of-the-night anxieties, all of these, but sometimes the morning isn't all that much better, because you wake up and there's so much still to deal with: the therapies you have to drive to—and have you chosen the right ones?—the kids who say mean things at your son's school, the school parents who don't talk to you because your kid is weird and they think you're a bad parent, the baby you adore but never have any time to play with because your other kid needs so much of your attention. . . .

Man, it's hard. If you're going through it now, you know how hard it is.

But know this, too:

It gets better.

Getting Better All the Time

When Andrew was ten, my husband and I went away overnight without the four kids, for the first time in ages. We stayed at a small hotel in Malibu, and as we walked along the beach that evening, we held hands and fantasized about retiring to a small cottage near the beach one day, just the two of us, when the kids were all grown up and on their own.

It was a nice dream. And hours later, it suddenly hit me—we had stopped worrying about Andrew's future.

For years, any discussion about the future was tempered by the nagging fear that we might still have to take care of Andrew, that he might be living with us or, worse, in an expensive institution. But gradually, as Andrew's skills grew and he started to catch up to his peers in most areas, that concern slowly faded away. Somehow, the thought "He'll probably need us to always take care of him" became "*Of course* he'll be an independent adult."

Admittedly, no one knows what the future holds, and it's possible that any one of our kids might still be living with us into his or her forties (hey, it happens). But the fear is gone, and the future looks pretty bright at the moment.

How Did We Get from There to Here?

The short answer is: interventions. The work we did with Andrew improved his symptoms and raised our spirits. Activity brings hope. Not doing anything because you don't know what to do—that's what brings on the bone-deadening "Why us?" kind of depression.

How did we know what to do? We didn't, at first, and that was definitely the darkest time. Fortunately for us, by the time we got the actual diagnosis of autism, Andrew was already seeing Roberta Poster, and she was a fantastic speech therapist. She referred us to Dr. Freeman, who referred us to Wayne Tashjian, a brilliant behavioral therapist (that is, someone who, like Dr. Koegel, approaches the child from a behavioral standpoint and uses positive reinforcement to improve behaviors and teach age-appropriate skills), and also to an occupational therapist and, over time, a recreational therapist and a tutor (although Andrew was a good student, he did need help in certain areas that required more sophisticated verbal skills than he had yet acquired, like word problems or reading comprehension).

All of this was expensive. We paid for some of it, got our insurance to pay for a few things, and eventually discovered that our public school system could be called upon to finance a part of it as well.

Good referrals led to more good referrals. We asked the experts we trusted, and as we met more and more parents of children with autism, we shared names and compared experiences. Not everything panned out equally well— for example, the same mother who gave us the name of an amazing music therapist who developed Andrew's love for song, rhythm, and playing the piano also gave us the name of a self-styled "computer therapist," whose services I found to be a complete waste of time.

You sift through your choices. You trust your gut.

And when Andrew was in preschool, a friend who had two sons with autism told us about this amazing clinic she'd discovered in Santa Barbara, run by a husband-and-wife team. She said their approach, which taught family-based interventions that focused on specific important areas, was doing wonders with everyone who went there. We met with Dr. Lynn Koegel as soon as we could get an appointment, and she taught us that virtually *all* interventions could be integrated into our daily lives and that leading the most normal lives possible was the best therapy for Andrew and for the entire family.

We were already working with some truly extraordinary people, and we shared Dr. Koegel's suggestions with everyone, so we could integrate them consistently into our daily lives. Dr. Koegel's advice helped us to refine and focus our interventions, so that Andrew made huge strides with the same amount of scheduled therapy time he'd always had—maybe even with less. And Rob and I felt more capable than we ever had before that we were steering him in the right direction.

Don't Lose Faith

Good friends of ours recently had dinner with a pediatrician. The subject turned to autism, and the doctor told them that his personal belief was that early intervention made no difference in a child's outcome, that his or her ultimate success or failure was hardwired at birth. "There's nothing *wrong* with most interventions," the doctor said. "They won't hurt. But they don't make any difference. I don't recommend them for my patients with autism."

My friends told us about this conversation because they were so horrified that anyone could go around saying that. They knew how we felt—that the interventions we'd put in place with amazing people like Dr. Koegel had pulled Andrew out of a dark, withdrawn place and helped him to overcome the worst symptoms of his autism.

We *know* that interventions turned Andrew around, and the research we describe in this book provides the scientific proof. From the very beginning, starting with our first speech therapist, we saw this kid who had been receding further and further away from us turn around and start moving back toward us. We saw systematic and scientifically validated interventions work.

No One Said It Would Be Easy

It's shocking how hard it is to keep a child with autism engaged in all the right ways, especially during the crucial early years. Although Dr. Koegel's interventions are engineered to slip into your day-to-day interactions with your child, the truth is that most kids with autism feel a strong pull away from any kind of engagement back into their own private world, and the energy parents need to keep pulling them back can be overwhelming.

At the very beginning of our journey, Roberta told us time and time again that we had to keep Andrew engaged as much as possible. I remember losing it. Just losing it. I had a fretful newborn who kept me up at night, and after a long day of caring for both small children and driving Andrew from one therapy to another, I was too exhausted to do anything but prop him in front of the TV or let him retreat into his mysterious world of lining things up and laughing to himself.

My husband was writing on a sitcom that had incredibly long hours. By the time he came home at ten or eleven at night, he was totally exhausted, and even on his rare early nights, he was wiped out. We'd both be collapsed on a sofa, barely able to move, and then we'd hear Andrew off by himself, playing his little self-stimulatory games and murmuring senselessly, and I'd be hit by an overwhelming sense of failure. Concern soon turned to anger—I kept thinking it was all Rob's fault, that if he would just go play with Andrew, I wouldn't have to feel so guilty about everything. I had spent the day with the kids—wasn't it his turn?

And Rob was thinking the same thing, of course—that he'd had a long day and didn't have anything left to give, but here he was feeling guilty, and if I would just get up and interact with Andrew, then *he* wouldn't have to feel so bad.

The truth was that we were both tapped out. Neither of us had the energy to engage our son, and we were resenting each other for it.

That was when we realized it was time to start hiring some extra help.

We're lucky. We can afford to spend money out of our own pocket for stuff like that. We hired an undergraduate named Pete Candela—who had worked with Andrew already at UCLA—to come every day for an hour or so late in the afternoon or early in the evening, just to play with Andrew and keep him engaged. These few hours improved our lives immeasurably in every possible way.

State centers will sometimes help pay for this kind of support, I know, and a lot of people can call on close friends and relatives to help, either financially or with the actual work. My sister Nell used to come in the evenings just to play with Andrew and give us a break. Her energy was unbelievable—at that point, she didn't have children of her own, so she didn't mind wearing herself out with Andrew. She made up great games and kept Andrew happy and engaged every time she came over.

So we discovered there *are* alternatives to sitting around and glaring at each other.

Doing the Research Together

Most of the time, Rob and I felt pretty confident about the interventions and therapists we had selected. Occasionally, though, doubt would creep in. For example, right after Andrew turned three, he had a down period (there were occasionally times when he didn't make progress or even appeared to slide backward for a few weeks), and we both felt a little panicky. We knew of some families who had made great progress with a series of interventions that involved long hours of the children sitting at tables being drilled by trained therapists. From the beginning, we felt strongly that we didn't want our very young child involved in any therapy that felt more like work than play. It just didn't feel natural.

But with Andrew plateauing, Rob and I wondered whether we were making a mistake not to try an approach that had so many previously nonverbal kids talking. So we started asking all the experts we knew and respected what their opinion of that particular approach was.

And not one of them thought we should pursue it. They all agreed that a bright, motivated kid like Andrew was going to make progress either way, but on the path we had chosen—where all interventions were playful and fun—he would simply become more and more motivated and social. And while it was true that Andrew's language might increase more quickly with drilling, most felt it would be at a cost, that he would become more robotic in his responses, more like a joyless trained animal and less like a normal kid.

Rob and I talked it all out, and we decided that we wanted to stick with interventions that mimicked the way most kids learn, through play and socializing. Maybe we'd lose a little time, but we were fairly confident the end result would be better.

We did the research, thought and talked about it, and in the end we continued on our way, feeling we had made the best choice for our son, who was soon learning and growing again.

And Here We Are

There was a time when I thought I would never hear my child say "Mommy," never be able to give him a simple direction and have him follow it, never send him alone on a play date to a friend's house, never drop him off at school without wondering if he would spend the day isolated and unreachable.

But back when we were finishing the first edition of this book, I stopped and took stock and realized how far he had come: there he was, excitedly planning his sixth-grade year at a regular private middle school, where we expected him to make his way like any other student.

Things change. They get better.

Ten Years Later

What a difference almost a decade makes: middle school already feels like a long time ago. Some of our hopes came true; some didn't. Andrew did fine at his classes and became much more independent during those three years, but he also sadly came to feel socially cut off. I remember dropping him off at the bus stop one day and watching him cheerfully greet the other kids, only to have them literally close ranks by making a small circle that excluded him. If you're a parent, you don't need me to tell you how I felt for the rest of that day. There was a lot of teasing—not just of him, of course, but he definitely got his share of it—and he now says middle school was rough, probably his roughest time. (To be fair, my other kids say the same thing about middle school—it may be par for the course.)

High school started off a little rocky but got better and we felt we'd made the right choice for him there. He went to a private high school near us that's known for its inclusiveness and support of kids with different learning styles. Andrew ended up with a few really close friends and real pride in his school: when his sister decided to go there too, years later, he cheered.

He goes to college now, in Vermont, about 2,500 miles away from home. We have no involvement in his daily life, aside from the occasional phone call or care package: he's responsible for choosing his courses, making sure he gets to them, and passing them. Last year he changed his major without even telling us, but when we found out, we approved. It was a good decision and he was on top of which courses he would now need to take.

When he's home, Andrew does a lot of the family driving: Rob and I depend on him to run errands and do school pickups. He insists on doing his own laundry and is the first to jump up to help if I have bags to carry in from the car. He's successfully held down a summer job, and wants to enter the work force right after college, although he admits that the task of launching a career is daunting.

His life isn't perfect—there are frustrations and disappointments, and I think they're probably beyond those that typical kids experience, but it's not my place to tell his story anymore. Andrew is a grown man now. His life is his own and, for the most part, it's pretty separate from mine. His dad and I love him and worry about him and try to help him any way we can, but the stories belong to him now.

Looking for Inspiration

Many readers of the first edition of this book have told me that learning about Andrew's journey was inspiring to them: it gave them hope and encouraged them to keep working hard, even when progress felt slow and limited.

I'm glad that sharing our stories has helped people, because after Andrew was diagnosed, I was desperate to meet older children and adults on the spectrum, but I had trouble finding many. I'm not sure why that is, but one guess is that people were less open about autism in general back then, so if someone had gotten the diagnosis but was doing well, maybe her family didn't want to use the label, and if someone had gotten the diagnosis and was still struggling, maybe his family wasn't taking him to social events as much as they might have. At any rate, I felt frustrated and ignorant, which made me even more nervous about what the future might hold for my little boy.

So it's wonderful that there are so many more adults out there now, proudly declaring themselves to be on the spectrum and writing about their lives. There's Temple Grandin, of course—a top-of-her-field professional who not only lectures around the world about autism but even had an Emmy-winning movie made about her life. There's Kevin Hosseini, a young and extremely talented artist whose pieces are on display in museums all around the world. John Elder Robison's *New York Times* bestselling books are about his life with Asperger's. And there are many more writers and speakers, all of whom say proudly, "This is who I am and I'm happy to be me." I wish that fifteen years ago I had had all these great example of adults on the spectrum who are successful and in the public eye. They prove that there are no limits to what your child can do, where he can go, what he can become. They are inspiring in the truest sense of the word.

How Society Has Changed: And How It Needs to Change *More*

I was asked to speak at a library recently about my writing career. I've written eight novels, so I figured I'd be asked lots of questions about fiction writing and how to get a book published. But as soon as I mentioned coauthoring two books about autism with Dr. Koegel, that was pretty much all the majority of the audience wanted to ask about. Even though the event was not about autism, most of the people in the room appeared to have a family member or friend on the spectrum. And this is something huge that's happened over the last decade: you don't have to seek out an autism support group to find people who know what autism is. *Everyone* does. Back in the early nineties, very few non-pros knew much more than that it was what the guy in *Rain Man* had, and they tended to assume that our kids' skills were pretty much limited to knowing how many toothpicks were in a pile on the floor.

Now if I mention having cowritten two books on the subject to new acquaintances, they'll almost instantly say, "My [grandson, nephew, friend's son, cousin's daughter—take your pick] was just diagnosed." Then they'll usually ask whether more kids have autism now than they used to or whether they're just being diagnosed more. (My traditional answer is "Probably both.") Then they'll want to know how my son is doing, and the best part of all is that when I say, "Oh, he's in college now," they no longer fall over in surprise. They nod and ask questions about where and what we think of it. And they don't want to know just because they're polite: they want to know so they can pass the information on to their friend or relative. Because people have stopped thinking, "A kid with autism can't go to college," and have started thinking, "What's the best place for a kid with autism to go to college?"

I love these changes. I used to feel like identifying my son as being on the spectrum marked him in people's eyes as the walking wounded, someone who was suffering and disabled—and that wasn't something we felt or wanted others to feel. Now he's simply one of a growing community, and people hope and expect to hear that he's doing well and continuing his education.

Educating Through Entertainment

In several of the novels I've written, I've included at least one character who falls somewhere on the spectrum. In my second novel, the protagonist is actually working in an autism clinic with young children, but in the other books, they're simply family members—quirky, loving, unique, accepted. I created these characters partially out of the old "write what you know" tradition, but also because I think that including people with differences in fiction is one of the best ways to make our society more accepting. I don't think there's any question that television shows with likable gay characters did more to help the gay rights movement than all the lectures in the world ever could have. People become comfortable through exposure—and entertainment is an awfully pleasant way for people to absorb new ideas.

I'm happy to see that many other writers are doing the same thing. There's currently a prime-time TV show (*Parenthood*) featuring a character on the spectrum, and there was a movie out not long ago about a young man with Asperger's, starring the gorgeous Hugh Dancy. (A crushable character with autism! We *are* making strides!) My brother-in-law Ken LaZebnik wrote a play called *On the Spectrum* that's been produced in two cities and has won a bunch of awards and is about a young woman with autism and a young male "Aspie" who fall in love. People speculate that the totally kick-ass title character in Stieg Larsson's *Girl with the Dragon Tattoo* has Asperger's. And so on.

It's a goal of mine—and I hope of other writers—to continue this momentum, to make a point of creating characters who cover the spectrum of the spectrum, who bring all the positives and frustrations of dealing with autism out into the open, and who say to the world, "We are your families; we are your friends; we are you."

Maybe the Biggest Change of All?

Ten years ago, the teaching all went in one direction: our kids with autism had to learn to fit in, to be more like their peers. Now we're beginning to see that while it's just as important as ever to encourage our kids to engage, socialize, communicate, and interact with their communities, those communities have their own learning to do: we need to do a better job at accepting those with differences and welcoming those who don't fit into a specific, narrow mold.

We all benefit when our society becomes more tolerant. Different perspectives, different experiences, different cultures—these things enrich our shared body of knowledge, and ideals of acceptance are the foundation of civilization. Let's all work on becoming more accepting, and let's encourage our friends and neighbors to do the same. The next time someone talks about "the weird kid in class" or makes a disparaging comment about someone who's different in any way, use it as a teaching moment. Remind that person that a tolerant society becomes a rich, varied, and caring one and that that's good for everyone.

And now I'm going to step down from my soapbox. Brownies don't bake themselves.

Chapter Two
Ending the Long Silence:
Teaching Your Child to Communicate

QUESTION: My grandson was perfect. He hardly ever cried. He crawled, sat up, and walked on time. He said a few words just before his second birthday, but a few months later he stopped using them. Now he's almost three, and he doesn't say anything and cries all the time, and the doctor told my daughter he may have autism. What can we do?

QUESTION: When my child was twenty months old, she could sing nursery rhymes. By twenty-two months, she could sing the alphabet song. We thought she was a genius. But by two years she wasn't talking to other people. Now she's two and a half and hardly seems interested in anyone. If we push her, she'll repeat what we say, but she never tries to interact with anyone on her own. Will she ever converse?

I remember when my daughter was born, I could hardly wait for her to start talking. I wanted to get to know the personality of this little person and learn her innermost secrets, her pain, and her joys. When she could still barely sit up, I started naming every item she came across and enthusiastically encouraged every little verbal attempt she made. Sure enough, not long after her first birthday, she started saying a few words. By a year and a half, she said many dozens of words and was such a good learner that I was able to teach her to call out "Dada!" in the morning, so my husband would have to get up while I got a few extra minutes of rest. Every day we marveled at her blossoming vocabulary, and somewhere around her second birthday, she could carry on a little conversation with her word combinations. Maybe it was the fact that I was a speech therapist that made me so obsessed with her ability to communicate—or maybe I'm just like any other parent, dying to experience the joy of having a conversation with my own child.

That brings me to the pain I feel for parents of children with autism who don't communicate. The very defining feature of autism includes communication delays—and that doesn't just mean that your child is a late talker. It means social communication is delayed, which affects all types of interactions with other people and often includes an apparent lack of interest in talking to or communicating with anyone, even Mom and Dad.

I had one family visit me a few years back. The dad was in the movie business and had been involved in one successful film after another. He was rich and famous and was happily married to a beautiful, intelligent woman. By most people's standards, he was a highly successful individual. He had a three-year-old child with autism who hadn't started talking. One day he confided to me that he would give up anything he had, even his own voice, if his child could talk.

Even his own voice.

This has always haunted me—the stress and agony of having a child who can't talk, who can't tell you he doesn't like a babysitter or that he has an earache or what he wants to eat. Even the children who have some language usually start out using their words only to ask for something, not to say those social things that are so meaningful to parents, like "Mama," "Dada," or "I love you."

What Does "Lack of Communication" Mean?

Although most children with autism have problems with communication, their difficulties vary hugely. Some never start talking at all on their own and probably never would if they didn't get intervention. Although they may make some noises, they don't develop any meaningful words or sounds on their own. Other children with autism may say some words early on but then stop. Incidentally, this unusual pattern of learning speech and losing it often leads to the parents' believing something has "happened" to their child, that some external event has caused a neurological problem that wasn't there at birth. However, it may also be a motivational problem—that is, communication is difficult, so why keep trying?

Another subgroup does develop some verbal communication, but it's delayed. These children usually use words and language to express their basic needs and wants but have little interest in communicating for purely social reasons.

Echolalia

Other children with autism develop what's called "echolalia" or "echolalic speech." Echolalia is when the child repeats part or all of the previous phrase spoken by another person, usually without understanding. Sometimes they do this immediately after hearing it, and other times it's a while later. When it is later, such as the next day, week, or month, it's called "delayed" echolalia. Adults often misinterpret echolalia as appropriate communication. I knew one mother who used to say "I love you" to her child, and when he repeated it tonelessly, she would give him a big, happy hug. It was heartbreaking. A common example of delayed echolalia is when a child repeats a word, segment, or phrase from a favorite video hours, days, or even weeks after watching it. Other children can sing entire songs without really understanding the meaning.

Sometimes children echo when they don't understand what has just been said, and other times they do understand but just can't use the grammar correctly. For instance, if you ask a child, "Do you want Cheerios?" and he responds with "You want Cheerios," it may be that he understands the question but simply isn't able to reverse the pronouns to say "I want Cheerios." Other times a child will echo whatever you say, so if you say, "Do you want Cheerios or chocolate-covered ants?" he will respond with "Do you want Cheerios or chocolate-covered ants," or even just "Chocolate-covered ants." There is a difference between these two forms of echolalia, and we'll talk about how to assess that later in this chapter.

Compensating for Lack of Language

Often the child's difficulty communicating is what makes parents first suspect that he or she may have a disability. Without a way to communicate, a child will have trouble having her needs met and is likely to resort to crying, tantrums, or other types of disruptive behavior to communicate her desires and frustrations.

To compensate for not talking, most children with autism display what has been called "autistic leading." That is, they'll take an adult's hand and lead that person to a desired item or activity. Since this can be a successful strategy to get most of their needs met without language, it makes it even harder to teach them to talk—without the drive to be social, and with all their wants taken care of, they don't feel the *need* to talk. Other children, like my nephew, will risk life and limb to do things on their own. Rather than try to ask for something or communicate with another person, my nephew used to climb up bookcases or onto the kitchen counter to retrieve a desired item or to get his favorite snack.

Can Kids on the Autism Spectrum Learn to Talk?

In the relatively recent past, only about half of all children with autism ever became verbal, even with intervention. However, we now have improved teaching techniques, and today most children who start early intervention with a verbal approach—which is what we'll describe in this book—are able to learn to use words and language to communicate. To be specific, if we start intervention for communication before the age of three, about 95 percent of children with autism who are *completely* nonverbal will learn to communicate verbally if the right approach is used, like the one we describe in this book. For children starting the intervention between the ages of three and five who are nonverbal, the probability goes down a bit, to 85 to 90 percent; and unfortunately only 20 percent of nonverbal children over five years old learn to communicate verbally.

Please realize that five years of age is not a magical number. The percentages are based on large databases, and many children do learn to communicate verbally after five. In fact, two summers ago we saw a fifteen-year-old boy who had never said a word in his life. Although he was toilet trained, he urinated in his pants during our first session because he wasn't able to ask where the toilet was. After about two hours of working with him, using the methods described later in this chapter, we got him to say "cracker," perfectly clearly, two times. His mother was shocked and elated to learn that he was indeed able to say a word. The family lived a distance away, but after a few months they returned for a week of training, and in those few months, using the approach described below, the mom had taught him to say about six different words with perfect articulation. We continued to work on more and more words, and by the end of a week he could repeat many words and said about twenty all by himself. Six months later he returned again, and by that time he was able to say about fifty or sixty words, so we started having him say two words together.

Now he's able to say short sentences. He doesn't express his feelings or thoughts yet, but he is able to let us know *verbally* what he wants. This was a child everyone, except his mother, had given up on. No one thought he could learn to talk, but his mom was determined and willing to work hard to turn things around.

But also consider that these are statistics from large groups of children and be aware that success isn't guaranteed right up until the day of the child's fifth birthday. I recently had a family visit from another country; the child was four years, ten months old and didn't say a word. According to the parents, no one had ever worked on verbal communication with him. The family stayed for one week and he really didn't have a clue that he was supposed to make a verbalization to communicate. He went through about every behavior in his repertoire— including biting, hitting, and throwing tantrums—and by the end of the week, while he did understand that the disruptive behavior didn't work to get him what he wanted (fortunately that decreased quickly), he still wasn't making any consistent vocalizations for items.

So *don't wait*. The longer a child goes without having to use verbal communication, the more difficult it will be to make that connection. Typical language learners say their first words between eleven and fourteen months. Boys may be a little slower, but if they aren't saying a word by eighteen months, it won't hurt to get that checked. And remember that by eighteen to twenty-four months most children are beginning to combine words: they need a pretty big vocabulary for that, so don't let your child get too far behind.

Typical language learners start with social words, like "Mama" and "Dada." Pointing and asking "Dat?" to get you to label things is also quite common. If your child exclusively uses words to request items—usually without looking at you, pointing, or engaging in any other way—it's a great idea to get an evaluation right away. There are so many things that can be done at an early age, and waiting just reduces your child's chances to have the best outcome possible.

The Complexities of Speech

When you think about it, verbal communication is incredibly complicated— given what's involved, it's surprising *anyone* learns to talk. Simple speech consists of a sound system involving vowels, consonants, groups of consonants, and complex combinations of vowels and consonants to form words. Each word has its own semantic meaning and must be combined with other words in a specific syntactic order to make sense. In addition, the words have to be spoken with the right volume, pitch, intonation patterns, and rate to sound right.

Finally, these word combinations have to be used in a pragmatically appropriate way, using the right gestures, eye contact, facial and body expressions, and empathy to develop and maintain relationships. Fortunately, the human brain is wired to learn all of this naturally and easily.

Unless, of course, you have something wrong with the part of your brain that controls speech and language. In that case, the simple task of saying "Hi" probably feels like what it would for the rest of us to try to do differential calculus. Not only do you have to figure out what to say and how to say it, but once you've done that, the other guy will most likely say something else that you've got to try to understand, and then you're supposed to say something else back that's even harder than the initial "Hi."

It's a lot easier just to avoid the whole thing, as many children with autism do, and understandably so.

TEACHING WORDS AND LANGUAGE TO NONVERBAL CHILDREN

A child with autism may not initially understand why it's so important to learn how to talk—it's hard work, and it's a lot easier just to take someone's hand and march him over to the orange juice when you want orange juice. Why bother?

Our goal is to make learning language rewarding and fun—so much fun that the child doesn't even realize he's learning this really difficult thing called talking.

Two Terms You'll Need to Know for This Chapter and All the Others: Prompting and Fading

Your child will probably need some help or "prompts" to learn many of the things you teach him. Prompts can be physical, verbal, or gestural. For example, when you're teaching first words you'll need to start by modeling the whole word. That's a verbal prompt. If you were teaching your child to hit a baseball, you might start out by standing behind her with your hands over hers on the bat and helping her swing at just the right time to hit the ball. That's a physical prompt. And other activities, such as reminding your child to put on his shoes while getting dressed may just require a point, or gestural prompt.

But our ultimate goal is to have our child be completely independent with these new behaviors. To do that, we'll need to fade our prompts. We need to gradually back off. This may seem like a straightforward thing to do, but many times a prompt-fading program isn't in place, and the child never becomes independent. You've probably heard of "hovering": this is a common expression, usually applied to school aides who help the child too much—sometimes so much that the child never learns to become independent. And that happens because there's no prompt-fading program in place.

I've also seen the opposite problem, when staff members fade their prompts so quickly that the child never really learns the new behavior. So make sure whenever you teach a new behavior—or when someone else does—that there's an intelligent, gradual, and systematic fading program in place.

For example, if your child doesn't interact at all with peers and is learning how to initiate greetings and get a conversation started, the school aide may need to accompany him initially and model an entire sentence for him, such as, "Hi, Ty, can I play handball with you guys?" But we don't want the aide doing that all year long. We want your child to initiate greetings and play bids independently. So the plan might be to prompt the child in greeting and joining in play ten times, then start to fade that full verbal prompt, perhaps by suggesting that the child go over, greet friends, then ask them to play while the aide steps back. Then the child can report back to the aide whether he greeted and joined in play, so you can all keep track of the progress, until she's engaging in these play initiations independently, and the prompts can be completely faded.

With first words, you may want to begin prompting the whole word, then fade that prompt to just saying the first sound or just one syllable of the word, then mouth it without sound, then wait expectantly until your child says the word independently. We'll talk more about prompting and fading language in the rest of this chapter.

With physical prompts, you want to provide less and less support until your child is engaging in the behavior without your help. It's the same thing with gestural prompts. At first you may need to point to your child's shoes to remind him what the next step is in getting dressed, but eventually you'll do less of the pointing until he can do it on his own.

A good prompt-fading program is well thought-out and applied very gradually and systematically until the child is responding correctly and independently without that extra help. And don't worry if you fade the prompt too quickly and then realize your child isn't able to be independent yet. It happens. You just need to move back to the step where your child was successful, then develop a branch step (a smaller, easier step) or fade more gradually.

This may all sound obvious and natural, but I can't begin to tell you how many programs I've seen where the prompting was faded too quickly, and the children didn't fully use their newly learned behaviors across different settings or over time. Let me give you an example. Often children with autism who are included in regular education classes will be given full-time aides, but once they're doing well, the school will recommend that the aide be faded. No gradual and systematic fading—just taken away. In cases like these, each school subject needs to be carefully examined, and fading needs to begin during times when the child is completely successful, and only during those times. The aide needs to check in with the teacher to make sure that the child was still successful during the fading, in the absence of the aide. And everyone needs to be aware that a child who isn't bothering anyone but who also isn't actively learning or is by himself on the playground still needs prompting.

Similarly, if you're working on improving socialization by having playdates, and your child does really well with planned activities, don't stop planning activities abruptly. Just gradually and systematically decrease your presence and assistance until your child responds at the same excellent level she did in the beginning when you were more significantly involved. A well-planned and intelligent prompt-fading program will help assure that your child will continue to use the new behaviors you've taught her in many different situations and for the long haul. Don't short-change your child or waste her valuable time by forgetting to implement a prompt-fading program.

Now here's how to get your child talking in six basic steps:

1. First Find Something Your Child Is Willing to Try Really Hard For

The first and most critical thing is to identify the objects or activities that are so important to your child that they are *worth talking for*.

Because children on the spectrum aren't socially motivated, they're not particularly interested in repeating people's names. But there's usually something out there the child definitely wants and will try really hard to get. Sometimes it's the obvious thing, like a bottle or blanket for small children, but sometimes you have to look a little harder.

When you're first starting out teaching language, we recommend using specific, concrete items, like toys and food—things you can hold and ultimately hand to the child when he tries to talk. (If you just can't find an item he likes, an activity he enjoys can also serve as a useful, concrete reward.) There are several reasons for this. One is that these kids are very literal, and showing them a picture or a label of something just isn't going to lead to the same kind of definite connection between word and object that you want and you'll get if the object is at hand. Another is that they can't always transfer their identification of a picture to the actual object, so while you might be able to teach them that a picture of a cup is a "cup," they may not generalize that to an actual three-dimensional cup. Additionally, if the children learn to identify common toys and foods, then whether they're at home or school or other kids' houses, they'll be familiar with those items and may even have learned to play appropriately with them. And finally, the positive reinforcement of actually getting a desired object is huge. We want them to learn that even though this talking thing is really hard, good things will happen if you do it.

Don't Worry About Spoiling Your Child with These Things

If we're going to expect the children to do this difficult talking thing, it has to be worth their while. So if the only thing your child wants is a piece of candy, use it. Even if it's before dinner. If the only thing your child likes is to turn the light on and off, use that as a reward. Don't worry about increasing the problematic behavior—you won't. In fact, it may even decrease once the child is using it in an appropriate context, such as saying "light" before she gets to turn the light on or off. The main thing is that you're offering something that the child wants so badly she's willing to work hard at this truly difficult task to get it.

The child *has* to find the chore of talking worth the effort. So if your daughter wants some kind of food and is willing to try to say its name to get it, then *you have to give it to her*. And give it to her right away, so she gets the connection.

She's got to see the way things work—Hey, I ask for something, I get it! Language is naturally reinforcing that way. Communication leads to attainment. For a child with special needs, that connection needs to be clarified and emphasized, and the simplest way to do that is to make sure the words you're teaching are immediately effective—i.e., you show the item, she attempts to say its name, you hand it to her. A connection has just been made, and she gets the idea: talking pays off big-time.

Reinforce, Reinforce, Reinforce

By using an item your child already likes and wants, you're providing a "natural reinforcer" (or "natural reward") for his attempts at language, putting it all in a meaningful context. If you try to teach him words that don't have that natural reinforcer, the teaching will go a lot more slowly. Why should he say

"Mommy" if Mommy's already sitting right in front of him? Or "rain" when that doesn't get him anything but a picture of a cloud?

Make sure the reward for talking is something your child wants, not something you think he should want. I heard a funny story once about a dad whose typically developing daughter was playing in a soccer game. She kept complaining that she wasn't in the mood to play and wanted to leave the game, but he wanted her to try a little harder. Finally, half joking, he said, "Make a goal, and you can sit the rest of the game out." She suddenly sprinted up the field, took possession of the ball, and shot it right into the goal. Her team scored, and she got what she wanted—to sit the rest of the game out. Obviously, not every kid can "score a goal" when motivated, but it does point to the powerful role a truly appealing reward can play—for most kids, just making a goal would have been enough, but for that one girl, it was only a means to get to her true reward, a nice long break.

Because the right reward is so crucial, our clinic playrooms look like toy stores. We want every kid to be able to find something in there that he really wants, and we know that different kids will be captivated by different things. For example, Lulu liked toys that stimulated her visually, so we bought all these toys that have balls that go down ramps. After she requested "ball," she got to watch the ball go down the ramps. Another child, David, loved music. His first word was "music," and every time he said "music," we turned on the musical toy. Once he was saying "music" consistently, we taught him to turn the knob on the toy to make it start, so not only could he ask for it, but when we handed it to him, he knew how to use it. His mom reported that he also started turning on other musical toys they had at home. Not only was he learning to use a word, but he was also beginning to learn how to play.

You need to find the right items for the child you're working with. You probably know better than anyone else what your child gravitates toward. Do be sure the toys you select are *age appropriate*—use items that would be used by a typically developing child of the same age as your child. For obvious social reasons, you don't want your middle schooler or high schooler walking around with infant toys you've been encouraging him to play with! For example, when a fourteen-year-old nonverbal boy named Marcus came to our clinic, he carried with him a number of musical toys designed for preschoolers. Although he greatly enjoyed these toys, it was stigmatizing for him to play with them in community settings. After a few sessions, we found that he also enjoyed listening to music, so we bought a small portable music player. We had hoped that he would enjoy listening to the music with earbuds, but he wouldn't tolerate anything on his head. So we settled for the player without the earbuds, which still looked a lot more appropriate for a teenager than the preschool toys. His mother gave him some cool music, which the other teens envied. Within a few months, he had learned over twenty words that he used as requests. Many were related to music: "radio," "on," "song," "more," and so on.

Activities Count, Too

Even when we use simple awards like toys or candies in our examples, remember that activities can also count as rewards. A child who likes to swing, slide, or go "up" in Daddy's arms will learn to say all those words if doing so leads to those favorite activities.

We taught "bye-bye" to one child who was having a tough time learning his first words and was making it clear he wanted to end the session. Thinking back, it was really kind of funny, because the family drove all the way from Los Angeles every week, several hours in heavy traffic, and when they got here, and he successfully said "bye-bye," we sent them home immediately—we wanted to be sure that he got his natural reward as soon as he said the word. Interestingly, when he realized that this newly learned skill of verbal words gave him control over leaving, he started playing with the toys for increasingly longer periods of time before he said "bye-bye." Eventually we were able to increase his requests to include the toys and other desired activities.

2. Model the Words

Now that you've put the time into figuring out what your child is most likely to work for—candy, a toy, a favorite activity, a TV show, whatever—it's time to get him to ask for it.

Hold that favorite object up. Now "model" the word for the child—that's a fancy way of telling you to say its name. Clearly and distinctly. Try not to say anything more than the object's label during this initial step, or you may confuse your child. So if you're holding up a blanket, say "blanket." Then wait.

Now It's the Child's Turn . . . Maybe

Obviously, if your child repeats the word perfectly, you give her the item or let her engage in the activity, and you're done. She's seen that saying a word gets her what she wants, her language is rewarded, and you can move on to the next word.

But if it were always that simple, you probably wouldn't be reading this chapter.

More likely, if your child is nonverbal, she won't understand what you want her to do at this point. This is often the most difficult part for parents and teachers, because the first thing the child usually does is revert to the disruptive behaviors that have always worked to get her what she wanted in the past—behaviors like crying and having tantrums.

It may be difficult, but try not to give in. Your child needs to learn to replace crying with words, and she's only going to learn how to do that if she realizes that words work and crying doesn't.

Calmly wait until she says something. It can be anything—a sound, a noise, part of the word, anything. Just something that sounds like your child's attempting to communicate. Then give her the desired item immediately. For example, Lulu wanted a ball. Her mom said "ball" and waited. After trying to grab it a few times, Lulu said "aaa," and her mom immediately gave her the ball.

Keep doing this—saying the word, waiting for an attempt, then giving the child the desired item—until it's clear to the child that a verbalization is the one and only thing that will get her what she wants.

Some children get the idea pretty quickly that crying won't work, so they go through their repertoire of other behaviors—doing anything and everything they can think of until they hit on the verbal attempt. That's fine. They're getting the idea that they have to do *something*. Simply wait to offer the reward until they make the verbal attempt.

We worked with one little boy who had a whole routine of things he did. First he cried, then he tried to grab the desired item, then he hit the floor with his fist. When those behaviors didn't work, he pushed his mom. Then he took her hand and tried to put it on the candy he wanted. Finally, he made a teeny-tiny little sound. It was more like a moan, but it *was* a sound, and his mom gave him the candy. The next time he went through the same routine in almost the same order, but he got to the moan a little sooner. This went on for a while, with fewer and fewer of the old behaviors each time, until finally he figured out that the sound thing worked to get him what he wanted, so he started using more and more sounds to communicate.

Some children will learn to verbalize words or sounds right away, in the first session or two, and others take months. Sooner or later, though, most young children learn to use words and language to communicate. In fact, very few don't.

I will admit, however, that it is hard work. For both of you. Which is why you have to follow my next tip, too.

Reward Good Trying—Don't Go for Perfection

Think about it. If you're trying to do something that's really hard for you, and someone says, "You're doing it wrong," how do you feel? Now take that same scenario and replace "You're doing it wrong" with "That's a really good try!" Doesn't that feel better? Same with children. Same with children with autism. Every once in a while a child who's learning his first words will have perfect pronunciation. Other times the words sound close but not perfect. In the old days, we felt that the child needed to have consistent feedback about whether the word was correct or not, so we said "Good" or "No." But we've now learned that if we encourage the child for *trying* (as long as it's clearly a genuinely good try), the child does much better.

Take toddler Mylie, for example. She was having a hard time saying "bottle." Once in a while she said it perfectly (well, "baba," which was close enough), but other times all she got was the "b" sound in there—not even close to "bottle." When we tried to have her say it perfectly each time, she got frustrated and stopped trying. However, when we rewarded all her good attempts, even the ones that didn't sound anything like the adult word, she started trying all the time. Eventually, with practice, she consistently said "baba."

The idea is to get the child motivated to want to talk, and to talk a lot, but that's not going to happen if he's getting frustrated because he can't do it perfectly yet. So reward good attempts with these difficult first words, both with praise and with the appropriate reinforcement—if your child says "ja" instead of "juice," don't hold out for the complete word. Reinforce the attempt with the cup of juice he wants, and you'll usually see gradual improvement over time.

Sounds Can Be Words

Similarly, when a child is having difficulty with whole words, you can sometimes help him by letting him choose an easy sound that can function as a meaningful word. The idea is to get him to understand that different items have different labels—the concept is more important at this stage than any specific words. Your child should find a sound he's comfortable with, but you can help him along the way. Be creative. "Shhhh" can be a word for water if a child likes to play with water. "Mmmmmm" can be a word for a particular type of candy he likes.

Listen closely to the noises your child makes when playing. Some children who are having difficulty saying different words actually have a bunch of sounds that they make at random times. Since you know that your child is able to produce these sounds, you can attach meaning to them.

For example, four-year-old Mick had the idea that he needed to make some vocalization to get things, but he always made the same sound. It just didn't occur to him that the sound might need to change—he figured what works once will work again. We wanted to get the idea through to him that different sounds have different meanings.

We noticed that throughout the day he made a repetitive sound that sounded something like the putter of an engine. It had no voicing but was simply air running past the lips, making them vibrate. Mick also had a lot of things he didn't like and made it clear by forcefully pushing objects away. We taught him to use the puttering sound, along with shaking his head no, in place of the pushing. Quite rapidly Mick started using the sound at the right times, which meant he had another "word" added to his vocabulary. Now that he had a second distinct word, it became clear to him that he could and should use different words at different times, and his vocabulary started increasing dramatically.

Get Your Child's Attention

If it's clear that your child wants something but just isn't getting the connection that using a word or sound will get it for her, it may be an attention problem. We noticed that some children were so intensely focused on the toy that they were tuning out everything else. We found that if we could briefly transfer the child's attention from the desired item to the adult's word, we had some success with the very small number of children who weren't learning words using the techniques I discussed above.

These "orienting cues" (our term for the ways in which we would get their attention) are different for every child. For some children a high five works; others we've had to gently swing them around a bit; and some respond to noises related to the desired object, such as saying "vroom-vroom" when the child wants a toy car. So the bottom line is that if a child just isn't getting the idea of using language to ask for something, and she's overly focused on the item to the extent of tuning everything else out, you might want to try using one of these orienting cues to get her attention off the desired item just long enough to quickly present the verbal model. This has been helpful for the small group of children who aren't learning to use words because they aren't attending to the modeled word. So be aware that a slow start in verbalizing sometimes boils down to an attention problem and doesn't mean the child can't learn to talk.

Model, Don't Overprompt

If no sound, or an inaccurate one, is coming from your child's mouth, you may be tempted to hold his lips in the desired position. Don't. It doesn't seem to help most children to learn a particular sound faster, and they tend to respond better if you just keep repeating the word with correct articulation.

We tried positioning kids' lips for them in the past—for example, if we were teaching the word "more," we often held the child's lips together—but found that many of the children got hooked on this prompt and only said the correct sounds when we were holding their lips. And while most of the children didn't seem to be bothered by the touching, it probably wasn't very comfortable.

Don't Physically Force the Child to Look at You

Similarly, although eye contact is an important part of social communication and needs to be taught, it's not a good idea to physically force a child to look at you. You won't see us doing it at our center, but some therapists do it: the adult will grab hold of the child's chin and turn it so that the eyes of the child are in line with the adult's. Often, it reads like a punishment—I've even seen adults roughly jerk a child's face back when he has looked away.

Think about this: If you have to jerk a child's face toward you, do you really think he's going to enjoy communicating with you? Or that he's going to want to initiate any social interactions with you in the future? I sure wouldn't.

You're trying to teach your child not only to talk, but to *want* to talk, and you're not going to do that by jerking his head around. This hard talking thing has to be really worth the effort. That's why you're picking out favorite toys and activities—to make the whole thing appealing. Physically correcting the child destroys the positive, comfortable atmosphere you're trying to create.

There are appealing, nonintrusive ways to help your child with social conventions. For instance, when the child is requesting the desired item, eventually you can just wait until you get some good eye contact before you give it to him. Another example: if your child says "chip" in a funny voice intonation, too loudly, or too slowly, just model it again until it sounds better. In other words, you can incorporate these areas into the teaching, so that you won't need a separate program later—they'll simply come to do these things naturally. Also, if a child is motivated and enjoying the communicative interaction, he'll be more likely to use good eye contact.

Add Words Slowly

Some children with autism get bursts of new words quickly when they realize they need to talk to get things, but others take a while. It can be overwhelming for parents to try to prompt lots of words when their child uses the same word over and over again for everything. In these cases, you can gradually require additional words.

For instance, four-year-old Erin said "more" for everything she wanted. Because talking was difficult for her, we decided to pick only one new word and let "more" work for everything else. So the next new word we picked was "up." (She liked when her dad picked her up and swung her.) It took a few days for her to figure out that it had to be "up" and not "more," but she did figure it out. After that second word, each word became easier. After "more" and "up," she learned "swing." We gradually and systematically added more and more words until she had a huge vocabulary.

Some children learn words with the help of a "carrier phrase." For example, we worked with one little girl who was five. First she started to say "go" for everything. That was all she said. When we thought about how she had learned the word "go," we realized it was from saying "Ready, set, *go!*" so we tried this with some other carrier phrases. We started saying "One, two, *three!*" then pushing her on the swing. Pretty soon we stopped after "one, two," and sure enough, she said "three." After about five carrier phrases, she started repeating new words without the carrier phrase.

Routines, Routines, Routines

Your life is going to change a bit now. We want your child to understand that talking can happen anytime and anywhere—and that we want it to happen *all* the time. It isn't enough for your child just to get speech therapy or work on communication only when she's with a therapist. We want her to talk *all day long.* This sounds daunting, but to make this task manageable, you need to get speech interventions into everyday routines. So whenever you have an opportunity throughout the day to encourage language, use it. If your child likes car rides, have her say "open" before you open the car door, "buckle" before you put the seat belt on, "keys" before you start the engine, and "go" before you start driving. Or if your child is excited about a meal, you can have her say "plate" when you're setting the table, "macaroni" to get a scoop full of her favorite food, and "water" when she wants a drink.

You can see how you can create these opportunities on a regular basis all through the day, using activities and objects that are genuinely and intrinsically motivating to your child. That way, she'll learn that she has to talk all day long—and that good things happen when she does.

3. The Next Phase: Getting Your Child to Talk on His or Her Own

At this point, you've worked on identifying your child's favorite things and activities, you've prompted words or word attempts, and you've given your child a sense of success by providing him with that desired item after a good verbal try. Your child is now saying the word—or at least *trying* to say the word—after you say it first.

Now we want him to start saying the words alone, or *spontaneously*. To accomplish this, show him the desired item and just wait a little while until he makes an attempt. Don't model the word. Give him a moment to come up with it himself. If your child doesn't make an attempt, go ahead and model it—we don't want him to get frustrated. But each time wait a little while, looking anticipatory, to give him an opportunity to say the word alone. Since he's probably pretty used to the routine of seeing the desired object and repeating the label, he's likely to pick up on this cue and say the word alone. And now the child has the idea of making a verbal request. Ask, and you shall receive.

Waiting for spontaneous words will also help you know that your child is really learning the words. Don't be concerned if he gets a little mixed up with the words. That sometimes happens. If he does say the wrong word, at least he's trying. Just model the correct word and give him another opportunity to say it. If you suspect that your child's not understanding your words, just echoing them, see the section on echolalia, below.

4. Remember, at Every Stage Keep Things Social and Interactive

Words need to be developed in the context of meaningful and functional interactions. Using real toys, taking turns, and using those toys functionally help the child begin to develop a sense of sharing and what it takes to be a good playmate.

The benefit isn't just that the child's learning to be more social, but that a lot more opportunities for language gain will arise while you're playing. For example, we have a little fishing game where the fish swim in circles. Their mouths open and close, and each fish has a magnet inside its mouth. Players catch the swimming fish using poles that have the attracting magnetic force. Six-year-old Margaret had learned to say "fish" when she wanted to play the game, but once she had the pole, she stopped interacting and played with it by herself. Although her mother also had a pole, Margaret seemed oblivious to the fact that anyone else was playing with her. To improve her interactions, we started playing the game with just one pole. Margaret and her mother now had to take turns with the pole, and before each turn, Margaret had to request the pole. This method provided Margaret with more opportunities to use her newly learned word *and* encouraged her to play interactively.

5. Moving On: Turning Requests into Conversation

Almost all children with autism learn to use words to request whatever they want using the above approach if you get them started in preschool. Once the children can use words to request their favorite items, some naturally pick up the idea that you can string words together to make more specific requests. Other children have to be taught.

Most kids won't start stringing words together until they have a pretty big vocabulary (fifty words or more) to draw from, so make sure your child can say lots of words, *by herself*, before you start thinking about getting her to combine them.

Stringing Two or Three Words Together

It's easiest to teach kids to string together two words that they already know and use. For example, we worked with one little boy who would scream loudly every time we tried to give him something he didn't want. This worked well for him and was therefore only getting worse. We started teaching him to say "no" when he didn't want something and then we took the object away when he said it. It took about a month of hard work, but it eventually sank in on him that "no" would work and screaming wouldn't. In his case—as in so many—the communication was a substitute for the screaming. Then we started to work on labeling objects. Once he had a pretty big vocabulary, we were able to combine the "no" with other words, like "no train," "no lettuce," and so on. We also taught him the word "more," so he could combine it with desired things, like "more cookie" or "more Elmo." Because putting two words together was challenging for him at first, we still let him use his single words for requests but occasionally interspersed the more difficult activity of having him say two words together.

Just as with single words, watch out for echolalia—make sure the child isn't just repeating what you're saying and that he can say the words spontaneously. Once he's able to say the two words after you, remember to pause and give him a chance to say the two words without your prompt.

Another way to prompt for two-word combinations is to add another word to your child's request. So, for example, if your child knows the word "open" and the word "door," when he says "open" you could respond with "Open door?" and wait to go outside until he has repeated "open door." But after a while you will want to pause again and make sure your child can say both words without needing you to model them.

Look for Different Combinations of Words

Another word of caution: make sure your child can put words together in *different, flexible* combinations. I can't tell you how many parents come in and say that their children can say "whole sentences," and then we discover that the children really only say one sentence, and it's "I want such-and-such." Sometimes they even say, "I want such-and-such, *please.*" While this can be a good start, a lot of these kids are using the sentence like it's essentially one long word. They can change the label of the desired item, but they don't use any other word combinations. Remember that children don't usually come out with three- or four-word sentences before they start combining two words spontaneously and independently, so if your child has a longer sentence he uses regularly but doesn't have any other sentences, he's probably not really creating any.

The bottom line is that we want the children to be able to use all kinds of new and novel two-word combinations. That is the start of true sentence use. Once they really get how to put two words together, we can take it from there and add more and more words. Colors, shapes, and numbers are good to start working on at around this time, too. Then you can get great little sentences going, such as "more green lollipop" or "open blue door."

Verbs

At around the age of two and a half, typical language developers start adding "–ing" to verbs and by four years they can use the past tense. Of course they often make some errors, like "I wented to the park," but they get the idea that they need to add something to the root verb to indicate that the action happened in the past. But we've noticed that when kids with autism start making big strides in their language, they often don't use very many verbs. And verb tenses are really hard for some kids to learn. Unfortunately, the past tense is hard to teach, because still pictures just don't capture action, and in real life, if you're trying to explain something like "the car *drove* by," the action is usually gone and finished by the time you're trying to explain it. So, after some trial and error, we found that pop-up books can be really useful to show action as it's happening or after it has just happened. It makes teaching verb tenses a heck of a lot easier.

For example, to teach verbs and verb tenses, get a pop-up book with a theme your child likes and start pulling on the tab continually, so the picture keeps popping up. Then prompt your child to ask, "What's happening?" Once the child repeats the question, you can answer using the present tense verb: "He's jumping!"

Similarly, to teach the past tense, pull on the tab so the picture pops up once or twice and then stop, so that it's like the action has just happened. Then prompt the child to ask, "What *happened?*" Now you can answer the question using the past tense: "He jumped!"

With this approach, kids learn the different verb endings while adding a lot of new verbs to their repertoire. Not to mention that "What's happening?" and "What happened?" are useful questions for everyday social interactions and a great way to initiate interactions (read on).

6. Encourage Initiations

One thing you may have noticed now that your child is using words is that most—maybe even all—of her verbalizations are *requests*. And that's fine. That's how we start, because we want to make sure we're able to give her something that's immediately rewarding or desirable after the request. And obviously, the most pressing need for communication is to ask for things—ask any mother whose infant is crying and can't tell her what he or she wants.

But language plays other important roles in human development. Through our research, we discovered that one of the most important indicators of a child's ultimate success was not how much language he had, but how much he used that language to enter into a conversation or start an interaction, such as by asking other people questions. Since many children with autism won't "initiate"—i.e., ask questions or interact socially for reasons other than requests, and thus enter into the potential beginning of a dialogue—it's important that we teach them to do so. Obviously, the child already needs some language to do this, but not so much as you might think—very early on, toddlers can point to objects, say "Dat?" and receive both information and attention. Once your child can request something spontaneously and is starting to use little phrases, you can start teaching initiations.

We teach the kids who have developed a good vocabulary and are starting to combine words to initiate. Typical children learn language by asking questions, and we've found that the closer we can follow the learning process of a typically developing child, the better the outcome for our children.

Teaching Initiations

Once again, we want you to motivate your child by collecting a bunch of favorite items, only this time put them inside an opaque bag and let him know they're in there. Once you have his attention, you're going to model the question you want. Say "What's that?" then pull out one of the desired items. Put the item back in the bag and let your child know it's his turn to try. If necessary, prompt him by repeating the question—but you may not need to. Once he says or repeats "What's that?" take out one of those desirable objects, label it, and hand it to him. We've found that it usually doesn't take much more than a few sessions of practice before your child will happily keep asking "What's that?" to get more and more of the unknown, but desired, items out of the bag. You're probably accustomed to asking your child "What's this?" or "What's that?" to get him to label things. Now we've reversed the process: We're getting *the child* to ask "What's that?" Can you see how important this will be for social and language development? It's not all up to you anymore—now your child can start some of the interactions that will eventually lead to learning new things and making friends.

Now that your child is asking his first question, and likes it because something good happens, you want to get him to ask questions about things he *doesn't* already know how to label, rather than those highly desired items you've been using to teach the initial question. Put some new items in the bag, something neutral like, say, a tissue or a pencil, something that's neither desirable nor undesirable. After the child has asked about and received three of her favored items, you can pull out one of these neutral items. Now you're genuinely supplying the answer to her question "What's that?" and she's learning how to ask about the label of something she doesn't already recognize. Gradually you can add more and more of the neutral items, until your child gets the idea that questions can get you useful information.

Using these procedures, most children will find the exchange of question/information rewarding and will start using their newly learned questions in other environments. In fact, one mom, whose four-year-old son had never asked a question in his life, told us that shortly after we'd worked on initiations, he started to get disruptive when she didn't understand what he was asking her for. But instead of launching into one of his full-blown tantrums, he pointed to a granola bar and said, "What's that?" When she said, "A granola bar," he then said, "I want granola bar." This child was using his new tool to learn vocabulary words—and it was in exactly the same manner that typically developing children learn new words!

Teaching Other Questions

You'll find that once your child understands how questions and answers work—and has found the use of questions rewarding—it will be easier to teach other questions, like "Where?" and "Whose?"

To teach your child to ask "Where is it?" hide one of his favorite toys and play a game of finding it. Model saying "Where is it?" then answer your own question with "Under the sofa," or wherever you've put it, and then uncover the toy. Then it's his turn to ask and be told. This is also a good way for the child to learn prepositions.

You can teach your child to ask "Whose is it?" and learn how to use "yours" and "mine" at the same time. Many children with autism have difficulty with pronouns, and when you think about it, they *are* complicated. When you say, "It's yours," the child has to know to reverse that and say, "It's mine." But usually they understand they'll get the object when they hear "It's yours," so of course they repeat that. Which leaves the adult saying things like "When I say it's yours you have to say it's mine because when you say it's yours, I'm going to think it's mine, not yours, so you have to say mine." Phew. It's hard to keep track of even on paper. Think how confusing it could be for a child with autism.

One way to work on the whole "whose" issue is to start with just teaching the child to say "mine." Again, select her favorite items and model asking "Whose is it?" When your child asks "Whose is it?" say "yours," then prompt her to say "mine" before you give it to her. If she says "yours mine," then you need to say "yours" softly and "mine" a little louder, or you can just say "mine," then fade in "yours" later. Pretty soon she'll understand the reversal and learn to respond with "mine" every time she hears "yours."

After your child is able to make this reversal, then you can start adding some neutral things, like pencils, pens, or anything else that may not be highly desired. This will allow you to work on teaching the child to say "yours" when she hears you say "mine." I've learned from experience that if you try to put some highly desired things in the pile and then tell the child these are *not* hers, she probably won't like it, so you need only things she doesn't value in there!

Be Creative

You can be creative in teaching your child just about any question, and we highly recommend teaching lots of them. For example, we worked with one child who was progressing nicely, learning various language structures, but she had the worst time with "did." When she asked questions, she always said, "Where it went?" or "Where Mommy went?" So we played a game with her using this little barking puppy toy that she loved. We had her cover her eyes, then hid the puppy toy in different places around the room. We prompted her to ask "Where did it go?" or "Where did you hide it?" She loved the game, and of course she got to play with the puppy every time she asked the question. At first she was a little confused about the tenses and started dropping the past tense in general, like "What happen?" but pretty soon she got the idea that the "did" worked for the past and that she still had to use verbs in the past tense when "did" wasn't in the sentence.

Initiations Are Social

When kids learn to initiate, it really changes the expression of their symptoms of autism. They don't just sit there alone and respond only when an adult demands it. The interactions look completely different. They're two-sided. They go back and forth. In short, when the kids initiate, they're *social*. Our research suggests that children with autism who don't learn to initiate these types of social interactions don't have as positive long-term outcomes as those who do. So always work on teaching your child to initiate. It will make a big difference in the long run.

IMPROVING THE LANGUAGE OF CHILDREN WHO HAVE ECHOLALIC OR DELAYED SPEECH

Imitation of words is a natural part of speech development, but children with autism are sometimes imitative in a way that *inhibits* speech development, a pattern referred to as "echolalic" (or occasionally as "echoic"). Echolalia is pretty much what it sounds like—the child repeats or "echoes" words, phrases, or sentences that have just been spoken, usually without a true sense of their meaning.

Echolalia is different from the average child's use of imitation, because, unlike most toddlers, the kids aren't repeating the words to learn them, and the repetition doesn't go away without intervention.

For example, every time I said "Hi!" to Aaron, he said "Hi!" back, which sounded pretty friendly, but when I said "Hi, Aaron," he would then say "Hi, Aaron." Aaron wasn't greeting me—he was simply repeating whatever had just been said to him. Many children with echolalia repeat the word or phrase with the exact intonation pattern they've heard. It's really easy for me to tell when a child's echolalic, since I, unfortunately, have a high, squeaky voice!

Why Does a Child Echo?

Children with autism often echo when they don't understand what you're asking. You see this clearly in children who appropriately answer questions they understand and echo the questions they don't understand.

Other children will simply echo when they don't want to make the effort to really listen to what the adult is saying, process it, and prepare an answer— all very time-consuming and difficult. It's much easier just to repeat a bit of what was said and hope that will suffice. You'd be amazed at how well this usually works. For example, if an adult says, "Do you want to go to the park?" and the child responds with "park," the adult will accept this as an enthusiastic affirmative, but if you ask that same child, "Do you want to swim in a bucket of ice cubes?" the child may well respond with "ice cubes."

It's not all that bad, though. You know your echolalic child has the ability to say words and phrases. Now your goal is to get him or her to use the words or phrases at the right time and place. Here are some ways to achieve that.

Teach "I Don't Understand"

Many children with autism aren't able to let you know that they don't understand what you've just asked them, so they echo the question back to you. It's important to prompt the child to say "I don't understand" at these times. You can practice this by picking specific questions that you know your child can't answer and prompting her to respond with "I don't know what you mean" or "I don't understand" or even "Can you help me?" depending on the circumstance. Once she's done it with your help, remind her to do it whenever she can't process a question. People will then rephrase questions in a way she's more likely to understand, leading to a genuine exchange.

Reword the Question

If you know that your child is repeating your words because he's not understanding them, try to reword your questions so he will.

For example, we worked with one junior high boy who didn't understand the word "where." Every time we asked him where he was going, he echoed the complete phrase. Then we realized that if we used "what place" instead of "where" he could understand the question and answer it. So his mom started pairing the two. She would say, "Kelly, where, what place did we go today?" After a while she was able to drop the "what place"—he now understood what "where" meant. By rewording the question and pairing it with a phrase he knew, his mother was able to cut down on his echolalia and increase his vocabulary.

Add Another Question

For children who echo just about everything, or who are just beginning to learn words, rewording or teaching "I don't understand" is not a viable solution. In these cases, it may be helpful to intersperse another question. For example, if we've chosen a highly desired item such as candy and we ask the child, "Do you want candy?" and the child says "candy," you can then ask, "What do you want?" If the child responds with "want," you'll know it's echoed. However, if the child responds with "candy," you'll know she understood.

If the child keeps echoing at this point, you can give a little prompt, saying the first sound in the word, like "ca." If your child still doesn't get it, go back to the whole word, and once she's repeating it, try saying the part of the word as a prompt again. As your child starts responding to the part of the word (by saying the whole word), you can gradually fade even the shorter prompt out, until the child is able to give you an answer without simply echoing what you just said.

Give Choices That Pair Undesirable and Desirable Items

Most of the time, echolalic children echo the last thing you said, so when you give your child a choice of items, like "Do you want an apple or an orange?" the child is likely to say "orange" because it was the last word in the sentence. If you see this happening, you may want to up the ante by using one desired and one *undesired* item and making sure the desired item is listed first. That way, the child has a reason to work a little harder to get what he genuinely wants.

We did this with a three-year-old who repeated everything we said. He loved chips but hated lettuce. He knew the word "chip," so we started asking him, "Do you want chips or lettuce?" At first, being echolalic, he always said "lettuce," so we handed him the lettuce. After a while, he started self-correcting, saying "lettuce, chip." Unfortunately he got some superstitious learning going, thinking that what he was saying (both words) was somehow connected to the outcome, and he started responding every time with "lettucechip" as if it were one word. So we backed up and asked the question again using the two choices, but modeling "chip" right after we asked the question: "Do you want chip or lettuce? Chip?" For a while he only said "chip" on occasion, and those were the only times he got a chip. Gradually, he started saying "chip" more frequently, and eventually he stopped adding the "lettuce." When he started just saying "chip," we faded the model. The great thing was that once it sank in on him that he was genuinely making a *choice*, and he could choose one thing (the chip) over another (the lettuce), it generalized to other choices, and pretty soon he was making clear and appropriate choices of all kinds.

Repetition for Its Own Sake

Sometimes echolalia isn't in response to questions but appears to be the child's desire to repeat whole phrases and sentences for the sheer pleasure of hearing them. It may be possible that there's a self-stimulatory aspect to this kind of echolalia.

It can be cute when a small child repeats an adult sentence or phrase without an appropriate context, but it can turn into a problem when some children with autism repeat phrases their parents have said or even lines they heard on a video or TV show at inappropriate times.

For instance, one family who was flying across the country just after 9/11 reported that their son got on the plane, buckled up, and then in a loud voice proceeded to announce, "Sky marshals will be placed on planes in the near future to decrease the likelihood of terrorist activity on airplanes." Of course, the mere mention of terrorists caused the plane to be greatly delayed while the flight crew investigated—and were ultimately given a crash course in autism by the frantic parents.

Although the child did relate what he had heard on the news to the right *context*, he needed to learn that talking about terrorists in an airplane is not acceptable. In situations like these, you can teach your child to reference the source. For example, if the child had said, *"On the news, they said that sky marshals will be placed on planes,"* there might have been less concern.

Another boy I worked with used to call me "Wilma," as in *The Flintstones* animated television show. I don't think I look or act anything like Wilma, but he sure did. We taught him to say, "You remind me of Wilma from *The Flintstones*," rather than just saying "Wilma" out of context. Again, teaching appropriate contexts can lead to some social conversation.

As we said earlier, the good news about echolalia is that it means your child has words and even some potentially useful phrases. If you work on turning those echoed words into spontaneous words and those echoed phrases into social conversation, you're helping your child both to acquire language and to engage in social dialogue.

JACK'S STORY

We met Jack when he was almost three. He lived in another state but had been referred to our clinic. The clinicians who had diagnosed Jack with autism before we met him had also informed his parents that he would probably never talk, and that even if he did, he would never sound normal, never go to college, and never have any friends or social relationships. They came to our center devastated and almost hopeless.

When we met Jack, he didn't say anything, nor did he even try to say anything, but he sure did cry a lot. He only had one interest: watching *Blue's Clues* videotapes. That little blue creature was the only thing that grabbed his attention; left alone, he would rewind the video to certain favorite parts over and over again. If any demands whatsoever were placed upon him, he flopped on the floor, crying and screaming, until that play button was pushed and Blue appeared on the screen.

We hate hearing kids cry, but we knew we had to stop the tantrums if he were going to make any progress, and since Blue was the only thing Jack liked, we put her to use. We put the TV up on a stand so the buttons were out of Jack's reach and started working on what we hoped would be Jack's first word: "on," to turn on the TV.

Jack started screaming for the TV. We modeled the word "on," but he just kept screaming. It felt like he screamed for several hours straight, but it was probably only twenty or thirty minutes—time slows down when you're with a screaming child.

Eventually, it did sink in that the crying was not going to get the TV back on. So next he started going through his repertoire of behaviors—running around, jumping up and down, trying to climb up the stand, and so on, everything that had ever worked in the past to get him what he wanted. All this time, we kept calmly modeling the word "on."

Eventually he made a feeble little attempt at saying "on." We immediately turned on the TV, and his face lit up with amazement. He just hadn't ever figured out how effective this communication thing could be.

After that first attempt, it was hit-or-miss. While he didn't cry as much, it still took him quite a while between attempts to say the word. But every time he did, the tape went back on, and he got to watch for a while. By the end of the week, Jack's parents had learned that Jack was willing to work for his Blue and how to use that knowledge to prompt some good verbalizations. They left our clinic ready to work hard.

A few months after their visit, they sent me a videotape of Jack, and he had indeed learned to say "on"—he was saying it pretty consistently whenever he wanted to see *Blue's Clues*. But that was the only word he said, and it was only under those limited conditions. So our task now was to expand his vocabulary.

They came back to the center for another week. This time we tried to find other things Jack liked besides Blue. We did hit upon a few things—not very many, but a few. One was climbing up his dad's back. His dad would scrunch down and he would climb up onto his dad's shoulders. Then his dad would stand up and help him do sort of a free fall back down to the floor. Jack loved this.

We told his dad, "You know what this means!" and from then on, every time Jack wanted to climb up, his dad prompted him to say "up."

I still remember how tired Jack's poor dad was after scrunching down several hundred times just to get that important second word. He was completely drained and exhausted at the end of each day, but it was well worth the sacrifice.

Soon we discovered that Jack also loved riding up and down the elevators, and so we started prompting the word "elevator" each time we went on a ride. Now, with a lot of effort—and some physical discomfort for his father—Jack had acquired three words. That was their second visit.

A few months later, I received a distraught call from Jack's dad. He said that although Jack continued to say the few words we had taught him, he had started to run around screaming all the time. Because I had no idea why Jack was doing this, I asked him to e-mail me a video clip immediately.

The clips were very revealing. It turned out that while Jack's high-pitched screams were undeniably loud and irritating, they weren't random. He only screamed when someone tried to engage him. And it didn't seem like he was screaming to get *rid* of the other person. It really looked to me like he had somehow developed this annoying behavior as an attempt to interact with people. It wasn't the same kind of scream that he used when he didn't have any words. He was screaming because he wanted to communicate and knew that vocalizing was the way to get it.

I talked to his father again and learned that, sure enough, Jack had already started coming out with more words. The screams had been social, and once his parents started prompting the appropriate words to initiate contact, he started saying more.

It had taken us many months to teach those first few words, but now they were popping up like weeds. It was like he had gotten the *idea* of words and was eager to make use of it. By their third visit to the center, Jack had developed a pretty big vocabulary, but he still only said single words. He was three now, and although he could talk, his language was still significantly delayed. So on this visit we worked not only on expanding his vocabulary but also on combining words, the first step toward forming sentences.

By the end of the week, Jack was able to use quite a few two-word combinations. He still liked the elevator, so we started having him say "Go up" and "Go down" before we pushed the button. He also, incredibly, learned to recognize and say each floor number after we'd modeled it just a few times. A little motivation will go a long way.

Jack was also really attached to his parents, so they would stand outside the elevator until he said, "Come, Mama" or "Come, Dada." We soon learned we had to be careful with this practice, though, because one time the door closed before they were able to get in, and we all frantically ran up the stairs, trying to find him. He had pushed the 5, so by the time we found him, he was wandering down the fifth-floor hallway by himself, happy as a clam. After that, we made sure one adult stayed with him while he asked for his parents.

Jack's language improved steadily, and by the time he was four, he could use little sentences of four or five words to communicate, like "I want two cookies, please," but most everything he said focused around what he wanted. He wasn't saying anything truly social. It was just request, request, request. No questions, no expressions, nothing to get attention, nothing to get help. So we decided to try to teach him to ask some questions.

As before, figuring out what most interested Jack was crucial to developing the right program. We discovered that Jack was now really into coins. Quarters, dimes, nickels, pennies—he loved them. We started out by putting one coin at a time in his piggy bank, shaking the bank, and prompting him to ask "What's in there?" before getting it out and giving it to him. Pretty soon he was asking "What's in there?" all the time. His mom started to hide coins everywhere—in the glove compartment, in her purse, in Dad's pocket— everywhere she could think of—and he asked about those coins all the time. Pretty soon she started prompting him to ask "where" the coins were and "whose" they were, and so on.

These initiations were such a dramatic divergence from the symptoms of autism that, as with most of the kids we've taught initiations to, he almost immediately started looking much better, much more social, much more like other kids. You can't be antisocial if you're initiating social interactions! His language no longer seemed nearly so delayed, because he was now appropriately seeking out information from others by asking questions. He was really starting to look like he was overcoming the symptoms of autism.

Of course we still had to work on his language skills, like teaching him the past tense, but we did this by teaching him to ask "What happened?" when someone got hurt or was crying. We also started working on academic areas, like having him count his favorite candies before he got to eat some; he was also learning his letters and how to draw a circle, square, and triangle around his favorite little toys.

Since Jack was doing so well, we didn't see the family as often, and they called us and e-mailed us less frequently. We would get an occasional card from them, thanking us and letting us know how well he was doing, but I hadn't seen him for a long time. So when my husband, Bob, and I were invited to give a speech in their state, I called them. We got together and spent the afternoon with Jack, who was then five.

Jack carried on a perfect conversation, made jokes, and played Trivial Pursuit—which he kept winning, because he was smarter than the rest of us. In fact, his mom said that the only complaint his kindergarten teacher had was that he was a "blabbermouth"! His teacher said that he talked to the other kids constantly and that she regularly had to remind him not to socialize in class.

Jack looked so good that I really tried to find symptoms of autism. I looked hard, and the only remnant of his autism was that when he got excited, he jumped up and down and flapped his hands in the air, and I only noticed this because I was looking for signs. But anyone else would have said he was fine, I'm sure. In fact, no one at school had ever mentioned that anything seemed to be wrong.

There's no question this was a long process. Not all children with autism do as well as Jack, but it is possible. For Jack, it took years and constant vigilance, incredible effort, and seemingly unbearable stress for his parents, but he's now a bright, articulate, and caring kid with lots of friends.

And Jack never says anything negative or mean. Never. He never picked that up. That's the part of language that I wish no one learned.

FAQ

QUESTION: My child talks, but no one can understand him, and even I can only understand him about half the time. What can be done?

Some children with autism use perfect articulation from the start, others learn sounds slowly, and still others have uneven development and will sometimes acquire difficult sounds before the easy ones.

If your child is just learning to say her first words, you may want to wait to see if they become clearer with more time and practice. If sounds continue to be a problem, you may want to pick one sound at a time and focus on trying to improve that sound. Most children with autism respond better if you keep the sounds in words, rather than drilling them on the sounds in isolation—it's just more motivating that way. Also, when you practice the sounds, be sure to use things that will be worth working for, items your child has chosen. A speech and language specialist can help you pick items that contain the sound you want to work on but that don't have a lot of other difficult sounds in the same word.

QUESTION: My child just doesn't get that she has to talk. We have tried using all the motivational procedures you discussed, but we still aren't making progress. What should we do now?

Our research suggests that most children with autism learn to use words and/or sentences to communicate when motivational procedures are used in the teaching so long as intervention for communication starts in the preschool years. However, there *is* a small percentage of children who will need to use a communication system that doesn't involve verbal speech. Picture systems are fantastic, and most portable computers and iPads have apps that can be used for communication.

We use the same motivational procedures as described above when teaching a child to use a picture system. The only difference is that instead of *saying* the word to get the item (or making an attempt at saying it), the child has to touch the item on the computer screen before he gets the desired object. Many of the computer programs are programmed to convert the word into a whole sentence, so if the child points to the cookie the computer may say, "I want a cookie, please."

Alternatively, laminated picture cards can be used with a variety of items. Start with one picture card and teach your child to hand you the card when you hold up a specific desired item. Once he's correctly picking up the picture and handing it to you to get what he wants, put another card out with a different picture on it—preferably of a nondesired item—and hold up the desired item. This way, you can teach your child to discriminate between the pictures. As he succeeds at this, you can gradually and systematically add more and more pictures. Make sure your child has constant access to the pictures, so he can communicate at any time.

In the past, many teachers and therapists were quick to use a picture system with nonverbal children as a "bridge" to verbal communication. However, recent research suggests that a verbal-only approach is just as effective, so we usually start with that. If the child isn't making progress, then we may switch to an augmentative system, but usually we like to give the verbal a good shot before switching. Kids learn at different rates, and while some have learned verbal words during the first session, we've had others who took an entire year before they started saying words—but who are now saying full sentences. So you need to give communication interventions a good long try. But if you're just struggling too much with those first words, or your child is making attempts to say words but is really hard to understand, a picture system can be helpful, especially for specificity. In that case, you can have the child make a word attempt then point to the picture so that he can clarify what he wants.

QUESTION: When my child talks, I can only understand a word here or there. She seems to be trying to say something to me, but most of it sounds garbled. Any suggestions?

I'm guessing that when your child says single words, they're pretty clear, and it's when the utterances get longer that she becomes more difficult to understand. Because some words are intelligible, people may still be getting her what she wants, so she may not be able to distinguish between successful and unsuccessful speech.

When you can't understand her, stop and remind her to use only the words that are intelligible. Try to stay positive. You don't want to discourage her from speaking. For instance, if you know your child wants orange juice and she says, "Gibberish, gibberish, orange juice," you may want to prompt her to just say "orange juice" before you give her the orange juice. If you can prompt her to say "I want orange juice" or "More orange juice," clearly, then that's even better. The idea is to give your child feedback on what others can and can't understand. This sounds counterintuitive because we've worked so hard to get your child's utterances longer, but if they aren't intelligible the message won't get across, which may frustrate her—you want everything she says to be successful. So better to have shorter successful statements than longer incomprehensible ones.

Sometimes children really don't know that you don't understand them. I remember reading a study about children who couldn't say their "r's." The examiner said, "Look at the wabbit," and the children responded with "It's not a wabbit, it's a wabbit!" They couldn't hear their own mispronunciation. Similarly, sometimes children with autism need the feedback to figure out which parts of their conversation aren't being understood. So shortening it up for a temporary time may make a big difference.

If a child has a lot of sounds that he says incorrectly, pick one sound at a time to target and improve, using fun activities that allow you to practice that sound. For example, one child we worked with couldn't say the "f" sound but he loved balls. So we got a whole bunch of balls and named them with "f" sounds—the fuzzy ball, the foam ball, the funny ball, and so on. When we played ball with him he had to name the ball. He quickly learned his "f" sound in the context of this fun game.

But if you are going to target sounds, make sure to check with a speech/language pathologist first so that you target sounds that are age appropriate and that your child should be able to produce. Some sounds, like "s" and "z" and "r," or any word with a bunch of consonants together will be difficult for all children at the beginning and come in later—remember when your parents used to have you say "spaghetti" and lovingly laughed every time you mispronounced it? Without any special work you eventually learned to say it correctly. Your child's sounds may come in, too, without any special attention, so again, check with a speech/language pathologist who specializes in this area before starting a speech sound program.

> **QUESTION:** My child doesn't seem to like anything or want anyone to interact with him. He just stims—engages in self-stimulatory behavior—all the time. I don't know how to get him interested enough in any items or activities to make him think talking is worth his while.

There are many children with autism who don't initially appear to be interested in anything, which makes teaching them more challenging—but still possible. We often select "bye" or "done" for a child's first word if he really doesn't want to interact. We won't leave him alone until he's made a good attempt at saying "bye" or "done." You'd be surprised at how motivating this can be!

Other times we use the child's repetitive behaviors as a reward for good communication. For example, we worked with one boy who repetitively played with a ball all day long. That was the only thing he did, so you've probably guessed by now that the first word he learned was "ball"—getting that ball back was worth making a stab at communicating. Another child only seemed to enjoy turning the lights off and on, so his first word was "light." Again, finding things that are motivating enough to talk for can really make a difference.

> **QUESTION:** Wait a minute—I'm trying to teach my child to do less self-stimulation, and now you're telling me to reward him with the stim! Isn't this going to make it worse?

This is a legitimate concern, but his stim isn't likely to get worse, especially if your child has to do something appropriate to get it. Keep in mind that this is just a start, and the first words can be so difficult that we want to be sure that the reward is really worth it to the child. Later we'll work on stringing a whole bunch of good words together so that more and more time is focused on communication and less and less time is spent on the repetitive behaviors.

The research tells us that self-stimulatory behavior won't get worse as a result of language acquisition. In fact, it generally decreases or drops out completely when it is used in an appropriate context.

> **QUESTION:** My therapist says my son needs to be able to imitate nonverbal activities before learning how to talk. Is that true? Should we wait to teach him until he's imitating us in other ways?

Imitation is a very important part of communication and of learning in general. However, most children with autism do not learn to talk as a result of learning how to imitate motor movements. And if you wait for him to learn to do that, you can lose a lot of valuable time. We recommend working on communication as early as possible.

There is value in teaching children to imitate others, however, and no reason not to teach that simultaneously, in a fun manner. Some activities, like Follow the Leader and Simon Says, are great games to help with nonverbal imitation and can get your child to start learning some fun ways to interact with peers. You can even simplify these activities to make them easier to learn, such as doing just one activity at a time, especially a favorite activity, like jumping or marching during Follow the Leader. Then add more over time as your child gets the idea.

A MOTHER LOOKS AT COMMUNICATION

When Andrew was two and a half, he didn't talk at all (although, oddly, he could make a fair number of animal sounds, like "moo" and "baa"), and our pediatrician suggested we consult a speech therapist he knew named Roberta Poster.

A few weeks later, we sat down for a good long talk with her. "He'll learn to talk," Roberta said, "but it's not going to be overnight. We're talking years of hard work here."

It turned out she wasn't exaggerating.

Making Language Worth the Trouble

Although we didn't know Dr. Koegel back when Andrew was first learning to talk, Roberta, our speech therapist, used a very similar system of teaching language.

Up until then, toddler Andrew had let us know when he wanted something by either leading us to the object—never pointing, just leading—or by raising his hand and waiting for us to take action. If he couldn't get a toy to work, for example, he would raise his hand and wait patiently for someone to notice and come to his aid. It never seemed to occur to him to do something more active. (Faced with that raised hand, his uncle—a teacher—would always call out, "Yes, you in the back? You've got a question?" Sadly, Andrew never did.)

Anyway, Roberta said we had to stop running to get Andrew his juice or food whenever he led us into the kitchen or sat down to eat. We had to learn to wait until he made a clear attempt to *say* what he wanted.

We did that every time he wanted a cup of orange juice—he was completely addicted to the stuff—and before too long he was saying "ju," and then, eventually, "juice," and not much longer after that, "orange juice." His first word(s)!

"Mommy," on the other hand, took forever. My memory is notoriously flawed, but I'm pretty sure Andrew didn't say "Mommy" until he was four. And even then it wasn't a "Mommy" the way most kids say "Mommy"—as in, calling out to her. If you pointed to me and asked him who I was, he could say "Mommy," identifying me the way you'd identify a toy or a character on TV. But it was a long time before he used it to call me to his side.

That's a hard one, not getting a meaningful "Mommy" out of your kid for years and years. Fortunately, he liked me to hold him and often fell asleep in my arms, so I knew the love was there, even if he couldn't put it into words.

Simplify, Simplify, Simplify

Roberta told us we had to simplify our own language as much as possible when talking to Andrew. She instructed us not to say complicated sentences like "We don't want you to hit, because you may hurt someone," but to keep our instructions to brief phrases, like a simple "Don't hit."

This strategy seemed to help Andrew's language development, and it sure did wonders for his younger brother. Leo was born right around the time that Andrew started speech therapy, and our overly simplified and exaggeratedly pronounced sentences had Leo speaking like a little professor before he was two.

With this approach, Andrew started using a fair number of words and after a while was actually able to *say* more than he could understand. I didn't realize how strange this was until I had three more kids and saw that kids usually under-stand way more than they can say for the first few years. Not Andrew. Labeling things and simple sentences—subject-verb-object—started to come fairly easily to him, but understanding the more complicated things people threw at him . . . that remained hard. A simple two-part instruction—"Pick up your shoes and put them in your room"—would confuse him, even though he "knew" every word in that sentence.

Echolalia

As his vocabulary grew, Andrew learned to put together simple sentences. Un-fortunately, a lot of what he said was just repeating whatever we said first.

The experts we worked with explained that this was called "echolalia" and said that Andrew saw sentences as wholes rather than as parts put together. A three-word sentence effectively functioned as a single long word for him. He could memorize its meaning but not get that it had separate grammatical parts.

Pronouns were essentially meaningless to him. If we said, "Do you want some-thing?" he would say, "You want something," which meant yes. We were calling him "you," so I guess he figured that was how this guy Andrew must be referred to.

Not long ago, my husband and I watched a videotape we had made while vacationing in Hawaii. (Remember videotapes? Those things we made before we could record things on our phones at the drop of a hat? Seems like ancient history). Andrew must have been about five years old. While he and his little brother played with Play-Doh on the terrace at the hotel, we asked them questions and taped their answers. I was shocked by what I saw on that tape—virtually everything Andrew said during the ten-minute video session was echo-lalic. I had already forgotten that he had talked like that for so long. Meanwhile his two-year-old brother was chatting away, asking lots of questions and de-scribing his creations. The contrast was amazing. And heartrending, even all these years later.

Still, the good news was that Andrew continued to make progress. Slowly he was saying more and more, and gradually he was learning not just to repeat phrases, but to respond appropriately. We had two amazing speech therapists in a row, and they put in a lot of long, hard hours working with him—at one point our second therapist was seeing him three times a week. They would play games and chat up in his room, and all the time she was helping him acquire new words and phrases.

Dr. Koegel's Advice: More Initiations

When Andrew was five, we took him to see Dr. Koegel for the first time.

She sat down and chatted and played with him for almost an hour.

I remember one of their exchanges. It went something like this:

"What did you do last night, Andrew?"

"I see a movie." (He hadn't mastered the past tense yet.)

"What movie?"

"*Toy Story.*" (Or whatever was out then.)

"Did you like it?"

"Yes."

"That's great. You know, I saw a movie last night, too."

Silence. Dr. Koegel waited expectantly, but Andrew didn't say anything, just waited until she asked him another question.

Later, Dr. Koegel said to us, "I'm concerned that Andrew doesn't initiate more—that he doesn't ask me more questions. For most children, questions make up a high percentage of their speech, but Andrew asked me very few questions. That's actually problematic."

She went on to explain that the kids who increase their initiations tend to improve strikingly in all ways.

"You need to teach Andrew to ask questions," she said.

Teaching Andrew to Ask Questions

Dr. Koegel told us that we could increase Andrew's initiations simply by prompting him to ask people questions—"Andrew, why don't you ask her if she liked the movie?" "Andrew, So-and-so just said he hurt his leg. Why don't you ask him how he hurt it?" "Did you ask Aunt Nellie if she had a good time in Ojai?" And so on.

So we started doing that. Andrew was an obedient guy. If we told him to say something, he'd say it. So when we told him to ask a question, he would. We also requested that all our regular therapists work on prompting him to ask questions during their time with him.

It was so simple—and yet breathtakingly effective. After just a few weeks of all this prompting, Andrew started to ask more questions on his own. And more and more. It was as though he just got the idea that asking questions led to a pleasurable exchange of information, and he wanted more of that—which was good for his language development and fantastic for his social development.

It reached the point where there were days when I wished he'd *stop* asking questions. I mean, we used to be able to talk about anything—and I do mean anything—in front of Andrew's face, and he'd be off in his own world, ignoring us. But after we'd done all this prompting and teaching, he always wanted to know what we were talking about and who was going where and why did we say that and who did we say had done what, and so on and so on. We started to have to watch what we said in front of him—and not just in front of him: we discovered he has exceptional hearing. If we tried to whisper in one room, he started to come running in to find out what we were talking about. We hadn't known he had such good hearing because he had been so uninterested in our conversation before!

And he blossomed.

Andrew's Language at Age Eleven

When he was eleven, Andrew had to explain to me what the word "chiaroscuro" meant, because he had used the technique in a drawing of his, and I didn't know what it meant. His vocabulary was getting broader by the day, and he had become a polite conversationalist who made sure he asked as many questions as he answered.

However, there were plenty of reminders at that age of how hard language still was for him. Frequently he would stop, midsentence, to correct himself, and, when he did, he often had to go back to the beginning of the sentence to find his place again. He was so aware of the need to stay "on topic" (something he'd been coached in, since he had a tendency to steer the conversation toward his own interests) that he would occasionally halt in the middle of saying something to apologize for having moved away from the previous subject, even when his change of subject was perfectly appropriate. And of course most kids don't apologize for changing subjects.

Also, prepositions remained difficult for Andrew for a very long time. It wasn't until he kept struggling with them that I realized how complicated our language is—it had never before occurred to me that we say things happen *on* a Monday but *in* October, *in* 1997 but *over* the weekend, *in* Missouri but *on* the beach, and so on. For Andrew, who had shown time and time again that his language was acquired through hard work and memorization, those distinctions were probably as difficult to nail down as it would be for me to learn all the irregular verbs of a foreign language.

There were bad weeks. One day when Andrew was seven or eight and had been saying "orange juice" perfectly for several years, he suddenly started asking for orange "juss." It was like he had just forgotten how to say the word right. I corrected him, and he quickly relearned how to say it correctly, but it brought home to me what hard work it must be for him to maintain the language he had to work so hard to acquire in the first place.

But he persevered and at eleven could carry on long conversations, talk on the telephone, get 100 percent right on his spelling tests, and was one of the most polite children you've ever seen. (Rote memorization serves you well when it comes to always saying "please" and "thank you.") Most people who met him at that age were surprised to hear he had been entirely nonverbal at the age of two and a half and still highly echolalic two years later. But we've got the videotapes to prove it.

And every single night, when I would say good night to him, he would say, "I love you, Mom."

Perfectly.

Ten Years Later

Well, one thing is for sure: I haven't gone in to say good night to Andrew in many years. Mostly because even when he's home from college, I go to bed hours before he does. And I do mean hours. I'm rapidly approaching the days when my kids will start tucking *me* into bed at night. So no more nighttime rituals or "I love you's" (sob).

On the plus side . . . speech therapy is a dim memory. That's not to say that all is as it should be, just that the days of working on it with someone else are past. He is, by the way, an amazing e-mail writer—when we're having a parent-child debate/argument/full-on-blow-out battle about some subject, sometimes he'll write the most eloquent, well-reasoned e-mails that will completely sway us to his side. I think it's simply easier for him to communicate that way than to try to put the same thoughts into spoken and immediate language. Which I totally get—I prefer e-mail to face-to-face interactions, myself.

I was talking to another mom recently, at a school event, and as we were chatting, I became incredibly self-conscious the way one does at a social event that doesn't involve any alcohol. (Oh, wait—is this universal or just my problem? Actually, I don't want to know the answer. I'm going to pretend it's universal.) At any rate, there I was trying to have a pleasant, casual conversation, and suddenly I became hyperaware of everything: Did I sound friendly enough? Did I sound too friendly? Did I sound honest and confiding or creepily confessional? Did I have something on my teeth? Was I talking too loudly because the room was noisy? Could I ask her to keep repeating things I couldn't hear because the room was so noisy, or did that get annoying after a while? Was she interested in what I was saying or just being polite? Was I supposed to stay there and keep the conversation going or at some point pretend to have something else to do on the other side of the room? And so on. (Sadly, I could go on for another paragraph about all my insecure thoughts.)

And I thought, "Talking to people is so frickin' hard." Except I didn't use the word "frickin'" in my head.

There's so much you have to be aware of when you have any kind of a conversation (and we'll talk more about that in chapter 5). Imagine how much harder it must be when you also have to struggle for the words and the sounds. And when everyone else is rattling away without any trouble. And when the subject keeps switching while you're still trying to figure out what people were talking about in the first place.

Honestly, it's enough to make anyone want to run away and be by himself and talk to his own hands.

This is why teaching and encouraging and keeping things fun and rewarding success are all so important. The more I look back on our early years, the more I realize that Andrew's difficulties with language were probably the main reason he was so withdrawn. My husband and I are almost ridiculously verbal— words are our trade (we're both writers). And our second son, who grew up at Andrew's side, mastered language with ease and was later considered such a good public speaker that he was asked to give the commencement address at his high school. In an environment like that, poor Andrew must have felt more shut out than I can imagine, all these words bouncing off the walls and people chattering away . . . a constant din that rarely coalesced into anything meaningful to him.

So speech therapy was, from the very beginning, our first priority. Hours and hours, as I described above. And that was the right choice: as the language came in, he pulled closer to us all, his frustration plummeted, and his motivation to socialize went way up. But it was such a difficult thing, and the idea of learning something hard just so you could do *more* of that hard thing— well, that's not exactly inspiring to a little kid. Which is why it's so important to make using language rewarding and meaningful, even if you have to resort to candy bars and swings to make that point. If ever there was a time to indulge your kid, it's when he's managed to use a word to make his wishes known. From that very simple beginning, a lifetime of social interactions will spring.

One Last Note

Remember how I said in an earlier section that a simple two-part command ("Pick up your shoes and put them in your room") would confuse Andrew in those early years? Well, just a couple of weeks ago, his father gave him this to-do list: "Go to the car rental place at nine a.m., pick up the car I've arranged for you, load it with the stuff from your dorm room, drive to your grandfather's house [a two-hour drive], look for the key and if it's there, carry everything into the house, but if the key isn't there [it wasn't], leave your boxes under the porch, then get back in the car and make sure you're back to the car rental place by two p.m., because if you don't make your three-thirty flight, then you won't make your connection to L.A." And all this was the day after his last paper was due, so Andrew had to pack up his entire dorm room the night before and still get up in time to make it all happen.

In case you're wondering: He did it perfectly.

Chapter Three
Tears, Meltdowns, Aggression, and Self-Injury: Breaking the Cycle

QUESTION: My three-year-old child sometimes has tantrums, flopping on the floor and banging his forehead on the ground until big, red, bloody welts appear. I try to hold him tightly so he won't get hurt, but it really scares me when he does this. This happens on a daily basis, and sometimes these episodes last for two or three hours. What's making him so angry?

QUESTION: I'm a classroom aide for an eight-year-old girl who is fully included in regular classes, and for the most part, she's doing well. But when something frustrates her, she'll break down and cry in front of everyone. The kids are starting to make fun of her, and I don't know how to help, because she just stops listening at that point. How do we stop the tears?

THERE are few things harder for parents than watching their children fall apart before their eyes. Tantrums, tears, head banging, screaming, throwing things—these are all disruptive behaviors that wreak havoc at school, in public, and at home.

The amount of stress these behaviors can cause is mind-boggling. Many parents report that they feel like prisoners in their own homes because their child's disruptive behavior makes it impossible to leave the house. One mother we visited recently said she hadn't showered in two weeks, because she couldn't leave her child unattended for even a few minutes.

Beyond the inconvenience, there's the emotional pain—we all signed on to protect and love our kids, so any sign that they're miserable is heartbreaking to us. When they throw tantrums or sob, we want to help, but we don't always know how, and we wonder if our efforts to make them stop are only making them worse. Meanwhile, we worry about the long-term consequences of these behaviors. Are people going to keep working with my child if he keeps injuring them? Is he going to have to get medicated until he's a zombie? Will he end up placed in a residential setting? Am I the only person who is ever going to love, or even like, my child with all this aggression?

The most painful thing to see is probably self-injury. At our center we see the same look of horror and shock in the eyes of every parent of a young child who injures himself. The parent jumps to hold the child tightly and protect him from harm at his own hands but feels overwhelming hopelessness at ever succeeding.

The Toll It Takes

All this means we're dealing with families under severe levels of stress. Families at a loss. Families whose circle of friends is dwindling and who are having trouble finding people willing to work with their children.

Even with those children whose disruptive behaviors are less violent, parents will find themselves frustrated. Whenever a child cries or melts down, he's not learning, he's not taking in information, he's not fitting in with his peers. All these things harm his progress, and sometimes it feels like you're never going to get a handle on controlling these behaviors.

So what do you do? A series of deliberate steps can break the cycle of disruptive behaviors and open the door to a whole new way of being in the world.

FIRST, DON'T PANIC

Problem behaviors are distressing. When a child is throwing a tantrum in front of you, your heart starts racing, your pulse speeds up, your head throbs—pure flight-or-fight syndrome in action. Just recently I was working with an eleven-year-old boy who was taller than I am and who weighed at least 50 percent more. Walking into our playroom, he already looked a little agitated and was pinching his mom's hand. Suddenly he was lunging at me, aiming right at my eyes. Even though I work with kids with autism all day, every day, I panicked—all I could think about was getting to the other side of the table to distance myself from him. My mind went completely blank and I even forgot that this is my field . . . I *know* what to do about this kind of behavior.

Staying Safe

Not that I was entirely wrong—maybe it would have been better if I'd stayed a bit more calm (at least inside), but the first and most important rule to remember when handling aggression is: *Keep everyone safe.* Toward this end, you want to try to determine if a severe incident of disruptive behavior subsides using any specific procedure.

For example, seventeen-year-old Mike frequently engaged in severe tantrums that included attacking anyone in the room. Mike was big, strong, and fast. We found that if we said "Sit down!" in a loud, stern voice, he responded. It wasn't a long-term solution—just a temporary fix—but it did help to keep everyone safe for that moment, while we worked out our plan for the future. Similarly, we've found that some aggressive children can be redirected to a new activity before their behavior spins out of control.

Waiting It Out

Often, though, keeping everyone safe means simply keeping our distance until the aggressive behavior has ended and we can resume teaching. It's important to realize that for the vast majority of children, no real teaching can occur during a tantrum. In other words, understand that you're probably *not* going to be able to teach your kid not to throw tantrums when he's in the *middle* of a full-blown tantrum.

What you can do is figure out what triggered the tantrum that time, so you'll be able to work to keep it from happening again. That's the next step.

Be Careful Not to Reward Disruptive Behaviors

Even though you'll need to wait out the tantrums, aggression, or self-injury, try not to reward any bad behavior. If your child is being disruptive because he wants something, giving it to him during or immediately after an incident will teach him that he's found a successful way to communicate. Similarly, if your child is trying to get out of a chore or activity by kicking and screaming, and you don't follow through and insist she still do it, she'll learn that's a pretty good way of getting out of something she doesn't want to do. Kids don't have disruptive behaviors because they don't work; they have them because they *do* work. They don't even have to work *all* the time to be reinforced: remember back to your Psychology 101 course—when behaviors are rewarded intermittently, they become even *more* established and *more* likely to reoccur than when they get rewarded every time. So don't think it's okay to give in once in a while: do your best never to reward the behavior you want to get rid of, and also make sure everyone in the child's environment understands that—siblings, grandparents, aunts and uncles, teachers, aides, babysitters, and anyone else your child interacts with. You don't want your child to learn or cling to bad habits because someone somewhere is inadvertently reinforcing them.

At the same time we're going to teach you how to help your child learn a better way to communicate. We want her to learn that asking nicely gets her what she wants and that screaming and throwing tantrums don't.

FIGURE OUT WHY THE BREAKDOWNS ARE OCCURRING

It's very important to figure out *why* the breakdowns are occurring. You'll need a data sheet for this. Make several copies of the full-size behavior data sheet from the appendix in the back of this book. If your child has lots of problem behaviors, you may need to make lots of copies. Make sure the sheets go wherever your child goes, so everyone who interacts with her can fill them out. You can also make extra copies of the behavior sheets to distribute to anyone who works with your child, and then merge the information once they're all filled out.

Now that you have the sheets, start filling them in. Every time your child engages in disruptive behaviors, reach for your data sheet and add another entry. Start by writing down the problem behavior at the top, such as "Hit Mom," "Bit sister," "Tantrum," and so on. Next, write when and where it happened. Then go down the list and make checks in the boxes to indicate what happened before and after the behavior, and why it happened. This sheet is designed to make the process quick and painless for you, while at the same time recording all the important information.

For the moment, don't worry about trying to change anything you're doing, just write down the information. You may feel like you're wasting time, but you're not—I promise you that doing this is the first step toward figuring out the solution. Fill in the boxes completely, because next we want you to try to find some patterns.

FINDING PATTERNS

This may seem difficult. Your first reaction may be, "I already know why my kid's screaming—he's angry." Or even, "I have no idea why he's screaming. There isn't a reason. He just *is*." But disruptive behaviors rarely occur for no reason, and what looks like simple anger is probably an expression of something more complex.

Remember: your child is getting something out of his behavior, or he wouldn't be indulging in it, and it's important to figure out what it is he's getting.

It may take a day or two, or even a week or two, to figure it out. But once you do, you can develop a plan to reduce or eliminate it.

Look at it this way—one day you scream at your kids, and someone asks why you're screaming at them. Your first thought might be, "I'm screaming because I'm mad at them." But it's not really that simple, is it? You're actually screaming because you want them to be quiet or because you want them to clean up their rooms or because someone spilled something and didn't clean it up and you don't want that ever to happen again. You're screaming because it gets their attention and leads to some desired result ("Hey, Mom or Dad's mad—we better stop yelling at each other"). To say it's simply because you're angry doesn't even begin to get at the truth.

Take Notes? Now?

By the way, I know it's easy for me to say, "Fill out the data sheet," but a lot harder for you to be clinical and focused when your child's engaged in a disruptive behavior. In fact, you're probably thinking, "My kid's screaming and hitting, and you want me to fill out a form?! Tell me how to get him to stop! Once he stops, *then* I'll think about filling out your sheet!"

I understand how you feel. Over and over again, the clinicians we work with will encounter a child engaging in aggressive behaviors, and after making sure the child can't hurt himself or anyone else, they'll come rushing into my office, saying, "We don't know what to do! What do we do?" These are professionals in the field, but even they are sometimes overwhelmed when a child falls apart. Nonetheless, when they say they don't know what to do, I always say, "Yes, you do." And they say, "No, we don't," and I say, "Yes, you do," and then they think, and then they say, "Oh, yeah—we do." And they get a data sheet and fill it out.

Figuring out *why* a child is engaging in disruptive behaviors is the first step to fixing the problem. It may not be as immediate as we'd all like, but *it's what works in the long run.*

Let me give you an example. Owen, an adorable little three-year-old, used to bite his fingers so hard there was scar tissue at the bottom of each finger. Telling him to stop didn't help—he'd just go back to biting. So we started keeping track of when he was biting, and we realized it was when he wanted something—it was simply his way of getting it. So, whenever he started to bite, we prompted him to use his words. We waited until he used the appropriate word, then, as positive reinforcement, we provided him with attention or the object or activity he desired. Of course, we had to be careful that he didn't learn, "First I bite, then someone prompts me to say the word, then I get the item." The last thing we wanted to do was to have him think that biting led to getting what he wanted. So we also practiced having him use his words throughout the day when he was *not* engaging in self-injury, so he would connect the success (getting what he wanted) with the use of the proper words and not the self-injurious act. This was critical. Pretty soon, language had replaced biting when Owen wanted something—it had simply become more effective for him to ask than for him to bite.

If you're having trouble figuring out why your child is engaging in some form of disruptive behavior, there's a list of very common causes to help you out on the data sheet. Once you have your data form filled out, you'll probably see a pattern that can be explained by one of the following possibilities.

To Avoid a Task

A child with autism may resort to aggressive or self-injurious behaviors to avoid doing something she dislikes—which very often can include most social interactions. Such a child might begin to bite herself as soon as the teacher approaches with the day's lesson or asks her to sit down.

We all know how this works. Teachers, parents, and therapists will often stop short if a child acts disruptively when she's asked to do work. In fact, there's some research to suggest that children with autism's disruptive behaviors can totally change the teacher's curriculum: I've seen plenty of teachers whose curriculum consists of such easy tasks that the child isn't learning anything. They basically simplify the workload to avoid bringing out a tantrum, so their fear of setting off disruptive behaviors actually harms the child's education. And the kids learn pretty quickly that all they have to do is act out and the teacher will completely withdraw his request.

Similarly, a child may be quietly playing with a toy, but when his mom tries to get involved by asking if she can have a turn, he may respond by forcefully pushing her away, just to avoid having to interact. Or when a parent tries to get the child to leave the TV to get dressed for an outing, he may hit himself on the side of the head with a closed fist. If the adult persists, he may lash out and scratch the adult across the face just to avoid having to transition to a less-desired activity.

Sometimes even something as simple as an adult's approaching and saying "Hi" can bring on an episode of aggression or self-injury. In all these examples, a child who's trying to avoid an upcoming task, activity, or person is using disruptive behaviors to attain that goal.

To Escape from a Task

A second common reason problem behavior arises is to escape a difficult task or situation that the child's already engaged in. This can happen when a task gets too difficult or the demands for social conversation are too great. For example, a child may be sitting nicely at circle time, but when the discussion gets too complicated to understand, he may try to escape the circle time by biting a peer sitting next to him. This usually works to disrupt the circle time, thereby terminating the unpleasant activity, which in turn reinforces the biting.

Similarly, when a task gets too difficult for a child, she may turn to aggression or self-injury. She may be cleaning her room, picking up and putting clothes away nicely, but when she gets to the last stack of laundry, she may decide she's had it and show you so by throwing the whole stack on the floor, then kicking and struggling until she's released from the task. Again, the disruptive behavior may escalate until the adult has given up trying to get the child to do the task, which unfortunately reinforces the behavior.

To Get Attention

Although most people think of children with autism as "driven" to avoid others, there is a subgroup of some who constantly and repeatedly seek attention—but the way in which they get that attention may not always be positive. For example, we worked with a four-year-old girl, Brooke, who used to scratch the skin on her arms and legs until they were bloody. As soon as her mother picked her up, the self-injury stopped—she never scratched herself while being held. So, even though Brooke was heavy, her petite mother still carried her around most of the day to avoid the self-injury. Brooke didn't know appropriate ways to get her mother's attention but *had* learned that scratching herself led to getting what she wanted. And I sometimes see children who are really interested in interacting with their peers—which is a good thing—but because social communication is difficult for them, they try to get a peer's attention by using an inappropriate behavior, such as hitting or pushing. The good news is that the child *wants* his peer's attention, but the bad news is he's getting it in an inappropriate way. It's very important that we teach him appropriate replacement behaviors for that, not only to reduce the disruptive behaviors but also to help him make friends.

To Get Something

Another common reason children engage in disruptive behavior is to obtain something they want or need.

During the year or so after birth, infants express most of their needs through crying, but at around a year, or shortly after, they start to learn to use words to communicate their wants and desires. However, if communication is difficult, as it is for many children with autism, they may continue to use early forms of communication such as crying to obtain a desired item or activity.

For example, one of our students liked to line up his favorite items. Anytime his mom didn't give him one of the items or one was misplaced, he screamed and stomped his feet on the floor, until she frantically searched for it and returned it to its proper order.

I've seen many children whine, cry, and grab for things they want, like candy, food, or toys, instead of using words. I visited a school one day to observe a little six-year-old boy with autism. At lunchtime he constantly grabbed the other children's food. When they didn't give it to him, he screamed and cried and aggressively lunged toward the food until he got it. The children pretty much just let him take their food to avoid the disruptive behavior, so his screaming was consistently rewarded.

Figuring out what your child is gaining from her disruptive behaviors is the first and most important clue to helping her overcome them.

RULE OUT A SIGNIFICANT PHYSICAL CAUSE FOR THE BEHAVIOR

It's important to rule out any serious physiological cause that could be underlying the disruptive behaviors before you start out on a course of interventions. Some physiological conditions, such as an ear infection, a cold, or a headache, can cause pain or discomfort and lead to disruptive behavior. For example, sometimes a young child with a bad ear infection will bang her head against the railings of her crib. Allergies can also result in some types of self-injury, such as repetitively picking at itchy areas of the skin—scabs form, and the child may pick at those until there's a cycle of never-ending sores. Other painful situations like a cold, headaches, or even PMS in adolescents may cause temporary increases in problem behavior. Obviously, you'd want to take care of the physical problem in all these cases, rather than leaping ahead to behavioral interventions.

Sometimes there may be a physiological problem that's less obvious. Let me give you an example. Gracie went to school on the bus every day, and when she got to class the teacher had a "job of the day" for each of her students. Nine out of ten days Gracie walked nicely to class, got her job, and completed it. However, about every tenth day Gracie would have a meltdown, lying on the floor, facedown, screaming and kicking, when she heard her job assignment. The teacher was really stumped, until she brought up the problem at a parent conference. It turned out that Gracie also had occasional sleep problems, and, on the days that she was sleep-deprived the least little demand would send her into the tantrum mode. Fortunately, Gracie's parents agreed to call the teacher before school after those occasional sleepless nights, so the teacher could be sure not to place too many demands on Gracie when she was fatigued.

Now that I've suggested you start by ruling out any physiological problem, I need to add a word of caution to that advice: be careful not to make excuses for *everything*. Good behavior can't be dependent on everything else being perfect. Let's face it, we all have sleepless nights, headaches, or other times when we just don't feel that great. Nonetheless, we still have to go to work, run errands, and even be nice to other people.

If you find that you're always making excuses for your child's behavior, you may be giving him too much latitude. For example, we worked with Jose, a cute little two-and-a-half-year-old who was throwing some pretty nasty tantrums on a regular basis. One day we were having a meeting about him and looking at our notes, and we realized that every day Jose's mom had a different excuse for his tantrums—he hadn't slept well, he had missed his nap, he hadn't eaten his lunch, he was getting a new tooth, they had gone grocery shopping (which he hated), his schedule was off that day, his dad was out of town, and so on. When we playfully went over the list of "excuses" with her, the lightbulb went on, and Jose's mother realized that she was finding excuses for some pretty well-established behaviors. She agreed it was time to start working on the problem.

So if you're constantly excusing your child for one reason or another . . . you know what to do. Drop the excuses and get to work.

LEARN WHAT NOT TO DO

At this point, you should have some pretty good records of when and why your child is engaging in disruptive behaviors. You're now ready to get to work on eliminating them. But before I tell you what to do, let me tell you what *not* to do.

Avoid the Temptation to Punish a Bad Behavior

The temptation to punish a child out of bad behaviors is huge—after all, you just want it to *stop*, one way or another. The problem is that while disruptive behaviors generally decrease when a child receives negative consequences, they usually return at a later time. Punishment is a "temporary fix" that doesn't result in long-lasting decreases in problem behaviors.

Back in the "old days," it was common for corporal punishment to be used on children with autism. This ranged from brisk slaps to electric shocks. Why were these used? Because they worked. Kids who were being shocked *would* learn to control their behavior—but there was a problem. The children usually only controlled their behavior when the person who slapped them or gave the shocks was in the room. The self-control didn't tend to generalize to other situations, because the actual reason for the problem behavior was never addressed, and the children weren't being taught another way to express themselves. Instead, it simply became about avoiding the pain of the punishment. And sometimes they even adapted to the punishment, so that it had to escalate in both frequency and degree to continue controlling the behavior.

No parent wants to punish his child physically. Add to that the fact that all the evidence points to its being an unsuccessful approach in the long run, and you can rule it out as an option.

Another Reason Punishment Doesn't Work

One mother told me that every time her preschool son knocked her glasses off her face, she spanked him. Her glasses were held together unattractively with a paper clip, and she explained that he knocked them off so frequently, it wasn't worth buying a new pair—they would just get broken immediately. With some observation, we realized that Barry had never learned how to get his mother's attention verbally. Once Barry's mom started prompting him to say "Mama" to get her attention, he gradually stopped knocking off her glasses.

The truth was, Barry *was* getting his mother's attention each and every time he knocked off her glasses. It may have come in the form of a spanking, which most of us would consider unpleasant, but in his eyes it was still a successful behavior.

The point here is that some commonly used types of punishment can actually feed into the problem and ultimately cause *increases* in disruptive behavior.

As we'll discuss in greater detail below, to eliminate undesirable behaviors, you must teach desirable behaviors that serve the same end (so-called replacement behaviors), while at the same time making sure that the undesirable ones are no longer effective. Barry's mother not only taught Barry a replacement behavior for knocking off her glasses (saying "Mama"), but she also stopped giving him any attention when he *did* knock off her glasses.

Schools and Discipline

Most schools deal with children's behavior problems through discipline, but the discipline tends to be oddly reinforcing of the bad behaviors.

For example, one principal of a local elementary school sent kindergartner Eldon home whenever he acted up. Pretty soon, Eldon had figured out that every time he didn't like an activity, all he had to do was throw a tantrum, and he would get out of the activity and sometimes even get sent home for the rest of the day. Once the principal understood that Eldon's behavior problems were increasing because being sent home was actually functioning as a *reward* for his inappropriate behavior, a different plan was implemented, and Eldon was no longer pulled out when he didn't like an activity.

At the same time, we developed a self-management program for Eldon. (For an explanation of self-management, see chapter 9.) For each period of school that was problem free, Eldon got to give himself a point. The points could be added up for small rewards, such as stickers, books, and get-out-of-homework-free passes the teacher used with her class. In addition, when Eldon got enough points, he would receive a special commendation from the principal. The teacher also started rewarding Eldon for every attempt he made at difficult assignments and gave him preferential seating toward the front of the class (before, she had seated him in the back, so he would be less distracting to her). Once he was being rewarded for behaving appropriately, rather than the reverse, Eldon's behavior improved enormously.

The bottom line is, think about what the consequence may be teaching the child. It just doesn't make sense to keep kicking out the children who don't find school very rewarding in the first place. By kicking them out, we're creating a vicious cycle: Kid finds school difficult and therefore acts out; Kid gets kicked out for misbehaving; Kid gets further behind because he misses classes and then finds school even more difficult when he returns, thus increasing his behavior problems. How about changing the cycle and creating rewards for every little positive attempt these children make, so that school becomes a rewarding, rather than punishing, experience?

ANALYZE YOUR DATA AND PLAN A STRATEGY

Okay. Let's get to work.

Sit down and look at your data sheet. Study the section about what happened right before the disruptive behaviors occurred. Do you see any patterns?

Precursors

Many children exhibit what we call "precursors" prior to an episode of disruptive behavior—i.e., some signal that the behavior is about to occur. Sometimes these precursors happen immediately before and sometimes a while before an outburst. If a parent or caregiver can learn to identify a precursor, he can potentially avert the negative behavior that would normally follow.

For example, Jessie occasionally scratched others so hard that it left bloody welts on their arms and faces. He also had a tendency to whine now and then. Given the severity of the aggression, no one was particularly concerned about the whining, until we figured out that the whining indicated a huge degree of agitation—agitation that, left unchecked, would often *lead* to the scratching.

For Jessie, it was all tied together—he was basically thinking, "I'm not going to use my appropriate communication. I'm going to start whining, and then if I'm still frustrated, I'll start scratching." So we focused on decreasing the whining: we ignored the whine, prompted him to say things nicely, then immediately reinforced the nicely phrased request. As soon as the whining decreased, we were able to greatly reduce his general agitation, and over time he stopped scratching.

By addressing the seemingly innocuous precursor (the whining), we were able to cut down on the more difficult behavior (the scratching).

Antecedents

While studying the data sheet, you may also find there's some event that always seems to trigger an outburst from your child. We call these events "antecedents," and if you can figure out what they are, you will once again be able to make changes that will prevent your child from falling apart.

Benny threw a tantrum every day when the bus pulled up in front of his house. His mother had to drag him onto the bus crying and screaming, which broke her heart. Obviously the arrival of the bus was distressing to Benny—but why?

We spent a few mornings at the family's home and learned that every morning, after he got dressed, Benny was allowed to watch his favorite television program. The arrival of the bus put an end to one of his favorite activities, watching TV, and signaled the need to go to school, which was hard work for him. Once we realized that, it was no longer a mystery why he fell apart—no one wants to leave a fun activity for a difficult one. The question was how to solve the difficulty of the transition.

We discussed this with Benny's teacher, who agreed to have a favorite activity or toy available to him to play with for a short period of time as soon as he got to school, so he'd have something to look forward to upon his arrival. Benny's mom helped out by taping a few episodes of his favorite television program to give to the school. She also gave the school a few of his favorite toys. When Benny got to school, the teacher gave him a choice of his favorite activities for a short period of free play.

Within three days Benny was happily running onto the bus, anticipating a fun activity at school. Benny's mom didn't even have to stop the TV at home—he didn't mind leaving it now that he knew there'd be another opportunity to watch a favorite show when he got to school. Something he had previously dreaded turned into something he looked forward to.

For Benny, the bus's arrival had been an antecedent to his bad behavior, because it signaled that he would have to stop his favorite activity and go to school to work. Once his arrival at school became pleasurable, the bus stopped being a negative signal for Benny, and he stopped throwing tantrums.

Other children engage in problem behaviors when a certain teacher comes to their home or if a certain workbook is taken out in class. If these patterns can be determined, an environmental change (see below) or appropriate intervention plan can be determined—the teacher can begin with an activity the child enjoys, say, or a different workbook can be used.

Manipulating the Environment

Sometimes the antecedent isn't obvious and takes some thought and effort to ferret out. For example, seven-year-old Mary hit her baby sister on a regular basis at the dinner table. Mary's mother yelled at her every time, but it wasn't helping. (Yelling rarely helps—like punishment, it may have a short-term effect, but it's probably not going to eliminate the behavior permanently.) At first we couldn't figure out what was triggering the hitting, so we asked Mary's mother to videotape the dinners. Once we watched the tapes and took notes, we were able to pin down some patterns. First, Mary was slapping her sister every time the baby banged her spoon on the metal tray of the high chair. Although the rest of the family hadn't noticed the spoon banging, Mary clearly found the noise unbearable and expressed her discomfort through an aggressive act. In this case, the simplest solution was to replace the metal tray with a plastic one. Second, Mary's mother had the two children sit at the table while she was finishing up the last odds and ends before dinner. During this "downtime," Mary frequently hit her sister. Boredom combined with a baby making irritating noises was really a recipe for disaster. So Mary's mom started waiting until just before the family was ready to eat before having Mary come to the table. Once Mary's mother did those things, the hitting subsided.

These are called "environmental changes" or "environmental manipulations"—by changing something in Mary's environment, we were able to curb her disruptive behavior. Obviously, Mary also needed to learn not to express discomfort through an aggressive act (more on that later), but by focusing for a moment on what came before each slap, we were able to make a minor change and keep dinnertime safe for everyone.

Be careful to make environmental changes only when they're appropriate. Let me give you an example of some inappropriate manipulations. Often we see schools that have special education classes on their campuses, and often these classes are fenced in so the children don't run away. Similarly, some families have locks on every door and window of their homes so their children won't run away. While this environmental manipulation may solve the problem temporarily, it doesn't teach the children not to run away—and in an unguarded environment, the child may do just that, since he hasn't been taught not to. While sometimes locks are temporarily important for safety, the child also needs to be taught to ask if he can leave—either with words or with a picture communication system if he hasn't learned to talk yet.

Here's one more example: One school I consulted with asked me what I thought about a student who threw items. The family's attorney had requested that everything in his classroom be bolted to the floor—desks, chairs, tables, everything. Bolting everything to the floor was not what you'd call a reasonable

request—all kids need to learn to live in the real world, and that child needed to be taught not to throw.

Here's the bottom line: If an environmental change can be made without feeding into the problem, then do it. It can really save a lot of work. But make sure that you're also addressing the underlying problem in a productive manner and not just sweeping it under the rug, thereby setting your child up for problems in the natural environment.

PLAN A STRATEGY TO STOP REWARDING THE BEHAVIORS

Now I want you to look at the "After" section of your data sheet, to see what your child's disruptive behaviors usually lead to. It's important to recognize that the consequences of the behaviors may be rewarding in many different ways, ways you may not be aware of. In other words, behaving badly may well be getting him what he wants.

For example, grocery shopping with ten-year-old Johnny was quite an event—he got anything he wanted by screaming relentlessly until his embarrassed mother reluctantly dropped the desired item into the basket. Giving in to him certainly succeeded in terminating the crying. It also relieved the family of a certain amount of public embarrassment, and Johnny's siblings enjoyed all the junk food that ended up coming home with him. Unfortunately, it also taught Johnny that screaming was an effective strategy for obtaining desired items and ultimately increased the likelihood that he would resort to it whenever there was something he wanted. Clearly his mother had to stop rewarding his crying by giving him what he wanted.

In this case, the reinforcement is obvious. In the case of Jared, which we described above, where the principal was pulling him out of the classroom, the reinforcement was less overt and only became noticeable under scrutiny.

Children with autism, who are often less aware socially, may continue to use inappropriate behaviors as they grow older, so it's especially important that they not find them effective. These kids may not distinguish between public and private behaviors. Most other kids, at a very early age, really care about how strangers are going to judge them—I've seen mothers yell at kids in public, and the kids look around and fall silent, embarrassed. But children with autism are much less tuned in socially. Johnny's supermarket tantrums embarrassed his mother, not him, so she was the one giving in.

You'll probably find that, at least initially, any attempt to control children

with autism by making them self-conscious about what others are thinking probably isn't going to work. Unlike other kids, who pay attention to peer pressure and public expectations, kids with autism will often continue to scream and cry and fall apart in public, so long as those behaviors get them what they want. Which means you have to be tough enough in public not to give in to them and reinforce their bad behaviors.

Efficiency

Another thing to consider when examining the consequences of a behavior is its efficiency—in other words, how well and how quickly it's working to get the child what he wants.

Aggression and self-injury can often be amazingly efficient—people tend to do whatever you want when they're terrified of what you'll do if disappointed. Slugging a classmate is easy and may well get you the desired toy, whereas asking politely is a complicated business and may only lead to a no in response. Hitting yourself when your mother says "You can't have that" will often shock her into giving it to you, whereas waiting patiently won't necessarily lead to much of anything.

Below we'll describe at length how to go about teaching a replacement behavior for a disruptive one, but first we want you to become aware of how effective the disruptive behavior has been and to ensure that it stops succeeding in getting the child what he wants.

You also have to make sure that the replacement behavior you're teaching is *as or more efficient* than the disruptive one. It's a two-pronged process: you have to make the bad behavior *inefficient* and the appropriate behavior *efficient* in order to get the child to switch from one to the other.

Let me give you an example: Four-year-old Suzy pushed kids at the park. Her mother spanked her every time, but the behavior did not diminish. After observing Suzy for a while—and filling out a data sheet on her behavior—we found the pattern: Suzy was pushing because she wanted the other children to play with her, and pushing was a quick and efficient way to interact with them. Suzy didn't yet have the social awareness to process the fact that pushing wasn't likely to be a successful long-term strategy for making friends. Her mother believed in manners and had been trying to get Suzy to say "May I please play with you?" when she approached the other kids. This sentence was difficult and unwieldy for Suzy, so she found pushing to be a lot more efficient. Realizing this, we simplified what she needed to say to "Play slide?" or "Play

sandbox?" Two words were well within her linguistic ability, and once she realized this behavior was both successful and efficient, the pushing immediately subsided.

TEACH REPLACEMENT BEHAVIORS

Once you've figured out what your child is getting from behaving badly (e.g., toys to calm him down, junk food at the market, being pulled out of class, and so on), it's time to stop reinforcing the bad behaviors by giving him those things. *At the same time*, you must teach him appropriate behaviors that *will* get your child what he wants—the "replacement behaviors" we mentioned earlier.

Remember: It's not enough to stop reinforcing the bad behaviors. The child also needs to be learning to communicate appropriately, or he'll simply revert to his old disruptive behaviors whenever he's frustrated.

Three-year-old Sammy frequently bit his hand while playing with his mother. He had deep red welts in his skin. We taught Sammy to say "Mama" whenever he wanted her attention and coached his mother to respond enthusiastically whenever he did so. At the same time, she ignored his biting rather than reacting to it. Within a week Sammy's biting was cut in half, and after about a month he always called his mother rather than biting. A previous behavior specialist had put a Velcro glove on him designed to hurt him whenever he bit himself but neglected to teach him an alternative way to get his mother's attention. The glove had little effect on his problem behavior, since he didn't know what else to do to express his needs. Once he had a successful alternative (saying "Mama"), he was willing to give up the self-injurious behavior.

Again, a child must be taught the appropriate way of asking for something, or he will not give up an inappropriate way that has served him over the years.

Practice, Practice, Practice

Appropriate replacement behaviors need to be practiced on a regular basis until they become easy and automatic. The child must be secure in his use of the new, appropriate behavior before he'll completely give up an old behavior he's grown used to. He'll need your help and the help of others to teach and reinforce the new behaviors until they come naturally.

For instance, whenever Ian wanted to shoot baskets at school, and someone was in his way, he would simply throw the basketball as hard as he could right at that person. Then he would say, "I'm sorry." Although this was effective at getting the other child to move, he also caused quite a few injuries. As a replacement strategy, we prompted Ian to say "Look out!" whenever someone was in the way, right before he threw the ball. To get this into his repertoire quickly, an aide went out with him every recess and lunch period. She started out standing in front of him, prompted him to say "Look out!" then immediately moved. After three days of practicing every time he threw a shot at the basket (a few hundred times in those three days!), Ian learned to say "Look out!" without prompting. The aide then recruited a few friends of Ian's to help him practice the replacement behavior. After two weeks the aide was able to fade completely, and Ian never injured another child while shooting hoops.

You'll probably find it necessary to set up a situation like that if you want to find enough controlled times to practice the behavior. You can recruit aides, teachers, parents, therapists, siblings, grandparents—anyone who's around and willing to help—to play the role of the other person in these scenarios, so your child can learn the correct replacement behavior under controlled circumstances.

Just how often the behavior needs to be practiced before it becomes automatic and the disruptive behavior goes away varies. Some children learn the replacement behaviors in a few days; others may take weeks, months, or even longer. It can depend on how long the disruptive behavior has been working for the child and whether it's still effective in some situations.

It's very important that you document how and when the replacement behavior is being practiced. Write down every time you prompt the good behaviors, and have the school, or anyone else working with the child, keep a tally, too. If your child isn't starting to use the replacement behavior without a prompt, then practice more often. If the child is starting to use the replacement behavior but still has disruptive behaviors, then take data again and start working on the next function that the behavior serves, which you identify by examining the column labeled "Why" on your recording sheet.

Once again, keeping records and notes will help you maintain a steady, consistent approach to your child's behaviors that will ultimately pay off.

It Might Get Worse First

One thing you have to brace yourself for when you're addressing behavior problems is that they may get worse before they get better—but remember it's only temporary. It's a simple rule of psychology that we call "extinction" or an "extinction burst," and kids with autism are no exception to the rule. In fact, if your child has a long history of getting rewarded for disruptive behaviors or is still getting rewarded for disruptive behaviors in some situations, she may carry on for quite a while before learning that those behaviors just aren't going to work anymore. Don't let this temporary increase confuse you and don't interpret it as a sign that your program isn't going to be effective. Most important: don't stop ignoring the disruptive behaviors, even when they temporarily get worse, or your child will *really* learn that the longer she carries on the more likely you'll be to give in. That will only increase those behaviors in the long run. Instead, have patience. Let her go through her repertoire and try every disruptive behavior that has worked in the past, while you just keep ignoring those behaviors. Pretty soon, she'll figure out that being disruptive just isn't an effective way to communicate anymore.

Extinction bursts aren't fun and you should warn people to expect them when you start ignoring those disruptive behaviors, but you'll be glad you followed through once they've passed and you start seeing the disruptive behaviors steadily decreasing.

Sometimes You Need a Combination of Programs

Some children need a combination of programs to get rid of disruptive behaviors quickly. While we always recommend teaching the functionally equivalent replacement behaviors, there are occasional situations where the child is at risk of getting kicked out of school or excluded from social activities while you're still teaching those. In these situations you may wish to use another program, such as self-management, a reward chart for good behavior, or increasing favorite activities while gradually interspersing the ones that cause a problem. But remember: If you don't teach a better way to communicate at the same time, the disruptive behaviors will probably return.

Try Self-Management for Older Children

The system of self-management we've developed is especially useful for decreasing problem behaviors while functionally equivalent behaviors are being taught. One of the great things about self-management is that it can be programmed to occur in the absence of an interventionist. (See chapter 9 for a detailed description of how to implement a self-management program.)

Danny's kindergarten had small bikes that the children could ride around the playground. When he was on one, Danny would deliberately run into the other bikers. After a few observations, we determined that he ran into the other children whenever they were in his way. Danny needed to learn to ask the children to get out of his way, but in the meantime he was at risk of getting excluded from being with his peers at recess, as the teacher was sending him to the office on a daily basis. Therefore, starting with small increments of time, we had Danny evaluate whether his behavior was appropriate. At the same time, we practiced having him use the appropriate replacement behavior (saying "Excuse me"). Within one week Danny no longer bumped the other children, and several weeks later he was saying "Excuse me" on a regular basis.

The self-management was effective in immediately reducing the problem behavior, while the replacement behaviors were taught for keeping it low in the long term.

Don't Let Little Things Slide

While you're in the midst of all this reinforcement of good behaviors and elimination of bad ones, it may feel impossible to stay on top of every little thing. You'll be tempted to overlook small outbursts. Don't. Addressing small behavior problems in a systematic way can reduce the larger problems. It may seem overwhelming at this point, especially with children who have many problem behaviors, but sometimes the smaller things are easier to deal with than the bigger ones, and eliminating them may also eliminate the greater problems, whereas letting them slide may well allow the worse behaviors to survive.

For example, Jerry used to shove people away every time they tried to interact with him. In addition, he assaulted adults on a regular basis, frequently leaving bloody scratch marks on their skin. The first time I met him, he was playing with a little farmhouse toy. I picked up one of the farm animals and ended up with bloody scratch marks all the way down my face—four perfect fingernail stripes starting on my eyelids, on both my nose and right cheek, along my lips, ending on my chin. I looked like I had walked off the set of a horror movie. That night Bob and I had promised to take our daughters out to dinner, and of course, as fate would have it, I saw everyone I knew. Sort of like when you run to the grocery store in your old sweats.

Anyway, I asked Jerry's mom if he was nonverbal, and she said, "No, he can say lots of words." So we started working on teaching him to use language instead of pushing or scratching. Interestingly, since the scratching was such a big problem, no one had addressed the pushing. What we discovered was that once we started addressing the pushing, his scratching went way down. They were basically all part of the same larger group of behaviors that he used instead of his words. The adults around him may have felt there was a huge difference between pushing and scratching, but to Jerry they were pretty much the same thing, a way to get what he wanted without having to ask for it. Once he realized that only the words were going to work in any situation, he stopped using either form of aggression.

COORDINATE YOUR PLAN AT HOME AND AT SCHOOL

As we've discussed above, eliminating disruptive behaviors is not a question of finding an appropriate punishment for every outburst. Rather, it's a systematic approach of examining the triggers, eliminating all reinforcement (deliberate and inadvertent), and teaching more appropriate behaviors that produce results for the child. It may sound complicated, but it's really very logical and simple.

It's crucial to coordinate a consistent program of dealing with your child's disruptive behaviors. She'll be confused if people are responding differently to the same problem behavior, and consequently it will continue in some or all settings. You need to be communicating with your child's teachers, therapists, clinicians, and relatives.

For example, we worked with one child who had no toileting accidents at home but was having regular ones at school. The school was insisting, for health reasons, that the parents put him in diapers while he was at school, but the parents refused, since he defecated in the toilet regularly at home. The school called us and pleaded with us to tell the family to put him in a diaper. Instead, we suggested that they have one parent come to the school and help with the toileting. That was when the school personnel discovered that the mother had a specific routine that she did with her son when she brought him to the toilet. As soon as the school used the same routine, he had no more accidents.

This is only one example of how consistency is crucial to any child's success. There are many ways inconsistency will work *against* your child's success. For example, if your child's teacher is handing her a toy to calm her down when she's having a tantrum, thereby reinforcing the tantrum ("Hey, look, I get a toy when I scream!"), that reinforcement is going to work against your attempts to ignore those tantrums at home. Your child's teacher needs to know how you want him to handle disruptive behavior.

So make sure there's a coordinated plan in place for dealing with disruptive behaviors, one that's *not* just the teacher calling you and telling you to come get your kid and bring her home because she's being bad. (Imagine how quickly that will teach your kid that misbehaving will get her home early. And yet many parents of kids with special needs get calls like that every day.) The school should be teaching appropriate behaviors on a regular basis and understand how to deal with problem behaviors in a way that won't be rewarding. For example, if your child hits another child to get him off the swing, make sure that she doesn't get to swing at that time, and make sure that asking nicely is being taught throughout the day. Again, it's a good idea to keep a record, both at home and at school, of when replacement behaviors are taught and practiced in addition to any incidents of the problem behavior you're working on replacing.

If an approach is clearly working, make sure it's being consistently used in *all* your child's environments.

Helping Your Child to Succeed at Tasks Everywhere

It's extremely important that a child learn to control his behavior in a classroom setting and other public places. Whether your child is fully included in a typical classroom, fully included with an aide, partially included with pullouts, in a special needs class, or in a special education school, he'll still need to learn to use appropriate behaviors even when he's frustrated or unhappy.

To help him do that, you must examine what's going on in the classroom setting and figure out ways to increase his success there. Yes, your child needs to learn to express his frustration in ways that aren't disruptive, but cutting down on his frustration will help him on that journey. Look at it this way—as parents, we know we should be patient when our child spills his milk, but it's a lot easier to be patient and smile about it if it only happens now and then, a lot harder if there are ten spills in a row. I learned that my oldest daughter (who constantly spilled her milk) was less likely to spill if I moved her glass as far back as it could go and still be within reach. You want to help your child learn to control his frustration by also controlling situations that are likely to set up a behavior problem. There are all kinds of ways the environment can be arranged to reduce the likelihood of a behavior problem.

I can't emphasize enough the importance of good teaching techniques with a child with autism. Recently a parent from the East Coast was visiting—

one I've known for many years. She told me that there's this impression that we don't work with children who have disruptive behaviors. When she told me this I almost fell off my chair laughing. I explained to her about studies we've published showing that good teaching reduces or even eliminates disruptive behavior. We'll discuss that more in chapter 10 on Pivotal Response Treatment, but suffice it to say at this point that outdated teaching techniques are one of the main reasons children exhibit disruptive behavior. Just make it fun. Kids don't get disruptive when they're having fun.

To help keep incidents of frustration to a minimum, try the following.

Tasks Should Be Meaningful, Fun, and Varied

All children are more motivated to learn if there are naturally rewarding consequences. For example, Mrs. Jones originally used worksheets to help her second-graders practice money concepts. The children had to circle various drawings of coins to equal the printed amount. Curtis, who was diagnosed with autism, let her know that the task wasn't interesting to him by aggressively scribbling all over the entire worksheet until it was shredded, laughing the whole time. However, when the teacher revamped the lesson and had the children work in pairs, buying items using real money in a pretend store situation, the task was much more meaningful, and Curtis demonstrated no disruptive behavior. (Obviously, this change benefited all the children—kids with autism aren't the only ones who enjoy a more meaningful and interesting curriculum.)

"Task variation" is an easy but important way to make curricular activities more pleasurable. Short tasks that are varied frequently help maintain attention and decrease disruptive behaviors. Janie's in-home therapist was drilling Janie for hours on end with flash cards. Janie was not allowed to proceed to the next task until she reached a 90 percent success rate on the previous one. This repetitive and demanding drilling resulted in tantrums, lashing out, and biting. Varying Janie's tasks helped to cut down on her disruptive behaviors.

Similarly, too many difficult tasks all at once can lead to meltdowns. Jake was learning to say words, but it was very difficult for him. In the past, his mother had given him what he wanted whenever he took her hand and placed it on the desired item. When she tried to insist that he use his words to ask for things, Jake was soon frustrated and acting out. Jake's mother decided to pick one frequently requested item (his bottle) and insist that he ask verbally for just that one thing—everything else he could lead her to. After one week Jake consistently said "bottle," so Jake's mom added another word, and then another, until Jake's vocabulary reached several hundred words. It took a while for him to learn the first few words, but each one after that came faster and faster. By interspersing the challenging task of saying a word with the easier task of leading her to the desired item, Jake's mother was able to forestall most of Jake's disruptive behavior.

Allow as Much Choice as Possible at All Times

Choice improves motivation and decreases behavior problems. Unfortunately, children with disabilities are generally given fewer choices than children without disabilities, but they can and should be allowed to make choices. This doesn't mean that the child has the choice of whether to learn or not, but within that one given, there can be plenty of smaller choices.

Jason never did his homework and would engage in lengthy tantrums when his parents tried to make him. Once his parents learned to provide him with a number of choices, he stopped acting out. For example, he got to choose what color pencil and what type of paper he wanted for his homework. He got to choose where he wanted to sit in the house, and he got to choose the order in which he tackled his assignments. He also got to choose what type of soft music he wanted in the background.

When he got to exercise some control over his environment, Jason stopped fighting the one thing he had no choice over—doing his homework.

Understand the Importance of Predictability for Your Child

Children with autism often demonstrate disruptive behaviors when there's a schedule change or unplanned activity. If you're a parent, you probably already know this—there's always fallout from any break with routine. Whenever possible, prepare your child for future events and especially any departure from the ordinary routine.

For example, Summer used to have a tantrum and be "off" the whole day whenever there was a fire drill at school. However, when we let her know the exact time the fire bell alarm and the drill would take place, she had no disruptive behavior—she could handle the noise and activity so long as she was anticipating them. Obviously, with this and many other similar events, we requested and received the school's cooperation.

Predictability is even important with school assignments. When children know how many math problems they're going to need to do or how many pages they're going to need to read, they're less disruptive than when they don't know what the future (even the near future) holds for them.

Every time Cammy was asked to start working in his third-grade workbook, he engaged in mildly disruptive behavior designed to irritate the teacher. This usually persisted until she sent him out of the classroom. However, we noticed that if she told him exactly how many pages he had to complete, he diligently worked away until they were finished. Knowing what lay ahead made all the difference.

While many children may not *like* it when things aren't predictable, they tolerate it. However, children with autism are more likely to let you know they're not comfortable with uncertainty, and unfortunately, if they have difficulties with communication, they may let you know with disruptive behavior.

Priming

Another thing you can do is to *prime* your child whenever possible—that is, introduce him ahead of time to academic and social activities that will happen in the future.

Story time is often difficult for children with autism—it's hard for them to follow an entire story the first time they hear it. Because of this, Willie would scream every time his class sat down for circle time. However, if his mother took home the book and read it to him the evening before it was read in class, he was a perfect angel the next day. That early exposure to the story allowed him to follow along with the class more easily.

Even special activities such as field trips can be primed. One girl we worked with was being excluded from all class field trips because she ran away from her classmates. Roxy's mom started taking her ahead of time to the location where the field trip would be. This increased her comfort level with the new environment to the point where she never ran away again during an outing.

Most recently, we've started priming kids during the summer when we know they'll be attending regular education classes in the fall. We simply get the books they'll be using during the upcoming year and spend a little time each day going over the concepts. We also record some of the regular routines in the classroom to show them during the summer so that they're familiar with how the class is run. All this practice in advance makes it easier to navigate a new situation, so it's not surprising that our studies show that disruptive behaviors are greatly reduced if you prime the child.

WILL THIS REALLY WORK?

If you have a child with strong tendencies toward aggression and tantrums, you may be feeling pretty overwhelmed at this point, and possibly even skeptical whether these interventions—so methodical and careful—are really going to do the trick. But if you follow through on *all* our advice, you should see a huge improvement. Just remember to take careful notes on your child's behaviors, identifying both their triggers and their consequences, then teach appropriate replacement behaviors for those negative behaviors. Don't forget to remove any causes of stress that can easily be eliminated from the environment, and always make sure you're not inadvertently reinforcing any bad behaviors. Make learning fun and life predictable.

Few kids are as difficult as the boy described in the story below—he was one of the most aggressive young children we have worked with. But even with someone whose behaviors were as extreme as his, we were able to turn things around and give him and his family back their lives.

CHRISTOPHER'S STORY

When I first met Chris, he was eight years old, chubby, and almost five feet tall. His hair had been chopped off at the scalp because he threw severe tantrums every time anyone tried to comb his hair.

By the time we started working with Chris, he was infamous for his disruptive behaviors throughout every county in which he'd lived. His parents hadn't been able to sleep together since he was born, because he threw a tantrum every time they left his bedroom at night. So they took turns sleeping on the floor beside his twin bed.

Chris's primary problem behavior consisted of repeatedly hitting the right side of his face with a closed fist, then loudly emitting a high-pitched, ear-piercing, shrill scream after each blow. He hit himself about forty to fifty times a minute during his episodes, and this had caused permanent damage to his right eye. Fortunately his vision was fine in his left eye, so aside from occasional difficulty with peripheral vision, he could see okay.

Another rather embarrassing penchant of Chris's was stripping. He always ripped off his clothes in the same order during his disruptive episodes—

first it was his shirt, then his shoes, which he usually hurled at the nearest person, then his socks, then the pants, and finally the undies. Generally adults were able to stop him before he got to the pants, but several times a day he succeeded in becoming buck-naked in public—at school, at the shopping mall, at the grocery store, anywhere.

Shoes weren't the only things Chris liked to hurl—he threw a lot of different objects and actually had pretty good aim. For that reason the family had no items on their tables, bookshelves, or any other location that Chris could reach.

He also kicked people's shins (frequently targeting any teacher who tried to give him an assignment) and spat at their faces.

Unsuccessful Treatments

Chris's problem behaviors had not gone unrecognized or unattended. Elaborate treatment plans had been developed and implemented. Unfortunately, they all had been based on punishment procedures and were therefore limited in their effectiveness. It seemed as if most of his treatment programs in the few years before he came to our clinic had involved "time-out." In fact, when we met Chris, "experts" from a state-funded program had recommended that his dad build a "time-out box" to put him in, since he was escaping the time-out corners and rooms they had used previously. They also recommended that Chris be left in the box until he was calm.

Following the advice of these experts, Chris's dad built a little box that just had enough space for a small child's chair, with a padlock on the door since he always tried to escape. And, as directed, every time Chris engaged in self-injury, aggression, property destruction, or other problem behavior, his parents dragged him, kicking and screaming, into the box and locked him in.

The problem was, Chris could tolerate the punishment better than his parents could tolerate his screaming.

So here's what always happened: When he got really bad, they locked him in the box, and he screamed nonstop while also injuring himself. Then, when his parents couldn't stand it anymore, they let him out of the box.

So what had Chris learned from this program? That if he screamed and injured himself long enough, his parents would finally rescue him. Sometimes he was in that box, screaming and hitting himself, for several hours. It was a deplorable situation for him and his family.

A Better Way: Figuring Out the Function of the Behavior

The first thing we did when we started working with Chris was to try to figure out what events were triggering his behavior problems. We set up situations that we suspected might cause disruptive behavior to see if each one did indeed cause a problem. That way we could fully understand the probability of disruptive behavior under a variety of conditions.

Since Chris's disruptive behaviors were often painful for the clinicians, we all had a good number of bruises, scratches, and bites by the end of our assessment, but we were able to pinpoint some things that reliably resulted in his problem behaviors.

One was when Chris wanted attention. When his parents tried to interact with anyone besides him, he engaged in self-injury, aggression, stripping, and so on. Of course, you can imagine how this limited their social lives. They were never able to do anything as a family with their friends. They couldn't have anyone over or go out, because if they talked to anyone, he'd start. Since he had a sleep disorder, they couldn't even have people over after he'd gone to bed. The only solution they'd found was for one of them to go out socializing alone, while the other stayed home with Chris. Not great for the marriage.

Another reliable trigger for disruptive behavior was schoolwork. Anytime we brought out a school assignment, Chris engaged in tons of escape behaviors, kicking us under the table, hitting himself, and so on. At school, the disruptive behavior was so bad that all the teachers had quickly learned to back off, leaving Chris to do whatever he wanted all day long.

A few other situations, like hair combing and haircuts, also reliably caused disruptive behavior.

Replacement Behaviors

We had to decide on some socially acceptable behaviors that Chris could use to replace each and every instance of disruptive behavior. We started by teaching him an appropriate way to get attention, prompting him to say "Look, Dad" or "Excuse me" every time he needed something. When he did, the parent immediately gave his full attention. We practiced this a lot—a few times a minute for hours each day.

After he was pretty good at asking nicely for attention, we gradually started having his parents interact with other people—something he had never liked. He had to understand that the disruptive behavior didn't work anymore, so we completely ignored any inappropriate behavior. Trust me, this wasn't easy to do. When someone's hurling a shoe at you and lunging at you with fingers bent in the "I'm going to scratch you" position, it's pretty hard not to react. However, we were able to ignore Chris enough of the time for him to learn that it was a lot easier and more efficient to say "Excuse me" than to attack anyone.

Eventually we were able to get him used to a delay, so that even if he couldn't get attention right away, he would wait nicely. We did this by having the adult say "Just a minute" or "Just a sec" right after he asked for attention. We waited just one second in the beginning, but gradually and systematically increased this to two seconds, then three, then five, and so on until he could tolerate a pretty lengthy delay. By doing this gradually and systematically, we were able to teach him that he *would* get the adult attention he so desperately desired, just not immediately. So, little by little, we took care of that behavior, but that was only part of the problem.

The next issue was school. Chris was starting a new class, and we really wanted him to be a successful part of it. So we made a little pseudoschool at our clinic, using the same type of work that would be expected of him the following year.

As I discussed above, the things that keep school interesting—like giving children choices, task variation, and natural rewards—are not always included in a class curriculum. Chris's situation was no exception. He was in a special education class, and the teacher (whom he would have for the next several years) was a stickler about having children sit in their seats and complete pencil-and-paper worksheets. The function of Chris's disruptive behavior was pretty clear (not to mention understandable)—he hated the boring schoolwork. Unfortunately, teaching him to say "I'm bored" or "Your teaching methods stink" (the "appropriate" verbalization of his feelings) would be unlikely to get him anywhere except the principal's office, so we had to take a different approach. We taught him to ask for help and to ask for a break, but because we knew that he still had to complete an awful lot of monotonous worksheets, we set up a self-management program that would simply reward him for doing his work.

We started out by having Chris come to the table and sit nicely, and when he did, he got to draw a little tally mark on a sheet on his desk. By using a self-management program, Chris was responsible for his own behavior evaluation; *he* had to tell *us* how his behavior was. Then he decided whether he deserved a point for the behavior. We had to teach him to evaluate his own behavior (i.e., was he sitting nicely, listening, not acting out, and so on?). Of course, we had to verify that we agreed with his self-evaluation, but the program was providing him with the skill to assess himself, which is critical for independence.

We started with a really short time period so he could be successful—just a few seconds—after which the adult asked Chris how his behavior had been. If there was no aggression, Chris got to put a sticker in the box. Then we went on to the next interval. After he got a predetermined number of stickers, he was able to pick out a treat. He liked candy and cookies, so it was easy to find something that he felt was worth working for.

After Chris could come to the table and sit nicely for those few seconds, we gradually and systematically increased his work time intervals. By the time the school year started, Chris was able to self-manage his behavior for half-hour periods, and he almost always had perfect behavior during the intervals. This program was adopted by the school, and he continued to show remarkable self-control with negligible problem behaviors throughout the school year. Of course, I would have preferred a different teacher who was able to incorporate motivational teaching procedures, but unfortunately we didn't have that option.

Now we pretty much had the behavior problems under control at home and at school, but there were still a few nagging times when the tantrums and problem behaviors would reoccur. One was during hair brushing and haircuts. I remembered fixing my own daughters' hair when they were young, and every once in a while you can get one little hair pulled the wrong way, which hurts a lot. It's a lot easier to avoid this if you do your own hair, so we taught Chris how to groom himself.

Haircuts were still a big problem, and to be honest, the approach his parents had taken of chopping his hair to the roots when he was sleeping made it look really unstylish. The problem was that he got upset at the very sight of a pair of scissors. So we developed a desensitization program for him (see chapter 6 for a more detailed discussion of desensitization). We started by having the scissors lying around in locations he could see (fortunately by this time he wasn't throwing objects anymore). Gradually and systematically we faded in first the sight of the scissors, then the sound. We did this so gradually that he didn't realize he was being "desensitized" to the haircuts.

Within about four months, by systematically figuring out the root causes of his aggressive and self-injurious behaviors, and by teaching him a system of replacement behaviors, we were able to eliminate Chris's seven-year history of problem behaviors. Interestingly enough, while Chris's disruptive behaviors had been severe, our program of interventions went quite smoothly, and he always learned quickly. The boy so many people had given up on was really a fast and eager learner.

Chris is an adult now. He lives in his own apartment, and he takes the bus to work every day and brings home a weekly paycheck. He earns enough money to pay his own bills. He has several close friends who visit him regularly, and he loves to watch sports with them. Chris is now a happy, law-abiding, self-sufficient member of society with no disruptive behaviors.

FACTS

Between 75 and 80 percent of disruptive behaviors are attempts to communicate.

When a child is being disruptive, 50 percent less teaching occurs.

Disruptive behavior arises 90 percent less often when motivational procedures are used.

FAQ

QUESTION: My child's teacher says that he sometimes injures himself for no reason. Can that be possible?

Your child is unlikely to injure himself for no reason, but that reason may be difficult to figure out, possibly because there's more than one single reason. In this case, start by addressing each cause, one at a time. Don't expect the disruptive behaviors to be eliminated completely when you've only addressed the first function, but they should be getting lower. Then go on to the next, and so on, until you've addressed them all.

There may be another problem in trying to address the "why"—some problem behaviors become a habit, and in addition to having problem behaviors for a reason, a child may also have them without real intent. Children who fall into this category still engage in the problem behaviors for specific reasons, such as avoiding a task or wanting attention, but they do it so often that they might also engage in the problem behavior for no apparent reason at all. It's still critical to address each of the functions and to teach the replacement behaviors, and at the same time to teach and reward behaviors that are incompatible with the problem behaviors. When we work on each function and get those down to a low level, the "habit" ones that look like they're happening for no reason usually tend to go down, too.

Finally, some problem behaviors may be self-stimulatory. For example, we worked with a child who screamed when he was frustrated, but he also screamed when he was alone. While his screaming fell into the category of disruptive behaviors in the first situation, it fell into self-stimulation in the second.

I also worked with a child who was constantly putting the tips of his fingers in his mouth, either biting his nails or sucking on the ends of his fingers. We collected some data to see when and how much time he spent doing this. Our records showed that he put his fingers in his mouth about 45 percent of the time during deskwork, not at all during recess, and only about 20 percent of the time during circle time: it seemed likely he was doing it for self-stimulatory reasons and not to get out of anything. Now, it wasn't really disruptive and to be completely honest most people probably wouldn't have noticed it, but his kindergarten staff had a thing about germs and thought it was completely unsanitary and wanted it addressed. We started a self-management program for him and in no time at all, he stopped putting his fingers in his mouth. Even though it had been an entrenched habit, the self-management quickly eliminated it.

Read chapter 4 for suggestions on tackling behaviors that appear to have no functional purpose other than self-stimulation.

> **QUESTION:** Zachary is a second-grader in my class and demonstrates frequent behavior problems at school, but his parents say that he has no problem behaviors at home. What do you suggest?

Our first suggestion is a home visit. It may be that he's given few demands at home and knows the routine, so there just aren't many opportunities for disruptive behavior. Another possibility is that the parents have a more effective strategy for dealing with the problem behaviors.

It's important to design a comprehensive program that has consistency across all environments. Remember, you're the teacher and you have lots of students. A comprehensive program needs to be developed and implemented by the whole IEP team. (Federal law requires that each student with a disability have an individualized educational plan, or IEP. A team consisting of the parents, school staff, and other relevant individuals creates the child's educational plan for each year.) Get the whole group on board, attacking the problem, at once, and you'll see a faster decrease in the problem behaviors.

QUESTION: I can't take my child with me on my weekly grocery shopping trips and other errands because she's too disruptive. But I need to do my shopping! What can I do?

It's quite likely your child is acting up because she's bored and doesn't enjoy shopping. You may want to try taking her to the store and buying one favorite item, then leaving immediately. Do this a few times until she realizes that there may be some natural reinforcers (i.e., if she's disruptive, she doesn't get the item) involved in shopping—in other words, it's not all bad.

Once she likes going to the store to get something special, keep going, only now buy one other item—something she hasn't requested but that you need—in addition to her favorite item. Gradually and systematically you can add more and more things, until she is able to help you with the weekly shopping. But don't forget to include a favorite item at the end.

Note that this isn't the same as "giving in" to a tantrum and buying a treat. Your child hasn't misbehaved, and in fact she only gets the desired item if she behaves well. In this case, you're reinforcing *good* behavior—if you waited until she threw a tantrum to buy her a toy, you'd be reinforcing bad behavior, so it's important not to wait until then to reward her, but to make it contingent on her behaving well.

QUESTION: My eight-year-old child is completely nonverbal and engages in disruptive behaviors. You keep talking about teaching appropriate words to replace the disruptive behaviors. That's not going to work for us. What are our alternatives?

Communication can come in many forms. Children who are unable to use expressive words or language can learn to use signs, signals, objects, pictures, computers, or other methods to communicate.

For example, one nonverbal child we worked with engaged in tantrums every time he wanted to take a break. As a replacement behavior, we taught him to manually make the sign for "break" (a simple sign, just like you're breaking an invisible stick in half), and his disruptive behavior went away. Interestingly, he never excessively asked for breaks, even though they were usually granted when he used the appropriate sign. Now, it may take some practice for your child to get in the habit of using a sign rather than a disruptive behavior, but if you keep practicing while ignoring the problem behaviors—and definitely not rewarding them—you should see some steady progress with the increasing use of appropriate behaviors.

QUESTION: My child engages in self-injurious behavior—he hits himself on the head. Stroking him calms him down. Is this okay?

Think about the lesson he's learning from the stroking: I hit myself, Mommy strokes me, I feel good. Essentially, you're teaching him to hit himself when he wants to feel good!

We once consulted at a school where a child was acting out with significantly disruptive behaviors. After each classroom incident, the teacher asked him what he wanted to do to calm himself down, giving him three or four choices of favorite activities outside the classroom (believe it or not, one choice was getting a massage from his aide—heck, I would have been disruptive too!). Not surprisingly, his problem behavior escalated to the point where he spent only about 20 percent of the day in his classroom. As soon as the school stopped offering him favorite activities after a disruptive episode, but instead only allowed him to engage in these favorite activities after periods of time *without* disruptive behavior, it decreased to negligible levels.

I've also seen this same thing happen at home. A few of the families I work with live in apartments and they're so worried that they'll be evicted if their child acts up that they give in to each and every disruptive episode. They pretty much live like they're walking on eggshells, terrified of saying or doing something that might set off a tantrum. But we've found that if we can change that pattern by providing the activities or desired items after *good* behaviors instead of after the bad ones, the disruptive ones decrease.

Let me give you a more specific example. One family I was seeing had an older elementary school child. Even though he was quite verbal, he often became disruptive, so his family had developed a series of "calming exercises." Dad would sit him on the floor, rock him back and forth, and soothe him. And he loved this special time with Dad. He would smile and eagerly engage in the calming routine, and it was clear to me that he saw it as a reward. Unfortunately, it was acting as a reward for his disruptive behaviors, which were occurring about every half hour. So I suggested that instead of waiting until he had a disruptive behavior to let him have the calming time with his dad, we try to keep him in a permanent state of calmness by letting him have them at regular, timed intervals, even—and especially—when he wasn't being disruptive. Since the disruptive behaviors were occurring about every half hour, we decided to cut them off before they started, setting the timer for his dad to do the calming exercises about every twenty-five minutes. Well, that immediately reduced his disruptive incidents by 80 percent. The disruptive behaviors might have been eliminated completely if the family had ignored them while they were doing the scheduled calming activities, but habits are hard to break and they lived in an apartment and were worried about getting evicted, so they did continue the calming activities after he acted up. But overall they decreased almost immediately, which was a good thing for everyone.

Always work to reinforce *good* behaviors, not bad ones.

QUESTION: You said to rule out any physiological problems, but a lot of times my kid has tantrums when he's hungry or tired. Does that count as a physiological problem?

Fatigue and hunger are definitely physiological states that may cause anyone to be more irritable (research shows marital fights occur most frequently in the late evening hours). Irritability may directly or indirectly cause behavior problems. For example, we worked with one kindergarten child who engaged in disruptive behavior *only* in the afternoons, never in the mornings. When the teacher discussed this with the parents, it turned out that they had become lax about her bedtime. An earlier bedtime and rewards for afternoons without aggression were successful in eliminating the afternoon aggression. Another child was throwing away his lunches and became extremely disruptive in the afternoons. A simple program of making sure that he ate his lunch fixed the problem. So yes, hunger or fatigue definitely can play a role in disruptive behavior so it's important to monitor that.

Now a word of caution. Obviously you should try to ensure that your child isn't tired or hungry whenever possible, but it's also important to realize that everyone gets tired and hungry sometimes—and we still have to control our behavior. Like the rest of us, your child needs to learn appropriate ways of acting when these states occur. It's also important to teach your child to express these states. I remember my nephew was quite capable of requesting a drink if it was visible ("I want juice, please") but never said "I'm thirsty." We had to teach him that and also "I'm hungry," "My stomach hurts," "I need to go potty," and so on. We used prompting: right before a meal (when we could be sure he was hungry) we prompted him to say "I'm hungry" and before he got a drink, we prompted him to say "I'm thirsty." Now he does a fine job of expressing these physical states even when food or water isn't right in front of him. And of course being able to express the state and request a drink or food reduces the likelihood that the child will simply fall apart, leaving you to guess *why*.

> **QUESTION:** You said to "manipulate the environment" if something's distressing your child, but you also said not to give in to his tantrums. How do you distinguish between the two?

Ask yourself two questions. One: Is it reasonable? Two: Would I do it if my child did *not* have a disability? If either of your answers is no, then you probably shouldn't make that change for your child with autism. Your child needs to learn to behave in the same way as his typically developing peers. As I mentioned above, the manipulations have to be within reason. The child has to learn that he can't rule the roost. If he does, he won't have many friends and won't be able to participate in inclusive settings. On the other hand, there are reasonable issues. No one likes loud, aversive noises, so it's fair to try to keep those to a minimum (also check out our section on desensitization in chapter 6). If he's upset when his baby brother is taking his toys, you can place his toys on a higher table so the baby can't reach them. That's reasonable. But driving a certain, inconvenient way every day to avoid a tantrum isn't. I even worked with a child who would throw a fit if anyone entered his home, so the parents were never able to entertain. That definitely wasn't reasonable! But it was also fixable: we arranged for a series of guests to arrive bearing a special rewarding item for him, and he started to look forward to having company. After a period of time he even began showing good behavior when visitors showed up empty-handed. Sometimes setting up the right things in the beginning can make a long-lasting difference. Think long term when you manipulate the environment. Are you dealing with something that the child will need to learn to tolerate—in which case, you should start to help him do so—or is the distress your child's exhibiting reasonable?

QUESTION: We're doing everything you told us to, and things are improving, but while we're working on the replacement behaviors and all that, our son is still getting enraged about once a day. What's our best way of dealing with his occasional bad behaviors so we can defuse them without unintentionally reinforcing them?

Sometimes the "low-frequency/high-intensity" behaviors are challenging to deal with. We've had some kids who behave pretty well most of the time but every once in a while have a big blowup. Again, make sure everyone's safe, and think of this as an assessment situation—you are going to figure out the "why" so that this doesn't happen again. Is he still lacking the appropriate replacement behaviors? You may not be able to stop the tantrum at this moment, but you can use the situation as a learning tool.

Always make sure the child understands that the disruptive behaviors are no longer efficient or effective—don't inadvertently reward them, and make sure no one else does, either. If Grandma still gives him a cookie when he screams and hits her, you'd better be sitting Grandma down for a talk.

Finally, think about the big picture. It may take time to reduce the behavior problems, but as long as they're going down, even gradually, you're on the right track.

QUESTION: I have an adult child who engages in disruptive behavior. Is it too late to help him? He's been aggressive for almost thirty years.

While it's certainly easier to decrease problem behaviors before they're well established, it's never too late. With intensive efforts using the procedures described above, many individuals of all ages have been able to reduce their problem behaviors. Verbal and nonverbal adults with histories of aggressive behavior can learn to use meaningful communication.

A MOTHER LOOKS AT AGGRESSIVE BEHAVIORS
Or Not?

When Dr. Koegel and I first started working on this chapter, I told her that I wouldn't have any personal stories to add to it. Andrew has never hurt himself or anyone in his life. He's virtually never thrown a temper tantrum. In fact, I remember when Andrew was probably about four and was in speech therapy with a little girl his age. Roberta, our speech therapist, said she had put the two kids together because they were so different: Ellie was fairly verbal, but prone to fits of rage. Andrew was almost completely nonverbal, but he was gentle and passive. Roberta felt the two kids would have a positive influence on each other. Ellie's mother and I laughed about how two such different kids could have the same diagnosis—it seemed to point to the craziness of the whole label of "autism."

Ellie's mother also told me something that I've never forgotten. One day, she had gone swimming with some friends, and afterward one of them had taken her aside and gently asked her if her husband was abusive—her bathing suit had revealed a mass of bruises on her arms and legs. Of course, it wasn't her husband who was battering her—it was her tantruming four-year-old daughter with autism.

I was surprised to hear that a kid with autism could kick and hit like that. Andrew had never so much as pinched me.

Which was what I told Dr. Koegel. She thought for a moment, and then she said to me, "What did Andrew do when he was little and he couldn't communicate his needs?"

"Sometimes he'd raise his hand and wait," I said.

"And if time went by and he didn't get what he wanted?"

"Sometimes he was okay with it," I said. "But usually he'd start crying."

"Did he cry a lot?" she said.

"Constantly."

"And now?"

"He still falls apart all the time," I admitted.

Lynn said, "That's exactly what we're addressing in this chapter: the child who finds communication difficult and gets so frustrated he falls apart. Andrew may not have fits of rage, but his crying serves the same function and requires the same series of interventions that any disruptive behavior would."

Oh.

So Here's What Used to Happen and Sometimes Still Happens

Let me start by describing a trip I took with Andrew when he was around two. No one had diagnosed him with anything yet, so all we knew was that he was an unusually withdrawn toddler and lagged behind all his peers in speech development. Although he was happiest playing at home by himself, lining up his foam letters in alphabetical order, I still thought it would be nice to take him to the East Coast to spend Rosh Hashanah with my family.

My husband drove us to the airport, and we said good-bye. I planned to be there something like five or six days.

Andrew didn't sleep on the flight, which was a problem, since it was the red-eye, and we both arrived in New York exhausted and on edge. But the main thing I remember is that later that first morning, he started sobbing inconsolably for no apparent reason. He cried and cried, and I couldn't calm him down. Then I noticed that he was clutching his stomach. He was clearly in pain, and I thought he had some kind of stomach bug.

I was a wreck. My son was sick, and we were far from home.

At some point, I brought him downstairs into the kitchen. I tried to distract him with a cookie.

He scarfed it. And cried until I gave him more.

That was when it hit me: Andrew wasn't sick. The boy was *hungry*. Starving. Traveling had thrown both of us off our schedules. I had probably offered him something to eat when he didn't need it yet and hadn't noticed that he hadn't eaten much. And it just hadn't occurred to me that he might be clutching his stomach in hunger rather than pain.

He couldn't tell me he was hungry. He didn't have the words to do it, and he hadn't even learned to point (an ability that for some reason tends to elude kids with autism, although I didn't know that then—hell, I didn't even know he *had* autism). Plus he was in a strange house and didn't know where the kitchen was so he couldn't even lead me to what he wanted.

Eating helped him for the moment, but he was still on edge in these strange new routineless surroundings, and I was convinced he had a cold coming on (he must have sneezed or something). I was already exhausted, Andrew was melting down constantly, and I just wanted to get us home before things got any worse. So I switched our tickets so we could fly back to L.A. the next morning. My husband met us at the airport. I was overjoyed to see him and somewhat disappointed in his less-than-overjoyed reaction at seeing us. I made some peevish comment about how he didn't seem to have missed us.

"Claire," he said patiently, "you were only gone a day, and I was at work for most of it. It just didn't feel like you'd actually gone away."

Just one day? It felt like a hell of a lot longer than that to me.

Later On . . .

On that trip, Andrew was still, admittedly, nonverbal. So if the tears and misery were a result of not being able to communicate, they should have faded out completely once he started talking, right?

Uh, well, no. Not completely. Some habits die hard, especially when they serve a useful function, like letting you get out of tasks that are difficult.

For quite a few more years, Andrew would still dissolve in tears when he was frustrated or overwhelmed. This was a kid who almost never cried from pain, but a tough homework assignment could bring on the waterworks. One night when he was in fifth grade, I checked over his homework and told him that a short essay he'd written was too messy—there were so many erasures on the page, it was practically illegible. I asked him to rewrite it. Andrew started blinking rapidly and swiping at his hair with the flat of his hand, both familiar signs of impending tears.

I hesitated. Should I back down, switch topics, and avert the tears? That was tempting, because once the crying started, Andrew lost all ability to listen to what I was saying, and we both usually ended up wildly frustrated.

On the other hand, if I backed down, wasn't I letting him get away with something? Like Dr. Koegel had said, I needed to think about what he was getting out of those tears, why he was resorting to them in the first place. In this case, if I let his crying steer me away from my original demand, as we'd done plenty of times in the past, then crying would have "worked" for him, and the next time I asked him to do something challenging or simply undesirable, he'd resort to tears even faster.

Ideally, I'd know how to do both—get him to stop crying and still do the work. I knew it was possible, because sometimes a positive tone of voice and a change in approach succeeded. But I was tired and didn't have the energy to be upbeat—the best I felt I could do was to wait out the tears, without backing down from my original demand.

This actually worked. He cried for a while, then, to my relief, he sat down and did a beautiful job rewriting the page. The breakdown hadn't gotten him out of anything, and maybe, just maybe, he'd be less likely to go there the next time.

Afterward, Andrew said to me, "I'm much better about crying now. I don't do it at school."

"Good," I said. "If you're going to cry, home's the right place to do it." I was pleased he had acquired a sense of public appropriateness. When he was little, he cried everywhere and anywhere, but he really learned that you don't want your friends to see you fall apart if you can help it.

Your parents are another story, of course.

Redirection, Antecedents, and Positive Tones

Getting Andrew to stop crying once he had started—or to listen to you while he was crying—was virtually impossible. You really couldn't break through to him once he was in the middle of a breakdown. You could wait it out, but you couldn't shorten it. Our brilliant behavioral therapist, Wayne Tashjian, had taught us that we needed to head off the tears at the first sign they were on the way, but without withdrawing the original demand on him.

We weren't always as organized in our approach as we should have been, but we did figure out what some of the antecedents and precursors were, and with Wayne's and Lynn's help, we learned some strategies for dealing with Andrew's tears.

For instance, whenever I saw the blinking and swiping (a consistent precursor to Andrew's tears), I would know Andrew was feeling like he was being pushed too hard. A lot of sincere praise came in handy at that point and could often turn things around. A typical comment would be, "I know it seems hard, but remember how hard your math was last week, and you figured out how to do it? I was so proud of you!" The point wasn't to let him get out of doing his work, but to make him feel less frustrated with the whole process. Sometimes it worked. Sometimes I waited too long, and it didn't. Sometimes I was too tired to change my tone and be positive, and we both would fall apart. (It's embarrassing, but I have to admit that his tears occasionally brought on my own.)

Tone of voice was huge with Andrew, who would often cry if he felt like an adult was angry at him or disappointed in him. Saying something like "I'm not happy with what you've done" was an antecedent that would send Andrew off the deep end. Far better to approach a serious topic with a cheerful "Hey, Andrew, you know what?"

I tried. I really, really tried, but like any mother, I'm not perfect. I knew how to say positive things, like "Your room looks great—if you just put away the papers, it will be perfect!" But I had four small kids, and I would get busy and tired, and sometimes I would just snap out, "Your room's a mess!" And sure enough, when I wasn't careful and said something too angrily, I would end up sending Andrew into blinking-and-swiping mode. And, honestly, sometimes I resented that. I wanted to be able to snap at him when I felt like it and not have it be such a big deal. But it was to him.

Well, most of the time it was—I may be the only mother in the world who rejoiced when her kid talked rudely back to her when she scolded him for something. I preferred to hear Andrew say, "I told you I'd do it!" with an edge in his voice than have him cry when I pointed out something he hadn't done.

Oh, I would tell him he wasn't allowed to speak to me rudely, but inside I triumphed because he sounded just like a twelve-year-old was supposed to sound when his mom was being a pain. Not that I wanted Andrew to be a snot—I was just glad to see him sticking up for himself without immediately going to a sad and worried place.

Getting Tougher

Andrew got tougher. Peer pressure did a lot of it. Once he started caring about what the other kids thought (something that only kicked in around third or fourth grade), he tried to control himself in front of them, and he reached a place where he could do it most of the time. He also seemed to be getting the idea that it wasn't the end of the world if one of his parents got annoyed at him about something. We stopped being at the mercy of his tears, stopped being afraid of saying something that might put him over the edge.

And when he got through something difficult without any tears at all, we learned to praise the hell out of him. He frequently returned the favor, and the other kids picked up on the whole positive reinforcement thing, so our house used to ring with the words "Good job!" "Awesome!" and "Way to go!"

It was kind of nice.

Ten Years Later

I was talking to an autism support group recently and a man who had been sitting there silently for most of the afternoon suddenly raised his hand and said, "What do you do if a child you're supposed to be keeping an eye on just suddenly *pops* someone?" (To illustrate what he meant, he struck the palm of one hand with the fist of the other.)

I—and some of the other moms—explained that it's important to try to figure out what made the child explode with sudden anger. Had something happened beforehand to trigger it? Was she going to get something out of it?

The man waved all that away. He wasn't interested in figuring out why the girl hit someone—he just wanted to know what he was supposed to do after she did.

We explained again that you can't really control the behavior unless you know what's causing it and that—

But he interrupted us impatiently. "I just want to know what you're supposed to do when a kid turns suddenly violent. What are you *supposed to do?*"

And I realized this was a cry from the heart. From the little information I was getting, it seemed this man was in charge of keeping things safe for everyone in this particular situation, and so when the child suddenly hit out savagely, he wasn't thinking about long-term solutions or behavioral interventions—he wanted simply to know what he was "allowed" to do to control the child.

So I said carefully, "It's important to keep everyone safe at that moment."

He nodded, pleased. Finally we were addressing the issue.

"And 'everyone' includes the child who's hitting," I added. Because I realized that a panicking adult with an aggressive child can be a recipe for disaster. "That means make sure the kid can't continue to hurt anyone, but don't punish her."

I'm not sure he was entirely satisfied with that response—I almost felt like he wanted some kind of additional permission that I wasn't giving him—but the conversation moved on.

One mother then told a story about how her son had been riding the same bus he always had, without any problems, when he suddenly turned around and punched the child in the seat behind him. People were horrified and accused her nonverbal child of being dangerously aggressive. And then the mother found the pinch marks on her son's leg: the kid behind him had been pinching him for days without anyone noticing or intervening. Her son couldn't communicate what was going on to any adult, and finally he had just reached his limit and wanted the pinching to stop. Far from being the initiator of aggression, he had endured it for longer than most kids would have, but to a casual observer his lashing out seemed sudden and arbitrary.

This is yet another reason why we have to approach aggression thoughtfully, caringly, and knowledgeably, especially when it involves someone who's nonverbal. Don't simply dismiss a child with disruptive behaviors as "violent" or "angry"—figure out what the meaning of the disruptive behavior is, what he's getting out of it, whether it's a kind of communication or a self-stimming behavior, or whether there's a trigger or reward that needs to be identified. And then take the appropriate steps to reduce the unwanted behavior while encouraging replacement behaviors.

And remember when there *is* an outburst that the goal is to keep everyone safe—and that includes the child who's being disruptive. You're the adult: stay calm, stay focused, stay fair.

And of course, when the crisis is over, feel free to go have a little cry in your room. We've all dropped a few tears into a pillow, or onto a faithful dog or soft warm cat.

Nothing's harder than dealing with disruptive behaviors, but know that with patience and hard work (I know—we say that a lot) you really can reduce and even eliminate them.

Chapter Four
Self-Stimulation: Flapping, Banging, Twirling, and Other Repetitive Behaviors

QUESTION: My child rocks and flaps his hands. My husband constantly yells at him to stop but the school psychologist says that he needs to "release" and we should let him engage in this behavior during recess and lunch. I'm confused. Why does he do it and what should we do about it?

QUESTION: My child hums and rubs a piece of cloth whenever she's alone, but she doesn't do it at school. Should I make her stop?

CHILDREN with autism often engage in repetitive behaviors that seem pointless. No one fully understands why they do this, but one theory suggests that all children need a certain amount of stimulation, and if they're not getting it from typical social and play interactions, they'll create it for themselves through these behaviors. The repetitive behavior makes them feel good, thereby providing sensory reinforcement or sensory stimulation. This theory has led people to refer to these behaviors as "self-stimulation," or "stim" for short.

Another theory suggests that repetitive behaviors serve a regulatory function. In some situations, the child may engage in the repetitive behavior to reduce sensory overload, increase sensory input, or modulate some type of erratic sensory input. Still other theories view self-stim as similar to behaviors like self-injury or obsessive-compulsive behavior. Some of these suggest that areas of the brain that control these behaviors are not working quite right or that these behaviors may produce some natural opiate through the production of endorphins in the nervous system.

Regardless of theoretical perspective, we do know that these behaviors can be decreased as a direct result of environmental manipulations and self-control. In other words, we can help our children find better outlets for their energy.

Examples of Stim

There are almost as many types of self-stimulatory behaviors as there are children with autism. One child we worked with would open and close the doors and windows on toy houses for hours at a time. She was equally fascinated with real doors and windows and would go in and out of any door she could find— she especially liked the automatic grocery-store type. If her mother tried to stop her or move on, she would flop down and throw a tantrum in public.

Another girl we knew masturbated on the corner of tables so often that a doctor sent her to us for treatment. He reported that her vulva was completely red and swollen, and a layer of scar tissue had formed on her genitals. She was so driven to masturbate that she sought out corners wherever she went, in schools, restaurants, and stores.

One boy picked his nose repetitively until he hit a major blood vessel and blood started pouring out of his nose. He did this several times a day, and everywhere he went there was always a trail of blood drops.

Most stims are not so severe. More commonly, the children rock back and forth, flap their hands in the air, wave their fingers, tap on objects, or hum or sing same song over and over again. They may be irritating for parents or teachers, but they don't cause harm or disruption.

Annoying, Yes—but Not Dire

Although repetitive behaviors are not well understood, we now know that they decrease without our having to punish the children. In fact, they tend to drop out naturally as the children's appropriate behaviors improve.

But while appropriate interventions lead to a decrease in self-stimulatory behavior, it's also true that the drive toward repetitive behaviors often lingers. People with autism, like anyone else, can learn when and where to indulge in behaviors that don't belong in a public arena—when you think about it, we *all* have certain behaviors that we've learned over the years to restrict to private places.

Furthermore, many children with autism learn to redirect their urge to stim into more appropriate activities, often ones that have the same type of sensory input that the original stim supplied. It may not be considered socially acceptable to wiggle threads or flap your hands in public; it *is* socially acceptable to knit, draw at a table, or play a piano for hours on end. You can help lead your child toward more appropriate behaviors, which may in time even become strengths. We know many children with autism who once had high levels of stim and who are now award-winning runners, accomplished artists, and successful musicians.

The Old-Fashioned Way

The way we used to deal with repetitive behavior is very different from what we do now. In the past, we were concerned that the children couldn't learn if they were engaging in repetitive behaviors. And this can be true. If a child is vigorously rocking his body while flapping his hands, he probably won't be able to give his full attention to you. In order to get the children "ready to learn," we included a whole program of teaching the child to sit still before we started any type of teaching. We often seated the child in a chair and said, "Look at me," and then rewarded her for looking. Similarly, if the child was engaging in hand flapping, we would say, "Hands down," then reward her for sitting still. This was a totally logical thing to do because the research had shown us that learning was slow or nonexistent if children were engaged in repetitive behaviors.

But now we have a different approach. Now that the teaching has improved (see chapter 10 on Pivotal Response Treatment), the children happily come to the sessions and engage fully—and the repetitive behaviors drop out without any need for direct intervention.

Unfortunately, I still see programs where the clinicians are working on eliminating the self-stimming behavior before beginning to teach. That's usually a waste of a young child's time. The children need to start right away with motivating activities, and when they do, the repetitive behaviors will probably decrease without needing any special program. Now, this isn't to say that your child shouldn't learn how to sit in a chair nicely—he'll have to do that at meals and in school for many years to come. It just means that, for the most part, motivated children really don't engage in repetitive and disruptive behaviors. They engage in the fun activities you've set up for them—the fun activities that also happen to be teaching them and moving them forward because we're targeting specific and important areas, like communication and socialization. We don't have time to spend on areas that really aren't necessary but take up a lot of your child's precious time.

Now, having said that, later on some new repetitive habits may develop and your child may engage in these while he should be learning or socializing. If that happens, we may need to address those with a different type of program, such as replacement behavior or self-management. But if your child is just getting started with intervention, make sure you dive right into the actual interventions using the motivational components, rather than spending time focusing on the stim alone, which your child may not need.

Staying on Top of It at School

Although in general we counsel parents not to worry too much about self-stimulation, since it tends to drop out by itself when the child gets intervention, we do feel it's crucial to curb the child's tendency to stim while he's at school and other public places. Because self-stimulation is a solitary pastime and can cause children to withdraw from social interaction, it's extremely important that they not stim during recesses and lunch periods, when the most important socializing of the school day takes place. Unfortunately, playground time is often when teachers and aides leave the children alone to do pretty much whatever they want.

Many children who stim when left alone will also be perfectly happy doing a more social activity, but they may require an adult to remind them and redirect them to that activity. For example, we worked with a set of identical twins who were doing quite well in the classroom academically, but you could always spot them during recess and lunch because they both paced around the perimeter of the playground for the entire period. However, when we prompted them to play handball—something they both enjoyed—their pacing ceased.

HOW TO REDUCE SELF-STIMULATION

Every parent knows that keeping children busy keeps them out of trouble. When our children are involved in supervised activities, hobbies, sports, and homework, they're not getting into trouble. We worry when our teenagers ask if they can stay out until midnight on Friday and Saturday night—it's not that we don't trust our kids, it's just the unknown. Will they get in a car wreck? Will they drink? Will they meet a bad person? The lack of structured activities and a clear course of action leads to a worrisome uncertainty.

It's no different for children with autism: We know that when they're engaging in self-stimulatory behaviors, they aren't learning. Their brains aren't making new neural connections, and they aren't developing socially. So we need to keep them engaged in meaningful activities. At first this may seem overwhelming, especially if your child engages in a lot of stim. But redirecting him will pay off in the long run. Find activities he likes, have him help you with each and every task throughout the day, enroll him in camps and programs that will keep him busy, and teach him how to play with toys and games. Here are some suggestions to help you with this process.

Run Your Child Around

Vigorous physical activity is a fun, easy, and effective way to decrease self-stimulation and improve learning. Regular exercise throughout the day is one of the first things we recommend to anyone trying to keep a child with autism engaged and focused.

Through careful research, we discovered that when we allowed our kids to run around and play outdoor sports for ten minutes or more at intervals throughout the day, it greatly increased their ability to focus without stimming. The physical activity must be vigorous—it's not enough just to take the kid outside and let him sit on the grass or walk around the perimeter of the yard—so check with your doctor first to make sure your child's in good health. And remember that this effect of vigorous physical exercise is short-lived—less than an hour—so spacing out bouts of physical activity throughout the day is best.

The truth is that physical exercise has positive physical, mental, and emotional effects on all individuals, regardless of age or ability level. Unfortunately for children with autism or other severe disabilities, regular physical activity is not always part of their daily routine as it should be. If vigorous exercise isn't already incorporated into your child's regular schedule, make sure you put it in there.

There are easy ways to do this. One family we worked with let their son jump on the trampoline (his favorite activity) for about twenty minutes every day before he went to school. This greatly reduced his repetitive behaviors first thing in the morning and helped him to concentrate on his schoolwork.

We've also developed effective classroom schedules that incorporate physical activity: the teachers at schools that use our schedule provide breaks every hour for the children to play games that involve running. The teachers at these schools invariably note that after the exercise program is put in place, the children are "better students." In addition—and not coincidentally—teachers also report that they find their days much more enjoyable when exercise programs have been incorporated.

Decrease the Stim Gradually

Whatever the drive is in these kids that makes them want to stim, it's such a strong one that you can make yourself crazy trying to eliminate it all at once.

You'll end up feeling overwhelmed if you try to redirect your child every single time he engages in a repetitive behavior. It's far less stressful to focus on decreasing it gradually over time, and ultimately it's just as successful. But keep in mind that this is a process. The more you work on it now, the less you'll have to do later. So if you have even a tiny bit of energy, go for it. You'll be glad you did.

Start by prompting your child to engage in just a few more minutes of appropriate behavior each day. If you want to use the stim as a natural reinforcer, that's fine. (See below for more on that.) Take Donny, for instance. When he was four, he rocked on his rocking horse for hours on end. Although his mother realized that he wasn't engaging in appropriate social and learning interactions during these hours, she was often busy with the household chores and his two younger sisters. Instead of forbidding him to ride, she simply required him to help her with *one* chore that kept him close to his beloved rocking horse, before he actually got to ride it. First she had him ask her for help moving the rocking horse away from the wall. Then he could climb on. Soon after, she had him help her clean up the toys around the horse so that he wouldn't trip over them. Once this became a regular part of his routine, she added another chore, and so on, until the time he spent on the rocking horse was minimal. Instead, he was engaged in appropriate behaviors for most of the day.

Self-Management

The system we've developed of self-management, in which kids learn to control and positively reinforce their own behaviors (see chapter 9 for details), works very well for those who are old enough to monitor themselves but who still fall into repetitive behaviors when left alone. One of the great strengths of self-management is that it can be programmed to occur in the absence of an interventionist. Since kids who stim are likeliest to do it when they're alone and unengaged, this self-reliance becomes crucial to their success in decreasing the self-stimulation.

We worked with one boy who repetitively played an imaginary trumpet. He played all day long in his regular education fourth-grade class, and it became quite annoying to his teachers and the students around him. We set up a self-management program at school: as a reward for periods of time without playing his imaginary horn, he could listen to jazz tapes with a headset. Not only was he able to engage in class periods without self-stimulatory behavior, but the reward of listening to jazz tapes provided him with a sensory reinforcer similar to the imaginary horn (but more appropriate), and after a while his stim disappeared.

Finding Socially Appropriate Replacement Behaviors

Many repetitive behaviors can be replaced with another activity that has the same sensory function for the child. For example, Mickey used to flap his hands repeatedly whenever he got excited. We taught Mickey to clap his hands instead of flapping them. This served the same sensory function for Mickey but didn't look stigmatizing.

Other children can be directed toward more functional behaviors. One child we worked with repeatedly played with small round items, rolling them between his fingers for hours on end. His mother gave him pencils to play with and eventually taught him how to draw with the pencils. He is now a talented artist—and his stim is virtually eliminated.

If you're using this approach, you'll have to figure out the exact sensory area that your child is engaging with the stim. Some stims are auditory in nature, some tactile, and some visual. The appropriate replacement behavior has to serve the same sensory function for your child. Many children who enjoy staring at patterns will also enjoy toys that have movement. Children who enjoy spinning objects may like "see and say" toys. If they like the noise that a spinning plate makes, look for musical toys.

In other words, look for toys and activities that are just as enjoyable as the stim, because they appeal to the same sense—they're fun to watch, they sound good, or they feel good.

Use the Stim as a Reinforcer and Reward

The drive to stim can be such a powerful thing in a kid's inner life that it can, somewhat ironically, play an important and useful role in interventions. In other words, if there's something your kid really likes to do (like opening and closing doors), have him *earn* the opportunity to do it. For example, many children with autism are fixated on turning lights on and off repetitively. So we prompt them to say "light" before allowing them to play with the switch. This is a great way to encourage appropriate behavior using a very highly desired activity. (Please see chapter 2, on teaching language, for more about this.)

A child with fewer support needs can earn periods of "time alone in private" to engage in repetitive behaviors, if he refrains from doing so in public. Of course, you don't ever want to allow your child to do any behavior that's injurious to himself or others. Those behaviors have to be cut out completely (for more on that, please see chapter 3).

FACTS

Up to 100 percent of self-stimulatory behavior can be eliminated with self-management.

Up to 67 percent of self-stimulatory behavior can be reduced after a jog of fifteen to twenty minutes.

Correct responding can increase by up to 100 percent after a jog of fifteen to twenty minutes.

JARED'S STORY

Jared was three and a half when we started working with him, and his defining feature was his nonstop repetitive behaviors. Strings were his thing. He picked up any string he could find and shook it in front of his eyes. He found strings everywhere, and if there were no strings around, he picked up a leaf or a stick from the ground and shook that in front of his eyes.

Jared also obsessively repeated requests when he wanted something he couldn't get—he would just keep asking for it over and over again until he got it. I remember one Mother's Day, Jared's dad asked his wife what she wanted as a gift. She responded that the best gift he could give her was to have Mother's Day completely to herself, without Jared. I felt so sad about that. I couldn't imagine not wanting to be with my children on Mother's Day, but Jared was a challenge. His mother worked with him constantly and was making good progress, but his repetitive behaviors were particularly wearing on her, and she chose Mother's Day for a break.

So that day, Jared's dad took him for an all-day hike. He planned a nice father-son day in the mountains with a picnic lunch on top of a scenic lookout. He packed a big lunch, loaded Jared's little sister in the backpack, and set out. Unfortunately, it didn't turn out to be the peaceful hike in the mountains he had anticipated. About an hour into the hike, Jared asked for a piece of gum. Jared's dad didn't have any gum and told him so, but Jared couldn't accept it. He repeated "I want gum" over and over again. Jared's dad said that after about the hundredth time of hearing "I want gum" he began to hike as fast as he could to get away from the endless requests, but Jared was right behind him at his heels. He repeated "I want gum, I want gum, I want gum" for six hours straight. Exhausted at the end of the day, Jared's dad brought the kids home, collapsed on the couch, and told his wife about his exceptionally stressful day. I actually think Jared's mom got a little sadistic pleasure from hearing about the gum incident, because she felt that her husband had never fully appreciated the effort Jared required. At any rate, Jared's mother got her one day of rest, and Jared's dad was more than happy to go back to work the next day.

As occasionally annoying as the endless requests were, however, Jared's habit of constantly shaking things in front of his eyes was the more persistent and worrisome stim. I was determined to get rid of that behavior. So during our summer preschool, I was on his case constantly. Every time he picked up a leaf and started shaking it in front of his eyes, I walked over to him and said, "What are your friends doing?" or "Go play with your friends." I never told him what to do specifically but just kept after him until he was doing what the other kids were doing.

This took such effort and vigilance that I fell into bed exhausted each night. I felt like I was running after him *all* the time. Because Jared had some good skills and was capable of imitating the other children, I consciously chose to give him just a general instruction, such as "Do what your friends are doing," rather than a specific instruction, such as "Go down the slide"—I wanted him to develop the skill of imitating the other children on his own.

After a few weeks of my constantly reminding him to go play with his friends, Jared was playing like his peers most of the time, and simultaneously his stim started to decrease. A few weeks later, he would drop the leaf or twig and run over to his friends when he just saw me walking toward him. One day I said to his mom, "I'll bet he hates me—I'm always on him to play with his friends instead of playing alone." To my surprise, she said, "No, not at all. In fact every morning he gets up and asks when he can go to Lynn's school!"

After that summer, Jared's parents enrolled him in a preschool for typically developing children. Unfortunately, stim still continued to be a constant problem for Jared. The school let him bring a blanket to school, and he pulled off loose threads from the edges of the blanket to wave in front of his eyes. His mother sewed, so I asked her to zigzag the edges of the blanket so he couldn't pull off the threads. That worked for indoors, as long as there were no threads or strings on the floor that he could pick up, but he still continued to pick up leaves and twigs to shake while outdoors instead of playing with the other students. So we had a clinician go over to the school to prompt him to play with his friends during all of the outdoor times, just as we had during the summer pre-school. It was slow, hard work, but he was improving gradually.

In addition, Jared's mother thought that if he could do something with his hands that was incompatible with the stim, it might decrease, so she started giving him music lessons. She was an accomplished musician, and she taught him piano for fifteen minutes every day. She decided that regardless of how much he protested, she would practice with him for just a quarter of an hour each day for a year, and after that, if he didn't want to continue, she would let him quit. Although the first year of lessons was a struggle, he eventually started enjoying playing the piano, and by the time he was in fifth grade, he had won a statewide award for his playing. He now spends much of his free time practicing the piano.

Around fifth grade, after several years of constant and systematic work in school and of channeling Jared's stim into piano playing, the behavior was virtually eliminated. One day I asked him if he remembered when he used to pick up things and wave them in front of his eyes all the time. He said, "Yeah, I do remember that." I asked him why he did it, and he said, "I don't know, I just remember that it felt so good."

Although I never see a bit of stim in Jared anymore, his dad told me that he still goes into his room and plays with strings on occasion, particularly if he hasn't exercised and has been sitting in school all day. His dad joked that he was going to buy him a rosary so that it would look like a "Catholic stim"!

FAQ

QUESTION: How do you distinguish between autism-related self-stimulation and the kind of habit any child might have, like biting fingernails or humming while eating?

This is an important distinction. The question is, basically, when to worry. There are a few things to consider when thinking about self-stimulatory behavior. First, is the behavior interfering with your child's learning? If the child is not engaging in academic or social activity because of the stim, you need to tackle it aggressively. Second, is the stim stigmatizing? Imagine your child at a job interview as an adult. If he engages in even five seconds of self-stimulation during a one-hour job interview, he may not get the job. Although it may seem insignificant at this time, you need to think of the long-term implications. Finally, you're right that all individuals exhibit some types of self-stimulatory behavior. The difference between its being a problem or being okay is how much, what type, when, and where the person exhibits it.

For example, if you drive down the freeway and look into people's cars, a good percentage of the people you observe will be picking their noses. However, these same people would be unlikely to pick their noses at work, in a shopping mall, or during a conversation with another person. Likewise, these people wouldn't pick their noses until they bled. Again, while it may not be necessary to eliminate stim completely, the child needs to learn when it's socially inappropriate to engage in the behaviors.

> **QUESTION:** You say I should get my son to exercise regularly if I want to cut back on self-stimulatory behaviors, but he hates playing ball and running around. I'm not so crazy about it, either. Is it really so important?

Getting started is the hardest part, but once you start engaging in regular physical activity, you will most likely find that the whole family benefits from this time together. If you, as a parent, are simply unable or unwilling, try asking a staff member at the school who enjoys vigorous exercise to take your child on regular exercise outings throughout the day. You could also consider buying a trampoline, since we've found that jumping works well with some children to reduce the stim. Bike riding is another activity that some parents find helpful. Recently I worked with a family who decided to bike to school rather than put their child on the school bus, so that some exercise would be built into the morning routine. Another family, whose child wasn't fit or motivated to exercise and who only wanted to stay home, arranged for someone to drop her off at various places a small distance from where they lived, so that she could have the natural reward of arriving home after a walk.

Remember, too, that sports are a huge social thing as kids get older, so acquiring the skills involved in these types of activities may have an entirely separate beneficial effect for your child in the future.

> **QUESTION:** If I use self-stimulation as a reward, won't it increase during other times of the day?

Many parents worry that if we take the child's most desired activity and use it as a reward, the child will want to engage in that behavior more frequently. Actually, the opposite is true—when we use self-stim as a reward, especially if it's tied into a naturally rewarding consequence, it doesn't increase at other times. For example, I've worked with many kids who like to turn the lights on and off repeatedly. Instead of letting them just randomly turn the lights on and off, I'll have them say "on" or "off" and *then* give them the natural reward of turning it on or off. Later we can work this up to a few words, like "on, please" or "turn off." It works like a dream. And because children are driven to engage in this type of behavior, they're often willing to engage in long and complex strings of behavior to earn the stim.

> **QUESTION:** Is my kid stimming because he's overwhelmed and stressed out? Do we need to pull back on our demands on him?

No one knows for sure what prompts these behaviors, but the fact that they often occur when the child is alone and no demands have been placed on him suggests that they're unlikely to be the result of stress. However, it is always important to assess whether there's a reason the child is engaging in the stim. For example, some children will engage in self-stimulatory behavior when school assignments are too difficult. In such cases replacement behaviors can be taught (as we discussed in chapter 3). Assessing the self-stimulatory behavior in the same way that you look for patterns for disruptive behaviors will help you figure out whether there's a functional cause—for example, you may find that your child is trying to avoid a task. And if she is, you can teach a replacement behavior.

> **QUESTION:** My son's teacher says he "needs" to stim and we should just leave him alone whenever he engages in those behaviors. Is this true?

No. Don't let anyone tell you it's okay for your child to stim at school. These children need ongoing programs at school and during other community activities so that they're engaged. Your child shouldn't be left alone to stim in these socially important venues. This is the time to actively teach important social communicative skills. And, as we've proven, if steps are taken to keep him engaged in enjoyable activities, he won't even *want* to stim.

QUESTION: But if a child isn't doing anything physically harmful, what's wrong with letting him stim whenever he wants?

Some people believe that these behaviors are harmful in and of themselves, because they interfere with learning—kids can get so involved with self-stimulation that they stop taking in any outside information. However, this isn't true of all types of stim; our research has shown that a child can learn while engaging in some types of self-stimulatory behaviors, but not others. In short, some types interfere with everything, and others don't. So you'll need to consider two things. First, is the stim interfering with learning? And second, does it make the child look different from his peers and have the potential to draw unwanted attention to him? If your answer is yes to either issue—it's interfering or it's stigmatizing—you'll want to make sure there are intervention programs in place.

QUESTION: Every time I take my child to the park, he spends the whole time sifting sand through his fingers. It's really frustrating, and I feel like just skipping the park altogether. Any ideas?

You may want to purchase some little beach toys that your child can use to sift sand with. Then help him learn how to use them appropriately. That way, he can get the sensation of sand sifting without looking different from the other kids. Using toys that other children are accustomed to may also encourage other children to join in play with him.

QUESTION: My son's favorite thing to do is to watch TV. In fact, he could spend all his waking hours watching television if we let him. We let him watch a few hours each day, but when he does, he rocks back and forth endlessly. This is okay around our house but somewhat embarrassing when we go to relatives or friends. Can this be stopped?

You may want to try using the remote control and turning off the TV every time he starts rocking. That way he'll learn that if he wants to watch the show, he has to sit quietly. If this doesn't work, you may want to try physical exercise or self-management.

> **QUESTION:** My child's therapist constantly says "Hands down" to my child. He said that we need to get him sitting quietly before we can start working on anything. Is this true?

There's no doubt that many kinds of stim are incompatible with learning, but I'd recommend working on it the other way—by teaching appropriate behaviors in as actively engaging, fun, and interesting a way as possible. Then the stim should drop out by itself without having to spend all that time working on it directly.

A MOTHER LOOKS AT SELF-STIM

When my cousin's daughter was three, she picked her nose constantly. They have a lot of photos to commemorate this period—apparently, it was fairly difficult to get a candid photo of her back then when her finger *wasn't* in her nose. My husband and I thought it was funny and kind of adorable and then one day I said to him, "You know, we're laughing about this, but if it had been *Andrew* who was always picking his nose, we would have had every therapist in L.A. working on getting him to stop."

That's the thing about having a kid with autism—you never know when a bad habit is a normal part of growing up or something that has to be clamped down upon immediately. Okay, maybe that's not entirely accurate—I mean, some bad behaviors you do know for sure about, like head banging or biting— but the weird little things, like making hand puppets in the air, lining shoes up in neat, obsessive rows, or sucking in your lower lip obsessively (all of which Andrew did) fall into the "Will someone please tell us if this is okay or not?" category.

When a typically developing kid picks her nose, you figure it's normal—you try to get her not to do it in front of other people, of course, but you don't read too much into it. When a kid with autism does it, it's self-stim. Or is it? Maybe you should cut her some slack. Then again, maybe you shouldn't. Everyone has bad habits now and then . . . but is *this* a bad habit or a symptom of the autism?

It's enough to make you crazy.

Not that Andrew picked his nose. He did other things, none of which I initially identified as anything so organized as a "self-stimulatory behavior." In fact, before I knew that my kid had autism and I was supposed to "keep him engaged," I actually thought it was great that he could amuse himself so quietly for such long periods of time. I'd lie there on the sofa reading a book while he gathered together all the kicked-off shoes in the house and put them in a nice neat row. Then he'd rearrange them. Then he'd rearrange them some more. I could read an entire novel while he lined those shoes up over and over again.

In his bedroom, he liked to line up his stuffed animals, always in the same order: first Ernie, then Bert, then Elmo, then Barney, then Cookie Monster, then a penguin. (Once, just to see how Andrew would react, Rob and I carefully laid his two-month-old baby brother right in the middle of the lineup, between Ernie and Bert. The only sign that Andrew noticed was that he stopped arranging the other stuffed animals. He just sat there, frozen, staring straight ahead, waiting. The baby started to cry, and we moved him. Andrew went back to straightening out the lineup.)

I later discovered that my lying-on-a-sofa-while-my-kid-lined-things-up approach to parenting was not my finest hour as a mother. Turns out I should have been a lot more active about trying to engage him. I wish I had been, but I did my best to make up for lost time.

The Problem with Hand Puppets

"Hand puppets" were another stim of Andrew's. Actually, at first, the whole hand-puppet thing seemed kind of cute. Here was this little toddler boy making his hands "talk" to each other by holding them up in front of his face, sticking out his fingers at odd angles, and making incoherent babbling sounds (of course they were incoherent—he was completely nonverbal in those days).

Anyway, it seemed kind of imaginative, and we probably cooed over it the first couple of times he did it.

But then, when Andrew continued to do hand puppets constantly and obsessively for the next four years, we stopped thinking it was cute and started wishing he would stop. He did hand puppets all the time, whenever he wasn't actually in therapy or being deliberately engaged by an adult. He did hand puppets in public places where people, even other kids, would give him strange looks. He did hand puppets instead of doing normal kid things like playing, socializing, talking, looking at you. . . .

I love my child, but I have to say, the older he got, the weirder he looked doing those hand puppets. His fingers were crooked, his arms were akimbo, his head was tilted, and he was completely absorbed in his own world. Plus he was chattering away in his own incomprehensible language. It was bad enough at home, but once Andrew was old enough to go to school and be with other kids, we became desperate to make him stop doing hand puppets. Not only did they alienate him from the other kids because they made him look so strange, but it was a solitary game, and he wasn't making any friends.

How Not to Get Rid of Hand Puppets

Here are some things we tried that *didn't* work:

1. Holding Andrew's hands still. He didn't like that, and we didn't like doing it, and anyway it only worked when we were actively clutching his wrists. The moment we let go, he'd escape, and in a few minutes he'd be back to the hand puppets.

2. Pretending our hands were also puppets and turning the stim into a social playtime. Andrew couldn't have been less interested in these attempts. He'd drop his hands, give us a funny look, and walk away. Once he was alone again—away from those crazy parents of his—he'd go back to doing hand puppets.

3. Showering him with real puppets and puppet theaters. We figured if he was going to play puppets, he might as well work toward a future career as a Muppeteer. Occasionally he'd carry a puppet around. But only his hands satisfied him for the stim.

4. Shouting at him. That never worked for anything.

5. Begging him to stop. He wanted to please us but couldn't resist whatever the pleasure was that he was getting from the stim. It was intrinsically rewarding and satisfying. We felt like we were no match for it.

Losing Patience

Hand puppets seemed to symbolize so much that worried me about Andrew then: his separateness, his withdrawal from the world, his weirdness. His autism.

It reached the point where I'd hear Andrew babbling away in the next room, making one hand talk to the other, and I'd want to scream out of sheer frustration. And sometimes I *would* scream at him to stop, and his hands would drop down to his sides out of pure shock and fear . . . but as soon as the moment had passed, and he wasn't actively thinking about it, they'd rise back up again. Only, then I felt guilty because I'd yelled at my kid.

So there we were.

What Dr. Koegel Had to Say About It

Once we brought Andrew to see Dr. Koegel, things improved—mostly because she assured us that there was no correlation between hand puppets and a bad prognosis. She also said that a lot of self-stimulatory behaviors just naturally fade out over time.

Most kids with autism stim, Dr. Koegel said. The important thing to focus on was whether or not they could be made to pay attention when you were actively trying to engage them. In Andrew's case, as she demonstrated, it was fairly easy to get him to stop stimming and do something else. True, the moment he was off by himself the self-stim returned, but that drive alone wasn't cause for concern. The fact that Andrew was willing to stop when presented with another activity was the key to knowing he would eventually learn to control and redirect the drive toward self-stim.

In other words, she said, *relax.* The stim wasn't that meaningful, and the odds were good he'd outgrow it when he learned to become more socially engaged with others.

Dr. Koegel's Advice

Still, Dr. Koegel agreed with us that we couldn't have Andrew stimming away in public places, especially ones that provided social opportunities, like school.

"Tell him," she said, "that he looks silly doing them and should only do them when he's alone. Quietly remind him whenever necessary to drop his hands and prompt him to interact with the other children. Try to find other activities that give him the same kind of pleasure, but that don't make him look weird in front of the other kids."

I was slightly shocked to hear her say we could tell Andrew to his face that something made him look silly. It had never occurred to me before that I could enlist Andrew's aid in his own behavioral interventions.

The truth, as I discovered once I approached Andrew directly, was that he had reached an age where he was both eager to please us and anxious to make friends at school. He wanted to know what he could do to fit in better and be like the other kids. Reminding him to put his hands down now brought forth an immediate compliance. Unfortunately—heartbreakingly—whatever urge it was that made him want to turn his hands into puppets was so strong that it always sprang up again the second he wasn't consciously working to control it.

Choosing Your Battles

Thanks to Dr. Koegel, we no longer felt we had to eradicate hand puppets—we just had to try to confine them to private times and places. That seemed like a much easier task.

Out in the world, whenever Andrew started to do hand puppets—which, at first, was all the time—whatever adult was with him would walk over and gently whisper a reminder, and Andrew would immediately drop his hands. Pretty soon they would rise again, the command would be repeated, and they would go back down. (Repetitive behaviors, we discovered, require repetitive corrections.) We would also urge him to go play with other kids rather than be off by himself. He now had an aide at school, and Dawn dedicated herself to playing such fun games with him that other kids would want to join in. This proved to be an over-whelmingly brilliant solution to the social difficulties of recess. And the busier he became doing normal kid stuff, the less he was inclined to stim.

At home, we tried to keep him busy doing fun things, but when there was nothing else Andrew was supposed to be doing and he was alone in a room, we turned a deaf ear and a blind eye to the frequent stimming.

Time went by. And very gradually, with no big noise or fuss, the hand puppets went away by themselves. Just like Dr. Koegel said they would.

Progress

That's not to say that Andrew's hands became still. It's just that, as Dr. Koegel predicted, he found more socially acceptable ways to keep them in motion. For example, these days, if you look at Andrew when he's quietly thinking about something, chances are good you'll catch him biting his nails. Of course, the same holds true for my sister and my father and about a dozen other people I could name. So I don't nag Andrew about the fingernail biting—people don't ostracize you for biting your nails.

(I sometimes wonder whether the strange pleasure we *all* get from biting our nails, peeling off scabs, rubbing our ears, twirling our hair, and myriad other weird but "normal" unconscious behaviors is akin to the pleasure kids with autism get from stimming. Maybe if we could figure out why *our* weird behaviors give us pleasure, we could figure out why theirs do.)

Better than the nail biting was Andrew's growing interest in drawing. He started to spend most of his free time with a pencil in hand. Drawing seemed to satisfy the need to keep his hands in motion and also allowed him to be satisfyingly repetitive without any complaints from his parents. He went through one phase where he would draw the four Beatles over and over and over again (changing them slightly depending on the year he was depicting and their actual facial and cranial hair during that time period)—we got a kick out of that one and had him design a Beatles ceramic remote control holder at Color Me Mine that's still in use in our family room. Not only is drawing socially acceptable, but his friends actually admired and encouraged his talent, and he was proud of his artwork. He also liked to draw intricate maps—some of real places, some of imaginary ones—and those were also pretty cool.

Other Stims and How They Changed

Hand puppets weren't the only form of self-stimulation that Andrew indulged in, just the one he was most passionate about for the longest period of time. For years he also flapped his hands and jumped up and down a lot, a behavior that stuck with him in certain specific situations. For example, when drawing, every few minutes he'd kind of lean forward over his drawing and kick his legs up (he liked to draw standing up), then rock back and wave his arms. Home was pretty much the only place he spent a lot of time drawing while standing up, so it wasn't a huge problem.

He stopped lining things up, but he continued for many years to enjoy making lists and drawing time lines.

Andrew never did the classic, ritualistic rocking thing that most people with autism do (at least in the movies). But he did love to swing. When he was a toddler, I stopped taking him to the park because it seemed so pointless—I wanted to wear him out, and instead I was wearing myself out, pushing him in the swing for what felt like hours. He'd cry if I tried to take him out and get him to do something else. It was so frustrating: I was trying to be the good mom who takes her kid to the park (even though I've never been a park person myself—more of a curl-up-with-a-book-at-home type), but those outings only left us both frustrated and annoyed at each other.

Of course, if I'd consulted Dr. Koegel about it (I didn't even know her back then, so that wasn't an option), she would have advised me to make the swinging a reward for doing something more interactive at the park: I should have told Andrew he could swing *after* he did the slide once. And then the next time I could have told him to do the slide and climb the jungle gym before swinging,

and the next time the slide, the jungle gym, and five minutes in the sandbox—
and so on. I wish I had thought to do that. Instead, I gave up on the park completely and bought a swing set for our backyard—nothing wrong with making
that available to him, but I completely lost out on any social interactions for either
of us at the park. And, trust me: I could have used an occasional few minutes of
mom talk back in those days. And of course Andrew needed a lot more experience socializing with his peers.

A Digression

It's funny to me now that, looking back, I can see clearly how I could have
turned something like Andrew's obsession with swinging at the park into a positive, by holding out and using it as a reinforcer for his doing something more
social (and which he probably would have ultimately enjoyed). Once you've
spent time with someone like Dr. Koegel—and once you're not too emotionally
overwrought to think clearly—you start understanding how to motivate and encourage your child using the very aspects of his life that have previously con-
founded and frustrated you. But when you're deep in the trenches, sometimes
you're so busy just trying to survive that you forget to think strategically.

Someone called me recently for advice about a boy who was having some
behavioral problems. I asked her some questions, thought "What would Dr.
Koegel do?" (WWDKD), and was able to make some helpful suggestions for
figuring out what the root of all the disruptive behaviors might be and how to
motivate him to give them up. It drives me crazy that I could never think that
clearly when the issue involved my *own* son—that I *still* have trouble thinking
clearly when I'm worried about any of my own kids. It's becoming a running
joke between me and my closest friends, all of whom give thoughtful, insightful,
useful advice when someone else is struggling with her kids, and all of whom
fall apart completely when the problem concerns their *own* children: "Here's
what you should do," we all say and then add, "Not that *I* ever succeed in
doing it." Wouldn't it be nice if the anxiety we feel for our kids made us more
clearheaded and thoughtful?

Yeah, it doesn't. But we can still make being clearheaded, thoughtful, calm,
and productive a goal and keep on trying to achieve it.

Back to Stimming

So anyway . . . we put up a swing at home, and I stopped going to the park.
I was *very* pleased when Andrew mastered the art of pumping—my arms

needed the rest. Then we got a big-kid play structure with two swings attached, and the first thing Andrew did for years whenever he got home was go out and swing for ten minutes or so.

I like a glass of wine at the end of a tough day and I've always wondered whether Andrew's swing time played a similar role, helping him transition from the stressful day to the more relaxing evening at home.

We bought a trampoline when Andrew was about ten (with a net enclosure), and he loved jumping on that for long periods of time. We all did.

We were lucky. None of Andrew's stimming behaviors were injurious to himself or to other people. Obviously, if they had been, we would have had to clamp down on them much more actively. Still, mild as they were, they worried us, because they took him out of our world and imprisoned him in another one, where a crooked finger could be the mouth of a wolf, and incoherent babble passed for communication.

Ten Years Later

It has been a very, very long time since I even thought about self-stimulation. It's simply not an issue in our lives.

Let's stop and think about that for a moment: Our kid used to make hand puppets and talk to himself obsessively for hours at a time. We worried and worried about it. If I visited him at preschool, I'd see him off by himself, walking in circles, making those damn hand puppets.

And it's all gone. There are plenty of things I still worry about, but self-stimulation isn't even a drop in the bucket of anxiety. It's a nonissue.

So don't waste too much time worrying about it in your own family's life. Follow Dr. Koegel's advice to keep teaching activities fun and engaging, do your best to convince your child to indulge in self-stimulating behaviors at home rather than out in the world, and then *let go*. Take a deep breath and move on. This isn't one of those areas to obsess over.

As far as where we are now . . . well, some things have fallen completely by the wayside, like swinging (I'm not convinced Andrew wouldn't still enjoy a fun, fast swing, but at some point he decided it was a sport for the younger generation and has eschewed it ever since) and jumping (our trampoline lost a few of its safety features over the years and eventually we realized it was more of a liability than a piece of exercise equipment; it's long gone).

But drawing . . . drawing's another story. Andrew did lose a certain amount of interest for a while. He never stopped drawing completely, but he did feel like maybe it was childish and started only doing it quietly, in private (sometimes I'd find drawings crammed into his pants pockets, almost like they were something to be ashamed of, even though they were perfectly acceptable and often lovely). But then he came back to it—and even changed his college major to graphic design in his sophomore year. The instruction he's gotten because of that has taken him from someone with a natural gift to someone who's a really good artist. I think his drawings are sort of spectacular. (Yeah, I know: of course I do, I'm his mom.) It's still one of the ways he spends a lot of his free time. Which, as far as I'm concerned, is terrific.

He also still bites his nails a lot.

Whatever.

Chapter Five
Social Skills: Turning Language and Play into Meaningful Interactions

QUESTION: My three-year-old grandson doesn't seem to be interested in other children. He's content playing by himself at the park, at preschool, and at family gatherings. Although he seems happy, I'm worried he's becoming isolated. What can I do?

QUESTION: My seven-year-old student does pretty well academically but spends all of her recesses and lunches wandering the playground alone. Is this okay?

WE lead social lives. It's virtually impossible to go through the day without a series of social interactions, from dropping off your kids at school, where you say hello to all the other parents, to buying your coffee where the baristas know you by name, to going to work, where you chat with coworkers and clients, to eating lunch with a friend, to meeting your spouse and another couple for dinner and a movie, and so on and so on. Life is equally social for kids, whose early interactions with their family members help them learn that they're part of a group and not just isolated individuals, a discovery that sets the stage for the friendships and romances they'll enjoy later in life.

The importance of learning to be social creatures looms large in the lives of parents of children with autism, because so many of those kids seem to lack the desire and ability to interact with others the way their peers do.

Social difficulties are an inherent part of the disability of autism, and they need to be addressed as early as possible. Left to themselves, children with autism won't usually get out there and take classes, start conversations, invite kids over, play sports with friends, go to parties, or feel driven to participate in other social activities that typical children are naturally drawn to.

Not learning how to be social can have a lot of negative long-term repercussions. Children who do not socialize well have more difficulties in securing jobs as adults, and when they do get jobs, there's a much higher likelihood that they'll lose them as a result of interpersonal relationship problems. It's not surprising that research has shown that adults who had social difficulties as children are more likely to be depressed or experience anxiety in social situations than those who didn't.

Children with autism are not likely to develop in the area of socialization unless specialized programs are developed and implemented, but with these programs, they can become social creatures. Of course, there's quite a bit of effort required—especially on the part of the school, where ample peers are available for social interaction, making it the perfect place to move those skills forward.

Approaching It Rationally

The good news is that socialization can be taught. The bad news is that it's hard to approach this issue calmly and methodically, because it touches on so many things that are vitally important to us, like love, friendship, and companionship.

I experienced this firsthand, when my younger daughter was about three: she was having a horrible problem with ear infections and her otolaryngologist was trying her on some rounds of antibiotics before resorting to surgery. Because there was always some fluid in her middle ears, she really hadn't been hearing much for most of the school year. One day the preschool called me for a parent conference. I met with two teachers and the director of the school, who dropped a bomb on me: they informed me that my child was having grave difficulties with socialization. They said that she rarely interacted with any of the other children, but instead spent most of her time perched on the top of the monkey bars staring into space, and that she didn't seem the least bit interested in group activities. I was stunned.

After the meeting, I got in my car, broke down in tears, and sobbed, barely able to suck in a breath, all the way home. When I got home and ran inside and told Bob what had happened, he said calmly, "And did you tell them what to do?" Between tears, I confessed that I hadn't. He gently reminded me that this was my area of expertise, that I knew exactly what to do, and that I simply had to get a comprehensive plan going. So the next day, when I was composed again and my face wasn't completely red and puffy, I went back to the school and informed them that she was having significant hearing problems and that her behavior was exactly what would be expected of a child in her situation. I said that in the classroom she was going to need preferential seating and more visual cues. Most important, someone needed to be there at recess and lunch to prompt her to get off the top of the monkey bars and encourage her to join in the group activities on a regular basis.

When I could think about it calmly, I *knew* what needed to be done, but my first reaction to hearing the teachers say, in essence, "Your child is failing socially" was to fall apart. As parents, we love our children and want the world to love them, too, so watching them reject the company of others—or be rejected by them—is often too painful for us to be rational about it. But we have to be.

Over time, with a combination of surgery and competent teachers taking the necessary action, my daughter improved, and now she spends most of her free time hanging out with friends.

Similarly, when my nephew was in preschool, I stopped by to observe one day. It was free time, and he was clearly hoarding the train set—his restricted interest at the time. Whenever other children tried to join in, he let out a huge scream, which immediately scared them off. So he had his own private little play set at school, and no one was intervening. (This is something I've seen at a lot of schools during unstructured time: if the kids are playing alone nicely and quietly, no one seems to worry, even if they're alienating the other children.) But seeing that was all I needed to swing into gear and get some social goals targeted.

We wanted to emphasize the importance of taking turns, so we approached the lesson systematically, looking for opportunities to incorporate it into his daily routine. We even targeted it at home. He had gotten into another repetitive behavior of always having to be the one to open each and every door all by himself. If he didn't get to open the door he would have a huge meltdown—screaming and crying. It had become such an issue that—to keep the peace—his parents just let him open the doors. He and his dad were in our clinic at UCSB one day, and his dad brought up the door problem. My suggestion was to say "my turn this time" at every other door and just to ignore whatever followed: Don't respond, don't get mad, don't give in. Just pretend it wasn't happening.

As they walked out the door, I heard his dad say, "This time it's my turn!" Then I heard a loud scream. Then the door shut after them.

And that was the beginning.

Slowly but surely my nephew came to understand what another person's turn was. After a bit of practice, he realized that crying and tantrums weren't going to get him a turn when it was time for someone else to have one. For several months after the crying stopped working, you could still tell that he didn't like it when someone other than him took a turn: he'd clench his hands and jaw and scowl. But now he's older. He's in team sports and plays lots of games with his friends. He's perfectly happy to give another person a turn. He still likes to win, but he's a pretty good sport when he loses, and he's a great team player.

So no matter how difficult it is to approach social issues rationally and methodically, you have to do it if you want to help your child succeed. And parents of children with disabilities report that having their child fail socially is more stressful and disconcerting than having their child fail academically. For a parent, if Johnny can't make friends it's far more difficult, psychologically, than if Johnny can't read. You'll feel a lot better if there's a comprehensive and effective social program in place for your child, and it's likely that your child will respond best if a whole bunch of different programs are being implemented simultaneously.

How Do Kids Play?

For most kids, the rules of social interaction come more or less naturally. It may not be *easy* to navigate the park or schoolyard, but the majority of kids find a way to do it successfully. Some of them find one good friend to hang out with; others find a whole bunch. Some always gravitate toward an ongoing sports game; others will cruise around, talking to their friends. Some will share food to make a new friend; others will ask to join an activity that's already begun. Some will walk boldly up to a stranger and introduce themselves; others will linger on the edges of a social group and hope to blend in.

The point is, while the way kids play may vary, most of them are driven to be part of the social life they see before them and will figure out a way to join in.

Kids with autism need you to help them do the same thing. Take it step by step, and you can actually *teach* them the skills they need to be part of the gang.

First Step: Check Out What the Other Kids Are Doing

Parents always ask me, "What should my child be doing in social situations?" and my answer is always the same: "What are the other children doing?" The reason this is critical is because social interaction varies. It varies at different ages, in different circumstances, and even in different communities. The games, the lingo, what's cool and what isn't—these are different in every school, park, playground, or other social environment.

So the first thing you're going to need to do to help your child become more social is to observe the children in his natural environment, or the environment in which you would like him to participate, and write down everything the children do and say in that setting.

If you're a parent, take your child to the store, to a fast-food restaurant, to a sporting event, to after-school lessons; see what your child does in those places and what the other children are doing, and take notes on both. If you're a teacher or specialist, go out on the playground, to the lunch tables, to the students' free play periods and take notes both on what the child you work with is doing and on what the other children are doing.

Be sure to write down *specifically* what your child is doing. For example, does he hang out with the other children and just not say anything, or does he socially isolate himself and seek out areas where there are no other children? If your child does interact with the other children, is it for the whole recess or just a small part of it? At the beginning or the end? If it is for the whole recess, what is he doing that's different from the other children?

Be equally specific about what the other kids are doing, focusing on the ones who are the same age and gender as your child. Are the other nine-year-old boys mostly playing football? Are some of them searching for bugs? Are the four-year-old girls playing in the sandbox or on the equipment? If they're playing some kind of imaginary game, what kinds of things are they imagining?

Now that you've done that, you may need some emotional support. You might be feeling a bit overwhelmed because the typical children you've observed are interacting so easily—*their* parents aren't standing next to them, prompting them to ask if they can play or join in the group! You may feel frustrated and slightly uncomfortable. But keep in mind that while it's very difficult for most children on the spectrum to socialize, and they need to be taught skills that often do come effortlessly for typical children, most of them will begin to socialize more once they've learned how to do it. And the literature tells us that most children, adolescents, and adults with autism report that they want to have friends, relationships, and significant others. So the desire is there, we just have to help them make it happen. And starting with a comprehensive program when the child is young will lead to much better outcomes than not addressing the issue at all. So give yourself time to feel a little bit sorry for yourself—and then get to work!

How It Works

I once observed a first-grade child who, from a distance, looked like she was interacting beautifully with the other kids. The school staff felt that she was ready to have her support fully faded at recess and lunch. However, when we approached her, we realized that Lila was repeating lines from a television show. In a perfect imitation of Angelica from *Rugrats*, she would order her classmates around: "Line up, you dumb babies!" "Lie down, you dumb babies!" Although her classmates reluctantly complied, she wasn't making any close friends this way.

So we watched to see what the other girls her age were doing. Interestingly, the games they were playing weren't all that different—they were also into imaginary play. But for them, the big thing was to pretend that they were cats or dogs or some other animal. They had elaborate play routines, which included eating, being cared for, making animal sounds, and so on.

I had mixed feelings about teaching a child with autism how to act like an animal—children with autism already have so many socially unacceptable behaviors, and it seemed strange to be teaching behaviors that, from an adult's point of view, had no socially redeeming value. But it was what the first-graders were doing. So we taught Lila to imitate us when we acted like a cat or a dog or a bunny. Then, at recess, we prompted her to look at the other children and pretend to be animals if that was what they were doing. It worked: gradually she behaved more and more like the other children and spent less and less time pretending to be Angelica.

Functional Analysis: Figuring Out Why Your Child Isn't Behaving Like the Others

Chances are, if you're reading this chapter, your child isn't playing like the other kids most of the time. The question is, why not?

If your child is behaving inappropriately or antisocially during playtime, it's important to figure out the root cause—what he's hoping to accomplish by his behaviors. A child who's hitting other children may be doing it for several different reasons, each of which requires a different sort of intervention.

For example, some children will engage in inappropriate behaviors deliberately to *avoid* social interaction. We worked with one very verbal child who had figured out a way to make people leave him alone—he would launch into a monologue about how he loved the idea of killing someone and watching the blood and gore drip from the body. Of course he was the nicest kid, who would never think of hurting a flea, but with one or two sentences like that, he could get rid of the other person immediately. Another girl used to stick her open palm into other people's faces to get them to stop trying to interact with her, and yet another young boy started barking like a dog every time someone tried to talk to him. These behaviors were all intended to get rid of the other person.

It's important to remember that not all antisocial behaviors are about avoidance. Sometimes they serve the opposite purpose, of *getting attention*. One adorable little fourth-grader I worked with spent all of his free time drawing elaborate pictures of skeletons, skulls, bodies with blood dripping from them, bodies with essential body parts ripped off, and so on. Unfortunately, he got a lot of attention for these drawings. Most people, especially other children, were quite interested in the drawings and his enthusiastic explanations of them, but they were interested in a shocked kind of way. To him, attention was attention—he wasn't attuned to their disgust—so he kept right on for years, and it got worse and worse, until his revolting drawings were pretty much his only topic of conversation. I've even seen kids on the spectrum hit other children when they're trying to interact. They just haven't learned how yet and don't realize that hitting isn't the right way to make a friend!

Different Functions, Different Approaches

Children who have limited verbal skills will use the same behaviors to achieve different results. We've worked with children who are aggressively hitting and kicking others in order to get rid of them *and* children who are aggressive to try to interact socially.

Knowing the "why" of the negative behavior, which is what functional assessment leads to, allows us to figure out the appropriate intervention to eliminate that behavior.

If the child is engaging in unacceptable social behaviors to *avoid* social interactions, you may need to set up some sort of reward system to increase his willingness to engage. For example, the young boy who talked about killing and gory scenes was taught to self-monitor during his conversations, so that they were full of questions, comments, and discussions about topics other than blood and gore. (See the discussion of self-management in chapter 9.) Initially, he earned small rewards for his appropriate comments. These rewards were gradually faded, until he could be counted on to engage in acceptable conversations with others. We also taught him acceptable and polite ways to end a conversation, such as saying, "Well, I better go now" or "Gosh, I'd love to talk but I'm in a hurry," rather than saying, "If you stick a knife in someone's artery, blood will squirt out all over you!"

However, if the child is engaging in unacceptable social behaviors to *obtain* attention, the motivation is there already—he wants to engage socially—and you just need to teach him more appropriate ways to get that attention. In these cases, the key is teaching appropriate ways to socially interact, such as initiating conversations, asking questions, and making pleasant or relevant comments. (Continue reading for a more specific discussion of teaching appropriate replacement behaviors.)

Often the attention the child receives during these appropriate social interactions is itself a strong reinforcement of those learned behaviors. For example, the child who drew the offensive pictures was taught how to listen to what other people were saying and then to ask them questions; he was so delighted with the response he got doing this that he no longer needed to draw his pictures to elicit the desired social contact—he had found an easier way.

So when you're writing down what your child is doing in social situations, make sure you've observed him enough to know not only what he's doing but *why* he's doing it. Is he grabbing a swing from other kids because he wants to swing or because he wants the other kids to notice him? Is he walking alone because he doesn't like to talk to others or because he's nervous and doesn't know how to approach them? Is he shoving another child because he's happy or because he's angry?

Inappropriate social behaviors tell us there's work to be done, but in and of themselves they don't suggest the nature of the work. We need to interpret their functions to figure out the next step.

What Are Reasonable Expectations for Your Child?

Push within reason. You need to figure out whether your child knows the desired behavior and just doesn't use it or if she simply doesn't know the desired behavior. If a child is capable of engaging in social interactions but simply doesn't want to, you may have to use an extrinsic reward system, in addition to teaching the child socially appropriate ways to politely terminate interactions. It would be great if the social interactions were always so rewarding that we never had to use extrinsic rewards, but sometimes kids with autism need that extra incentive when they're first learning a difficult social skill. The good news is that the need for extrinsic rewards will gradually lessen as the new social skill becomes a regular part of your child's repertoire.

And don't be too concerned if your child doesn't want to interact. Things change. As children become more competent at social interactions, and these interactions become rewarding, their motivation to interact usually improves.

An Important Note on Fashion and Trends

Although we're focusing on social interactions here—i.e., play and conversation—don't overlook the importance of appearance in helping your child fit in socially. While you're observing the other children at play, take notes on what they're wearing, what kind of lunchboxes they're carrying, how their hair is styled, whether their shoes are tied with laces or attached with Velcro, and so on. Kids with autism tend not to be as aware as others of changes in styles and what's currently hip for their age group. While this may not be such a bad quality (remember how our mothers used to say, "You don't have to be just like your friends—it's good to be different"?), the wrong shoes or clothes *can* make it much harder for a child to be accepted by his peers, and you want your child to have every bit of support and advantage you can give him. I've actually seen our children get teased because they were wearing styles that were popular the year before, and if you can eliminate that whole area of potential embarrassment, you might as well.

Most kids will come home and demand the latest thing in clothing, and our job as parents is to teach them that they can't have everything they want. Ironically, parents of children with autism may have to play a different role and insist their child *get* the latest thing. Because these kids are oblivious to trends, they'll be left behind if you don't start paying attention.

Staying on top of the trends can have an additional social benefit. We recently invited a few of the classmates of a fifth-grader with autism to come shopping with us to help her pick out some trendy clothes. The other girls loved the trip to the mall, and Jenny got all kinds of stylish clothes. Another student was using a roller backpack while his classmates all had the more common backpack that you actually carry on your back. A big group of boys accompanied him to a cool skater shop and helped him pick out a more stylish one.

Although, from a philosophical point of view, it may bother us that our society demands a certain amount of conformity, remember that every culture has its accepted attire. Children with autism have enough difficulties already. We don't want to add another stigma because they're wearing or carrying an item that's more appropriate for a younger child. Eventually, they can progress to a stage where they can choose to ignore trends, as opposed to simply being unaware of them.

Working on the Problem

Okay. You've done your observation and your functional analysis (figuring out the "why" of your child's behavior), and you should have the following information at your fingertips:

1. What the other kids are doing during these periods of freedom. (Your "goal," essentially.)

2. What your child is doing that's different.

3. Why your child is doing these things. (The function of these behaviors.)

The answer to the first category depends a lot on your child's age. Preschoolers tend to play with toys more than with each other at first, then they move on to sharing toys and playing imaginary games. Outside, they like to dig in the sand and climb around on a jungle gym. And older preschoolers are already pretty good conversationalists. They'll listen in, contribute to the conversation, and tell short stories. During the elementary school years, some kids will start to gravitate toward playing sports whenever possible, while others like to hunt for bugs, swing and climb on the playground equipment, walk around chatting, or play imaginary games.

Based on the enormous differences in types of play, we've organized this chapter into several parts, moving from the most basic kinds of social interaction to the most sophisticated, starting with simple play (with toys and games), then moving on to playing at school (navigating recess and making conversation at the lunch table), then socializing during classroom time (using buddies and setting a routine), and finally cementing friendships outside of school with play dates and parties. Depending on your child's age, school situation, and capabilities, some sections may be more relevant than others at the moment, but they all should come in handy eventually.

Look at your list and see what the majority of kids your child's age and gender are doing, then follow our advice for that category of play.

Enlisting Some Help

While some of the interventions can be worked on at home (how to make social conversation, for example), the majority of play activities will need to be prompted and practiced out on the schoolyard or park or wherever your child needs to change her behavior. And even if your child is pretty good with socialization at home, you'll need to make sure that she's interacting socially with others at school and other settings. I've seen plenty of kids with autism who can engage beautifully with an adult but don't say a peep to other children. This is true for all ages. So don't assume your child is socializing with peers just because she looks pretty good at home.

Odds are you'll need some adult help in this endeavor.

Many schools have no social programs in place during the recess or lunch periods, so you may need to start from scratch and request that someone be assigned to go into those social settings to help teach your child. If she has a one-on-one aide, that's great—you have the help, you just have to organize and track it. If you don't have that support in place, there are resources at hand. A number of schools coordinate with their local high schools, colleges, and community groups to arrange volunteers who regularly go to the schools to help children with special needs. You can request that the school's speech/language pathologist or the school psychologist include social components in the intervention sessions, which can be implemented during recess, lunch, or free time. In other words, these special educators can work on goals—such as entering playgroups, taking turns during ongoing activities, and engaging in interesting conversations—in the context of your child's regular activities. Remember, social areas are just as important as academic areas for your child's well-being and long-term success and need to be addressed on a regular and ongoing basis.

In a pinch, a parent could come at those free period times to help the child, but in most cases the school can and should come through with the additional support.

Once you've determined that there's adequate support when necessary, you can start with some systematic programs.

SIMPLE PLAY
Playing with Toys

If your child is still a toddler or in his early years of preschool, chances are his peers are spending most of their free time indoors playing with toys. This is when they learn how to take turns and share toys. They engage in simple little play routines—most preschools have trucks, cars, and trains, a playhouse, sand toys, dress-up clothes, and a variety of other activities that appeal to the imagination. The toddler and preschool years are when you want your child to learn to play appropriately with toys and follow the rules of a simple game, to take turns and share with other children, and to engage in pretend play.

An inherent part of early play is verbal interaction: toddlers and pre-schoolers learn to repeat sounds and words and to use these sounds in a social way. While children with autism usually don't have difficulties with motor movements and are physically able to keep up with their peers, they do need help in the verbal and social areas. And while most typical children will play with lots of toys in an imaginary and social fashion, children with autism tend to play with fewer toys and to do so in a repetitive manner.

So how do you get your child to play appropriately with toys when other kids are around?

Toy Match

One easy thing parents of a child with autism can do is to buy and donate to the school the toys that their child already likes and knows how to play with. This way, you can be sure that your child will enjoy the activity and will use it appropriately. (You're essentially stacking the deck in your child's favor—never a bad idea!) If your child has pretty good verbal skills and is the only one who knows how to play a new game, not only will she know how to use the toy, but she can even take a leadership role and explain the rules to the other children.

Even if your child doesn't have any games at home that she's especially good at, consider taking her to the toy store and buying a few that she seems to take an interest in. Make sure the toys are age appropriate—don't get an infant toy for a preschooler, even if your child likes it, but do try to figure out what she likes about it. Is it the musical sound or the visual stimulation? Then try to find an age-appropriate toy that will provide that same type of sensory pleasure.

Take the chosen toy home first and practice playing with it with your child, then send it or an extra one to school once your she's able to play with it pretty well at home. Not only will this help your child, but in these times of tight educational budgets, the school will really appreciate it. Plus, kids tend to gravitate toward brand-new toys and games, so you may discover that having your child walk in with something new makes her popular immediately. And it doesn't have to be a toy—books and games work, too. Just make sure you've taught your child how to engage with the toy in a social way.

We worked with one preschool child who was reading already (he was also doing calculus when he was five). He loved books, so we had him bring his favorite ones to school and read them to the other children.

Borrowing

Similarly, most schools will allow you to borrow toys overnight to use as teaching tools, so borrow things that many of the kids are playing with at school and practice using them appropriately at home. You can also use these times to teach your child the right things to say when he's playing, like "My turn," "Your turn," and "Good game." (See "Playing with Others," below, for more specific advice on that.)

Keep in mind that it may take a fair bit of time and practice for your child to learn to use each toy appropriately. It's best if you can start by finding a toy he likes. Even if your child wants to play with it in a repetitive way, have him make one or two appropriate responses before letting him play with it the way he wants. Gradually help him play with it appropriately for longer periods of time, ultimately holding off the reward of playing with it repetitively until he can play appropriately long enough to play with a peer. Gradual is better than forcing. You want to make sure that the activity remains fun and enjoyable. Keep a positive attitude—be silly and funny and goofy. Anything to help your child stay happily engaged.

Tackling Spontaneous Play

Since a lot of play is spontaneous and can't be pretaught, your child needs to learn to look at the other kids and imitate what they're doing. You can practice this at home by getting out toys, playing with them, then having your child imitate what you just did. You can also practice with another child, a friend, a cousin, or a sibling. Point out what the other child is doing and suggest your child do the same. For example, if the other child is putting pieces in

Mr. Potato Head, you can say things to your child with autism like "Look, Suzy put eyes on hers, can you put eyes on yours?" This teaches your child to observe and imitate what someone else is doing, which is especially helpful for play.

Keep in mind that, as your child gets older, you may not want him to imitate some of the things the other kids are doing, so you'll want to make sure he can distinguish the right kind of imitation from the wrong. On occasion I've seen typical students egg on a student with autism to misbehave, so make sure you also teach your child about school rules and knowing right from wrong. Imitation doesn't always come naturally to children with autism spectrum disorder so it's important to teach them that skill, but it's also important to teach them when, what, and how much to imitate.

At your child's school, coordinate with his aide or teacher to make sure someone is prompting him similarly during free play activities, to ensure that he continues to imitate others and to play appropriately.

You can work on pretend play at home, too. Start with a natural reward and a common activity. For example, one child we worked with seemed to have no interest in anything but food, so one of our clinicians decided to see if she could teach him to pretend to have one of the plastic animals take a bite of the food before he did. She prompted him to give the toy a pretend bite before letting him go ahead and eat (a natural reward). Within a few minutes, he was offering the animals a bite without any prompts. Now remember, tied into that was the fact that he got a bite if he gave the animal one first, so there was some motivation there! Pretty soon, he discovered that he actually enjoyed this kind of pretend play and began to spontaneously feed the animals and everyone around him—eventually the goal is to pretend play with other children—while laughing at the whole idea. It's always a good idea to have some natural rewards built into your playtime together. And don't forget to keep the game lighthearted. Your child may find it humorous if you surprise her with "Yuck!" and pretend to spit out the food. Or you can make a happy sound and pretend to gobble it down. Again, anytime you can get your child to enjoy the learning interaction, you'll have the wind at your back.

PLAYING WITH OTHERS

In addition to teaching her to play appropriately with toys, you may need to help your child learn to play appropriately with others.

Play Initiation and Joining In

To get started in a play activity, your child will need to learn how to recruit playmates to play with and how to join in an ongoing activity—both challenging activities for someone with limited verbal and social skills, but very important ones. We recently published work showing that if the children aren't taught to initiate activities—even their favorite ones—they usually end up playing alone when no adult is there to help get them involved. Now remember, these were children who played alone when no adult prompted them to play with other children, but who, when an intervention was put in place, played nicely and frequently with their peers. You'd think that they'd continue to play with the other kids even after an adult faded out, since they'd been doing it for weeks with the adult intervention, but that didn't happen: they went right back to playing alone when the adult wasn't facilitating the play. But when they were taught how to *initiate* the play interactions—how to ask other children to play with them—they continued to play with peers without adult support. Further, the literature on neurotypical children suggests that the most popular kids in school are the ones who start activities. So let's teach your child how to be the mover and shaker by starting activities.

As always when teaching a child a new and difficult task, remember to keep it as rewarding as possible for her by beginning with activities that she already enjoys. Activities built around your child's restricted interests are often the most motivating and fun for her: they're naturally reinforcing, which will encourage her to participate and be social. They just need to be tweaked a bit to make sure they're also fun for your child's peers.

First, prompt your child to go up to other children and ask if they want to play. We've worked on play initiation with children who have language delays, and simply saying "Play ball?" or "Play slide?" works. But if your child can handle it, a whole sentence can be used, such as "Do you want to play with the blocks?"

Joining in an ongoing activity is as important as starting an activity. Joining in an ongoing playgroup can be done verbally or nonverbally. The child can simply join in the other children's play, or he can ask if he can play with prompting from an adult. But make sure to observe first, so that you teach your child to enter like the other children. We were working with a first-grader recently, prompting him to ask if he could play. He went home and told his mother that we were teaching him to "play like a girl." He said, "Boys don't ask, they just start playing!" This child was unusually aware of the subtleties of social relationships (most kids would depend on the adults' being aware of the differences), but his reaction again points out why your initial observations are critical.

Now that you have prompted your child to try to join in, the unfortunate truth is that some kids are not so nice and may say no. I've been to preschools where there are rules that you can't say no if another child asks to play, and I've been to other schools where the rule is that if a child says no, that has to be honored. We've discovered that if an adult stays nearby when a child asks nicely to play—and looks the other child *straight in the eye*—that other child will almost always say yes. If the child does still say no, teach the child with autism to persevere and approach another child. You should also encourage your child to seek out the children who are most likely to say yes, so that she doesn't get frustrated. And if the child she asks still doesn't seem interested in the suggested play activity, she can also try suggesting a different game. Again, perseverance is important.

You can also set your child up for success by asking another child if yours can play with him *before* you prompt her to try. For older children, you can talk with the nondisabled peers about your goals and even recruit children to help you by not rejecting the child you're working with. Many children are happy to help when directly approached, especially if you explain to them what you're doing and why you're doing it. Sometimes children don't fully understand the challenges of an "invisible" disability and may think the child with ASD is ignoring them or acting inappropriately on purpose, but once they understand the situation and the goals, they can be very helpful.

While teaching your child to initiate interactions, you might want to send desired and valued items to school or the park with your child. For instance, if she brings a handball from home and handballs are in demand, the children are likely to want to play with her.

Finally, if children do seem to be rejecting the child you are working with, you may want to ask them why. You may get information you didn't expect. Once the children told us that they didn't want to play with Dennis because he picked his nose in class. We only worked with him on the playground, so we hadn't noticed this, but once he had learned to use a tissue instead of his finger, the kids stopped rejecting him. We would never have known this if we hadn't asked. Again, the more we know about your child's social interactions, the easier it is to respond to them with appropriate interventions.

Taking Turns

Taking turns is obviously an important part of any kind of play, and it's one that's especially challenging for kids with autism, whose frustration tolerance can be low and whose interest in game playing is often fragile to begin with. One of the things I've noticed is that many children with ASD don't like to give up what they're playing with because they think they'll never get it back. They don't fully understand that the concept of a "turn" is that they *will* get it back again. That's often why they protest so much when someone else tries to take a turn. So here's a way to solve the problems of taking away a prized possession while also teaching the child that he *will* get it back again.

When teaching turn taking, you want to start with games that don't have a lot of rules, so you can just focus on the one important one. A lot of children with autism like toys that create visual or auditory stimulation, such as a set of ramps that a ball can roll down or a toy that plays music. These kinds of toys work well for turn taking, because they're simple, the turns aren't too long, and it's gratifying to be a spectator, too. Also, it's sometimes helpful to start with an activity that your child enjoys but that isn't his absolute favorite. The truly precious toy, book, or whatever it is may be more difficult to part with even for a brief moment.

The first time you teach turn taking, you can be the other player. Keep your turn extremely short at the very beginning—one quick moment, and then it's back to the child. Once your child tolerates not having the item for just a brief second, you can very gradually add to the length of your turn until he's able to tolerate longer and longer periods. Don't try to make this happen too quickly. It may take a little bit of time to gradually work up to a reasonable amount of time. Remember, you don't want it to be painful for the child, and it won't be if it's taught gradually and systematically.

Also, try to make sure that your child is still watching the game when it's not his turn. Wait to go until you're sure he's watching, prompting or redirecting him as necessary. Sometimes, in extreme cases, we've used a self-management program (see instructions for doing this in chapter 9) to ensure that the child with autism continues to watch when it's the other person's turn. Kids with autism have a strong pull toward disengaging—they may revert to self-stimulation or simply zone out—but they need to learn that an important part of interacting is showing interest in what's happening with the other person.

Again, if your child is just starting to learn how to play with others, don't worry if you only get one turn in. This is a good start. The next day or week you can work on two turns, and so on, until your child can play for an extended period. Once he's learned how to take turns and will play socially for a while, you can try other, more difficult games. But, remember, always try to find games that your child will enjoy, so just getting his own turn will reward him for waiting through yours.

Play Termination

Just as your child must learn the appropriate way to enter a game, she needs to learn the appropriate way to *end* one. You'll have to teach her the right things to say, based on the situation.

For example, if she simply doesn't want to play anymore—she's reached the end of her ability to play appropriately at that moment—prompt her to say, "Could we finish the game later?" before running off.

If the game is over, and she's won, she should learn to say "Good game!" If she lost, maybe she could say, "You played really well."

This is another area where it's good to observe the other kids and see what they're likely to say under these situations. (Just make sure you're not observing a sore loser!)

And Speaking of Winning and Losing . . .

Quite a few of the children we work with don't seem to get the idea of winning and losing—that is, they don't seem to care one way or the other. Maybe it's a good quality not to be too competitive, but these children do need to learn the difference and to make an appropriate comment at the end of a game.

Other children on the autism spectrum get exceptionally upset when they lose. One child we worked with would go into a full-blown tantrum every time he lost a game. For those children, we usually start with games or activities that they don't seem to mind losing. Parents can be really helpful in developing a hierarchy of games—those that the child *has* to win, those that the child doesn't care if he wins, and those in between. Then we start with a game that the child enjoys but that he doesn't really care if he loses. We point out that he lost the game, but it's no big deal, you win some and lose some. At the same time we teach the child to make good sportsmanship comments like "Great game!" "That was fun!" or "I lost, but that's okay." Once we've practiced on these neutral games, and he seems okay with the idea of losing, then we start introducing the games that had previously caused a problem. If one particular game continues to cause a problem, we warn the child that we won't be able to play it any longer if he can't accept losing at it now and then. After that, if he still can't control his anger, then we discard that game and go on to others. That's rare, though—most kids have learned to deal with it by that point. We've helped other children learn to control their anger by giving them a reward for not being angry after losing a game. After a while, we fade out the reward. We taught another child to cheer wildly for the person who won the game. This completely distracted him from the fact that he had lost.

Finally, sometimes self-management can help a child control his urge to get upset when he doesn't win: he can keep track of the times he loses the game without losing his temper and get a prize when he's exercised control an agreed-upon number of times.

FREE TIME AT SCHOOL—NAVIGATING THE PLAYGROUND

For many kids with autism, recess and lunch are the most challenging parts of the school day. Classroom activities tend to be structured and clear-cut: the teacher tells you what to do, and you do it. But life's a lot more complicated when you go outside. Other kids seem to know instinctively where to go and what to do during recess. Our kids may need some more help finding activities, making friends, and having fun.

Rules

Kids understand rules and like consistency. If your child is repeatedly behaving inappropriately during free time, you can set some clear rules for that period. They may actually help him understand what's expected of him at a time when the loose structure can feel confusing.

For example, we worked with a kindergartner who always climbed to the top of the monkey bars, where there was a little crawl space. Unfortunately the enclosed area only fit one child, and no one could see him up there, so he was socially isolated. We decided to make that area off-limits to him. After a few reminders, he remembered the rule on his own. Interestingly, he really didn't seem to mind not going in that area once he knew he wasn't supposed to.

If your child has a tendency to wander around alone, you can make a "Don't be alone" rule. Tell him that school is a time to play with his friends and he needs to go find a friend to play with. Many kids, especially those who spend their entire recesses alone, need constant reminders and prompts to go find a friend. You may want to look for some willing peers to assist with this.

Fortunately, most young children thrive on adult attention, and I've found that simply asking a peer if he can help get a socially isolated child involved in a playground game or activity can be a great way to get many children with autism involved. Of course, the adult still needs to be there to teach, but with a little searching, it's usually easy to find ready and willing helpers out there.

This isn't to say that you should make everything rule-bound. That can be a problem, too. In fact, we're working with a college student now whose behavior is so rule-driven that he has major meltdowns (so bad that the police have had to intervene) when his schedule is disrupted. Too much structure and too many rules can cause problems: kids have to learn to be flexible and to adapt to changes in routines and rules. But a few rules to help your child during free play periods may be helpful in facilitating socialization, so use them wisely and well.

Again, let me emphasize that the literature is very clear that in most cases social isolation can have damaging consequences later in life and should be addressed at all times. So as much work as keeping your child focused during free play may be, it's necessary. Unfortunately, there's a tendency for people to view outdoor time as "free time" for themselves as well as the kids, so an adult may take the opportunity to relax and just let the kid roam around. Some may not fully understand the long-term consequences of being socially isolated. Explain to them that free time is a crucial part of the day for these kids and that letting them roam free can actually be damaging to their social growth.

Line Up with a Friend

Elementary school children almost always line up with a friend or group of friends when recess is over and they have to wait in line before going back into their classrooms. Unfortunately, we've noticed that our children usually walk back to the classroom alone, and when they line up, they rarely talk to anyone. (Of course, the kids aren't supposed to talk, but they all do, and this is one case where you want your kids to follow the unwritten rules, not the written ones.)

If your child is walking in by herself, whatever adult is out there with her should suggest that she go up to a buddy and walk in with that person. Most of the children we've worked with, once prompted, will actually look around and find a group of children to join. The same adult can also remind the child to start a conversation or join in if one's already under way. After she's been reminded a few times, she'll probably start remembering on her own—especially if the adult gives her a meaningful look—and once she gets it into her routine, you'll see her looking around to find someone as soon as the bell rings.

Once again, a simple small prompt can lead to huge gains in social appropriateness.

Question Banks

Another strategy that may help your child during lining up or free play time is something we call "question banks." Listen in on what the typical peers are asking their friends and write each question you hear on an index card. Then teach your child to initiate these questions and practice them at home. For example, you can prompt your child to ask, "What are you going to do over the weekend?" with appropriate voice volume and eye contact. We often practice dozens of questions so that our children have a huge variety to choose from to start a conversation. And by listening to your child's peers, you'll be sure all the questions are age appropriate and covering the right topics—sometimes what we adults find interesting isn't so fascinating to kids. You can start practicing questions at home or at school, and if your child needs some prompting at school when he's with his peers, make sure to coordinate the program with the support that's available there.

Develop Structured Activities

Since a lot of what makes recess difficult for kids with autism is the lack of structure—you can do pretty much what you want when you want—many children do better when structured activities are available. When my own children were in elementary school, they used to love Friday lunch periods because one of the teachers taught a hip-hop class in the auditorium. Although most children may report that recess is their favorite time of day, our research suggests that they're even more interested and happy if structured activities are available during recess for them to choose from.

Some of the schools we work with have developed a number of semistructured activities, such as crafts, art, gardening, and games, during the lunch periods. Those kids who tend to drift aimlessly during playtime will be more comfortable with activities that have clear rules and directions and will usually happily join their friends doing one of these projects. Parents who have special interests may be especially helpful in assisting with these lunchtime activities, and—better yet—if your child enjoys a particular activity, you can add that to the activity table.

If the school can't provide this, then whatever adult is out with your child can, by organizing a game of Simon Says, Hide and Seek, or Freeze Tag or making flower wreaths, singing songs, or doing some other simple activity that will attract other children and keep the child with autism focused. And if you go the extra mile and teach your child how to initiate the games, she'll most likely play with peers even when an adult isn't present. Unfortunately, if a child doesn't know how to invite peers to play with her, our research suggests that she'll most likely be alone whenever there's no adult to facilitate. So make sure part of any monitored activity includes having your child ask peers to play. You can even practice having your child initiate activities at home with family members. Don't forget that important piece for the best outcome.

Fixation Games

If your child has a particular fixation, using it as the foundation of a game can turn that into a strength.

For example, one of our students worked with a kindergartner, Nicholas, who had never gone to school before and showed no interest in the other students. He was, however, fascinated by traffic lights. There was a traffic light outside his classroom, and Nicholas spent most of the day jumping up excitedly and flapping his hands whenever the light changed from yellow to red to green.

One day I visited at recess to discover that the brilliant aide had organized a game of Red Light, Green Light. Wow. For once, Nicholas was actively participating in a game—and not *just* participating: he was laughing and having a great time, while following all the rules. In fact, he didn't look any different from any of the other children. The fixation that had previously been a problem behavior had led to some truly positive social interaction.

We decided to see if this approach—using a child's fixation as the basis of a social game—would work with other children. Sure enough, it was a great success.

One child loved the United States, and luckily there was a huge outline of all the states painted on the pavement at his school. His aide made up a tag game where the caller had to name a state and a mode of transportation (jump, hop, walk) to get to that state. Of course, our little boy was the only one who knew all of his states, so he was the most valued team player—after all, he was the only one from California who could find Nebraska, Iowa, and Illinois!

Another kindergartner who loved the Disney characters was taught to play Follow the Leader with Disney characters—each child wore a different hat from Disneyland. A fourth-grader memorized dialogues from movies, so we developed a way to play tag using that dialogue as the cue to run over to the safety line.

Over and over again, we've seen children who would normally withdraw to engage in stereotypic ritualistic behavior readily and happily engage in a social activity that somehow incorporates that interest. You may need to use your imagination to find a game that works for your child, but give it some thought, and you'll come up with something. The interesting thing about fixations or restricted interests is that they're inherently reinforcing—your child really wants to engage in them—so it doesn't take much to get him socially involved if the fixation is the theme of the activity. Just be sure that the game is set up in such a way that it can only be played with a group of peers. Best of all, if your child has accumulated a lot of information on the topic, he'll be the most valued player in the group!

SPORTS

Sports are a big thing these days. It seems like almost every kid gets involved in some type of organized sport. Organized sports can be difficult for children with autism, as they require the child to engage in social interaction, follow rules, and demonstrate appropriate behavior. To make matters worse, many of the coaches have little or no experience with children with disabilities and can be competitive. So you end up with someone yelling at your kid instead of rewarding him for his efforts. But if you can find a sport your child likes, it can be a great opportunity for teaching.

Here are some suggestions for making it work. First, if you or someone close to you can be the coach, that's fantastic. You know how to work with your child and can teach a friend to do the same. If this isn't possible, see if you can recruit one of his teammates to be a buddy and help him out, or consider hiring a local high school student to help at practices and games.

You can also help your child during free time at home, by priming him on the rules and traditions of the game and by having him practice what to say and how to interact with his teammates and coaches. With your camera or phone, record the practices so that you can go over them at home with your child, but make sure that you don't just talk about the problems; always show your child examples where he's doing the right things and compliment him for those. And don't forget to practice being a good sport—that's something we really had to work on with my nephew. If he won, he'd gloat, and if he lost, he'd cry. But we practiced the right things to say with him and gave him rewards for being a good sport, and he learned how to say "Good game" or "That was fun playing with you"—regardless of whether he won or lost.

And if competitive types of organized sports just aren't working, you may want to try less competitive activities like karate, track, or swimming. Some of our children can excel at jump rope or hopscotch but find quick-moving sports like basketball more difficult. Keep trying those that already exist, and if you just can't find one that's ongoing, you may have to dream up some new ones that are easier for your child and can be started at the school.

Sports are often the main activity at recess and lunch during the school day, and the kids usually join in readily and easily. If your child doesn't join in but instead isolates himself, you can practice some of these activities at home and over the weekends. For example, we worked on one child's basketball skills, and he got pretty good at making baskets. This really helped him to join in with his classmates during recess and lunch games.

Of course, some children just aren't great at sports, so you may have to work hard to find something that your child likes and can be successful at. And remember, if the sports thing just isn't successful, don't be discouraged—just search for alternative activities (like gardening or bug catching) that some of his other peers are doing during lunchtime, so that your child can still learn to socialize.

MAKING CONVERSATION AT MEALS

Because classroom time is usually teacher driven, most student-to-student conversations occur during lunch and snacktime. By older elementary school, conversations will continue even when the kids get up from the table.

Unfortunately, most children with autism just sit and eat and don't say anything. In fact, a school psychologist once told me that in her opinion children with autism are *unable* to eat and talk at the same time. She was wrong—they can, if we teach them.

Lunch and snack tables actually provide a great opportunity to teach social conversation, because the kids are all sitting in one place, not moving around. Once again, observing and listening to the kids ahead of time is the most valuable way we have of finding out what our kids need to know to join in.

Food Talk

We've spent a lot of time just listening to what kids talk about at the lunch and snack tables, and believe it or not, most of the conversation revolves around food—what the kids have at home, what's in their lunches, what the other kids have, whether the food is disgusting, ugly, sick, delicious, and so on. This is great, because there are visual cues for our children, and food is something simple and concrete to talk about.

Out at the snack table, the adult who's with your child can prompt the child to comment on the food in his lunch—"I have gummies in my lunch today," or simply "Gummies!" if the child's language is delayed. He can then comment on other people's food—"Your mom made you a great lunch today" or "Yummy!" Also, you can prompt the child to talk about what he has at home—"My mom made cookies last night"—or what his food looks like—"This pasta looks disgusting." The idea is to get the child to start conversations, and a good place to begin is commenting about the food that's right there.

You'd be surprised at how easy it is to make conversation about food and how you can fill up a whole period of free time with that conversation. You may have noticed in your observation that kids aren't always polite in their discussion of food—"Ew, what's that? It looks gross!"—so don't force your child to be too polite.

You can easily practice this food talk at home during family meals. With enough practice, and a bit of prompting if necessary, your child can also learn to socialize with classmates at lunch and snack times.

Finding Another Topic

Another way to encourage chatting at the table came from a mom I know. She would look things up in a children's encyclopedia, find some fascinating bit of information, like which animal is the fastest or which planet weighs the most, and jot it down in a little note to her son on the napkin in his lunch. He would read it out loud, and it always started a good discussion.

In fact, pretty soon after she started the napkin facts, kids were running up just to find out what interesting tidbit of information Louie had brought to school that day, and he enjoyed being the center of attention.

Sharing at the Table

In our observations at schools, we've noticed that, whether adults like it or not, sharing and trading food is a social custom that happens with just about every group of young people. Sharing in general is a way for kids to bond and connect, and teaching your child to share his food is a good way to help him interact with the other kids.

We coordinate with the university's summer camp program so that our children with autism can be included in their large summer day camp. We found that many of our campers ate by themselves. So we asked their parents to send some extra snacks with them—especially the desirable ones like Gummy Bears, chips, and candy. Not so healthful, admittedly, but awfully appealing to kids.

Bringing extra snacks immediately helps in a bunch of ways. First of all, it brings other kids physically closer—the kids with the desirable extra snacks are like magnets, and kids come out of the woodwork to sit nearby. Second, I have never been to a school or camp that didn't have at least one poor little soul whose parent didn't send any snack at all. Those kids really appreciate the extra snack. Third, having extra snacks provides great opportunities to prompt social interactions. The adult with your child can prompt her to ask the other children if they would like some of the treats, then prompt her to respond with "You're welcome" if the kids say "Thank you." Then she can be prompted to ask whether the kids want more, and so on.

Not only is your child learning to initiate socially and to be a good friend, but you'll find that other kids are much more accepting of any child, however different, who's got the good stuff at snack time.

MAKING CONVERSATION AWAY FROM THE TABLE

Conversations are an important part of life, but they're wildly complicated. Not only do you have to be able to formulate grammatically correct sentences, but you have to use them in an appropriate context, with the right intonation and nonverbal cues, and only when it's your turn, and so on and so on. There are just so many conformities when you get to social conversation.

For kids who have very little language, please read chapter 2, which discusses not only the basics of teaching language but some early conversational skills like initiation, which is asking simple questions. For children with more sophisticated language, read on for some advice on teaching them to start and maintain a sociable conversation.

Starting a Conversation

Your child needs to learn specific cues for entering into or starting a conversation. Teach him to listen for a pause in a conversation between others; when neither one says anything for a moment, that's a good time to plunge in. If someone is alone or looking around and not talking to anyone, that's probably a good time to strike up a conversation.

Your child may not know how to get someone's attention. We often use school pictures to teach our children their classmates' names, so they can call them when they want to start a conversation. Gently tapping another child is also an appropriate way to get attention (just make sure the taps are, indeed, gentle). During these initial stages, an adult may need to prompt the child to initiate an interaction.

Of course, starting a conversation is one thing. Keeping it going is another. Here are some suggestions for helping with that challenge.

Commenting

Typical kids comment a lot. They comment on other children's things, and they comment on their own things. Often these comments are as simple as pointing out what someone else has or that two things are the same. Many children spend half their time saying "Look!" to whoever's with them.

As we mentioned in chapter 2, children with autism don't often initiate conversations by making a spontaneous comment, so this is something you may need to teach your child. Start by teaching her to say "Look!" to you right before she engages in a favorite activity or plays with a favorite toy. That way, a natural reward is tied into the learning activity. (When she says "Look!" she gets to do something she enjoys, so she'll make a connection and want to keep saying it.) Don't have your child say "Look" about something she has no interest in. Try to relate it to desired activities.

Children can be prompted to say "Look" to their peers during school activities. Some activities, like art, have lots of opportunities. When your child works on a project, prompt him to say "Look!" to another student as the work progresses. Once he can do that, you can prompt him to add on a little more, such as "Look, a dog," or "Look, it's red."

Once you've taught "Look," you can teach your child to comment on states, such as "I'm tired," or "I'm having fun," and so on. To do this, prompt her to say something like "This is fun" right before she goes on the desired merry-go-round ride. Or have him say "Yummy!" right before he eats his favorite food or "I'm tired" just before he dozes off. Prompt your child to express these feelings, and with practice he should eventually start using these verbal expressions on his own.

Commenting is a great conversation starter and an important part of social conversation: it brings people together and ensures that they're looking at the same thing. But remember to listen to your child's peers to make sure that the lingo he uses is the same as his friends' (who would have ever thought that the word "cool" would be resurrected as a main staple of kids' vocabulary?).

Learning to Be Appropriate

Some children with autism have difficulty with conversations because they can't string words together easily, but others have just been socially isolated for so long that they haven't learned what's appropriate conversation and what isn't. In all innocence, some children with ASD may bring up sensitive subjects like skin color, age, weight, religion, money, and so on, without realizing that other people may be offended by their comments.

For example, our building on campus is right next to the ROTC building, so every once in a while we see ROTC students wandering by in full regalia. I was walking once with a six-year-old boy who walked right up to one of the ROTC students and in a loud, clear voice asked, "Are you Forrest Gump?" Another child we worked with, who was nine years old and large for his age, told an African American man that he needed to take a shower to wash off all that black dirt on his skin. Fortunately the man was understanding and realized that there was no bad intention there, but it was still pretty embarrassing.

I remember when my own daughter was about two or three and an obese woman walked by, my daughter loudly asked, "When is she going to have her baby, Mom?" Of course, she was so young that no one was going to get angry at her. Furthermore, I could explain things to her, even at that young age, so she could learn from the experience and not repeat the social error. Children with autism who have communication delays may not have the advantage of fully understanding when you try to explain subtle social clues. Further, even if they do understand the particular situation, they may not generalize it to another. So they may still be making social faux pas even when they're older, and people who'll overlook something rude that a two-year-old says may not take it so well when it comes from a ten-year-old. So you need to teach your child the difference between an appropriate and an inappropriate comment and practice the appropriate social conversation as frequently and in as many different contexts as possible. And be prepared to explain once in a while that you're still working on teaching your child social graces, in case there's a blunder.

Starting Conversations—Appropriately

You can actually help your child learn appropriate ways to start a conversation. One way is to use visual cues. Teach your child to pick out something someone is wearing and say something nice about it, like "That's a nice necklace" or "Those are pretty earrings." We usually have the kids practice this a lot at home first. You can sit with your child and let a few seconds of silence be a cue that he should start up a conversation and then prompt him to say something complimentary.

Everyone likes a compliment, and, once you start paying attention, you'll realize that adults frequently initiate conversations with each other by picking out something to compliment. But be careful not to go overboard. We worked with one child who learned to compliment beautifully, but when she got with new people, that was all she did. Without taking a breath, she would say, "I like your earrings, I like your necklace, I like your shirt, I like your sweater." We had to help her learn to make different comments and wait for a response. Eventually she learned to make a compliment, such as "I like your necklace," then wait for a response, such as "Oh, thank you," then make another *different* response, such as "Where did you get it?" With some practice, she became quite good at simple conversations, but it did take a fair amount of teaching and prompting to get her there.

Another easily learned conversation topic is favorite things. The children can learn to ask, "What's your favorite food?" or "What's your favorite TV show?"

Simple questions can lead to good conversations. You can ask what someone did recently, like "Did you have a good weekend?" or "Have you gone to any good movies lately?"

Of course, once a conversation gets started, it has to be maintained. Your child may willingly start a conversation or answer a simple question but balk at having to continue it for longer—it's a lot of work listening to what the other person said and formulating the next question or comment. Many children with autism don't know how to respond, and others just don't want to respond. In the case of the children who don't know how to respond, try teaching "empathetic responses."

Empathetic Responses

When you're having a conversation with someone, you don't especially want the other person to tune out while you're talking. No matter how "accurate" his responses may be, if your companion doesn't seem to care much about what you're saying, you're probably not going to enjoy talking to him. If, on the other hand, he responds with interest and attention to something you say, you'll probably want to talk more.

Children with autism don't always show a lot of empathy in their interactions, but they can be taught to make empathetic responses to another person. The first thing we teach is for the child to listen attentively to the conversational partner. Sometimes we have to "check" to make sure they're listening by having them repeat what the other person said, and other times we just have to remind them to listen. This can be accomplished by simply asking the child what the person said. If the child didn't listen, prompt the child to ask, "What did you say?" "What?" "I didn't hear you," or "Sorry, could you say that again?" Then, when the speaker repeats it, you can ask the child again what was said.

In addition to listening, the kids need to learn to respond appropriately and empathetically, so that the person they're talking to knows they're genuinely interested. Start by saying something like "I had a great lunch today." Many kids with autism will not respond at all, and others are likely to respond by saying something like "Oh," followed by a dead silence. Some will even bring the topic back to their own interests, as if you'd never said anything.

If your child doesn't respond to your statement, repeat it, then prompt her to ask an appropriate follow-up question, such as "What did you eat?" Once your child is repeating the question—and you're answering it—you can then encourage her to come up with a question of her own by saying something like "What would a good question be now?" If your child has enough language, you can even have her repeat back part of the information, like "Oh, you had a good lunch, what did you eat?" People like to hear their words repeated—it makes them feel listened to.

Children who haven't asked questions in the past or who have more language impairments will have some difficulties with this. For some of them, it's the grammar that's difficult—they'll frequently say, for example, "What you ate?" or "What did you ate?" But don't worry. Just keep helping them with the appropriate prompt and, with practice, they can and will learn to use the right sentence structure. Another challenge they often have is asking the same question over and over again. One child we worked with asked "Why?" all the time. You'd say, "I went out of town last weekend," and she'd respond with "Why?"

Then, if you said, "I had to give a speech," she would say, "Why?" You can actually keep a conversation going for a pretty long time with the question "Why?" but sooner or later the other person is going to get the feeling no one's really paying attention. Make sure your child learns to vary his questions.

Once your child is pretty good at asking questions in the context of conversation, you can move toward teaching more empathetic responses. Pretend to bump into something and say "ouch." If your child doesn't respond, prompt him to say "Are you okay" or "What happened?" Tell your child you had fun with a friend and see if she can respond in a way that shares your happiness. If not, teach her to say "That's great, Mom," or "I like seeing friends, too."

Teach your child how to be a good supporter if something isn't going well. If you say, "I'm not feeling well today," he should learn to respond with a concerned statement like "Oh, that's too bad—what's wrong?" Or if a peer says, "I'm having trouble with this homework assignment," your child could learn to say, "Can I help out?" You get the idea. If he's struggling to come up with appropriately empathetic statements, you may have to practice them. A straightforward way to teach empathy to children with ASD who have the language skills, is by giving the child a formula, such as "First respond with a statement indicating concern, then ask a question or make a helpful suggestion, such as 'Oh, you didn't finish your homework. Can you ask the teacher for more time?'" With the formula and a little practice, your child will learn to create empathetic responses during conversation.

It takes practice and a lot of hard work to teach social communication, but gradually you'll notice that your child is taking not just a *learned* interest in others, but a genuine one. In other words, even though the interest is taught by practice initially, once the child starts asking appropriate questions, he'll often become genuinely more curious and interactive. So don't give up. Many kids and adolescents who initially show no interest whatsoever in other people can learn to fluently engage in social conversations. The more we help the children with strategies to get involved, the more involved they actually become.

SOCIAL LIFE IN THE CLASSROOM

For the youngest children, toddlers and preschoolers, life in the classroom isn't that different from time on the playground: they're mostly just playing with toys and games and making comments about this and that to one another. For the child in elementary school, however, the classroom offers some unique opportunities for socializing.

Social Routines

Everyone knows a habit is hard to break, which is a bad thing when you're talking about biting your nails but a good one when you're trying to get your child used to interacting socially. The idea here is to get a "social habit" going. Most kids put their backpacks away when they arrive at school, and then they start socializing without needing any specific instruction. Unfortunately, children with autism don't usually initiate these social interactions, so we need to make them a regular and definite part of their daily routines.

For example, every day when you arrive at school with your child, prompt him to say hi to the teacher, then to say hi to one other child. Once greeting two people becomes routine, you can fade your prompts gradually, until your child is doing it completely on his own. You've now set in place a pattern that will help him start interacting with other students the moment he walks in the door at school.

Once he's regularly greeting classmates, you can add on a question. Teaching your child to say "What are you doing?" or "Can I play with you?" can be the key to getting him involved in an ongoing activity.

But remember, if your child is learning his first words, don't start with greetings. They don't usually have a natural reward that your child wants and may not motivate your child to talk more (see chapter 2, on communication).

You can set other routines in motion, too, like answering the phone, talking to a clerk in the store, saying "Bye" when leaving places, and greeting Mom or Dad when she or he comes home from work. All of these situations provide repeated and regular social practice for your child. The idea is to get them to become a routine so that you don't have to prompt them every time.

Show and Talk

We've already seen how desirable snacks can increase and improve your child's social life at the lunch table. But the positive return from having something appealing to offer doesn't have to start and end at food—you can send other things to school with your child to help get conversations started.

Let me give you a personal example that may give you some ideas. We have a friend who's a neurologist. After we'd been to his house several times, I noticed that he always had something interesting to show us. I think the most interesting was an X-ray of the skull of a prisoner he had treated. In prison this guy had been attacked by another prisoner, who had managed to stab him in the head with a foot-long metal rod. The rod had gone into one side of his head and out the other with *no* brain damage—actually, no harm whatsoever other than the discomfort of having to have the rod removed. The X-ray was quite a novelty and stimulated a lengthy and fascinating discussion. Another time, the same friend brought out a book of walking trails in England, once he brought out from his wine collection a bottle of wine with quite a history, and yet another time he brought out photographs of his trip to France. It's always great fun going to his house, and no one ever has to worry about making conversation—he always has something special and fascinating to talk about!

Similar strategies can help kids with autism. Send in pictures of family members, a playlist of some favorite music, stubs from the last movie your child went to, a favorite toy, or anything you can think of that will help get a social interaction going. Of course, you may have to prime your child ahead of time on how to start a conversation while showing the item, and, for some children, an adult or aide may have to help initiate the showing part of the interaction, but even if your child has a language delay, a visual prompt can really help jumpstart a conversation. And if you can find something as unique as that X-ray—only more age appropriate, of course—you may manage to raise your child's "cool quotient" at the same time.

Peer Assistance

There are many social things peers can actually teach more easily than adults, like the kinds of things kids *really* say to each other, the cool places to hang out, the current fashions and fads, and even simple survival techniques, like who and what to avoid.

Children love attention, and children love to help. At all ages. When I go to schools to work with a child, invariably another child or two will come up to me and ask me what I'm doing. When I explain, "It hasn't been as easy for [this child] to learn to talk as it was for you," they almost always ask if they can help. I teach them how to help get those words out, and we have little mini-therapists for the child all day long.

Once I was at a preschool with a child who was just learning to say his first words. We were prompting him to request items in the playhouse. To do this, we got his favorite things together, modeled the labels, and when he attempted to label each item, we gave it to him. An adorable little girl came up to me and said, "What are you doing?" I replied, "I'm teaching Charles how to say these words. Do you want to help?" She said she did, so I showed her how to say the name of the toy Charles was looking at, then to quickly give it to him when he tried to say the word. She learned this within a few minutes, and of course I gave her tons of praise for her successful interactions with him. When I came back a few days later, not only was she repeatedly getting him to say words, but she had recruited a number of other little girls and taught them how to get Charles to talk. A few weeks later she had decided to marry him, and clearly felt it was critical that her future husband learn to communicate. In fact, Charles was spending most of his free time at preschool saying words to his peers. Just what we want to see happen.

Buddies

We have enlisted peer buddies in elementary through high school to help children with autism get from one class to another or from recess back to the classroom. Some teachers prefer to have one particular child volunteer to be the special buddy, and other teachers opt to have a group of children help. The research suggests that in the older grades it's best to enlist an entire group of friends, so the child with autism can become part of a peer group, and so a single child doesn't have to break away from his friends to help. When you connect the child with autism to an already established friendship group, usually more socialization will go on during and after school. With peer buddies, the child's social interactions are increasing while he's getting some help navigating around the school.

There are creative ways to enlist the aid of other students. A third-grade teacher we worked with wrote each child's name on a Popsicle stick, and every day before lunch she picked two at a time to create many pairs of "lunch buddies." The lunch buddies had to line up with each other and sit together during lunch. Although I was a bit concerned that the children wouldn't want to be forced to sit with someone they weren't particularly interested in, it turned out to be an overwhelming success. Many of the kids admitted that they wouldn't have picked their buddy to sit with on their own but said they ended up enjoying the experience—and no one was left out at lunchtime. It was so successful that the next year several other teachers adopted this system for the upper grades in the same elementary school.

Some schools offer special courses and credits or community service hours for their typical students that allow them to assist with peer socialization and even help their "buddies" work on specific target areas. With the limited number of services that many children with ASD receive for socialization, trained, committed peers can be a great resource for putting together a supportive social structure.

Pulling It All Together

One of the programs we have going in a few elementary schools is a schoolwide social support system. The idea is to have no child left alone at any unstructured time. Not only children with autism, but a number of children who just have difficulties finding friends end up socially isolated. We use several different approaches to make it work.

For the younger kids, we start project tables during each lunch period. We've had gardening projects, art projects, beading, coloring, and so on. We try to pick activities that the children with social difficulties like. One adult, such as a special education aide, runs the table and helps with the project, while another invites children into the group. Of course, if a child with social difficulties is already playing appropriately with a group of friends, that's fine, but if not, we help him get involved in one of the group activities.

For older children, we've implemented more formal programs of social interaction. Interestingly, this project was named "Chain of Friends" by one of the children who participated. We talk to the whole class, gather together a group of kids who are willing to socialize with our child during recess, and hold weekly or biweekly meetings to brainstorm any social difficulties that arise. We've found that kids are wonderful helpers when recruited directly. (Please see chapter 7 for more suggestions on peer involvement at school.)

HOME SUPPORT

There are also things that can be done at home—after school and over the weekends—to increase your child's social interactions.

Work on Getting to Know Classmates

For a lot of obvious reasons, your child will benefit from knowing his classmates' names and being able to recognize their faces. Use photos to help your child memorize his classmates' names at home. Follow through at school: when he sees a classmate, an adult should prompt him to greet her by name. At the end of the day, have someone prompt the child to say "Bye!" along with each friend's name. And, as mentioned earlier, throughout the day you can prompt your child to call other classmates by name to get their attention. If your child is able to comment, you can have him include the classmate's name: "Alex, that's a good drawing." Using names can also be practiced at home with Mommy, Daddy, a sister or brother, Grandma and Grandpa, the babysitter, and others.

As any good politician or game show host could tell you, people like hearing their names used—it makes the speaker sound friendly and caring.

Priming

The idea of priming is to go over activities *before* they happen in real life. Although we first used priming in an academic context, we and other researchers have discovered that it can help out with social activities, too.

Go over the events to come in the day ahead while driving to school in the morning, and remind your child of her social obligations. For example: "Emma, when you get to school, don't forget you'll have some free time—I want you to look for your friends to play with." Other times priming can be more specific, such as "Paul, say 'Hi' to Mr. Brown when you see him," or "If you lose the game, don't forget to say 'Good game' afterward." There's also some research that shows that if you prime the child in playing specific games at home, she's likely to play the same ones with her schoolmates without needing any special instruction from an adult. But you will have to practice enough to get her comfortable and competent at those games.

You can also prepare even more directly by taking a bunch of pictures of scenes from your child's own school or activities. The two of you can then go over them, step by step, discussing how to interact on the playground or wherever. Videos are similarly helpful. For example, you can say, "Here is where we keep the balls. First you need to ask the teacher if you can take one outside, then you can ask a classmate to play with you, then you can take a turn. After your turn, you need to wait in line until the other people have a turn," and so on. And if the school will let you, record the classroom activities and recess times in the next grade, then go over those videos in the summer with your child. Discuss, in detail, what will happen in the next grade and what will be expected of your child there.

The more your child is prepared for what's ahead socially, the more she'll be able to jump in and do what she needs to in order to interact successfully with the other kids.

MAKING FRIENDS AND HAVING PLAY DATES

Children need friends. Friends support, assist, help resolve conflicts, and even give feedback about socially acceptable behaviors. Adults can also do some of those things, but they can't completely take the place of a good friend your child's age.

No child—with or without special needs—can make friends unless he has plenty of opportunities to interact with other children. Many of the kids we see are so occupied by therapy hours or so isolated by their communication difficulties that they're just not around other children enough. Understand how important that social exposure is and make sure socializing is on the agenda. There are lots of spontaneous opportunities for interaction, such as going out for ice cream after a sports game or lingering after school. Others can be arranged.

Scheduling Play Dates

Typical children usually have play dates a couple of times a week, and it's important for children with autism to do the same.

I realized how much work setting up play dates can be when my own children were younger. I could have sworn that there were some mothers who dedicated their lives to their children's socialization—they had play dates every day of the week and were always getting their kids together with other children on the weekends, whereas I always felt like if I could throw a few dates together in a week, it was an exceptional week. But hard as it can be to set up and see a play date through, it's important if your child is going to make and maintain friends at school.

Here are some suggestions for successful play dates.

Finding Someone with Potential

With most kids, you can identify potential play dates simply by asking who they want to play with or by watching who they play with at school. But children with autism may be less forthcoming—they may not instinctively be thinking about anyone as a potential play date. So when you set up your child's first play dates, you may need to ask her teacher or aide to recommend children who get along well with her at school. If you're a teacher, be sure to tell the parents of children with disabilities who their child seems to play with or who takes an interest in that child. That allows parents to then call the other family and say, "Ms. Brown said that my child seems to enjoy playing with your child, and I wondered if he might be free on Friday to get ice cream after school."

Some teachers will even suggest children who they think would be good role models or who come from families familiar with autism and who are therefore used to being around similar children. Since teachers and aides are around the students all day long, they're great resources for potential play dates.

The Initial Phone Call, Text, or E-mail

Many children today have busy schedules, so make sure you call the other parents well in advance of the desired play date. If you've planned a great activity (see below), you might want to mention that when you make the invitation, so the other child knows he's got something to look forward to and will be eager to come over.

After you've made that first phone call, you might want to have your child call the other child, either to invite him personally or just as a reminder before the play date. This will give your child an opportunity to learn the little social things you say when inviting someone over. Have him practice first. You can ask a relative to play the part of the playmate on the phone, while you prompt your child during this trial run, so he'll know what to say during the real thing.

Stay nearby during the real phone call—if your child gets stuck, you can take over. Remember that phone conversations have no visual cues, so they can be quite difficult for children (and even some adults—my husband says he hates talking on the phone, even though he's a great conversationalist). If the phone call is too overwhelming a challenge for your child, you may need to start out small, like just having him say "See you tomorrow" or something simple.

Ironically, we have also worked with children who repeatedly call other children, to the point that it irritates them. If this happens with your child, limit her phone calling to a reasonable number of times or even to one specific, supervised time each day. Ask classmates what constitutes an acceptable number of phone calls and when are the best times for talking.

Another alternative is texting, e-mailing, or communicating via some other type of social media. This is especially helpful if your child doesn't like talking on the phone. These days kids use their phones to text more than to talk, and these electronic communications can be a great way to get social events organized outside of school. But make sure they're appropriate in length and detail. This may take some supervision and practice. Just like phoning too frequently, too many texts may also turn off a potential friend.

Starting Short

I have had so many parents tell me how disappointed they were after their child's first play date. When initial play dates haven't been successful, parents almost universally say that they started out just fine but ended up disastrously, with the child with autism going off and leaving the playmate alone. What we've discovered is that when the initial play dates are kept short, they're much more likely to be successful all the way through.

What works best in our experience is to plan a very short structured activity right after school. For example, take your child and the selected playmate out to the local ice cream parlor for an ice cream cone after school and then take the playmate right home. Even though this may seem like an awfully short play date, you'd be surprised at how grateful other parents can be to get a chance to relax at home for an extra thirty or forty-five minutes.

Fast-food restaurants also work out well, because you can get a snack and then have a few minutes in the climbing structure, ball area, or any other fun activity the restaurant may have. Local parks are also great. Just bring a favorite snack and let them play on the equipment for a while.

If your child tends to have time-absorbing solitary pursuits, like playing on the computer or watching television, or even if he spends hours swinging alone at the park, it's especially important to have play dates where these activities aren't available. Then you won't have to worry so much about his abandoning his playmate or your having to constantly redirect him.

The important thing to remember is that even if the play date is going well, keep it short at the beginning. Make sure the playmate wants to come back for more. If both kids are begging for more time together, then you know it's been a success, and that's the time to end. Don't drag it on until there's a problem. Once you can count on a successful hour or so, you can try lengthening it.

Planning a Longer Play Date

Once your child is ready to have play date that will last longer than a trip to the ice cream store or restaurant, it's important to plan some fun activities ahead of time. This is especially helpful if your child has social and language difficulties. While you're choosing the activities, make sure they're equally appealing to both children. Your child may be great at Monopoly and love to play, but if Monopoly bores the playmate, she won't want to come back. Similarly, if you try to entertain the guest with something your own child dislikes, you'll wind up with your kid wandering off again.

You and your child can make a list of her favorite activities, and then you can have her call her friend on the phone and ask which ones the friend also likes—that way, you'll end up with activities you know both kids will enjoy and won't have to deal with either of them saying, "Nah, I don't want to do that," after you've set something up.

If the play date is going to take place at your house (which is usually preferable at this stage), you should free up your schedule—and/or find another adult to help out—so you can help the children with an art project, cooking project, craft project, or whatever activity you've chosen.

You can prime your child on these activities the night or afternoon before the play date, and that way you can ensure some success. In fact, sometimes the extra priming allows the child to reach a level of competence with the activity that then allows her to take a leadership role when she and her playmate are together.

When planning ahead, remember that some activities are to die for. Others are just plain boring. We have a ceramics studio here where the kids can pick out a piece of pottery and then paint it. After it's fired in the kiln, they can come back for it. This is a to-die-for activity. While you may not have a kiln at home, try to think of something special and exciting so the other children will be eager to maintain their friendship with your child and be invited back. Andrew loved spin-art, an activity that required turn taking but was pleasurable for those watching as well, and one that almost all kids seem to love, so that was a guaranteed-success activity.

PARTIES

Most typically developing children love parties and love being with a whole group of other children. Parents of kids with special needs sometimes feel their children are left out of the invitation loop, that they don't get invited to as many parties as the other kids. There is a fix for that problem—be the one to throw the party.

Birthdays may be the most obvious opportunity to throw a party, with

Halloween and Valentine's Day running close behind, but you don't have to wait for a special day of the year to invite a bunch of kids over and give them a good time.

Be Creative

I worked with one family whose child was in a regular education class but still had some language difficulties and needed some help with her social interactions. The parents wanted to improve Lizzy's social life, but play dates were hard for them to schedule and supervise, so they came up with the idea of having theme parties once a month.

The first party they had, in September, was a pizza party. They picked seven other kids to join them at a popular local pizza joint that had lots of games, play structures, bins with balls to play in, and other desirable kid activities. Lizzy and her mom sent out handmade invitations and, a few days before the party, called the kids to remind them.

I was at Lizzy's school the day of the party, and a few kids asked if they could go, too. Lizzy told them that she was only able to have a small number of children but that she would invite them to the next one (and she did, if they were truly interested).

The next month came—October—and they had a Halloween party at Lizzy's house, with bobbing for apples and all kinds of other fun games. Every month from then on, they came up with some type of cool party, Thanksgiving, April Showers (the mom heated the pool for the kids to swim in), Cinco de Mayo, and so on—and that's what the kids talked about for days before and for days after. These parties became the biggest thing in school, and everyone wanted to be included. It didn't matter that Lizzy had difficulties with communication and socialization—she was still really fun! And the kids who were especially nice to her were always invited every month. Talk about an incentive.

BEING A GOOD FRIEND

Once your child has some friends to play with and talk to, you'll still need to monitor the socializing.

Sometimes children with disabilities who have communication and social difficulties may not let their classmates know how important their friendship is. You can help your child by making sure she remembers to make gestures of appreciation on a regular basis.

For example, stuff a few extra candies in the valentines of favorite friends, or have your child buy them a special gift before the winter break. Kids also love cards with thoughtful messages or a few extra cookies packaged up just for them. These small attentions can make buddies, playmates, and friends feel special and appreciated.

HARD WORK

Remember how I said at the beginning of this book that there was going to be a lot of hard work involved? Few things are more time-consuming and exhausting than keeping your child socially interactive. Whether he's three and you're working on redirecting him at the park—constantly getting him to stop walking in circles by himself and go play in the sand with the other kids—or eight and in need of constant play dates, which you then have to monitor and run, you're looking at a lot of hours of hard, sweaty, and occasionally frustrating work.

On the list of the million things you feel you have to do for your child, getting him to play a game with a friend may seem a lot lower down than, say, getting him to speak correctly. But it's not. The most important thing for your child is to have friends and close relationships throughout his entire life.

It's the most important thing for any of us.

PLAY DATE ACTIVITIES THAT
OUR FAMILIES HAVE FOUND TO BE SUCCESSFUL

Rock climbing at the local gym	Getting ice cream
Cooking	Decorating cupcakes or cookies
Art projects	Going to a video arcade
Making bookmarks	Going to a fast-food restaurant
Swimming	Going to the carousel
Making valentines	Going to a toy store
Surfing lessons	Visiting the zoo
Going to a local sports game	Making holiday decorations

Going to Mom or Dad's workplace

Beading

Visiting a bookstore

Bike riding

Going to a music store

Horseback riding

Playing video games

Going to a parade

Going to the movies

Going to the park

Inviting a high school cheerleader over to teach some simple cheers

Making hot chocolate

Making ice cream sundaes

FACTS

Without intervention, children with autism spend, on average, more than 80 percent of their recess and free time alone.

When children with autism learn appropriate social interactions, disruptive behavior decreases.

MARCY'S STORY

We started working with Marcy when she was in a special education preschool. Back then, her favorite activities were playing in the dirt (especially if it was wet) and sifting sand through her fingers. Needless to say, she came home filthy each day. Her mom even sent an extra change of clothes to school each day, but both sets usually came home soiled and grimy. To make matters worse, she was only partially toilet trained and wet her pants about half the days. She was, quite literally, a mess.

Marcy could talk, but her language was significantly delayed, and she never talked to other children. Marcy's parents were concerned about her language, her socialization, and her behavior problems, which consisted of making inappropriate vocalizations during circle time and other unstructured activities. She had a little brother with whom she never interacted, even though he tried to approach her all the time. She occasionally interacted with her parents but usually only to lead them to a desired item or activity. Marcy had some words and could make some short sentences, but she only talked when it was absolutely necessary.

Our Work Begins

Over the next year, we primarily worked on behavior. The school had hired a one-on-one aide for her, but although Marcy's IEP had specifically stated that the aide should have experience with inclusion, autism, and behavior management, she had none of the agreed-upon criteria. She basically watched Marcy and kept her from harm, but that was it. We needed someone who would help develop and implement programs and actively prompt her to engage with the other children. So we found another aide for Marcy. Fortunately, since the IEP had stated that a trained person was critical, the school was more than willing to replace the first aide.

We started by creating a self-management program to reduce Marcy's vocalizations in class. The aide made a rule that she couldn't play in the dirt during outdoor time and redirected her toward playing with the other kids instead. We also worked on teaching her the other children's names, using photographs, and prompted her to greet them when she came into the classroom.

By the end of kindergarten, Marcy's disruptive behavior was quite low. She was no longer wandering away from the students during group times, she wasn't making loud, inappropriate noises during class, and she was easy to redirect during outdoor times. These disruptive behaviors had been off-putting to the other children, and as they faded out, we were able to focus more on socialization.

In first grade, we found a fabulous aide—and a good aide is critical to a child's success. She was taking a year off to get some experience in schools before getting her teaching credential. She spent every recess prompting Marcy to interact and developed some great games for the children. During unstructured times indoors, she prompted Marcy to comment on and compliment the other children's work.

I remember visiting one day when Marcy was with a group of children, all decorating a pumpkin. The aide had arranged this pumpkin decorating so that it *had* to be a group activity. One child was in charge of the pins, another in charge of the pieces, and yet another put them on the pumpkin—they had to work cooperatively to get the job done. The aide did this with everything—she turned every activity into teamwork—and Marcy improved dramatically in social areas over the year.

Marcy's parents were also doing their part to work on socialization after school and on weekends. They arranged parties once a month, invited the whole class to her birthday party at a local pizza parlor, and enrolled her in after-school clubs and activities. She always had an adult with her to help her interact during all of these activities.

By third grade, she had a small group of friends and had play dates with them regularly. She still had a language delay but was able to engage in simple conversations. She was being invited over to other kids' houses and to birthday parties.

In sixth grade, Marcy's interest in others continued to grow. If another child fell or got upset, she approached him with concern and asked what was wrong. She didn't have a huge vocabulary and had some difficulties with phrases that had double meanings, like "mud pie" and "break a leg," but her friends didn't mind helping her out.

In preschool and kindergarten, Marcy had no interest whatsoever in other children. Now she has friends, frequent play dates, and a love of being social.

FAQ

QUESTION: You say to teach my child to imitate the way other kids play, but I'm worried he'll start to imitate some of their bad behaviors as well. For instance, there's a boy in the class who hits—if I tell my son to do what the others are doing, won't he start hitting, too?

You're right. While it's important that your child learn to imitate, you don't want him imitating inappropriate behaviors. To reduce the likelihood of this being a problem, you'll need to make sure that good role models are chosen for your child to imitate. Ask the teacher, aide, and other school staff which classmates will be good role models for your son, and be picky about who he's teamed with for activities and play dates. Make sure the teaching is implemented with children who have good competence in the focus area. If your child does happen to start imitating inappropriate behaviors (and this does happen on occasion), you'll need to figure out their function and teach replacement behaviors (see chapter 3).

QUESTION: You say a good aide is critical to a child's success in social interactions, but our aide is so-so at best. The school says she's fine, but I don't think she's taking an active enough role with our daughter. What do I do about this?

If the aide isn't effective or able to work on social interactions, you're going to have to find another person or have her get training. Sometimes the school already has someone on staff who can train the aide and provide reading materials, like a speech and language, inclusion, or resource specialist. If not, the school will need to hire an outside consultant to develop programs and train the aide. Sending an aide to a workshop or having her watch an online training program usually isn't effective; aides need direct feedback from professionals on how they're implementing the interventions. You can do this in several ways. Many schools around the country send us digital clips of their aides in action. We can then provide feedback. If there's a competent teacher or specialist at the school, it's sometimes helpful for that person to observe the aide and provide direct feedback on how to prompt specific behaviors then fade back as the student picks up on the skills. It's so important that your child doesn't waste time with an aide who prefers to chat with other aides at recess (I see this a lot); who stands too far away to be helpful then yells at the students when they get into trouble (I see this far too often); or who hovers so much that the student just isn't getting a chance to interact with peers (and, yes, I've seen this way too many times). An aide's interventions need to be thoughtful and skilled, so your child gets what he needs to make steady progress.

> **QUESTION:** My child is in fourth grade and has never had play dates. I have called a few of the parents, but they always say their children are busy. Any ideas?

You may need to get some help from the teachers in identifying classmates with whom your child interacts well. You also might want to try having one of the "parties" we discussed above or a spontaneous get-together after another social event. Sometimes it's easier to get a group of children together than to set up a one-on-one play date. Try not to feel discouraged. Keep trying, and you should be able to hit on a person or an activity that works.

> **QUESTION:** I host play dates frequently, but my child never gets invited over to the other kids' homes. I'm getting discouraged. What should I do?

When my daughter was young, she preferred to have the other children come to our house rather than go to their houses. After a while, the parents stopped inviting her over. One day I was talking to another mom, and she mentioned that she never invited my daughter over because she thought that she didn't want to go to other kids' houses. When I explained that she was over that phase, the mom immediately invited her over. In short, talk to the other parents. Find out what their concerns are. You may get some useful information that will help you turn things around.

You may need to help your child adjust to going on play dates by offering to stay for the first couple then gradually fading off as the other parents feel comfortable with your child. Or you could send some activities that your child enjoys and has some competence with to help a play date go smoothly. Again, keep the play dates short and fun initially so the kids are begging for more. This is especially important if your child tends to isolate himself or is happy to play alone.

> **QUESTION:** I hate calling other parents because I usually have to call three or four before we hit on a play date. It always makes me feel so rejected every time a parent says her child's busy. This may sound selfish, but I don't plan too many play dates because I hate calling. Do you have any thoughts?

One family we worked with had the same concerns, so they had their son create handmade invitations. Kids love to get mail, and if you send the invitations out early enough with an RSVP request, you can avoid having to make the phone calls. We've also had the staff at the child's school help with creating after-school play dates. They know the classmates and can get them enthusiastic about an activity so that they're begging to go over to your house! Texting can also take the pressure off of a potential rejection or conflict. And sometimes planning early enough can be helpful with kids' busy schedules.

A MOTHER LOOKS AT SOCIAL SKILLS

I couldn't figure Andrew out when he was a toddler. The same kid who was happy as a clam at home, crawling around, watching TV, and lining up his toys, would spend his entire time out in the world moaning and crying. I wanted so desperately to show him off to my friends and family (he was so cute!), but how can you show off a kid who won't stop crying? Other people just don't find that particularly adorable.

We used to go to my brother-in-law's all the time back then (they lived nearby), and from the age of two to four, Andrew always did the same thing there. He never acted like he recognized anyone—no greetings—but he obviously knew the place, because he would go straight to his cousin's room, where he would pick out the same two stuffed puppets (Ernie and Bert), and then he'd head unerringly for the back door and the play structure. He would plop himself down on the swing, clutching Ernie and Bert—one in each hand—and wait for someone to push him. As long as he had Ernie, Bert, and the swing, he was okay. Problems arose only if someone else wanted a turn on the swing—then he'd fall apart and wouldn't really be happy again until he got back on the swing or we went home.

At least at his uncle's he could find Ernie and Bert and make himself comfortable. Most other places we went, he was a miserable wreck, whining, whimpering, and crying, until we brought him back home, where he was immediately calm and content again.

We were one of the first couples among our friends to have a baby. There was only one other kid we knew well, a girl who was six months older than Andrew. She was immediately and entirely so far ahead of him in every way—verbally, physically, socially—that she seemed like a different species. We chalked it up to her being a girl. Girls were traditionally more outgoing and sophisticated than boys, right? She ran up to everyone who walked into their house and chatted away; Andrew liked to put his arms around his mother's neck and bury his face when strangers were around. Different genders, different personalities.

We told ourselves that was all it was.

Starting School

I knew it was time to get the kid socialized and a little more independent. I was pregnant with our second, and two-year-old Andrew was still completely in my lap and around my neck at all times. So we started doing a "mommy and me" class at our local temple. The leader was a former hippie who played the guitar and had a gorgeous singing voice. She was kind and easygoing and didn't see anything to worry about in Andrew's delayed speech—"His intonation is very musical," she assured me. "That's what we look for."

But it was in this class that I really started to notice how different Andrew was from the other kids. Not just the girls but the boys, too. They all ran around and played games and shouted and examined toys and made a lot of noise together. Andrew mostly sat in my lap. Sometimes he would look at the chairs that were stacked in the corner of the room and trace their edges with his finger.

During circle time, the teacher always dumped a big box of musical instruments in the middle of the circle, and all the other kids would run to grab one. Sometimes they'd fight with each other over a special tambourine or something. Andrew would stay in my lap, staring off into space, indifferent to the instruments. I'd try pushing him toward them, but he'd just cling to me. So I would stagger forward with him attached to me, grab something for him, and fall back down into place. Even then, he showed no interest in playing the instrument. I could get him to hold it by folding his hand around it, but I couldn't get him to actually play it. Meanwhile, the other kids would be dancing and singing and making loud music. I could feel the other mothers looking at us, wondering.

Once we all met at one family's house for a special class get-together. The mothers wanted to take a group photo, and all the other kids lined up. Andrew clung to me and refused to get in the line. I tried to coax him and then to drag him into line, while the other mothers exchanged more looks. I finally told them to take the photo without us.

Birthday parties were bad. Andrew would cry if I tried to set him down anywhere other than my lap. He wouldn't do any of the activities, wouldn't participate in the games, wouldn't even eat the food. I started to turn down all the party invitations—why go when I always left parties in tears? I felt alone and alienated. Other moms connected over their kids. No one was connecting with me.

You get tired of being the mother of the weird kid. One day at snack, I quietly told the leader that we had just taken Andrew to UCLA's Neuropsychiatric Institute to be looked at. I guess I wasn't being quiet enough—all the other mothers stopped talking and eagerly listened in. When I said the word "autism"—it was one of the first times I had mentioned the diagnosis in public—a mom cried out, "I *knew* it! I knew there was something wrong with him!"

Was that what they were all saying behind my back all that time? That they all knew there was something diagnosably wrong with my beautiful little boy? It was one thing to have a professional diagnosis, but something completely different to know that people had been whispering about us and speculating.

I was done with that class.

Many years later, the teacher of that mommy and me class contacted me on Facebook and we started chatting online. I told her how much I had admired her as a teacher, but how hard that class had been on me—especially that one moment when the mother had said there was "something wrong" with Andrew. She told me that she had actually called the mother up that very night to ream her out for saying something so callous. I wish I'd known she had my back! I thanked her and we've not only stayed in touch since then, but she's become one of my dearest friends. It's sad that I was such a bundle of raw nerves back in those days that I couldn't reach out to her as much as I should have, but at least we found each other again.

Transition Class

After that, our recently acquired speech therapist arranged for Andrew to go to a different class at a temple near her, one that was supposed to teach kids to separate from their moms in preparation for preschool.

So here I was in a new class, at a new school, and everyone seemed very nice and friendly. The first day, Andrew and I sat on the floor during free play, and he reached for some toy—I can't remember what it was exactly, but it had parts that had to be put together. Andrew took the pieces and did what he always did with toys: he lined them up in one long neat row, which he kept straightening over and over again.

Our speech therapist had told us that we had to take an active role in changing the way Andrew played. She said we had to show him how to play with toys correctly and make him be aware of someone else while he played. So I picked up the toy pieces he had just lined up and said, "No, Andrew, not like that. We play with the toy this way. . . . " And I showed him how the pieces were supposed to be used.

A mother sitting nearby overheard this. She looked over and, in a friendly tone, said, "Oh, let him play with the toy any way he wants. There's really no right way to do it at this age, is there?"

I wanted to cry. I wanted to cry and yell and scream and shout at her that she didn't understand, that I had always planned to be the kind of mother who let her kid play with toys any old way he wanted, who sat back and was relaxed and easygoing, who understood that creativity springs from a child's freedom to play the way he wanted to, who was playful and open-minded and spontaneous and loose. . . .

And then I *had* a kid—a gorgeous, blue-eyed, curly-haired angel of a baby—and I let him play the way he wanted to, and he lined things up all day long and couldn't look anyone in the eye, and now people I trusted were telling me I had to be a different kind of mother, the kind who got in her kid's face and told him how he had to play, who couldn't just let him be. Because if I didn't, he would withdraw further and further into a world we weren't part of.

But I didn't cry or scream or yell or say anything like that to this woman. She meant well. I don't remember what I said—just laughed and agreed, maybe. What I do remember is that the parking lot outside the school was always a haze to me, because there were tears in my eyes almost every time I ran through it on the way to my car, Andrew slung over my hip, far in front of all the other mothers who were lingering and scheduling play dates while their kids ran around, shouting and laughing and playing games together.

Alone in a Group

In those days, Andrew had no interest in playing with other children. None. Throughout preschool and even into kindergarten, his idea of playing during recess was to wander around the periphery of the playground, doing hand puppets and muttering to himself. Back in a classroom full of other kids, he was still in his own world, and while you might find him *next* to someone, it was never because they were playing together.

The good news was that he didn't seem to care that he didn't have friends. I suspect that the world Andrew lived in was densely populated with various characters who felt like friends—the hand puppets who spoke to him, the stuffed animals who reassured him, the Sesame Street characters who sang to him on videos. . . . It never occurred to him he was isolated. That came later.

Elementary School

In kindergarten, Andrew's speech was still severely delayed and highly echolalic. He reverted to hand puppets whenever he could. He could read and write and was clearly bright, but the fog that surrounded him was thick.

Dawn Davenport, our one-on-one classroom aide, immediately understood that the key to helping Andrew was to attract other kids to play with him. Every recess, she'd start some kind of socially interactive game. Because she was a kid magnet—warm and friendly and maternal—and because she played games that really looked like fun, there was always a group of kids hanging around her. And because she stayed close to Andrew, that meant there was always a group of kids around him. Thanks to Dawn, he rarely wandered around alone anymore.

The game playing and constant contact with other kids had an amazing effect. For the first time, Andrew seemed to get the idea that other kids could be fun. It also helped that at home his little brother was now at an age when he could play games and talk, and Leo was always calling to Andrew to come play with him. And Andrew, amazingly, often did.

At school, he was paying more attention to the kids around him. Mostly this was good—he was now motivated to improve his social skills. The downside was that he was still an odd kid with a language delay, and kids don't always respond the way we wish they would to overtures of friendship. I was always bracing myself for rejections (which, when they came, hit me harder than they hit him, truth be told).

Andrew could also still be socially inappropriate. At one point in kindergarten, he became fascinated with a girl in his class. She was very sweet, but Andrew's constant attempts to sit near her and follow her around were discomfiting and occasionally made her the target of other kids' teasing, so she grew impatient with him. I couldn't blame her, and at times I almost wished Andrew would just go back to ignoring the other kids. It was less excruciating.

Improvement

For the most part, however, Andrew's mounting interest in socializing was a good thing. More and more we were seeing in him a desire to be part of a group and to play with other kids. He was interacting beautifully with his ever-increasing family of siblings, who truly adored and looked up to him, and his language was catching up to his peers'.

In first grade, he actually found a friend, a kid who admired how smart Andrew was academically and who had a strong nurturing instinct. He liked being Andrew's "helper" out in the less-structured environments of the playground and lunch table. With Dawn still at his side, and his friend there to guide him, Andrew felt more and more part of the social scene at school.

There were still a lot of hurdles. For one thing, Andrew has never liked sports, and while that wasn't much of a problem in kindergarten and first grade, it became one as the boys in his class started to play first handball, then soccer, then basketball at lunchtime. Somewhere around third grade, Andrew did start to play handball. He got pretty good at it, and it helped him enormously with socializing at school—recess always found him playing with the other kids. Unfortunately, halfway through fourth grade, the boys stopped playing handball and turned to basketball, which was way too fast and challenging a game for Andrew. Once again, he just didn't have the right skills to be part of the dominant social group.

Another problem for Andrew socially was that when he got frustrated, he would cry, and he got frustrated a lot. All that weepiness definitely marked him as a "different" kid, and while most of the kids in school liked him well enough, they weren't exactly crowding around asking for play dates. Nor were their parents encouraging them to.

By the time Andrew was in fourth grade, thanks to the hard work of a whole team of people, he no longer needed speech therapy. He was too well coordinated to qualify for continued adaptive PE; academically, he was at the top of his class and getting great report cards. But we were still worried about his socialization. He was kind and cheerful and supportive of the other kids and had no enemies that we knew of, but he wasn't making close friends, either. His former friend was still around, but Andrew wasn't so crazy about being nurtured anymore. He didn't want another aide—he wanted friends like his brother had: boys his age who came over all the time and who invited him over all the time. He just didn't have that.

Social Skills Groups

We threw ourselves into improving Andrew's social skills and found a special class to help us take some initial steps.

It was a structured twelve-week program, run out of UCLA's Neuropsychiatric Institute. One night a week, Rob, Andrew, and I would leave the other kids with a babysitter and spend two hours learning about social skills. The kids would all go off to one room, while the parents stayed in another and had their own meeting. The mix of kids in the group was interesting. Andrew was probably the only one with an autism diagnosis. The rest ranged from extremely shy to extremely aggressive. The only thing they had in common was the desire to improve their skills at making and keeping friends.

Each week, the parents and kids had "homework." We were assigned things like having Andrew call someone on the phone or taking him to the park, where he'd have to join in with kids who were playing there, or arranging a play date for him with someone from school. We left each session with written instructions on how to carry out these tasks.

I found it all absolutely terrifying.

I was always terrible about arranging play dates for all my children— with four kids, I had enough juggling of schedules and driving as it was, and adding in a bunch of play dates just made everything harder. My other kids learned to make plans themselves if they really wanted to do something, but poor Andrew definitely suffered from having a busy mother and from not connecting enough with other kids to be able to arrange his own social life. And I have my own social anxiety issues, which got in the way of my reaching out to other mothers to see if their kids wanted to play with him.

So this "homework" of helping Andrew become social was a pretty major task. Fortunately Rob, who's much more outgoing than I am, took a lot of it on himself. And Andrew was a great sport, cheerfully, if haltingly, making his phone calls—I hadn't realized until then how badly he needed to practice that skill—and trying hard to join in the games being played at the park.

I think this intellectual, structured approach to socializing helped us all. For Andrew, who found most subtle social cues bewildering, the more information he could have written down in front of him, the easier things got. For Rob and me, it was a kick in the butt, a reminder that we needed to simply get our kid out there more.

At the last session, the instructor said to us, "A parent who did this a couple of years ago said she was relieved when it was over because she wouldn't have to arrange any more play dates." The instructor fixed us with a steely glare. "But of course she did, and you do. The need for play dates isn't over just because the class is. You *have* to continue doing this if you want your child to continue to improve socially."

That other parent and I would have gotten along well—I had been feeling relieved, too. And now I felt guilty for feeling relieved.

Video Games and PG-13 Movies

Over and over again, my natural instincts as a parent had to give way to Andrew's needs as a child with autism. Remember how, when he was still a preschooler, I had to stop being laid-back when I played with him and learn to get in his face and make him play "the right way" with toys? Well, I continued to have to adjust my way of thinking in order to do the right thing for *him*.

For example, I hate video games. Truly. Sometimes I think it's a male-female thing, because my husband and sons find them fascinating, while my daughter and I resent their existence. I didn't like it when Rob used to play Nintendo a lot, and when the boys discovered PlayStation 2, I couldn't stand the way they wanted to play all the time and fought me whenever I asked them to stop.

But here's the thing about video games: preteen and teenage boys play them. A lot. And they not only play them, they talk about them. In fact, from what I've seen, the two main things that boys talk about are sports and video games. Since Andrew never really had any interest in sports, it was that much more important for us to encourage him to talk about video games. And in order to talk about them knowledgeably, he had to actually play them. Which meant I was in the strange position of urging my son to play more video games.

Same thing with PG-13 movies. And even the occasional R-rated one. I've never been in any great rush to expose my kids at an early age to a lot of violence and bad language (and stupid bathroom humor), but when I discovered that 70 percent of the kids in Andrew's class had seen some slightly adult movie, I let him see it, too. Once again, he needed to be able to participate in the social conversation at school. And I was lucky: those kinds of movies never seemed to bother Andrew in any way—no nightmares, no discomfort, no distaste. I think he just kind of let them wash over him. (My youngest son had a very different temperament and for years hated seeing any movie that was disturbing in any way. All on his own, he would look up parent reviews for whatever movies we were thinking of seeing and sometimes he'd come back and tell us that he didn't think it was appropriate for him to see yet!)

Here's What I Feel Guilty About

Just writing this section has made me realize that I missed the boat in some areas. I wish I had pushed sports more with Andrew when he was little. It's true he was pretty resistant, but he might have gotten over that initial hump (which he's done with swimming and handball) and really started enjoying himself. I was so worried about how the other kids and parents would react to him if I put him on some kind of team that I postponed doing it until he was too old to be a beginner, and it became an even more awkward proposition. Once he was deep into elementary school and I saw what a huge role sports play in most boys' lives, I regretted not pushing harder on the sports when he was five.

And I know I didn't do my best by Andrew with play dates, either. He learned to be a kind, courteous host, but I always dragged my feet over making plans happen: calling parents of kids who may or may not want to play with my own counts as one of the most agonizing things I've had to do and one I would have done almost anything to avoid.

But I should have done it. And in all honesty, I think Andrew is still paying a price for my social anxiety issues. Which is a pretty painful thing for a mom to admit. But if my regret inspires any of you to push a little harder for your kid to get out there and make friends, then at least it's not completely wasted regret, right?

Here's what I wrote in summary, ten years ago, for the first draft of this book:

"Andrew is a great kid who's kind and good-natured but who doesn't let himself get pushed around. He has a strong sense of right and wrong, and is a fair and generous player who sincerely admires and compliments his friends for the things they do well. He's eager for play dates, and we've found some kids he can really have a good time with. We have a big extended family, and when we all get together he no longer isolates himself—he runs off happily to play with his cousins. He and his brother are good friends, and he's unbelievably gentle and kind with his younger siblings. When I drop him off at camp, kids I've never even met before run up to say hi to him.

"So I guess he's doing just fine."

Ten Years Later

Now that Andrew's in college, most of his social life is a bit of a mystery to me, which is probably how it should be at this stage of things, partially because college kids lead independent lives and partially (okay, *mostly*) because

I think we parents would be horrified to find out what a college social life actually consists of for the majority of our kids. So I think I'd better draw a curtain over Andrew's personal social life, for the sake of both his privacy and my sanity.

But here are some thoughts and suggestions, as I look over the last couple of decades and think about the past.

First of all, make sure your child is truly enjoying the friends you're setting up play dates with. There's a trap we parents of kids on the spectrum can fall into, and that's assuming that we know what they want better than they do. Sometimes we do, but sometimes we have to pay attention to what they're trying to tell us. For example, Andrew started to turn down play dates with a kid he had formerly been eager to play with. I assumed he was just trying to avoid being social, so I kept coaxing him into inviting the boy over. Eventually he told me that he didn't like the boy anymore, for reasons that were understandable once I knew them. The problem was, he thought he would disappoint me by telling me that he didn't like this friend, so instead of simply saying, "I don't like some of the things he does," he kept trying to invent reasons to explain why he couldn't have a play date that day (and his reasons weren't very good, so I kept pushing!). Moral of the story: pay attention to what your child is communicating, even if he's not doing a good job of putting it into words. Not all friends are created equal, so if your child is more enthusiastic about some kids than others, follow his lead. And remember that the way some kids play when there are no adults around can be different from when they know they're being watched, so stay vigilant, especially if your child has trouble relaying information.

And here's another thing I've been trying to figure out: I honestly worry that we may have emphasized the whole "Do what the other kids are doing" thing too much when Andrew was little, because we found ourselves having to back-pedal when his peers started smoking and getting drunk. He knew, of course, that those weren't the kinds of behaviors we wanted him to imitate, but it must be a little confusing to grow up trying to fit in and looking to others for examples of how to do that, and then one day find yourself a teenager surrounded by teenagers acting like . . . well . . . teenagers. I'm not sure what the solution is. I do think that in the last ten years we've all learned a little bit better how to encourage our kids to play appropriately and socialize happily without necessarily making them feel like they have to be exactly like everyone else. Which is of course what we want for *all* our children. So I guess I'd say let your child be different in the ways that make him unique and wonderful—but not in ways that could lead to isolation or ostracism. And if that distinction sounds complicated to figure out, well, welcome to the wonderful world of parenting, where you get to spend years trying to figure out what's best for your child at any given moment!

Finally, I want to reiterate what Dr. Koegel has said, only with more fervency and maybe even a touch of sorrow: nothing is harder than knowing your child feels lonely and isolated. Nothing.

Good friends are far more valuable than anything you can buy your children, and I'm not saying that in a sweet, chicken-soupy kind of way or because I'm a nonmaterialist (I love my little luxuries), but because I've been a parent whose kids have at times been lonely, and it sucks, it sucks, it sucks. So do what you can to help them learn some social skills, even if it's hard. And it probably will be hard.

I think Dr. Koegel is so right when she says that encouraging your child's specific and heartfelt interests is one of the best ways to help him find friends. I know plenty of quirky kids who have terrific friends just like them, because they all play Dungeons and Dragons together or Magic: The Gathering or arrange to see every single fantasy movie the first night it comes out, and so on. If your kid loves train schedules, bring him to hang out at a model train store. If he loves sports stats, see if he can do some kind of scorekeeping job at his school. If all he likes to do is play video games, make it a rule that he can play as much as he wants so long as he's got a friend over—but not when he's alone. (Parents have to be good at manipulating situations to make some things more reinforcing than others!)

And while I agree with Dr. Koegel that mainstreaming is the best way to keep your child growing, learning, and improving, if she's showing signs of social strain and feeling like she's not connecting with the other kids at school, look even harder for extracurricular activities that will put her in touch with peers she can relate to. You might have to check out some special social skills groups or maybe even see if she can join some activities at a school for kids who are on the spectrum. (The research suggests that while some kids find social skills groups beneficial, others don't get much out of them, so again, listen to your child and assess the situation for your own family—Andrew made a friend in one of them, so that definitely was a gain, but he also loathed a couple of the groups and we pulled him out of those quickly.) I've learned over the years that your kids' best friends don't have to go to the same school, so don't assume you're limited to the kids her class can offer. Shake the trees, climb the mountains, check out the possibilities.

We all need friends. And some of us need help finding them.

Chapter Six
Battling Fears and Fixations: Bringing Your Child Back to the Real World

QUESTION: Our family get-togethers are severely limited because my niece covers her ears and cries when there's a loud noise—it's almost like it's painful for her. It causes her family a lot of problems in public. What can they do about this?

QUESTION: My son insists on following the same routines at all times. When we go to therapy, he throws tantrums if he can't go in the same door, walk the same route, and use the same room that he did the first time we went there. Any suggestions short of stopping therapy at that setting?

WE all have strong feelings that aren't always logical. I have a friend who's terrified of snakes and therefore won't go for hikes in the hills. I know several people who collect one specific kind of object and know every detail about every piece in their collection. And I also know a lot of people who, while claiming not to be superstitious, will still avoid stepping on cracks. These fears, fascinations, and fixations don't make much sense, but they persist in all of us, maybe because they impose a certain amount of order in a chaotic world, maybe because they're vestiges of something that happened when we were younger, or maybe just because.

For most of us, though, these inexplicably intense fears and attractions to various objects stay in their place and don't interfere with the normal routine of our daily lives. It's different for kids with autism, who sometimes become unaccountably and wildly fearful of certain noises or events and equally unaccountably and wildly fascinated with certain objects or routines—so much so that much of their time is spent in avoidance of the former or in search of the latter.

People speculate about why these kids are more likely to cling to exaggerated fears and beliefs than the rest of us, but no one is totally sure.

There may be lots of reasons. Maybe they don't feel the social pressures that force the rest of us to ignore our overactive imaginations in public, or maybe a cycle of repetitiveness developed and is now difficult to break. Maybe their inability to generalize and their tendency toward rigidity make it harder for them to abandon feelings established early on. Maybe they find the world even more chaotic and confusing than the rest of us do and need to impose on it their own structure and rules for it to make any sense to them at all. We don't know, but whatever the reason, these fears and fixations can lead to difficulties for their caregivers.

How do we deal with the child who insists on driving a certain route and who'll throw a tantrum if there's a road construction detour? What about the child who refuses to ride in the backseat of the car? How do we help a child who appears to have a horrible physiological reaction to an everyday noise, like a vacuum cleaner? What if your child gets aggressive anytime one of his toys is moved or touched?

Such fears and fixations are not uncommon, and you're going to have to tackle the problem head-on if your child with autism is reacting in a way that limits your family's ability to function.

CONTROLLING FEARS AND FIXATIONS THAT SERVE A FUNCTION

Sometimes a child's excessive fears or insistence on routine may serve a useful function in his life, just as many disruptive behaviors do (see chapter 3). In other words, you may find, upon close analysis, that the child likes the consequences he's found to be associated with maintaining the behavior.

Having said that, let me also warn you that you probably aren't going to be able to figure out the "why" on many fears or fixations. Some may have had a function at one time but now are just habit. Others may fall into the self-stimulatory category, an area that no one fully understands (see chapter 4 for more on that). Some may be the result of "superstitious learning"—in other words, the child may connect an action with a positive consequence where actually there is no cause and effect at all. We all do this from time to time—for example, you get into a little fender bender in your car, so forevermore you avoid the corner where you had the accident. Day after day you don't get into an accident, so you feel validated in your decision to continue avoiding that corner. Sort of like clapping to keep the elephants away. You clap . . . no elephants . . . so it worked, right? This sometimes happens to children with autism—they walk a certain way to get to therapy, then they have a great

session, so they insist on walking that same way every time. We can still intervene and improve these functionless behaviors, as I'll describe below, but for
the moment, let's focus on the times when you can determine specific functions
that the behaviors fulfill.

Getting Started

Make copies of the behavior data sheet in the appendix at the back of this
book and use it to see if you can figure out if there's a reason why your
child is displaying fears or clinging to fixations. Write down what your child
did (e.g., wouldn't leave the automatic doors at the grocery store or screamed at
the thought of swimming), then write down what happened before and
what happened after, and then hypothesize as to why he did this. With fears
and fixations, sometimes you'll be able to see a reason, and sometimes you
won't.

Finding Patterns

Once you've filled in all your data, look and see if there are any patterns.
You may, upon analysis, determine that nine out of ten times your child is
being unintentionally rewarded for his excessive reactions—getting attention for a behavior that seems otherwise inexplicable or maybe even getting
out of an undesirable conversation or academic assignment. If you can figure out a pattern, that will direct you toward the appropriate type of intervention.

For example, Ryan always became disruptive before swimming class. He
refused to leave the classroom and repeatedly said that he was afraid of the
water. He began tipping desks and throwing papers each time the teacher tried
to get him to go. His fear of water seemed so overwhelming that the teacher
decided she would let him stay in the classroom and play by himself while she
graded papers. This created a problem, however, because she couldn't leave
him alone in the classroom, so she didn't get a break to go to the bathroom, visit
with other teachers, or run errands the way she normally would have during
that period. Following a brief functional analysis and an interview with his
parents, we found that Ryan absolutely loved to take baths and spent most of
his summer at the beach. He actually didn't have a fear of water, as he had convinced the teacher, but rather had learned that he could avoid social interaction
and get some free time if he stayed in the classroom.

When a fear or fixation appears to have a function, here are some things you can try.

Stop Rewarding the Behavior

As we discuss in chapter 3, many children engage in inappropriate behaviors to avoid or escape an activity. Take Ryan, for example—although he didn't have a true fear of water, he behaved as if he did to get out of a demanding activity and have some time alone.

We approach a case like this the same way we would any disruptive behavior that's being maintained by the fact that the child desires its consequence—by making sure we stop reinforcing the wrong choice and by rewarding the right choice. In Ryan's case, instead of letting him roam around freely in the classroom, we told him that if he stayed there, he would have to choose one of several fairly demanding activities to work on. After just a week of this new structure, his "free time" became a lot less appealing. We also told him he could engage in free swim for the first half of the swim lesson. Since the swim activity thus became less demanding, and the classroom time had become more demanding, Ryan began to prefer to go to swim lesson. Once he was choosing that regularly, we gradually and slowly decreased his free time during swimming, until he was able to participate in the swim lesson for the full class period like his classmates.

Reinforce the Right Things

Similarly, if your data suggest that your child is getting *attention* from clinging to a fear or a fixation, you must once again make sure you're giving attention to good behavior, not the inappropriate behavior.

Freddie couldn't walk past a telephone without stopping and playing with it, and he cried and threw tantrums when his mother tried to keep him moving along. A careful look at his history revealed that when he was first learning to talk, his mother had made up a phone game, during which she would pretend to talk on the phone and then hand Freddie the phone whenever he requested it. She had purchased several play phones that had fancy buttons, made amusing sounds, and lit up with bright colors. The phones had been Freddie's favorite toys and had helped him make great gains during intervention, but in the process they had become associated with his mother's attention. Even now, when he walked past a phone, his mother always discussed it or let him play with it, in order to continue to encourage his communication, so he was still getting a lot of phone-related attention from his mother.

Once we had figured out that Freddie associated telephones with playing with Mom, we worked out a way to make them less appealing to him. Instead of trying to abruptly pull Freddie away when he stopped to play with a phone, his mother gave him a warning that they were going to have to leave in a minute, then she walked a few steps away and ignored him during that minute. Since Freddie was no longer getting her attention (even her attempts to pull him away had functioned as a reward, since it was a kind of interaction), he'd lose interest and leave without an incident.

Similarly, we once worked with a child, Molly, who cried and threw fits every time there was a school assembly. Molly was well behaved the rest of the time, so everyone assumed the tantrums were sparked by genuine distress, probably a fear of crowds. Because she seemed so overwhelmed, the classroom aide would remove her from the assembly and play with her alone in the classroom. But once the school staff really observed what was going on and analyzed it, they realized that Molly wasn't actually afraid of school assemblies—she just preferred being alone with the aide, and the crying was her way to get into that preferable situation. To overcome this problem, the aide began to give Molly attention *only* when she engaged in assembly-related activities. For example, when she walked with the class toward the assembly, the aide chatted with her, and when she sat nicely in assembly, the aide enthusiastically pointed out interesting things and kept her amused. After about four assemblies, Molly no longer got upset when asked to go to one, so the aide gradually and systematically faded her attention until Molly could attend the assembly without it.

Again, if you're able to determine a function for your child's fears or fixations, they can be addressed by the steps described in chapter 3, on disruptive behavior. If not, you may want to try some of the suggestions below.

CONTROLLING FIXATIONS THAT SERVE NO FUNCTION

We all like predictability and are thrown by the unexpected, but some children with autism cling much too rigidly—almost superstitiously—to certain repetitive actions, routines, and ideas. In this case, there may be no obvious outward reinforcement of the behavior; instead, it has become so ingrained that it reinforces itself.

For example, we worked with a cute little preschooler who became fixated with chain saws. I'm not quite sure when it started, but that was all he talked about. His mother wanted to bring him to a new preschool but was afraid that the staff wouldn't accept him if he brought up the subject of chain saws. This little guy was trying so hard to control himself, but as soon as he got into the classroom, he looked up at the director and said, all in one go, "Are there any chain saws here? We're not talking about chain saws now." He had said the thing he just had to say, then he immediately proceeded to self-instruct, repeating the response he had heard so many times before. The director looked at him in shock—she'd never had a preschooler ask about chain saws, then go on to say we aren't talking about them!

The following are specific things you can do to decrease your child's difficulties with activities that he or she seems to have an abnormal drive to pursue. Every child is different, so if one technique doesn't work, try another—or you may want to try a combination of techniques.

Reward Your Child for Breaking a Pattern

Some fixations are simply patterns that the children get in a habit of completing, so they become upset if they feel the pattern is not completed. For example, one child we knew insisted on spending hours at a time lining up her shoes in exactly the same order whenever she put a pair of shoes away, and if not allowed to do so she would throw a tantrum. Other children will be bothered all day long if Mom or Dad doesn't drive a specific route to school.

If that's the case with your child, one thing you can do is to reward him for breaking the pattern early in the sequence. You essentially want to stop this kind of fixation before it really gets started, so *distract, then reward*: distract your child before the ritual has gotten to the point where it looks unnatural and then immediately reward him. To be specific: well before your child begins to engage in the fixation, get him involved in a fun activity. That way, he won't be so "stuck" on the fixation. For example, one child threw huge tantrums at the mall if he couldn't go up and down (repeatedly) in the elevator. But he also loved to count and to go the toy store, so before they even got near the elevator, his mom would engage him in fun counting activities, and then, after they passed the elevator, she would immediately ask him if he wanted to go to the toy store. The counting helped to break the ritual, and the toy store provided another rewarding—but appropriate—activity.

Remember, the further on into the chain your child gets, the more inappropriate it looks and the harder it is to distract him, so try to break the pattern early on. If you can consistently break the pattern before it gets fully under way, you'll nip the habit in the bud.

In the example of the girl above, we focused on distracting her immediately after she put the shoes in the closet by bringing her to another favorite activity, so that the chain was broken and she never settled into lining them up. One child who was upset if his mom drove a different route to school was distracted *and* rewarded by a beloved CD. When his mom gave him headphones and his favorite music, he didn't mind if she drove another route.

Offer Rewards

We can break some repetitive cycles by offering the child a reward for *not* engaging in the problematic behavior or for engaging in an appropriate alternative behavior that competes with the problem behavior.

Take Megan, for instance. We have our own center now, but we were in a different building back in those days and had to use a small shared clinic room the first time we saw her at UCSB. After that, she insisted on using the same room each time. She also insisted on walking in the same doors and following the same path into the building each session. The problem with this was that we couldn't guarantee that the room would be available, and more than once Megan walked in on some adult getting psychotherapy—her mother also had a baby to watch, and no matter how hard she tried to get Megan to stay with her in the waiting room, Megan regularly succeeded in escaping into that same first room. To make matters worse, Megan proceeded to engage in a full-blown tantrum if someone was in "her" room. Let me tell you, when someone's in the middle of confiding her innermost secrets and problems to a therapist, she's not too thrilled when a little kid—no matter how cute—interrupts and tells her she has to leave!

We finally solved the problem by meeting Megan at her car, then offering her a treat (licorice was her favorite) if she walked in a different door and went into a different room. By catching her before she had already started walking a certain way, and instantly priming her as to which way she would be going, then rewarding her flexibility, we were able to break her pattern. After a few sessions, this pattern was broken, and she no longer required the reward.

Try Self-Management

Self-management (described in detail in chapter 9) ties into the reward system and can also be effective in decreasing fears and fixations. Basically, what you want to do is reward the child for having periods that are free of the fear or fixation, but with self-management, the child is in control of monitoring herself, rather than having someone else tell her when she's done well and gets to be rewarded. That means she has to understand what the new desired behavior is, engage in it, then evaluate her own behavior. After a specified number of charted successes, she can earn a chosen reward.

For example, one day Mimi noticed that her name looked cute if she dotted the letter "i" with a heart. Everyone complimented her on how creative she was and how nice it looked, and within a few weeks, Mimi was drawing hearts all over her paper—up and down the sides, across the top and the bottom. The heart drawing was taking up most of her class time, and she was rarely able to complete an assignment. When the teacher tried to take the paper or pencil away, Mimi refused to let go and caused a disruption that led to chaos in the classroom.

We decided to set up a self-management program. Mimi got to reward herself with a heart-shaped sticker in her sticker book every time she finished a worksheet *without* drawing hearts on it. That way, she still got a taste of her fixation, but in a way that helped instead of interfered with her work.

One teenage girl I met had one of the more interesting fixations I've come across: she was fascinated by belt buckles. The bigger the better. Unfortunately, whenever she saw one, she was compelled to kiss it. To make matters worse, she lived in Texas, where just about every guy (and a lot of women, for that matter) wears a belt buckle too big to miss. Walking down the street with her was a formidable task for her mother, who found that explanations didn't always go over big with strangers whose belt buckles her daughter was trying to kiss. We set up a self-management program so that she could reward herself for going out in public for short periods of time *without* kissing a buckle. Gradually over a period of several months we increased the amount of time we took her out, while continuing to have her self-manage, which eventually eliminated the problem.

Offer Choices

We adults have a tendency to try to control our children by telling them what to do, but often the same goal can be accomplished more happily by giving them choices.

For example, we began working with a teenager who had endured lots of drill-type therapy, which he disliked; as a result, he was reluctant to enter our clinic rooms the first time his family brought him. Although our rooms are filled with toys and fun activities, A. J. hid behind a brick column in front of our building and refused to come inside. When his parents tried to move him along, he dropped to the floor and began kicking, crying, and screaming when they tried to get him up. He truly acted as if he were terrified of entering the building. Deciding to see how A. J. would do if *he* could have a say in making a decision, we said, "Would you like to walk inside, or would you like us to carry you?" Amazingly, he was able to calm down and make a choice; he chose to walk into the room. It didn't matter that the end result of the choice was the same, and that both of the choices were what he hadn't wanted to do in the first place. He now had some control, because *he* got to make the choice.

This strategy can also be effective with fixations. Paul was fixated on the automatic doors in the grocery store. Whenever his mom went shopping, he repeatedly went in and out of the automatic doors and would throw a tantrum if she tried to move him away so she could do her shopping. However, when she gave Paul a choice of other desired things, such as "Paul, do you want to get animal crackers or fruit leather?" he instantaneously left the doors.

It may be that making a choice offers a child some dignity and independence, or simply that it distracts them from the activity, but for some children it's a far more successful strategy than providing them with only one option. And, interestingly, it doesn't always have to be a choice between desired objects (although that probably helps)—even if neither choice is all that appealing (like walking or being carried into the building), the simple act of choosing seems to help kids accept the end result.

Suggest a New Activity Before Ending the Current One

Many children have difficulty making a transition away from a beloved item or activity. If this happens, try offering another fun activity when your child is having trouble leaving a highly desired one.

For example, Robbie loved going up and down the elevator. This was great for working on his verbal skills, as we had him ask for it ("Elevator, please"), say whether he wanted to go up or down, call his parents to come with him while we held the door open ("C'mon, Mom/Dad!"), and learn his numbers by pushing the buttons. However, whenever we tried to move on to a new activity, Robbie screamed, fell to the floor, and refused to leave. We found that if we offered another desired activity, such as going to get a soda at the store, *before* we tried to leave the elevator, he went with minimal difficulty.

Use Counting Consistently

Counting can be an effective way to let kids know that they have only a few more seconds to finish or complete an activity, and it can weaken the reward the fixation is giving the child.

Ali loved to play in the park. When his mother tried to get him to leave afterward, he lashed out at her. So, right before she was ready to leave, his mother would say, "Ali, time to go," then start counting. She didn't count punitively, but as a transition to another reinforcer. When she got to three, she always followed through by making him leave. The first few times she did have to carry him away—kicking and screaming—but once he realized that three absolutely and definitely meant he'd have to go, he learned to drop what he was doing before she got past two.

Similarly, Lucy liked to play with toys and hated to stop and clean up. But once her mother started with the countdown, she learned to put them away immediately. Of course, the first few times, her mother had to assist and direct her with the cleaning up, but eventually she learned that Mom meant it and started picking the toys up by herself.

From time to time, all parents give their kids a warning that they don't follow through with. And kids are incredibly smart, so they figure this out and know when they can get away without obeying. On the other hand, they can recognize certain looks and tones of voice that say we really mean it. You want this to be the case with counting, so consistency is key. Make sure your child knows what action will take place at the count of three, and *stick to it every time*. If you get distracted and three becomes three and a half or four, your child isn't going to respect the counting.

Keep It Short

Similarly, you can make it clear ahead of time that the behavior can't go on too long. Some fixations are not a problem in and of themselves—it's just their intensity and duration that cause problems, and you simply need to control those variables.

For example, Mindy liked to play board games with her friends. Unfortunately, whenever it was her turn, she would just keep shaking the dice while counting—she would sometimes count into the hundreds. The other children, irritated by her nonstop shaking, would lose patience with her or even quit playing the game. We talked to Mindy about the fact that many people have a little routine when they roll the dice, but hers was just going on too long. We tried having her count to three and then throw the dice, but it was hard for her to stop at three once she'd started counting, and she'd often just keep on going. Then Mindy's mom came up with a fantastic idea. She had her count backward: three, two, one. When she got to one, that was it. There was nowhere for Mindy to go after that, so she always threw the dice. (Fortunately, no one had told her about negative integers yet.)

Another child liked to go up and down the escalators at Nordstrom and would scream, cry, and grip the escalators with all her might when her mom tried to get her to leave. The mom wasn't a frequent shopper at Nordstrom, but because her daughter liked the escalator so much, she used it as a reward for good behavior during the day. To decrease the problem of leaving, her mom changed the routine so that Mari got on the escalator, rode all the way to the top of the store, then rode straight back down again. This shortened the overall amount of time Mari rode on the escalator, but because the new routine was clear and consistent, Mari accepted it and left easily once she'd had her ride.

Make a Rule

As we saw in the example above, setting firm and consistent rules can help. Kids with autism can be very good at learning rules and sticking to them, so long as they're clearly laid out. For example, we worked with a preschool child who insisted on carrying a small toy with her everywhere she went. This turned into a problem—her school had a rule that children couldn't bring toys from home, and the item usually interfered with her therapy sessions. But since Briana screamed and cried whenever her mother tried to get her to leave the item in the car, her mother usually gave in and let her take it. One day her mother decided that the only way to tackle the problem was to stop it cold turkey. Prior to starting, she warned all her child's therapists and the school, so they would be prepared for some fallout. Then she told Briana that she could no longer take the item out of the car. For about three days, Briana had a complete meltdown every time she had to leave the car without her treasured item, but soon the meltdowns became shorter and less intense. After about eight days, Briana had learned the rule and no longer became disruptive when she had to leave the toy in the car. She had learned that taking it wasn't even an option.

But remember, you have to make the rule very clear and simple and stick to it for some time if you want it to work. The other thing to remember is that sometimes behavior gets worse before it gets better. This is a well-known phenomenon discussed frequently in the psychology literature and it is true with all kids. So if you're going to ignore or disallow an inappropriate behavior, your child may exhibit higher-than-usual levels of the inappropriate behavior before it starts waning. Like Briana's mother did, be prepared for that: warn everybody and stick with it—and you'll be glad you did.

Channel the Fixation into an Appropriate Activity

Sometimes fixations can be channeled into an appropriate activity. Although many parents worry that this will cause an even greater problem, it doesn't. The point here is to use the theme that is so fascinating to your child and change it so that it becomes an appropriate social activity—not one that isolates your child.

We worked with Habib, a first-grader, who spent most of his free time talking about birthdays. If you told him what your birthday was, he would tell you what day of the week it would fall on that year. One day his older brother entered them both in the talent show at his school. The act consisted of the brother's calling on people in the audience to give their birth date and then asking Habib what day of the week the birthday would fall on. Habib's brother had a large calendar to show the accuracy of Habib's amswers. They turned out to be a hit at the talent show.

Similarly, April was fixated on her multiplication tables. She constantly approached other children and asked them if they knew their times tables, and if they didn't, she would rattle them off. April's teacher felt that the manner in which she was approaching the children was socially inappropriate and that April's knowledge could be put to better use. She decided that she would make her the "multiplication aide" in her classroom—April was in charge of drilling the other children during math period. By helping April learn an appropriate and helpful way to use her math skills, the teacher turned a potential disadvantage into an advantage, and the kids learned to admire April's knowledge.

The difference is surprisingly narrow between a specialist—someone who knows a lot about one subject and is therefore a good resource for everyone—and someone who's fixated on one thing and won't talk about anything else. If your child is fixated on one area, try to turn that area into a strength, rather than a weakness, by using it to increase social interactions. While a child who stays in his room talking to himself about the solar system may require intervention, that same child presenting a report on the solar system at school and answering his friends' questions is a success.

Interrupt Self-Stimulatory Behavior

We often see children engaging in repetitive or self-stimulatory behaviors while at the same time they appear to be obsessively engaged in an activity, and the pleasure of the stim may be the reinforcing agent in these cases.

Dani loved going to the car wash every day after school with her dad. She could spend hours watching the cars go into the building, the water spray the cars, the big rollers suds up the cars, and the spray rinse it all off. Although this had initially been an enjoyable father-daughter activity, the father was losing patience with it—Dani insisted on staying for hours and became disruptive when he wanted her to go. The father didn't want to stop taking Dani to a place that made her so happy, but he couldn't deal with her refusals to leave.

When our staff joined them one afternoon, we noticed that while Dani was watching the cars go through the wash, she was also engaging in repetitive behaviors, flapping her hands constantly while arching her back. Clearly, the stim was a large part of what she found addictive about watching the car wash. Once we realized that, we told the dad to break the cycle of repetitive behavior by engaging Dani in another activity with him while at the car wash, such as singing a song, listening to a tape, or reciting a poem—one that didn't allow her to get lost in the stim. Once he did that, she was able to leave the car wash without a problem. For Dani, it was actually the repetitive behavior that she did while watching the car wash that was making the transition difficult. Getting her involved in another activity interrupted the stim and eliminated the transition problem.

TACKLING FEARS THAT SERVE NO CLEAR FUNCTION

Fears are essentially the opposite side of the coin to fixations: whatever it is in some kids that makes one activity wildly fascinating and necessary seems to make other things equally frightening and unbearable. In the same way that we break patterns of ritualistic behaviors so the child stops reverting to them automatically, you can "break" the fear cycle by gradually and carefully acclimating the child to whatever was causing the irrational terror in the first place, until his fear stops being habitual.

Desensitization

Desensitization is a commonly used technique that effectively reduces or eliminates fears (or phobias) in adults and has been used successfully with children with autism. The overall procedure involves gradually and systematically introducing the problematic stimulus in tiny steps, so that it's not aversive to the child.

For example, Logan seemed to experience pain every time the toilet flushed at school. He had no problem flushing his home toilet, which was much quieter, so it appeared to be the excessive noise that distressed him. Whenever he was taken to the bathroom at school, he covered his ears and refused to use the toilet. Not surprisingly, he began having toileting accidents.

To help Logan overcome this fear, we developed a desensitization program. There were two areas involved. One was to get him used to being in the bathroom, since he refused to go near it, and the other was to teach him to be less sensitive to the flushing noise. First we figured out where in the hallway he tended to begin covering his ears, then we walked him to a point in the hall that was just before that spot while one of us discussed his favorite topics with him (you can also have the child engage in an enjoyable and preferred activity during the desensitization). After several little strolls to the location before the spot, we began going a little farther—not to the point where he would cover his ears, but just far enough to be a little closer. When he was able to walk there comfortably three or four times, we added on a few feet. Gradually, after about twenty little walks, he was able to walk past the boys' bathroom without covering his ears. Next, we began walking him past the bathroom with the door partially open (we used a doorstop). Then we opened the door a tiny bit wider and tried again. We continued doing this, always in such small steps that Logan really wasn't bothered.

Once he could walk past the bathroom with the door completely open, we began the flushing. We played with him back down the hall while another person flushed. And flushed, and flushed. We started where the flushing was barely audible and someone repeatedly flushed the toilet. Although Logan looked up a few times at the sound of the flush, he didn't cover his ears. We very gradually moved him ever so slightly closer to the bathroom each session while continuing to flush, until he was able to go into the bathroom without covering his ears and successfully use the toilet.

Anytime Logan seemed overwhelmed or anxious during this process, we moved back a step to where he was comfortable and made sure our next step forward was a small, gradual one. The idea is to keep things moving so gradually that the child gets used to the thing that formerly caused fear without even realizing he's becoming accustomed to it. We've effectively used desensitization with all kinds of fears—hand dryers, hair dryers, hair cuts, blenders, vacuum cleaners, and so on. Using gradual steps while engaging your child in a fun activity can eliminate fears that make family life trying.

Cog-Mod

Cognitive behavioral therapy (CBT) has been shown to be helpful for some children with ASD. Studies show that CBT is often effective at reducing anxiety, social phobias, and repetitive behaviors. Most often CBT is used with older elementary students through adults, and generally the intervention works best if the child has pretty good language skills, since most programs require some dialogue between the therapist and patient. Most of the CBT programs involve having the patient explain in detail what the problems are and generally help the patient take a different perspective on whatever is challenging.

There are several ways that CBT can be implemented: often the child is asked to develop a hierarchy of least to most fearful or least to most difficult situations and then is rewarded for attempting to engage in those situations in small steps. Say a child has an irrational and excessive fear of dogs: he could make a list of least scary to most scary interactions with dogs. At the top of the list might be watching a movie about a dog; on the bottom, actually playing with a dog. With the therapist or a parent, he could then start at the top of the list and "rethink" the fear. In this case, he could learn to substitute the thought "Seeing a dog in a movie is completely harmless" for "If I see a dog in a movie, it might be dangerous and I couldn't handle it." When he's successfully watched a certain number of minutes of a movie without reporting or exhibiting the fear, he would get a reward. This would be repeated several times to ensure the step was mastered. And then the therapy would move on to the next scariest task, such as visiting a park with dogs playing far away from him but within his eyesight. Most programs also involve getting detailed feedback on the anxiety or fear levels, often charting the patient's level of anxiety at regular intervals in different settings.

The children are also coached on how to help their perspective-taking skills in terms of rethinking situations that may cause anxiety: for example, in a social situation, the child may be taught to ask herself how a friend might feel about her if she offered the friend some of her chips at lunch, creating an awareness of other people's points of view that might not come naturally to a child on the spectrum and that might help her alter her behavior to be more sociable.

Similarly, the child may be taught to deliberately alter the way he thinks about situations that are causing anxiety. For example, a child who feels anxiety about people not liking him in social situations, or about not knowing what to say to new acquaintances, may be taught to rethink the situation and to self-instruct, changing the patterns of his thoughts from "What if no one likes me? I always fail in social situations" to the far more positive "My friends like me and will be there to support me." Or if he has a tendency to think, "I never know what to say to my friends," he can learn to change that thought to "I can ask my friends a question, like how was their weekend, or what did they do last night." Learning to review those automatic negative thoughts and then self-instructing to change them to something positive can help a child reduce fears and anxieties. Research has shown that it *is* possible to change the way you think about things—you just have to go about the process systematically and gradually. Most importantly, negative beliefs about fearful and difficult situations change the most when self-instruction on positive ways to think about the situations is combined with actually facing the situations in small steps.

The best CBT programs usually have a parent education component, since parents can be very helpful in implementing programs and can support them in natural settings. Interestingly, these types of programs can also help the parents. Many parents of children with ASD get depressed and blame themselves for their child's behavior problems, which makes effective parenting more difficult. A CBT-trained therapist can teach them to stop thinking, "I can't help my child; I'm not doing a good enough job," and instead tell themselves, "I know how to deal with this problem behavior"; studies show that just changing the way they think about their children and their problems allows parents to become more effective.

CBT can bring about an improvement in self-confidence, self-reassurance, and positive thinking, all of which are helpful to children on the spectrum, as well as their parents, especially if used in conjunction with other effective programs.

JEFF'S STORY

When we started working with Jeff, he was a three-year-old who had all the symptom areas of autism, including difficulties with social communication and restricted interests. However, most problematic for the family was Jeff's apparent hypersensitivity to certain noises.

Jeff's mom first noticed that he didn't like some sounds when he was about eighteen months old, but his reaction had worsened over time, and now it seemed like the noise of vacuum cleaners, blenders, hand mixers, and many other similar things caused him physical pain. This problem had greatly affected the family's daily routines and consequently their quality of life. For instance, they could only vacuum when Jeff was asleep or out of the house, and often weeks went by when they weren't able to vacuum their home at all. Similarly, although Jeff's mother enjoyed cooking, she was limited to what she could make without using the blender and the hand mixer. Finally, because they had to avoid the sound of a blender, they had to stop going to their family's favorite smoothie and juice bar.

The problem had become so severe that at the mere mention or sight of a vacuum cleaner, hand mixer, or blender, Jeff would run away, crying, screaming, grinding his teeth, and slapping his hands over his ears.

Jeff's desensitization program for the vacuum consisted of fourteen steps. Each individually designed step in a desensitization program is based on making a bit of progress toward the end goal, but in such small increments that it will desensitize the child to the irrational fear. For Jeff, the first step was to get him used to hearing the word "vacuum" without going into a panic and also to get him comfortable with the sight of the vacuum. To do this, we played Jeff's favorite games and activities while the vacuum cleaner was in the room. Once in a while, we'd look up and point out the vacuum, saying its name.

Next, we moved on to getting him used to the noise. We started by turning on the vacuum in his parents' room with both the bedroom and hallway doors shut—you could barely hear the noise. We continued to play with Jeff with that slight sound in the background. Again, this step was so tiny that he was okay with it. Then we gradually opened the hall door. When he didn't appear bothered, we gradually opened the bedroom door—first a quarter of the way open, then halfway, then all the way. We moved the vacuum to different rooms, so he would be used to the sound no matter which direction it came from. Finally, we turned on the vacuum just outside his playroom but out of sight. By this time it was pretty loud, but we just kept playing calmly with Jeff. Although he looked up a few times, he didn't seem to be excessively bothered, and he just went back to playing. In fact, most of the time he didn't even seem to notice the vacuum at all.

Again, each step in his program consisted of either increasing the decibel level of the vacuum or decreasing the distance between it and Jeff in gradual increments. This whole process took just a few weeks, which was a relatively short time in comparison to the years that his fears had been an ever-increasing problem. Jeff only showed anxiety a few times, and these were mostly during the first week of therapy. When he did, we moved back on the hierarchy. If, for example, he had difficulty with the door being halfway open, we moved back a step so it was open less than that, then we reopened it more gradually.

The final steps involved gradually moving the turned-on vacuum cleaner into the same room as Jeff. Overall, it took about *five weeks* to get Jeff to the point where his mom could vacuum any room in the house at any time.

Unfortunately, while his phobia of the vacuum was completely eliminated, there appeared to be no generalizing to blenders, so we had to develop a hierarchy for that, too. We started by having Jeff and his mother go outside their house to engage in some of his favorite activities while the blender was turned on—so far away, it was barely audible. The two of them slowly moved closer and closer to the door, then gradually entered the house into a playroom area that opened onto the kitchen. Once Jeff was comfortable inside the house with the noise, we began turning the blender on and off, just as they did at some of the family's favorite juice, ice cream, and coffee shops. Next, we took him to the shops. Again, we continued to play Jeff's favorite activities just outside the stores that had blenders while gradually moving him closer to the door. After he showed no discomfort, the program was complete, and Jeff's family was able to go to any restaurant or shop without a problem.

Interestingly, once Jeff's desensitization program for the vacuum and blender had been completed and we tried yet another appliance—the hand mixer—Jeff had no adverse reaction to the new noise, no screaming or crying or covering his ears, as he had previously. This boded well for all future unexpected noises.

Jeff's behavior had been worsening to the point where it was severely affecting his family's life. It took just around a month or two to desensitize him to each noise with sessions only a few times a week, and finally, the family could engage in activities that had been off-limits for over a year.

FAQ

QUESTION: A student in my class is obsessed with lining up items. He has flash cards with the numbers one through ten, and he can put those in order even though he hardly knows any words. Should I discourage him from lining up items?

You may be able to channel the lining up into appropriate activities.

We worked with a four-year-old boy who also knew only a few words but liked to line items up. His mother bought him alphabet flash cards, and within a day he could line them up from A to Z without any trouble. He also could line them up from Z to A just as quickly. Because his visual abilities were so superb, we started teaching him to spell words of desired items. Eventually he was able to use a small computer to spell words. Although he continued to have some difficulties with verbal communication, he could easily recognize words.

Channeling fixations into appropriate contexts can lead to new strengths for the child.

> **QUESTION:** My granddaughter likes me to pick her up. However, I can never seem to get it right. She keeps repeating "Not like that," then makes me put her down and try again. I never get it right, even after dozens of tries, and it makes us both frustrated and upset. Any ideas?

We worked with a child who had the same problem. We tried putting a rule in place that her mother would pick her up, and if that wasn't right, she would try just one more time. Then that was it. Although it was rough the first few times, eventually she learned that if she wanted to be picked up, she would have to be satisfied with the first or second try. This is another example of how setting a firm rule and sticking to it can make your life easier.

> **QUESTION:** My seven-year-old daughter likes to wear the same outfit every day. If I don't let her, she cries and throws tantrums and it's difficult to get her to go to school. So I often just let her wear the dirty outfit. Is this bad?

For both health and social reasons, your daughter has to learn to change her clothes. We've found some ways to help with this. We used a self-management program with one child: we started with just one item, such as his socks, rewarding him when he put on clean ones, and gradually added more items until all his clothes were different.

Another preschooler we worked with insisted on wearing a Mickey Mouse dress every day. One day her mother just put it away, and while she protested for a few mornings, she was always fine by the time she got to school. Another mother of a fourth-grader found that the fabric of the clothing was the variable that made her child want to wear the same outfit every day. Taking her shopping and letting her pick out clothes that felt comfortable solved the problem and increased her wardrobe.

> **QUESTION:** A student in my class is fixated on cars. He repeatedly names the different cars when we go out. It can get really irritating, and the other children make fun of him. Any ideas?

You may want to start teaching him to use the car naming in an appropriate way. For example, we worked with a young adult who was fixated on old movies. His favorite activity was to repeat lines from various movies and talk fixatedly about various characters. Since he seemed to enjoy the movies so much, his mother began using them to help his conversation skills, getting him to discuss the lines and characters in a more social way. After about six months of this approach, he began working at a movie theater and was a great consultant to ticket buyers. As a perk, he also got several movie passes a week and almost always invited a friend to accompany him to the movies, which was a treat for both.

So, in short, you may be able to teach this child to name the cars in a social way, like talking to you in a dialogue about cars, rather than simply naming the cars to himself, thereby providing him with an appropriate way to use this skill when he's out in the world.

> **QUESTION:** My son likes to pretend he's a character or an animal. It's impossible to get him to stop and speak normally once he's declared himself to be Batman or a spider or whatever. He'll even go to school that way and growl when someone talks to him. What do I do about that?

First of all, you may want to try to figure out if there's a reason for this. For example, if he's growling at the other children, he may be trying to get their attention and socialize with them. In that case, he needs to learn more appropriate replacement behaviors (see chapter 3) or appropriate ways to interact socially (see chapter 5). Also described in chapter 5 are ways to turn such behaviors into appropriate social games. Again, tweaking these desired activities to turn them into appropriate games can help your child engage in a desired activity while also learning to socialize with peers.

A MOTHER LOOKS AT FEARS AND FIXATIONS

Along with some more useful traits, I inherited from my father an intense and ir-rational fear of spiders. The man used to empty an entire can of Raid onto an unsuspecting tiny arachnid, and I soon learned to follow suit, although tissues were my chosen weapon. A fold, a squish, a toss, a flush, and the world had one fewer Charlotte in it.

I don't know how it happened, but I gave birth to a child—my second, Leo—who for years absolutely loved anything that crawled, crept, or flew. He especially adored spiders. He learned enough about spiders to know that most breeds in southern California don't bite, and as a result he would pick up any spider he saw and let it crawl over his hands. He would also bring it over to show me.

I like to support my kids' interests, even if they're not mine, so I would smile and nod and try not to let him see how totally freaked I was.

Leo also liked watching spiders in their natural habitat and would call to me to come see an unusually beautiful web, an egg sac that had just hatched, a spider that was red and gold and shone in the sun. . . . I actually liked looking at these things—especially if there was a window between me and the sight—and found it easier over time to move closer to the spiders we were watching. At times, I honestly agreed with him that these things were wonderful to see and even awe-inspiring.

Leo started to collect spiders in jars. He would catch moths and small in-sects and put them inside for the spiders to eat. At first I made him keep the jars outside, but gradually the spiders moved into our house. One day I looked around the kitchen and realized I was surrounded by eight spiders in eight little jars. And it didn't bother me at all.

Not long after that, I found myself holding out my hand when Leo brought a spider to show me. I let it crawl around my palm while we both admired its markings and cute little face.

And I realized I was no longer afraid of spiders.

Since then, I've petted tarantulas, caught wolf spiders, watched tiny house spiders scurry across a wall or over my desk, and not once have I been tempted to get out a tissue.

I had been *desensitized*, acclimated to the sight and even touch of spi-ders so gradually and consistently that I didn't even realize I was getting used to them. Leo didn't set out to desensitize his mother to spiders—he did it without even trying. But it's an amazingly effective approach to irrational fears. Trust me, I know.

Back to Andrew

We've been lucky with Andrew. He hasn't had a lot of irrational fears. Sounds have never bothered him any more than the rest of us. Smells sometimes do, but his reaction isn't fear, just a general nausea. He's always been able to sit through a scary movie filled with blood and gore and tension and not be fazed at all.

The one thing that did make him fall apart consistently for years was when we were late picking him up from somewhere. If I were as little as three minutes late, he'd be quivering with nerves, and if I were ten minutes late, he'd be a total wreck, crying out of sheer terror that I'd never show.

This was a tough one to fix. One day we were supposed to pick him and his brother up after a tennis lesson, but the traffic was awful and we were fifteen minutes late, and it took Andrew a full hour to calm down—he just couldn't stop crying. Meanwhile, his younger brother was waiting at his side, completely calm, slightly bored, certain we'd be there soon.

We tried working on this fear in various ways, preparing Andrew ahead of time on days when we knew we might be a few minutes late, suggesting activities he could do while he was waiting, promising him over and over again that we'd never forget, that we might be late but we'd always come eventually . . . but still he'd fall apart.

When I mentioned to Dr. Koegel how tense it made me to know that Andrew would fall apart publicly if I got caught in traffic and was late picking him up, she suggested we get Andrew his own cell phone. This was long enough ago that we had to clear it with the school (now every single kid has a cell phone—back then, not so many), and it turned out they were fine with cell phones, so long as they stayed in backpacks and off during the school day. The phone changed everything. Andrew's breakdowns were based on the fear that we'd never show at all or not until everyone else had left; the cell phone allowed us to reassure him that we would, in fact, be there soon.

Andrew always liked to impose order on a world that must have seemed even more chaotic to him than it did to the rest of us. When he was little, he lined things up, putting everything in its (same exact) place time after time. As he got older, he memorized his daily schedule and, if anything changed, grew anxious and had to know why. And to this day, when the family is in a new, strange place, like an airport or train station, he doesn't like the younger kids to wander more than a few feet away from us—he worries. So this irrational anxiety probably sprang from his need to feel that everything would happen according to plan and that events were under our control. Unfortunately, no matter how hard you try, there are times when you can't predict what's going to happen (and traffic in L.A. is, at best, unpredictable—at worst, it's intolerable), and the cell phone at least gave us a chance to let him know that, while we might be a few minutes late, the world wasn't about to spiral out of control as a result.

Fixations

Like I said, Andrew hasn't had a lot of fears. Fixations, though . . . those he's had in abundance.

While Andrew's fixations worried us initially, once Dr. Koegel told us we could use them as the basis of games and socialization rather than spend all our time trying to steer him away from them, we started appreciating the fact that he had some pretty interesting interests.

Andrew's first noticeable fixation was with letters. He loved the alphabet and would spend hours arranging foam letters in order, A to Z and back again. Since he was only two when he started, we thought it proved that he was a genius in spite of his lack of language. We bragged about his mastery of the alphabet to his first speech therapist, who looked more concerned than impressed at being told Andrew knew all his letters. "Of course he does," she said. "Kids like this usually do. You need to get him to play with age-appropriate toys and with other people."

So we did what we could to get him interested in shape sorters and stacking rings, but at least the letters did lead to Andrew's being an early reader. Even better, one of the first times I saw him truly laugh in a social way was when a friend sang the alphabet song to him and deliberately reversed a couple of the letters. Andrew thought that was hysterical—it was basically the first joke he ever shared with someone. So for all that letters could make him withdraw from the world, we discovered that, with a little effort and creativity, we could also use them as the basis of a shared game. Once we met Lynn, we discovered that our friend had stumbled by accident onto a strategy that the Koegels had been using successfully for years.

Moving On to Presidents

At some point around kindergarten, Andrew fell in love with the presidents of the United States. I can't even remember how it started. He saw a grouping of them somewhere, I guess, and they seemed to strike the same kind of chord that the alphabet did—a distinct arrangement of similar objects that can be put into order time and time again. Within days he had memorized the order of all the presidents, something I'd never come close to knowing. He also drew them constantly.

Weird, yes, but also strangely appealing. We discovered that a lot of our male friends had a similar obsession with the presidents when they were kids (none of our female friends had, for some reason), and everyone liked to talk to Andrew about them. Presidents' Day, which used to mean nothing more to us than a day off from school, suddenly became one of the most important days of the year for our family. We'd throw a party and invite lots of people and make Jell-O flag cakes, and Andrew would get up in front of everyone and list all the presidents from Washington to whoever was currently in the White House. Then we'd all cheer. He was the hit of the party.

His fixation on presidents continued to come in handy all through elementary school, where his teachers frequently called on him to tell the class which president was in office during which time period or who someone's vice president was. The other kids were, I think, genuinely impressed by Andrew's knowledge.

At Dr. Koegel's suggestion, Andrew's aide at school once made up a running game where the leader named a president and you had to shout out his vice president to continue. Andrew totally ruled at it, of course, and it added yet another boost to his budding socialization skills.

The Beatles

I know a *lot* of kids with autism who love the Beatles. Once again, I suspect it has something to do with a group of objects that are similar yet different enough to merit arranging and rearranging. (Their music is good, too, of course.) At any rate, Andrew fell in love with them and pretty soon was drawing the four Beatles on every piece of paper he could find, carefully dating each one—1964, 1968, 1972—and making sure their facial and cranial hair was accurate for that time period.

A couple of our adult friends are into the Beatles, and Andrew set up his own "Beatles Club" with them and their kids. They met every now and then, and Andrew used to call them all when something big happened, like Paul McCartney's 2003 announcement that his new young wife was pregnant. The Beatles were a great restricted interest, since they lent themselves to lots of different family activities—we listened to their music together, watched movies (I've always thought that *A Hard Day's Night* was one of the best films ever made), bought posters, and collected books about them.

At the same time, we worked with Andrew on understanding that not everyone was as interested in the Beatles as he was and that if he wanted to talk about them to someone else, he had to make sure that person was interested. If he saw signs of boredom (yawning, looking away, attempts to change the subject, and so on), he had to stop talking about them. (I kind of wish everyone I knew used these guidelines when making conversation.)

Greek Myths

My absolute favorite fixation of Andrew's was Greek mythology. (Think about all the Greek gods—yet again, you have a bunch of similar figures with slight differences that can be grouped and arranged in hierarchies.) When he was nine or ten, he came across *D'Aulaires' Book of Greek Myths* and loved it. His younger brother started reading it over his shoulder and got equally interested, and over the next few months, they both went on to read every collection of myths they could get their hands on.

I loved Greek myths when I was a kid, so this was one fixation I really got excited about. I took both boys to the Getty Villa; we went to the antiquities section, and I had my ten-year-old and my eight-year-old running around, examining different vases, and enthusiastically crying out, "There's Apollo! Look, it's Dionysus!" And so on. It was great.

We tried to expand Andrew's range of interest to other ancient mythologies, like the Egyptian ones, by buying books that weren't just about the Greek gods. We also bought more general books about ancient Greece and Rome, hoping the interest in one part of their culture would spur some curiosity about its other aspects, but he mostly just looked up the sections on mythology. His interest never really moved past the actual Greek myths.

Some fixations last longer than others, and Andrew lost his interest in Greek myths before I was ready for him to. His interest in the Beatles resurfaced, probably because so many people admired his Beatles drawings and responded so enthusiastically to the Beatles as a conversation subject—Andrew had reached a point in his social development where he valued something that helped him to connect to others.

A less-fortunate fixation also cropped up—a passionate attraction to the characters of the video games he was currently playing. One of my favorite Andrew drawings was one he did when he was probably about ten or eleven, showing the four Beatles—side by side with the Mario Brothers. Like they belonged together.

So . . . Are Fixations Okay?

I once met a boy with Asperger's who was extremely interested in fruit bats and who would quote long passages from a field guide to bats, entirely from memory. Tons of people like to listen to the Beatles. Not so many are devoted to fruit bats, and unfortunately, this boy's rote memorization in that one area didn't help him make casual conversation.

But there's no question in my mind that, with a little effort on our part, Andrew's early fixations did him more good socially than harm. He went to a summer camp where the director knew him well, and every summer "Coach" Steve Morris made sure he included some games that he knew Andrew—who wasn't usually crazy about sports—would play. They had a Beatles Day, when the four competing relay race teams were named John, Paul, George, and Ringo, and one summer they held the Greek Olympics. Andrew happily participated and, as the resident expert in these areas, strutted around like he was the boss of the whole thing.

It's an odd thing that so many kids on the spectrum share similar interests (I've met a bunch more who liked the Beatles, the presidents, and/or the Greek gods), but these fixations brought so much good into Andrew's life—socially, artistically, even physically—that I didn't really ever see any reason to question why they were there. Because we worked to modify them and turn them into social activities whenever possible, his fixations created a bridge between him and the rest of the world that might not have existed otherwise.

Ten Years Later

I liked Andrew's fixations. I miss the Beatles. And the Greek gods. They're not part of our daily lives anymore, although I do think that the hours Andrew spent drawing both contributed to the artistic talent he has today—and the feeling of satisfaction he gets when he can draw something simply for his own amusement.

There are still some subjects that interest him more than others (he's incredibly knowledgeable about celebrity birth dates and theme parks now), but I don't think I'd go so far as to say he has restricted interests. Or maybe he does but keeps them to himself—thanks to the Internet, you can spend a lot of quiet time reading about things that interest you without having to inflict them on anyone who lives with you (speaking of which, if you know any great cooking blogs, send them my way—I love wasting time reading recipes and no one else around here shares my fascination with cooking). Anyway, when Andrew's hanging with us, he makes an effort to talk about whatever we want to talk about, which is the important social thing.

Anxiety

Without getting too specific, I think I can safely say that Andrew battles anxiety. This isn't a huge shock to anyone in my family: my husband and I are anxious people ourselves, and of our four children, only one is truly free of anxiety issues. So when I think about Andrew and anxiety, I go back to the question I asked in an earlier chapter: how do you know what's autism related and what's just . . . you know . . . personality? Isn't he likely to have been an anxious person whether or not he had autism, given the family genetics? And, if so, should I even be bringing it up in a book about autism?

Well, here's the thing: people need support and help with excessive anxiety, whether or not they have a diagnosis of any kind. And my experiences with Andrew, my friendship with Dr. Koegel, and the actual research have all taught me that a behavioral approach is the most efficient, effective, and long-term way to improve areas of discomfort, so that's where we've turned—mostly—for help with the anxiety issues that bedevil our family.

You *can* rewrite the way you react to situations. It just takes some effort. ("It just takes some effort" should be Dr. Koegel's and my motto: we'll have to have T-shirts made.) Cognitive behavioral therapy is a well-regarded approach, one that can teach some people to stop old unhelpful thoughts in their tracks and replace them with new, positive ones. So we've pursued that kind of therapy at various times and in various ways.

But Dr. Koegel has taught me that it's even more important to work on the root cause of the anxiety—helping to refine shaky social skills, say, or using desensitization to reduce excessive fears. Confidence comes from feeling competent and prepared.

I won't sit here and tell you we've had an easy time dealing with anxiety in our family, that a few interventions have blown it all away for any one of us. But, bit by bit, we're all figuring out how to beat the demons back and extend to ourselves the same courtesies we extend to our friends: trust that we're capable, patience when we make mistakes, and respect for what we manage to accomplish. Anxiety and fears can be paralyzing but they don't have to be. So long as you do the work.

Chapter Seven
Education: Finding the Right School
Placement and Making It Even More Right

QUESTION: My three-year-old child is ready to enter school, and I'm not sure what to do. There are some "autism classes" through my school district, but I like my neighborhood preschool that his older sister attended. What do you recommend?

QUESTION: My fourth-grader is attending a regular education class with a pullout special education program. She's falling far behind, and the school is recommending that she attend a special day class. The other children are fabulous with her, and I'm concerned that she'll be upset if she's moved. Do you have any suggestions?

THERE are many school options for children with autism, and parents usually have a pretty good intuitive feel for what's best for their child. Still, decisions regarding school programs can be very challenging. It's not easy wading through options about placement, IEP goals, specific programs, level of support, and so on. There's just so much to take into account—most important, your child's needs.

The choices for placement can range from full-inclusion settings, where children go to a regular classroom in a regular school and participate with typically developing peers, to special day classes that have only children with disabilities. In between those vastly different choices are programs with varying numbers of opportunities to interact with nondisabled children. Some families are more comfortable putting their child with other disabled children, and some prefer to see them in a fully included classroom. But regardless of what educational placement you decide on, you need to make sure your child is in a good program with trained staff, who will provide the quality and quantity of intervention your child needs.

The Benefits of Full Inclusion

My personal belief is that, whenever possible, children with autism should be included with typically developing children throughout the day—what we call "fully included." However, full inclusion doesn't come without its challenges and stressors. We'll discuss these below, but first let me tell you why I prefer full inclusion.

First, children with autism have difficulties in communication and social areas. If we place them with other children who have those same difficulties, they don't have opportunities to practice newly learned behaviors and learn what is age-appropriate behavior and what is not.

Next, typical children are fabulous models and helpers. Forget what you've heard about children being mean to each other. For the most part they aren't. If the program is set up properly, the typical children will be mentors, helpers, and friends. At every school I've visited, I've found students who were interested in what we were doing and eager to be an active part of the program. Even without any special effort, these kids help our kids: the research clearly shows that children in regular education have many more social opportunities to interact with typical children than those who are kept in special education. That's important for the development of social skills.

Furthermore, we often find a large discrepancy between the behavior required of children in special education classes and that of those in regular education classes. Children in regular education classes are expected to pay attention to the teacher, line up quietly, and respond to the teacher's instruction the first time. When a child with autism is fully included, these same expectations also apply to him, as they should. However, many special education classes are not able to have these same expectations, largely due to the difficulty of educating ten or fifteen children with disabilities that vary greatly in severity. For example, a special education teacher may be willing to repeat an instruction several times, while a regular education teacher expects the students to follow directions the first time. By having to "play by the rules" of the regular education teachers, your child will be more likely to behave like typically developing children. And if children in the special education classroom have disruptive behaviors, your child may learn those behaviors and not understand that they're not appropriate. To put it simply, a child's environment has the power to move him in both positive and negative directions, and you want as positive an influence as possible.

The curriculum is also usually vastly different in regular and special education classrooms of the same age. For example, the ten-year-olds in one special education class I visited spent the morning getting pedicures. Although the children seemed to be enjoying this activity, there was no curriculum involved, no teaching activities, nothing academic. I have never seen this type of activity being implemented for a whole morning in a regular education classroom. We want our kids to be doing whatever the typical children are doing, with some modifications if necessary, and that's simply more likely to happen in a regular education classroom.

Finally, many years of research have shown that children who are fully included have better outcomes than matched control children who are placed in special education classes. And these outcomes are not just academic—they also do better behaviorally and emotionally. So if your goal for your child is to have him function within society's mainstream, remember that it's never too early to work toward that. In fact, the younger the better.

Let's talk about another issue. What happens to the general education students when a child with disabilities is included in their classroom? If you're thinking it might harm their education in some way, you're wrong. In fact, research suggests that when a child with disabilities is included into a general education classroom, *all* the students perform better. Maybe it's because there's added support; maybe it's because the general education teacher learns to individualize the curriculum and implement other strategies to improve behavior, which benefits everyone; or maybe it's because it broadens the perspective of the peers, which leads to additional learning. Inclusion is beneficial from an emotional and psychological standpoint, too: it increases the students' empathy, creates diversity in their everyday lives, and opens their minds to greater learning. In fact, many students who assist with specialized educational programs end up going into the field as a career.

Now that I have expressed my preferences about inclusion, I will also admit that going the inclusion route does have its challenges.

Schools Aren't Always Open to Full Inclusion

The first and most fundamental obstacle is that education is an evolving science, and inclusion is a relatively new process. Although your child is entitled by law to participate in the "least restrictive environment," some schools don't even have a fully developed inclusive program.

I worked with a preschool child from a small community in southern

California whose parents elected to enroll him in their local preschool, where his sister went. They contacted the director of special education to request an aide for six hours a week to help him with communication and socialization. The director said that if their son had autism, he would have to be in their special autism program. He refused to bend on the subject, so it went to fair hearing. I testified on behalf of the child, pointing out that he was succeeding quite well in the regular education preschool classroom, and that what he really needed was to learn how to interact socially and verbally with his peers, something that this setting was providing an ideal opportunity for. The child was already attending the preschool—successfully—but just needed some additional support to encourage socialization.

The testimony of the fair hearing trial gives you a pretty good sense of how unwilling the school was to give the family what they were asking for. The testimony went something like this:

SCHOOL'S ATTORNEY: *Lynn [he seemed to find it humorous to refuse to call me Dr. Koegel], have you ever worked in the public schools?*

ME: *Yes, I worked in the public schools as a speech and language specialist.*

SCHOOL'S ATTORNEY: *Did you ever work with any children who were in special education classes?*

ME: *Yes.*

SCHOOL'S ATTORNEY: *And did you ever help any of them?*

ME: *Yes, but back then there weren't really many children who were included.*

SCHOOL'S ATTORNEY: *I didn't ask you that. Let me reiterate my question. Did you ever feel like you helped any of them?*

ME: *Yes.*

SCHOOL'S ATTORNEY: *Lynn, let me ask you another question. Do you testify often on behalf of families?*

ME: *Not often, but occasionally. Usually the districts try to work out their differences before—*

SCHOOL'S ATTORNEY: *Lynn, I don't want any additional information. Just answer the question.*

FAMILY'S ATTORNEY: *Objection, Judge. If Dr. Koegel doesn't give her the answer she wants, she harasses the witness.*

JUDGE: *Please let Dr. Koegel answer the question.*

SCHOOL'S ATTORNEY: *Let me ask another question. In your court experience, Lynn, have you ever testified on behalf of a family who wanted their child in a special education classroom?*

ME: *That is a complicated question. Placement is an individual decision, and I have trained and worked with many teachers and staff who teach in special education classrooms, but in regard to testimony, usually the reason the cases go to court is because the only option the schools provide to the parents is a special education classroom—*

SCHOOL'S ATTORNEY (IN A NASTY VOICE): *That wasn't what I asked. Just answer "yes" or "no."*

FAMILY'S ATTORNEY: *Objection. Judge, if the school's attorney thinks she knows everything, let's swear her in and let her testify. She is badgering the witness. If the witness doesn't give her the answer she wants, she cuts her off.*

JUDGE (TO SCHOOL'S ATTORNEY): *Please let the expert witness give her opinion and fully answer your question.*

This type of questioning went on and on for hours, but several months later the ruling came. The family won everything. Not only did they get the aide in the regular preschool, but the judge ordered that the entire tuition be paid by the school (something that the family hadn't even asked for) and that the school reimburse the family for all past expenses, including the previous year's tuition and aide time. We had won, but it took a lot of time and effort to fight that battle. It may seem like this scenario was from the dark ages, but it wasn't. This happened in 2002. What's worse, that was more than a decade ago and I'm still dealing with the same issues. I'm working with a family now whose son is in a special day class in the third grade. His test scores in every area are average to above average yet he's mainstreamed for less than an hour a day. One day the parent was observing him in his regular education classroom, and she overheard some of the students complaining that they don't like it when the "special education" students come into their class. This is wrong in so many ways, and it's the kind of stuff that makes my blood boil. The way to defeat that kind of thinking is by including the students *more*, not less: when students with disabilities are just a regular part of the classroom—as in full inclusion—they're usually simply accepted as "one of the group." Their presence isn't even questioned—it's *not* including them fully that makes their peers think they don't belong there at all.

The story continues. That same parent asked for her son to be included for the full day so that social areas could be targeted while he was around his typical peers, and the public school responded that they don't fully include special day class students, and they don't provide any specialized intervention programs in the regular education setting. So . . . now we have an unsigned IEP (since the parent refused to sign because the school wouldn't include the child in regular education), a gifted child (who excels in math) spending almost the whole day in the special education classroom, the school saying that they can't provide any special education services in the regular education classroom (not true), and a big fight on our hands. This makes me unhappy.

While schools are becoming more aware of the need for inclusive programs, we are still in a transition period from a time when no children with autism were included in any public education program. Unfortunately, moving forward takes time and for students with disabilities sometimes it takes decades—which means some students aren't getting what they need while they're still in school. This shouldn't be the case. Parents should have the inclusion option. While some schools are willing, there still is discrimination—and battles to be fought.

JAY'S STORY

Many years ago, I included a child with some disruptive behaviors into a regular education classroom. During difficult assignments he engaged in escape behavior, and when he wanted an item, he sometimes engaged in aggression because he didn't have the words to request it. The school was adamant about having the child in a special education classroom, so, after repeated meetings and a lot of stress, the family eventually compromised on half time in the regular education classroom and half in the special education classroom.

Because a first goal was to eliminate the disruptive behavior, we took data on each incident. Interestingly, he had much lower levels of disruptive behavior in the regular education classroom than in the special education classroom. Part of the reason his disruptive behavior was higher in the special education classroom was because his classmates' disruptive behavior bothered him. He constantly put his hands over his ears when the other students made inappropriate noises or were loud or disruptive. Once they realized he behaved more appropriately in the regular education classroom, his parents wanted him in there all the time—they knew it would lower his disruptive behavior overall. So they requested an IEP. Unfortunately, the director of special education was firm in her belief that he shouldn't be included at *all*, much less spend all day in the regular education classroom, where, she made it clear, he was not welcome. Hearing that, the mother, who was the head nurse at a local hospital, became quite agitated and told the director of special education that the next time she was admitted to the hospital, the mom was going to make her leave because *she* wasn't welcome.

Two things struck me. First, it seemed like it was okay with the director if the child aggressed toward other children with disabilities but not if he aggressed toward typically developing children—after all, he was far less likely to be aggressive in the regular education classroom, so she wasn't concerned about cutting back on his overall aggression, she just wanted him far away from the typically developing kids when he acted out. That was a chilling thing to realize.

Second, many people—like that special education director—don't realize the prejudice they show toward individuals with disabilities when they exclude them from all sorts of experiences. People like that don't stop to think how they themselves would feel to be cavalierly excluded from an important place (like, yes, an emergency room). It's almost like they treat the child as a problem that needs to be shut down and not as a human being who can grow and learn.

Just last week I was consulting with a family whose child, an older elementary student, was placed in a special education classroom and was mainstreamed for only a half hour a day. The child happens to be on or above grade level in all subjects; however, the school told the parents that he had trouble "staying on task" in both the regular and general education classrooms. But the staff hadn't implemented any programs to address his off-task behavior other than "frequent redirections." They had never attempted to understand the root cause of the behaviors and didn't know how to set up a self-management program. So they weren't trying to address and fix the problem at all; they were just using it as an excuse to pull him out of the classroom.

In addition, the school indicated that he only interacted with adults and didn't engage appropriately with the other students except to direct them when he felt they were breaking the rules. Their goal was to stop him from being "bossy" to the other students—they didn't even stop to think about whether this was his attempt to connect socially to his peers.

What the student needed was to be in the regular education classroom with a self-management program to address his off-task behavior; he also needed to be taught appropriate replacement behaviors so that he could interact positively with the other students when they were breaking school rules; and he needed lots of social instruction so that he could build up his repertoire of appropriate peer interactions and develop friends. None of these areas were being addressed, and what's more, the staff told the parents that no specialized services (speech therapy, occupational therapy, etc.) could be provided in the regular education classroom or during recess if he was fully included. (Sounds a bit like blackmail, doesn't it? "You can only get the services you want when you do what we want.")

When I began consulting, the mother said she knew her son didn't have the best program at school, and she felt terrible that she hadn't done something about it earlier. She was a very famous medical doctor with extensive training in pediatric cardiology, so I sent her an e-mail that said: "I feel so badly for you—if a parent took their child to you for medical advice, you would never expect them to come up with their own treatment plan, nor would you provide them with what *isn't* state of the art. It's too bad the school can't do the same for your child."

The point is, we still have a long way to go with preprofessional and professional training, and we need to make sure our schools are updated on the latest state-of-the-art procedures, so they can do what's best for our children.

How can we avoid situations like this? We all know that a big battle isn't good for anyone, especially our children. The best thing is to make sure the program is set up correctly from day one and that it includes evidence-based interventions. Parents need to be familiar with the interventions so they can suggest strategies that work well with their child. Team meetings, monthly if possible, are always helpful for coordinating programs and making sure everyone is doing his or her part. Trust me—getting in a battle is no fun. If you do your homework, handpick a teacher, get the right support with the right programs at the right time, your life will be a lot simpler. Your child will learn more, and when you drop her off each day at school knowing that she has a good program, your stress level will be lower and you'll be a lot happier.

Parents Aren't Always Open to Full Inclusion

One of the surprising truths I've discovered is that while kids are usually fine with children with disabilities, a lot of parents of typically developing children aren't. Believe it or not, some parents refuse to let their child participate in a class that includes a child with a disability. And the ironic thing is that, in my experience, the kids of the parents who object most strongly usually have some kind of behavioral problem themselves.

Take Brendan, for example. His forceful and assertive mom actually passed around a petition the first week of school to the parents in the class demanding that a child with autism not be included in the class. She did get about ten signatures, but the school did not change either child's placement. Turned out that every time—and I mean *every* time—I worked in that classroom, Brendan was getting in trouble for behavior problems, not my kid. Amazing.

Usually these parents (and sometimes the teachers and administrators) worry that having a child with a disability in the class will negatively affect the curriculum. Does a child with autism, who needs specialized programs, drag down the rest of the class? *No.* Actually, the opposite is true. When children with disabilities are included in regular education classes, *all* the children perform better! As I mentioned above, I'm not sure why, but it's a good thing.

Hard for Families to Compare

Sometimes it's emotionally hard on parents constantly to see their child with peers who are the same age but developmentally ahead in many areas, and this can become a psychological stumbling block to putting their child into a fully included environment. That's totally understandable. Just try to remember that the gains for your child are what's important here, and that his inclusion benefits the whole class. Only by placing your child in this environment will you consistently expose him to the types of activities children do in typical settings. Further, although your child may have areas of need, you'll be able to develop appropriate academic and social goals by assessing what typical children are doing in their everyday settings.

GETTING TO SCHOOL HAPPILY

Most children with autism interact more comfortably with adults than with other children, as most of their therapy has been with adults. This may make them reluctant to go to school, where they have to be with kids their own age all day long. Sometimes the child expresses this passively, by acting lethargic and making it tough for you to get him ready; other times, he might actively protest or even become aggressive.

Here are some ideas to get your child heading happily to school.

Use Rewards

When you think about it, many children have a legitimate reason for not wanting to go to school—there they are, having a great time at home with fewer demands (and maybe the intervention provided at home has motivational components included so that it's fun—see chapter 11)—and then suddenly they have to go to school, where it's all about work. Not a lot to look forward to there. And in many regular education classes, school days start with circle time, a highly verbal activity that's often difficult for children with autism. If your child is having trouble going to school, you may want to ask the teacher if you can bring him in early for a few minutes of his favorite activity, like playing with a cherished toy, watching a video, or reading a familiar book. If he knows there's something to look forward to upon his arrival in the classroom, he's likely to be a lot more enthusiastic about heading there.

Help Your Child Keep Track of the Time

Let your child know how much time he has left before he needs to leave for school. Ten-minute warnings, then five-minute warnings, then two, and so on can often help a child accept the transition more comfortably.

You can also use a timer for the same effect—either an egg timer or a kitchen timer can be helpful and provide a visual reminder of the time remaining. But be sure to leave right when the timer goes off, or your child will learn not to respond to it.

A word of caution: some kids learn how to turn the timer back, so make sure it's out of reach if this becomes a problem.

Priming with Pictures

Try using a picture system in the morning to let your child know what activities are coming up. Take pictures of your child going through his morning— eating breakfast, getting dressed, getting on the bus, and so on—and make sure you include a picture of his teacher greeting him at school. After each finished activity, the parent can prime the child for what's coming next—some parents like to put Velcro on the back of the pictures and move them to the "finished" side of a cloth board after the activity is completed, while other parents prefer putting all the pictures onto a ring and flipping them over as each activity is completed. Later in this chapter, I'll explain how to use priming to prepare your child for all school activities: this system can be used for transitions throughout the day. That way, the child feels prepared for the next thing and isn't taken by surprise. This can really help a child who has difficulty with transitions.

MAKING SURE SCHOOL IS ENJOYABLE FOR YOUR CHILD

My younger daughter had one tough year in elementary school. About a month into the school year, she started saying her stomach hurt and she didn't want to go to school. After this happened a few times, I started probing. It turned out that her teacher, who was new that year, constantly yelled at the children. My daughter was never personally yelled at, but it really upset her when the teacher yelled at her friends. I have to admit that outside the school context, this teacher was a lot of fun and had a nice, friendly personality with a great sense of humor, but everything was different when she was with a whole bunch of kids. I went into the class to observe and saw that the teacher would goof around with kids until they got too rambunctious, then she'd yell at them to get them back under control. Some students may have been fine with this teacher, but she wasn't a good match for my sensitive daughter. The principal wouldn't allow me to transfer her to another classroom, so I spent a lot of time at school that year. I wasn't the only concerned parent, but I must say that we had a pretty miserable year.

Teachers and aides in both regular and special education classrooms can be punitive if they aren't good at behavior management. And some teachers aren't good at making the curriculum interesting, so the children will act out because of boredom, and then the teachers will react to the disruptive behavior in a negative way, rather than warding it off in the first place. As I describe more thoroughly in chapter 3, on disruptive behaviors, punishing bad behaviors is far less effective than reinforcing good ones and much more likely to make school an unhappy experience for all involved. It's just as easy to say, "Let me see how nicely you can line up," and then reward the children for lining up quietly, as it is to punish them for not doing so, and it's far more likely to lead to a classroom of children who take pride in behaving well. In addition to learning to control behavior through positive procedures, some teachers will need support in developing curricula that are interesting to their students (see below for more on that).

How to Choose the Right Teacher

Finding the right teacher is critical, especially for families of children with autism, since there's so much personal interaction involved in the special programs. Generally, principals are supportive of our parents' requests for a particular teacher and let our staff and our parents observe teachers. They'll even make time for the teachers to meet and observe the child to help everyone find the best possible match.

When you're observing a teacher, here are a few things that are helpful to consider:

- **DOES THE TEACHER HAVE GOOD BEHAVIORAL CONTROL OF HER STUDENTS?** Some teachers just don't have good control over the children. They haven't learned how to use reinforcement to encourage the children to behave. But don't assume that because a classroom is noisy and busy, the teacher doesn't have control: wait to see whether the children listen and follow the teacher's instructions when she speaks.

- **IS THE TEACHER ABLE TO INDIVIDUALIZE THE INSTRUCTION FOR THE VARIETY OF STUDENT ABILITIES IN HER CLASSROOM?** Every child in the class will be at a different level, but some teachers find it difficult to adapt the instruction so each child can be challenged without being overwhelmed. Try to find teachers who can teach to different levels.

- **IS THE TEACHER WILLING AND ENTHUSIASTIC ABOUT HAVING YOUR CHILD IN HIS CLASS?** Some teachers love having children with special needs in their classroom and will even request them. But even if a teacher you like doesn't seem enthusiastic at first, talk with her. I've found that sometimes even really good teachers are afraid that they'll fail. By reassuring them that you'll work together so that they can develop the "special skills" to help your child achieve, you can often help them overcome their concerns. On the other hand, if the teacher has a reputation for not being enthusiastic about having a special needs child in his class or isn't willing to expand her knowledge to learn techniques that may be helpful with your child (and probably the typical children as well), you should probably steer clear.

- **IS THE TEACHER ORGANIZED ENOUGH SO THAT PRIMING CAN OCCUR?** Priming—which, as I discuss below, simply means preparing your child ahead of time for future lessons—can be critical to your child's success. Teachers who don't have a lesson plan usually aren't that great to begin with and definitely won't be able to provide priming assignments.

- **DOES THE TEACHER USE A COMBINATION OF VISUAL AND AUDITORY CUES TO HELP DIFFERENT TYPES OF LEARNERS?** Children learn in different ways. Some learn faster with visual cues and others with auditory cues. So the teacher who can present both visual and auditory cues will have the most success with different types of learners in the classroom.

- **DOES THE TEACHER USE POSITIVE BEHAVIOR SUPPORT STRATEGIES TO CONTROL BEHAVIOR, RATHER THAN PUNITIVE STRATEGIES?** Again, a teacher who relies heavily or exclusively on punishing strategies will not provide a pleasant environment for any student. Remember, we want our children to learn because they're excited about learning, not because they're trying to avoid a punishment.

- **DO THE CHILDREN IN THE CLASSROOM INTERACT WELL WITH AND ENJOY THE TEACHER?** Do the students hang around the teacher at lunch and recess and while she's walking to the teachers' lounge? A good student-teacher bond is important, as your child will be spending the next year with this person. Further, kids will work harder for someone they like and will seek information more readily from someone who's approachable.

- **ARE THE TEACHER'S CLASSROOM ACTIVITIES AND CURRICULUM MEANINGFUL?** Children have a harder time learning information if it's not presented in a practical and meaningful way. It's a lot more work for a teacher to develop meaningful activities (more on that below), but those who do are much better teachers, especially for children with special needs.

- **DOES THE TEACHER INCORPORATE MOTIVATIONAL STRATEGIES INTO THE TEACHING?** Learning can and should be fun. Specific strategies are described in chapter 11 that you can look for when you visit the classroom. For instance, do the activities have natural reinforcers? Are activities varied frequently to keep the children's interest? Are the children being rewarded for trying? Are the students provided with choices? All of these strategies help keep a child's interest.

- **IS THE TEACHER WILLING TO WORK WITH YOU AND THE SPECIAL EDUCATION STAFF TO SET UP SPECIALIZED PROGRAMS?** Your child may benefit from strategies such as a peer buddy, sticker chart, or self-management program. This means that a specialist will be in the classroom to develop and coordinate the program. A teacher who looks forward to learning such strategies will make the whole process easier.

- **IS THE TEACHER A "TEAM PLAYER"?** The best programs require a coordinated and consistent effort. Some teachers and special education staff members aren't open to any other opinions. They have their way of doing things and that's it. I've been in this field a long time—since before some of these teachers were even born—and I've seen a lot of children struggle because of a lack of coordination. The research clearly shows that a consistent and coordinated program results in the best outcomes and without that—without the teamwork—your child will not have the best outcome.

- **IS THE TEACHER COMPETENT?** This may sound like a silly thing to say— after all, teachers have to go to graduate school, student teach, and complete all of the state requirements to get a credential. So it seems self-evident that a teacher would know how to teach, but there's a lot they need to master in the time that it takes to become a teacher. And some teachers just don't have a whole lot of tricks in their bag. They may lack important skills, like how to implement a good systematic reading program with measurable goals or how to address behavior problems that may arise in the classroom. A few extra questions may be helpful to determine competency. In fact, I was recently interviewing candidates for a special education staff position at a school where I consult. The school had narrowed the search down to two people. I developed a standardized set of questions to ask so that I could systematically compare their answers. I asked them about discipline and one of the teachers said that if a child is acting up in his classroom, he has the child sit on a big round yoga ball (I'm not sure if this was supposed to be a punishment or a technique to help the student focus—either way it isn't a traditional behavior management technique) or has the student stay in from recess. The last thing we want is for a student to stick out like a sore thumb or to be punished and have to miss important socialization opportunities. Fortunately, the other candidate had a whole lot of positive behavioral support strategies in her repertoire, so it was an easy choice!

INSIDE THE CLASSROOM

I frequently go into classrooms where the child with autism will be sitting in the corner with an aide, working on a completely different assignment from the rest of the class—he might as well be in his own classroom! One time, I found all the other children in the classroom singing songs, while the child with autism was stacking blocks with his aide. This was a kid who *loved* singing, and he kept looking over at the other children longingly, but every time his attention drifted, the aide redirected him back to the block-stacking task. Obviously he should have been right in there with his class.

You might be wondering how a child with autism could work on the same assignments as the others if she has difficulties in communication, but it is possible. Here are some ways to make it work, no matter what your child's level.

Curriculum

Before we start talking about ways to help your child succeed in school, I want to make sure that you pay attention to the curriculum. Many students with disabilities are expected to follow curricula based on standardized testing—but children with autism often have behaviors that interfere with accurate testing. And because most standardized tests don't have any naturally reinforcing consequences, many children with autism aren't interested in trying hard on these tests, so standardized tests tend to be more representative of a child's behavior rather than his ability. We have research that shows that standardized tests often underestimate the abilities of a child who's on the spectrum. And if her IEP is based on these standardized tests, your child may be spending the rest of her life with a curriculum that's below her academic level.

I've seen a similar situation, where a child becomes disruptive during academic tasks that are difficult, so rather than making the curriculum more interesting and therefore more engaging, the instructors develop one that's far below his level. So if you're feeling like the goals are too easy for your child, you're probably right. Show the staff what your child can do under the right circumstances, and make sure the IEP goals will help your child progress and learn new skills.

CLASS'S MATH PROBLEM:	YOUR CHILD'S PROBLEM:
14	4
+ 15	+ 5
———	———

Partial Participation

Partial participation involves having your child work on the same *type* of task or assignment as the other children, but scaled to her own level. Say the class is doing a math assignment, such as adding and subtracting using two-digit numbers, and your child can only add in the ones column. The assignment can be simplified accordingly. For example, your child is still participating in the math assignment with her classmates, but since she's still working on adding figures in the ones column, the tens column has been omitted.

Other assignments can be adjusted similarly. If your child is working on the initial sound of words, and there's a spelling test, the rest of the class could have blank sheets of paper, and your child could have all the letters *except* the first one on the sheet.

Just about any assignment can be reduced into parts so that your child can partially participate in all class activities. These curricular revisions can be made by special education staff at your school—all the teacher needs to do is make sure she gives them the class's assignments ahead of time. Or you, yourself, can make the alterations, again with the teacher's assistance in acquiring the assignments beforehand—but don't feel obligated if you're too busy. This is the school's responsibility, and the materials they develop will be helpful for many future students, so they should see the benefits of making the effort. And so long as you make sure it's written in your child's individualized educational program, the school *will* need to do it.

Shorter Assignments

Similarly, your child may be able to complete the same work as the other students but need a little more time. No problem. Most teachers are happy to reduce the number of problems. In fact, this technique worked great for my oldest daughter when she was in fourth grade. The class had dozens and dozens of math calculation problems. Even though she was great at math, she started making lots of mistakes. We noticed that most of her mistakes were at the end of each assignment. Luckily she had a wonderful teacher, Jackie, who agreed to let her do only as many problems as she wanted and simply grade her on the number she completed. In other words, each problem would count for more points, so it was even more important she get them correct. Not only did her accuracy increase, but her enthusiasm did as well. And it didn't hurt her in the long run—she's a medical doctor now! In fact, it may have helped her motivation.

Pointing Out Relevant Cues

Children with autism often have difficulty attending to the most critical cues in an assignment, and that can affect schoolwork. For example, a child with autism may not notice whether the problem is an addition or subtraction problem. If you heighten the cues—in this case, by darkening the plus and minus signs—you can ensure that your child pays attention to them. Similarly, you can highlight relevant parts of the directions to make sure that your child completes the assignments correctly. Even during reading lessons, you can emphasize (if you're reading aloud) or highlight (for silent reading) relevant parts of the text. Of course, these cues will need to be gradually and systematically faded over time, so your child can respond like the others, but starting this way may help him learn to attend to the right cues.

Aids

If your child is really having difficulty in a certain area, he can try using aids like a calculator or a speller. If your child needs to use these tools to help complete assignments, that's fine. Just be sure to keep in mind his areas of need, and if necessary, teach those areas outside of class time, so he won't always be dependent on the aids.

Doing Error Analysis

An error analysis is where you try to understand an underlying problem by analyzing the errors—it's fairly similar to figuring out why behavior problems occur by analyzing the underlying motivation, as described in chapter 3.

Your child is going to make mistakes. When he does, you may find it helpful to do an error analysis. Often, the solution will then be a simple one. For example, you may find that your child is getting low grades on complicated math problems because she doesn't know her multiplication tables. Knowing this, you can focus on practicing the multiplication tables, rather than simply assigning more of the same sort of work without addressing the core problem. Or if your child misses the last few math problems of every homework assignment because she gets fatigued, fewer problems can be given with more points for each problem.

Again, you want to figure out what the basic underlying problem is whenever your child has difficulty, so you can figure out the simplest solution to it.

Priming

Priming is a great way to help your child succeed in school—it involves going over the assignments prior to when they are presented in class. The purpose of priming is to familiarize your child with the material in a relaxed, undemanding way. It should be fun and encouraging for your child, and it should *not* feel like he's being tested or penalized in any way. You want him to enjoy the material more, not less.

We have implemented priming programs with all grade levels, preschool through high school, and with all kinds of assignments, ranging from the work that will be done in class to the activities your child can choose from during free time. For a preschooler, it might mean reading a book at home one night that will then be read in the next day's circle time. For a high schooler, it might mean exposing him early to the next day's history lesson.

Priming can be individualized to the child's needs. For example, we worked with a third-grader who had difficulty understanding directions but not in completing the assignments. In her case, we simply went over the directions, then had her complete just one or two problems to make sure she understood them. That was all she needed to improve her class work dramatically.

Priming can be implemented by school staff, parents, or any other willing person. Some choose to prime the child in the morning before school, some in the evenings, and some right after school. For older children, a study hall or resource period provides a great opportunity for priming. But, as I mentioned above, for priming to be successful, you must have an organized teacher. When you're searching for good teachers, make sure you let them know that priming will be in the IEP—a teacher who likes to "wing it" in the classroom may not be a good fit for your child.

Make Things Predictable

Everyone has a problem with lack of predictability, but it seems to bother children with autism more than others. A written schedule or a picture schedule (for the child who doesn't read—see more specific directions for priming with pictures in the section on going to school happily earlier in this chapter) on the child's desk or in his binder allows him to keep track of his day and know what to expect next, while consistent warnings before each transition can make them all go much more smoothly.

If the schedule is going to change for an unexpected reason, such as an assembly or fire drill, make sure you'll be informed of this so it can go on the child's schedule that day.

Teach Flexibility

Having said that it's good to make things predictable, I also need to caution that following a schedule too closely without teaching a child how to be flexible in the face of change can cause big problems later on. I've seen families that always maintained such a tight and predictable schedule that the children continued to have meltdowns if there was a change, even after they had grown up and become adults! In fact, one adult we knew was detained by the police because his behavior spun out of control after his schedule was changed.

There are some things you can do to teach flexibility. Self-management works well, as you can teach the individual to use self-control when something changes. To do this you'll need to follow the steps we outlined in the self-management chapter. First teach your child to discriminate between the appropriate and inappropriate behaviors (in this case, you would teach her to stay calm when something unexpected or new occurs), then help her set up a system for keeping track of the number of times she succeeds in using the appropriate behavior. Make sure you set up rewards for achieving specific goals (e.g., she gets something she wants when she has successfully stayed calm and reasonable throughout a certain number of transitions and surprises).

Reward charts for engaging in appropriate behaviors when something unpredictable happens can also encourage a child to hold it together.

You can also teach the individual to self-instruct when there's a predictable pattern to the inappropriate behaviors: he can learn to say things like "It's okay if I go out to recess a few minutes late; I'll still have time to play with my friends" or "My teacher is helping me to be a better student by having me finish my homework," rather than having a meltdown. The child may need to be reminded on how to recast these thoughts initially, but with practice it should become easier and "self-instructed," not teacher instructed.

But make sure that everyone is coordinated on this. If one person is "fixing the problem" after a meltdown ("Oh, never mind, you don't need to stay in and finish your work during recess, go ahead and play"), that person is rewarding the behavior, making it especially difficult to get rid of.

INSIST THAT TRAINED STAFF BE AVAILABLE

School programs *never* seem to work if the school's staff members aren't trained. Everyone who will be interacting regularly with your child in any way needs some training in disabilities—the teacher, the inclusion specialist, the aide, the principal. Everyone. Although this seems logical, it doesn't happen in many schools. And training doesn't mean going to a one-day workshop on autism. It means the staff members need to have a comprehensive understanding of research-based programs that work (and work well) for children with autism. They need to understand behavior principles, how to deal with disruptive behavior, how to teach (in a motivating way) children with autism, how to create a meaningful curriculum for the classroom, how to include children with autism into regular education classrooms, and how to develop comprehensive social programs. It's also critical that the school staff be willing and able to coordinate goals across the child's environments, communicating with the parents and private therapists, so consistent programs can be implemented. And finally, new staff members need feedback from a trained professional on how they're implementing the procedures. Without this specialized training, your child may not progress.

Quality of Time, Not Quantity

It doesn't matter how good your goals are if they aren't being taught—or taught often enough.

Let me give you some examples. I recently went to a parent-teacher conference where the teacher told us the child was having difficulty reading. Now, this was a pretty sharp kid—he excelled at math—and I knew he had learned his phonics and could sound out words, so I was having some trouble figuring out how decoding could be so challenging for him. His reading rate was far below his classmates', and the teacher indicated that it was a huge problem and even suggested that he might have some major learning disabilities. I asked if

I could observe him during his reading instruction. The teacher gave me a date to visit the class during a "typical day"—a day when there would be no testing, special assemblies, field trips, and so on—which turned out to mean that I had to wait several weeks.

I arrived on the designated day to see that she had two students (mine and one other) at her table in the front of the room while the other students were quietly doing their work at their desks. The reading instruction began. The teacher asked the students to open their books to a particular page, and while they were doing so, several students came up to the teacher to ask questions. Each time a student approached her and asked a question she replied, "Remember, I told you when I'm working with a student you aren't supposed to interrupt me"—and then proceeded to answer the question. Mixed message indeed!

Next, an adult entered the classroom and chatted with the teacher for several minutes (I couldn't hear what they were saying but it definitely didn't have anything to do with the reading instruction). Finally, she attended to her reading lesson and had each child read one sentence. One sentence. That was all. Then there were more interruptions, and she had some discussion with the two students about the story. To my surprise, she then proceeded to roll her eyes and tell me how difficult the class was this year (which I didn't see at all—they were all very well behaved), and then she moved the two students to the floor (while telling me that they didn't have the focus she needed them to have at the table—from what I could tell, *their* focus wasn't the issue, hers was!) and had them read one more sentence each.

More students came up to ask her questions, which she continued to answer while simultaneously reprimanding them for interrupting her when she was "working" with students (notice I put "working" in quotes). When the reading period was over, I counted the sentences each student had read: in a half hour, they'd completed two sentences each. That was all. After that, the two students went to a pullout reading program for students who were struggling with reading. During this session the students were reading lines from a play they were going to perform. My little guy got to read another two sentences during the half-hour session—sentences he clearly had practiced reading many times before and had completely memorized.

So what did my observation show? That not much teaching was going on, to put it plainly. The sum total of the reading was four sentences in a full hour! And I also noticed that the teacher quickly jumped in and read any words my guy was having trouble with, so he didn't even have to sound them out himself, and the specialist just had him reading sentences he had already memorized. No wonder he wasn't making progress.

Simply put, if there isn't teaching going on, your child probably won't make much progress. And this isn't only an issue with academics. I consulted at a school where a child was working on social skills. The parents (accurately) felt that no one was working on socialization, so to make sure that the child was actually getting practice with social areas, the parents included the number of times the child should socially interact during the lunch recess in their IEP. One goal was that the student would approach a peer at least ten times during recess and either ask the peer to play or make a verbal comment to her and/or verbally respond to her. So here's what I witnessed when I came to observe how well this goal was being implemented: the aide walked the child up to a typical peer, prompted the child with ASD to say, "Do you want to talk?" then encouraged the other child to ask a series of questions, while prompting the child with ASD to respond. The aide had a little tally sheet and marked a hash each time the child responded. Within about two minutes, the aide had ten tallies and disappeared. Of course, the child with ASD went back to playing by himself, and for the rest of the lunch recess no teaching went on. At all. So, while the aide was fulfilling the actual number of recommended trials, the spirit of the goal—having the child engage in socialization with peers during the lunch period—was far from being fulfilled.

You need to make sure that the aide, teacher, and any specialized staff have the enthusiasm, energy, and commitment to make a difference in your child's life. They should be using each and every opportunity for learning and creating an environment where your child has ample learning opportunities— or it's just not good teaching.

If the school is lacking in these areas, the administration will need to hire an outside consultant to help. Many districts have been successfully sued by families because their staff members have not had training. In fact, this is such a common reason for schools getting sued that these days most schools are actively sending their staff for training or are bringing in specialists to provide it.

TACKLE SOCIAL ISSUES CONSTRUCTIVELY

The choice of teacher is obviously incredibly important in determining how happy your child feels in school, but the way he relates to the other students— and how they relate to him—can also strongly affect how comfortable he is in his own classroom. While there's no question a certain amount of luck is involved in the particular mix of students in any given class, you can use many different strategies to help your child reach out and make friends at school.

How Much Should You Disclose?

One of the biggest questions parents face when their child with autism enters a new class is whether to talk to the other children about their child's disability. Unfortunately, there's no one single answer to that question. It depends on the situation.

Ask yourself whether this knowledge would help or hurt your child. We have worked with some children who are so mildly affected that singling them out in that way would only have harmed them socially, but for others, increasing their peers' knowledge leads to more understanding, support, and empathy.

These days most people know what autism spectrum disorder is, but kids vary so much that, in general, the more others learn about your child's unique strengths and challenges, the more willing and able they are to help.

Information about disabilities and a particular child must be presented in a clear, well-thought-out manner. The presentation can be given by a parent, teacher, or a specialist, but it's important that whoever you choose knows the child well.

Presentations vary tremendously. Some focus only on a general discussion of disabilities without singling out any individual child, while others focus on a specific child with special needs. Some presentations are developed to span several different classroom visits over several weeks, and others are just a one-shot deal. Either way, a classroom discussion should be coordinated with or by the family and carefully planned. Most parents choose not to have their child there if the conversation is going to be specifically about that child. However, some more general programs have all the children participate.

Keep It General at First

When you talk to the children in your child's class, it's helpful to present the general topic of disabilities first. The presenter can touch upon common types of disabilities, such as impaired vision and the need to wear glasses. If you really want to give the children an idea of how it feels to have a disability, you can borrow some glasses, a hearing aid, or a wheelchair and let the children try it out. (I remember when I was taking classes in audiology and one professor required us to wear a hearing aid for a while. It was an eye-opener for me, as I had never realized the effect of having all things amplified equally. It was so weird being able to hear the people who were talking behind me just as well as the people who were talking in front of me!) I've seen kids get excited during disability awareness programs and start confiding their own difficulties in certain areas or relating stories about family members' disabilities. This will help to set the stage for talking about the individual child.

Then Discuss the Individual

Next, and only if the family is comfortable with it, the presenter can provide some specific information about the child with the disability.

We've done this in several ways. One parent whose child was in a regular education kindergarten but who was nonverbal brought a videotape with short clips of her child engaging in his favorite activities—swimming, eating ice cream, roughhousing with his brother, and so on. She talked to the class about how he was just another kid with similar interests to theirs, who just hadn't learned how to talk yet.

The idea here is to help the other kids get to know the individual child and to feel comfortable around him. Some parents like to discuss autism specifically (one parent sent a letter to each parent in her son's class when he was diagnosed), and other parents feel it's not necessary to label the child, preferring to discuss his symptoms. This is an individual preference.

Once the classmates understand your child's unique strengths, interests, and challenges, it's time to move on and provide some constructive advice.

Teach Strategies for Positive Interaction

It's important to teach the classmates *specific* strategies for interacting with your child and helping him to communicate. This is the time to be positive. Stress your child's strengths and focus on why the strategies you're discussing will help your child. Stress what a big challenge your child has had to overcome and give examples about how difficult it would be for all the students if they couldn't express themselves and couldn't ask for something simple like juice or water, or how they might not have as many friends if they couldn't learn to pick up on subtle social cues. Children *are* understanding and empathetic and will be able to put themselves in your child's shoes if they can relate your child's experiences to their own lives.

If the child you're discussing is disruptive and needs to learn replacement behaviors, talk to the children about helping to prompt these behaviors and about how to react when problem behaviors happen, such as ignoring them. (See chapter 3 for more on disruptive behaviors.)

If the child needs to learn how to make friends, this is a great time to recruit interested classmates to develop a formal "circle of friends." Many programs meet regularly with classmates and have them brainstorm ways to help the child with autism. In fact, we started a club for a fifth-grader with autism who was always alone. The club met every other week for pizza and discussion. By the end of the year, thirty kids had joined the club, and the fifth-grader never spent another recess or lunch alone. Kids are great interventionists, and we have found that with a little direction from the student's aide or a specialist, they're enthusiastic helpers. Let them help. It will be an invaluable experience for them and for your child. It's also helpful to find out from the peers—in a sensitive way—what social areas they feel would be helpful to target. We're sometimes surprised at how different their suggestions are from the goals we've developed, but peers know even better than we do what's age appropriate and relevant to their lives!

Encourage the School to Take a Role in Your Child's Social Life

Many teachers have a very good feel for a child's social needs and can easily pick out typical students who are likely to become good friends with your child. However, many schools simply don't develop comprehensive socialization programs for children with autism. In fact, most schools I visit allow children with autism to wander the playground aimlessly during recess, lunch, and free play periods. Some schools even offer the excuse that the kids "need a break." This is not okay. Children with autism need to learn how to interact socially, and often school is their only opportunity. Each and every recess, lunch, and free period is an ideal time to work on those areas. (See chapter 5 for more social skills interventions.)

Some things work, and others don't. It's critical that your child's behavior be measured on an ongoing and regular basis. If a program isn't working, changes need to be made. But only objective data, collected on a regular basis, will tell us this.

Start with a Baseline

When you write an IEP or develop an intervention plan, insist that each goal be measurable and that the child's progress be documented. To do this, you'll need to get an accurate and recorded baseline in each area—that is, how your child is currently doing. Is she spending 100 percent of the lunch period alone or only about half the time alone? When she's engaging in interactions with another child, what is she saying? What types of behavior problems is she having in the classroom?

I recently worked with a family whose kindergarten daughter had met all of her social goals according to the school staff, who were recommending that services be terminated. But just by observing her at school, we noticed that she never interacted with her peers. Upon further querying, we found out that all of the goals had been measured in "pullout" settings. None were measured in the classroom or at recess, and the success in the specialized environments hadn't generalized. So we had the staff retake the data in natural settings and, lo and behold, they agreed that there wasn't any social behavior going on outside of the isolated settings where the treatment had taken place.

Also, it's helpful if more than one person independently observes the child to make sure both adults are seeing the same thing. Your child needs to be evaluated by live observations during the normal school day, not just by what the test scores say when he's in a little office.

Once you have your baseline, you can make comparisons to it over time to see if the program is working.

Now Chart the Progress

You need to continue to collect the data in the same manner to chart the course of your child's progress (or lack thereof). For example, if your child spends all of his lunchtime in the corner of the playground watching the cars drive by, and the goal is for him to interact with other children, then someone on the staff will need to observe him regularly during lunchtime. Progress can be assessed while someone is working with your child, and also when that person backs off a bit, to see if your child can do it on his own. If the goal is for the child to talk to the other children at the lunch table, make sure that data are collected at the lunch table, with both quality (what he said) and quantity (how much he said) recorded.

Schedule regular meetings—biweekly or monthly, depending on the child—with your entire team, including the teacher, aide, and any specialists who are working with your child, to discuss programs, review progress, and create new goals. If programs aren't working, they should be adjusted. Things that work and don't work can be discussed by the team at these meetings. Remember that the goal is to improve the life of the child, so everyone needs to be on this wavelength. No hostilities, no accusations. You're all working together.

Pulling It All Together

We've discussed getting to school, finding the right teacher, addressing curriculum issues, and increasing social interactions. Billy's story will help you understand how everything can come together to help a child succeed in all areas.

BILLY'S STORY

Billy started coming to our clinic when he was three years old and not yet going to school. Billy's language was delayed, but he could communicate verbally. He had a lot of repetitive behaviors—he was absolutely driven to pick up anything off the ground that he could shake in front of his eyes. He would shake the object at the side of his head and watch it vibrate out of the corner of his eye for hours on end.

Billy also had some disruptive behaviors. When he was seated at a small table, he would often laugh continuously, scream individual words out of context, and knock the papers off the desk. Although he usually shaped up when we incorporated motivational procedures, we were aware that not all assignments are motivating, and he wasn't shy about letting people know if they weren't. He was a great kid to place with our beginning clinicians, as he would give them immediate feedback as to how well they were implementing the motivational procedures! With intensive work, Billy was learning to interact pretty well with adults, but he had no interest in other children whatsoever, so we decided he would benefit from a school experience.

When the school year started, Billy's parents enrolled him in a preschool for typically developing children. Stim still continued to be a constant problem for Billy, and he spent most of his recess time alone, shaking leaves in front of his eyes, so we had a clinician go to the school to prompt him to play with his friends during all of the outdoor times. It was slow, hard work, but he was improving. At the same time we kept plugging away at his language. His parents worked with him every night, and we taught them strategies to improve his communication and decrease his behavior problems.

We arranged for Billy to partially participate in all the classwork. This meant that he would engage in the exact same activities as his peers—all of them—but that the work would be individualized so that he could complete the parts of the assignments that were within his ability level. One really funny thing happened during an art assignment on a day when the school district had asked a psychologist to come observe Billy. The particular task that day was to glue curly brown acrylic hair on the head of cutout paper dolls. Billy wasn't great at art, and he really had no interest in it, but he had learned to partially participate in the activities, so he took a small handful of hair, dipped it in the glue, and plopped it down wherever it landed. Well, it just happened that it landed smack-dab in the middle of the paper doll—essentially the crotch area. The psychologist had a heyday with that. Although we tried to explain that Billy hadn't intentionally tried to create pubic hair for the doll, the psychologist refused to believe that there wasn't something devious going on in Billy's little mind. At least the teachers didn't seem to attach much meaning to the hair incident.

Despite that, Billy made significant progress in preschool. He learned to sit with the other children during circle time, to line up, to play with the children when redirected, and to participate to some extent in all the activities.

After the year of preschool came Billy's kindergarten year and a move from the private preschool to a public elementary school. Even though he had so far been included with typical children, this was the mid-1980s, and children with autism were not yet being included in general education classes on a regular basis. The principal didn't want him in a regular education classroom. The kindergarten teachers didn't want him in a regular education classroom. Even the director of special education didn't want him in a regular education classroom. But we wanted him in a regular education classroom, and so did his parents.

It was clearly going to be an uphill battle.

We started with the director of special education. His main concern was budgetary—Billy needed lots of support, and that was going to be expensive. The director told us that at that same school he had a deaf and blind student whose parents had sued the district to have him fully included. He actually said that since he was going to have to pay the bill on that one, he didn't want to have to provide intensive support for another child. So I told him that our autism center would provide the support. I actually liked it better that way; I knew the inclusion was more likely to be successful if we were able to implement the programs that were already working with Billy, using our own staff. Although highly trained aides can be expensive, we had a federal grant from the Department of Education to develop strategies to include disruptive children in the community, and Billy fit the criteria.

I also figured that if we could show the school system that including Billy was successful, they might be more willing to include other children with autism. One of the biggest problems is that many children with autism are included in the public school system with an untrained and unskilled aide. Because the aide isn't trained, the inclusion fails, the teacher wants the child kicked out of the class, and the child goes back to special education. But if someone skilled develops a comprehensive behavior support program from the beginning, the child is far more likely to succeed.

The next hurdle was the teacher. She was fresh and young and not too long out of graduate school. But she had never worked with a child with autism before—it wasn't that she was prejudiced against a child with disabilities, but she was the best teacher in the school, all the parents requested her, and all of her students reached a high level of success in her classroom. She was worried that she couldn't live up to her own standards with a child who had autism. We invited her to Billy's home to meet him. We served lemonade and cookies and had Billy's favorite toys available, so he behaved beautifully during her visit. We assured her that Billy was just another child with some challenges in some areas, whose needs could be best met in a regular education classroom environment. She decided that, while he did have some communication delays, she would be able to deal with him.

The most difficult person was the principal. He was a real jerk. His idea of solving a problem was to bully the parents and say nasty things about their child. But now that we had the director of special education and the teacher on board, he couldn't prevent Billy from being admitted.

The first two days of school, we decided not to intervene and to see how Billy would function without support. Those two days were a disaster. We had kind of hoped that there would be some positive carryover from his previous programs, but there wasn't. Billy screamed out-of-context words an average of two times a minute all day long—words like "refrigerator," "Chuck E. Cheese," and "triangle." He would laugh hysterically after each scream. The truth was that Billy was bored with the lessons, especially those that were highly verbal, and he had figured out a way to liven up the atmosphere. He also asked to go to the bathroom every twenty minutes. When he got into the boys' bathroom, he plugged up the sinks and toilets with paper towels, which caused the boys' room to flood. At recess time, all he did was shake twigs and leaves in front of his eyes. It was clear that, without the right programming, Billy's inclusion would have been a disaster.

After two days of figuring out that Billy wasn't going to adjust on his own, we threw ourselves into action and immediately implemented the programs that had previously worked, and things changed overnight. Every evening, we previewed the next day's class materials (priming), going over the tasks he would do in class and the stories he would read during circle time. We instated a self-management program for good behavior, and his pediatrician authorized us to let him go to the bathroom only during recesses, at which time he was accompanied by an adult who didn't let him engage in his water play and clogging games. We sent extra snacks to school with him every day to share (see chapter 5 for more on encouraging sharing to make friends), and we stayed on top of him during every recess, prompting him to play with his friends. Unfortunately, those first two days had left their mark. By the end of the week, after considerable pressure from the school principal, the director of special education had called an emergency IEP. We knew what was on the horizon. Although we had implemented a number of programs, and the significant behavior problems were now at a minimum, it was too late. We were completely expecting the school staff to send him to a special education class under no uncertain terms.

However, there was an interesting turn of events at the emergency IEP. It started out pretty badly, with the principal blasting the parents for the lousy kid they had and asking how they could ever have thought of putting a child with autism in *his* school with *his* best kindergarten teacher, and on and on and on. It was torture. If I'd been Billy's parent, I would have burst out in uncontrollable sobs, but they sat quietly and patiently listened to his diatribe.

But then, to our surprise, the teacher spoke up. She said, "I think Billy will do well in my class, and I want to keep him there." I was in complete shock when she said that, as Billy's parents and I knew that she'd been apprehensive about the whole inclusion thing from the start. I could have kissed her—finally there was one person, and a critical one at that, on our side. There was dead silence in the room for about thirty seconds while everyone, including the nasty principal, stared at her.

With the teacher saying she wanted to keep Billy in her class, the principal couldn't find an argument for taking him out. We had succeeded. After the meeting, I privately asked the teacher what had made her change her mind about Billy. She told me that just prior to our emergency IEP, she had had another meeting with a parent whose child was also having difficulties in kindergarten. She said that the principal had treated that family badly, and she hadn't had the courage to speak up, but when he did it again, she just couldn't keep quiet any longer. So it was really a matter of lucky timing.

Interestingly, about ten years later, this same teacher had a child with Down syndrome. I always thought what a lucky little boy he was to have her as a mother. Not only had she developed a number of skills, but her attitude regarding disabilities was now positive because of her experiences. In fact, I found out that every year after Billy was in her class, she requested that a child with significant disabilities be fully included in her classroom!

By the end of Billy's kindergarten school year, he had stopped the screaming and could generally engage in the same activities as his peers. Sometimes he needed a little help, but he did participate the whole day. Eventually the teacher took over the self-management program, so Billy's aide was actually able to fade during parts of his three-hour kindergarten day. The principal did manage to suspend him a few times during the kindergarten school year, but he was never able to transfer him into a special education classroom like he wanted.

Billy also developed a budding romance with one of his classmates, a cute little blond-haired, blue-eyed girl named Lexi, who followed him everywhere. She especially admired Billy for being the only boy in the class who was willing to go into the playhouse. Billy would play the dad and she could be the mom, and for her it was a lot more appealing than having to argue another little girl into being the daddy. Even though Billy was not a talkative father, he was perfectly able and willing to hold the dolly and give it a bottle while Lexi did the household chores. She sat by him at every recess and circle time. If he moved to another spot during circle time, she followed him like a starstruck fan. To encourage the friendship, Billy's parents took Lexi out a few times a week after school, for ice cream, McDonald's, or whatever seemed like fun. They kept the play dates short and centered on specific activities, because if there was any unstructured time, Billy isolated himself and started stimming. But Billy now had a friend.

The summer after kindergarten, Billy's dad lost his job in a mass layoff at his company. The family moved to another state but kept Billy fully included in regular education classrooms. They continued with the same types of interventions at school, and Billy continued to improve.

In high school, Billy got As and Bs and was in all regular education classes. He had lots of friends and loved playing the piano. He joined the track team and was one of their star athletes. He ran marathons and went dirt biking. He dated, went to his school dances, and called girls on the phone. And girls called him. He was a tall, talented, and really nice guy.

By high school, he was a great conversationalist, but it took some effort using self-management to get him to ask questions during social interactions. The one thing that worried me then was that he still had some attention-seeking behaviors, like belching and farting, but my teenage daughter assured me that all boys had these habits, and although the girls thought they were disgusting, he *was* a normal teenage guy.

Now Billy is an adult. He has a job and pays his own rent for the apartment he lives in. Although his parents describe him as a "late bloomer" in relation to the opposite sex, he has a long-time girlfriend whom he spends all of his free time with. She's a talented singer, so they enjoy music together—he plays the piano and she sings. It was a long haul in the beginning, but each year got easier and now he's a completely independent, employed adult, with hobbies and a girlfriend.

FACTS

No conclusive data suggest that children perform better in special education classes, but a growing body of research suggests that inclusive settings offer social and academic benefits. In fact, recent research using two groups matched for parity, with one group in regular education and the other in special education, suggests that the children in the regular education programs outperform those in the special education classes. And what's more, the typically developing students perform better when children with disabilities are included in their classrooms.

FAQ

QUESTION: My child's teacher says that he has academic limitations and I should put him in a special education classroom. He has no behavior problems but can't keep up with the other students. Is this a reason to find a more restrictive placement?

Your child's teacher may not know about partial participation (see the section on it earlier in this chapter). If he does the same things as the other children, he will continue to be exposed to all the things typical children are exposed to.

This is important, because if you want him to be able to participate in typical settings as an adult, he'll need to learn what to do in these settings. You can't learn what you're supposed to be learning if you're being given a completely different curriculum from your peers.

You really can't—and shouldn't—predetermine a child's academic limitations. I can speak on this from personal experience. When my daughter was in fourth grade, I came to school one day and found her outside the classroom, working at a small table with one other student. When I asked the teacher why she was outside, he replied that those two girls were bad at spelling, and so he was giving them fewer words than the rest of the class. I responded that if she was such a bad speller, wouldn't it make more sense to give her *more* words, not *fewer*? He looked me straight in the eyes and told me that my expectations for her were too high and that she would never be able to have an academic career. Well, this "nonacademic" person got straight As in high school, was class president and coeditor of the school newspaper, participated in Mock Trial and Model UN, was a biochemistry major at one of the best universities in California, completed medical school at Stanford University, and is doing her residency at Harvard. I can't imagine what she would have been like had I believed that teacher! In short, don't give up on your child based on one person's opinion. Kids often can do things we never expected—but we need to make sure they have the opportunities to do so.

This example shows why you need to make sure that your child is working at his maximum potential. Don't assume he needs all assignments simplified, and don't go overboard in making them easy: make sure you've done a functional analysis first. If you remember, I did have a teacher give my daughter fewer math problems on tests one year, but that was because I had determined fatigue was a factor in her making careless errors, not to "go easy" on her. In fact, this is why I usually like to try priming before I start having a child partially participate in an assignment—I would rather give him a boost that way than immediately start altering the work for him. But partial participation is a good resource when necessary.

QUESTION: I'm a fourth-grade teacher. A child in my classroom doesn't need a full-time aide at school but has trouble getting started on assignments and takes up an inordinate amount of my time. Any ideas?

You may want to find a peer buddy for your student—that is, pair him with a child who's willing and able to steer him in the right direction. A peer buddy who's competent in the subject area may be able to help this child get started on assignments. The buddy would benefit from this responsibility as well. Also, consider having the parents or a special educator prime him. This can work well with following basic instructions.

> **QUESTION:** My child falls asleep a lot during the afternoons at school. Her teacher has suggested that she attend a half day of school instead of a whole day. Would you recommend this?

Before deciding to have your child attend school for fewer hours, you may want to assess a few things. First, is the sleeping a function of the activities? For example, I observed a child in a high school special education class who slept through some activities but not others. His sleeping was a result of boredom during some of the activities. By rearranging his schedule a bit, we were able to have him take his physical education class during the activity he slept through and then return to class for activities he enjoyed. Second, how is your child sleeping at night? A program designed to improve her nighttime sleeping (see chapter 8) may result in more awake time during the day. Third, have the school keep your child awake during the day even if this means building in frequent walks or other activities that invigorate her. Sleeping in school or on the bus can interfere with nighttime sleeping.

Again, there are a number of reasons why your child may be sleeping, and these should be investigated first, before you pull her out of school.

A MOTHER LOOKS AT SCHOOL

In the chapter on social skills, I wrote about how Andrew's first school experience was in a regular mommy and me class. "Full inclusion," right? Only we didn't know what full inclusion was yet—we didn't even know our kid had autism. At that point, he was just the difficult kid in the class who didn't talk or play like the others, and I felt lonely and isolated. No one was asking us for play dates. In fact, none of the other moms talked to me much at all.

After Andrew was diagnosed, we switched him to a different mommy and me program because our speech therapist felt that the teachers there were skilled at including kids with special needs into their regular classrooms. The teachers had been fully informed, and it wasn't long before I was telling every other parent there that my kid had autism. It just felt so much easier than trying to pretend my kid wasn't different, and moms went from looking down their noses at both of us to being quite sympathetic. I was no longer treated like the bad mother of a strange child—I was the brave mother of a child struggling to overcome a neurological defect.

Still didn't have any play dates, though.

Andrew was supposed to learn to separate from me in this class, but that just didn't happen. He was way too nervous and used to being with me—he had been my constant companion for two and a half years, and even the birth of his infant brother hadn't changed that, so he'd cry hysterically anytime I'd try to say good-bye for a quick coffee break as the other moms were already doing. Unlike the other kids, he just couldn't understand the concept of "Mommy comes back"—Mommy was either there or she wasn't, as far as he was concerned. One day I realized that for weeks I'd been the only adult other than the teachers in the room. Alone again. Naturally.

In the Hospital

Since we were struggling with the separation issue, Dr. B. J. Freeman, who had diagnosed Andrew with autism a few months earlier and was continuing to counsel us, recommended that we put him into her Early Childhood Center Partial Hospitalization Program at UCLA's Neuropsychiatric Institute—a very long, fancy name for what was effectively a day school for kids with autism. Andrew didn't seem to be making any kind of progress where he was, so we decided it couldn't hurt to give special education a try.

Wow. What a relief. Andrew went from being "the weird kid" in class to being one of the two most beloved students in the entire school. There was a little girl there who was also three years old, who had black curly hair and the biggest, most beautiful brown eyes I'd ever seen, and everyone fussed over her and Andrew because they were both so adorable. In fact, Dr. Freeman told us at one point that she had to tell the caregivers and teachers in the program to start demanding more from Andrew and the cute girl. "They just bat those big ol' eyes of theirs, and everyone lets them get away with anything," she said, laughing. I loved that people were finally appreciating my kid.

Now remember that Andrew had never separated from me up till this point, except to be with his dad or the one babysitter he knew well. So when we brought him there the first day, we weren't sure what was going to happen.

"Just leave him," said the nurse who ran the self-help skills part of the program. "He'll be fine."

"Really?" I said.

"Really," she said firmly. So we did. We left Andrew with her and walked out. His screams were so loud we could hear them all the way to the elevator.

I was close to tears all the way home. All I could think about was whether Andrew was still screaming for me. The phone rang an hour or so after I got back, and it was the nurse.

"He's fine," she said. "He stopped crying right after you left."

I immediately felt better, and even though he continued to scream every time I said good-bye (and again when I picked him up), the nurse assured me he never screamed for long.

Turned out that nurse was a kind, lovely liar. One of the undergraduate volunteers at the clinic back then told me years later, "I never heard a kid scream for as long as Andrew did. Those first few days he was there, he basically didn't stop crying and screaming all day long."

I don't blame the nurse for lying to me. I think it was the right thing to do. Andrew ultimately did learn to be happy at that school and just had to get over that hump of not being able to say good-bye to me. It wouldn't have done me any good to have known he was crying so much—I would just have felt worried and upset, but I still would have made myself leave.

The good-byes were painful, but I loved having Andrew at that school. For one thing, that nurse got him out of diapers and into underpants, something I don't think I could have done for another year or two. With her help (and incredible patience—she just put him in underpants, took him to the bathroom regularly, and didn't seem bothered by any accidents), he "got" the idea of using the potty, and once it clicked, he was 100 percent trained, even at night.

The other caregivers and teachers (all young, most of them UCLA students or recent graduates) were also amazing. Andrew was learning a lot, but in a loving environment where people knew his strengths and weaknesses.

I would have kept him there forever.

Forever Not an Option

Unfortunately, that program wasn't set up for long-term stays. Also, because it was run out of a hospital, it was wildly expensive. Think of any hospital stay you've ever had and how much you've been charged for every single little item and scrap of food, and you have an idea of what I'm talking about. Our medical insurance was willing to pay for a few weeks of it as "treatment," but they would only okay a week or two at a time, and after about six weeks, they wouldn't okay it anymore.

Dropping kids off and picking them up always turned into an impromptu support group session, and one day we parents were talking about the cost of the program and how difficult the insurance companies could be, and one of the other moms said, "I have this family ring that my mother handed down to me. It was my great-grandmother's originally. I'm selling it so I can keep my son here a while longer." She looked at all of us: she was close to tears and I think we all were too. "He's making so much progress—and what better use could I make of the ring? I mean, this is what matters, isn't it?" She was right, it was what mattered, but that didn't make her sacrifice any less heartbreaking.

At any rate, the insurance company stopped paying, and Dr. Freeman said it was time to move Andrew back into the real world anyway. Like Dr. Koegel (whom we hadn't yet met), Dr. Freeman felt it was extremely important for Andrew to be around his typically developing peers.

We had to find a new school for Andrew.

The Special Ed Preschool

Our local public school district drove me nuts. The staffers were absurdly, almost comically disorganized. I spent hours on the phone and in person with various people answering questions and filling out forms, even having Andrew checked out by one of their medical doctors. They said they would call me back with a placement for him. I didn't hear from them for a month. When someone finally called me, she said, "So . . . let's get started. I'll need some information from you. How old is Andrew?" It was as if the hours and hours of previous interviews and exams had never even happened. I actually burst into tears, out of sheer frustration.

Finally we got a recommendation from them, checked it out, and enrolled Andrew in a public preschool class for kids with language disorders that met for a couple of hours each morning. We loved the teacher, but, a few months after Andrew started, she got promoted to an administrative job, and, once she left, the class no longer seemed well run. Andrew always did best with structured activities (he could stay engaged if an activity kept his interest), but every time I came by, the kids weren't doing anything much at all, which meant he was wandering around, making hand puppets. That school was also on the other side of town, and I was tired of abandoning my newborn baby to a babysitter just so I could cart Andrew halfway across L.A. and back. (One of the unwritten laws governing the lives of parents of kids with special needs is that decent special education classes are always on the other side of the universe from where you live.)

The "Regular" Preschool

Meanwhile, in the afternoon, Andrew was testing his feet in the waters of a neighborhood preschool that had come highly recommended by several friends, who said it was warm and nurturing. When I first approached the school about Andrew, they couldn't have been nicer. "We'd love to have him," they said. "We feel like kids with special needs improve everyone's experience."

Great, right? Only when Andrew actually started going there, it was a total bust. Part of it was my fault—I should have hired an aide for him but thought we could do without one (more on that below). But part of it was their fault—for all their welcoming attitude, the school's staff didn't want to actually change their approach to help Andrew assimilate. For example, his teacher believed in talking endlessly to the kids whenever they seemed upset, rather than distracting or redirecting them. I would say good-bye, and Andrew would cry, and this teacher would pull him on her lap and say, "Are you sad Mommy's gone? Because Mommy will come back, you know. I know you're sad that Mommy had to leave. But Mommy loves you." And so on. The problem was, Andrew was nonverbal then, and his comprehension was pretty delayed. So the teacher would go on and on, and all he was hearing was, "Blah blah blah *Mommy*. Blah blah blah *Mommy*." She was essentially *taunting* him with my absence. He'd cry even more, and eventually they'd call me and tell me I had to come right back, because my kid couldn't separate.

I, of course, suggested that the teacher try redirecting him to a favorite toy when he was crying. She refused. She said she knew what kids needed and that distracting him was a denial of his feelings. I said that was what they had been doing at his previous school, and it had worked. She said if he was sad, she had to validate his feelings, and that she had been a teacher for a very long time. I said I had been Andrew's mother for a very long time and knew what he needed better than some arrogant, inflexible stranger. (Okay, I didn't actually say that, but I wanted to.) I still can't believe that she refused to try a technique recommended by a mother who had seen it work successfully at another school!

Anyway, I went from having a boy who could separate to having a boy who cried more at separation than ever, from having a boy who was everyone's favorite student to having a boy whom the other parents and even the teacher seemed to find distasteful—after all, he was crying or clinging most of the time.

We had hoped that in a regular preschool he would start imitating the other kids' social interactions, but without any interventions in place, he just spent most of his time there wandering around doing hand puppets and ignoring the activities. Both Rob and I felt that, far from making progress in social skills, he was losing ones he'd gained at the hospital.

Why It Failed

Looking back now, I realize I should have been much more active at both schools in coordinating interventions for Andrew that might have increased his participation and interactions, but at that point, I was still relatively new to the whole autism thing and hadn't realized how incredibly involved a parent had to be. This was especially true at the regular preschool, where they simply weren't trained to work with special needs kids, but it was also true at the public special ed class. I wanted to just drop him off there and assume that an expert would take care of him, the way people had at the UCLA school, but the staff members weren't as well trained (although they were all very nice and probably would have been willing to accept some pointers from me), and the loss of the teacher led to even more confusion.

The truth was, I wanted school—any school—to be the place where I didn't have to be in charge of Andrew, where I got a break from all the work and worry, but when you have a kid with special needs, you really need to stay on top of things all the time.

I realize all this now, but at that point I was stressed out and exhausted from dealing with both a newborn and a child with a disability, and all I wanted was for Andrew to be settled somewhere where we knew he'd make progress. So far, we'd only found one place like that, so we sent him back into the UCLA program for another six-week stint. Once again, his improvement was dramatic, and we were relieved. But once again, we had to face the fact that it wasn't a long-term solution.

Finding a Long-Term Solution

When Andrew's special ed teacher left and the class fell apart, I had decided I was done with the public school system. So now I tried to find an appropriate private preschool on my own, but it was hard—I liked the warm and relaxed ones, but experience had proven that that kind of class was too unstructured for Andrew, and he'd end up doing hand puppets and walking in circles all day. On the other hand, he was still practically nonverbal, so a structured and academic preschool wasn't the answer, either. What was?

The public school employee in charge of special needs for our district called and said, "I have the perfect class for Andrew." I was so fed up with the district at that point, I said, "I'm not interested." But she insisted I check it out, and at Rob's urging, we went over.

The class was fantastic. There were about fifteen kids, most of them typically developing, but every year they accepted one or two kids with special needs. Because of this, the teacher was both trained and experienced. We chose not to have an aide for Andrew, because the two-hour class was so structured that it kept him engaged (except during recess, and my one regret about the class was that we didn't tackle that, because he did end up off by himself the whole time). Kids were required to memorize the spelling of their names and addresses, which played right into Andrew's strengths—he was just starting to talk and loved letters and spelling.

The class was prekindergarten and meant to last only one year: in the spring, the students were expected to graduate and go on to kindergarten. Andrew had a fall birthday, though, so we had the luxury of waiting to start him in elementary school, and we knew other parents at other schools who gave their kids an extra year of preschool, or even had them repeat kindergarten at two different schools, to give them an extra year to grow physically or emotionally. We discussed it and decided that Andrew just wasn't socially or behaviorally ready to tackle kindergarten yet, so we arranged for him to do another year at that same pre-K class. The kids were all new, but the teachers were the same, so he felt comfortable but not bored.

But that year, we had to face a dreaded task: finding the right kindergarten for him.

Where Will This Kid Fit In?

So what do you do with a kid whose language is still tremendously delayed, who stims whenever he's not actively engaged, who's strange and withdrawn and not like other kids his age—but who's bright and capable of learning and whose future is still very much unwritten?

We looked at everything, starting with public school classes for kids with autism. To be blunt, those were horrifying. The ratio of students to teachers was usually decent, but the kids always seemed miserable and bored. We saw one teacher yell at a kid for not listening and then grab the kid angrily by the arm, hard enough to bruise him. No one was ever doing interesting work—just some photocopied worksheets—and few of the teachers seemed trained in any kind of behavioral intervention. They just seemed to be marking time, essentially babysitting the kids. We visited a couple of these classes and then said to each other, "Never." I even said I'd homeschool Andrew before we sent him to a place like that. (This was quite a few years ago, and my understanding is that these classes have improved significantly since then. I hope so.)

But if we weren't going to do the special ed thing, what then? We thought maybe a private school would work, if we could find one that was open-minded and willing to include a kid with some delays. Admittedly, that hadn't worked out so well in preschool, but he had grown a lot since then.

Unfortunately, private elementary schools were hard to get into and not set up to offer any support to Andrew. We didn't think he could keep up at most of the larger private schools, and the really small ones that seemed nurturing just didn't have space.

So, feeling like our options were narrowing, we went on a tour of our local neighborhood public school and, somewhat to our amazement, fell in love with it. We saw a first-grade class, which was wonderful, and afterward the beautiful young teacher told us that she loved having kids with special needs in her class. On that basis alone, we settled on that school. (Of course, that teacher got pregnant *that year* and left the school before Andrew ever had her. Fortunately there were many other wonderful teachers at our school, but it was definitely ironic that we made our choice based on a teacher we never saw again.)

Getting an Aide

By now we had learned a little, and we knew Andrew needed support—we couldn't just throw him into a classroom and expect him to thrive. One of the experts we'd worked with didn't believe in aides at school. She felt (with some justification, as most of the aides she had seen weren't trained and tended to hover) that kids can get too dependent on them. We had stayed away from using an aide in preschool for just that reason, and we'd paid the price in wasted recesses and probably some wasted opportunities in the classroom as well. Since the social and academic demands of kindergarten seemed so much greater to us, and Andrew still had language delays and problems with excessive stim, we decided to at least *try* having an aide, who would be paid for by the school district. What could we lose? If we weren't happy with the situation, we could always change it. Better to start with more help and pull back, we figured.

The administrators at our school agreed that Andrew should have some support, especially in kindergarten, where the class was going to have over thirty kids. One day, the principal told us she'd found our aide. "Dawn has never done this work before," she said, "but I think she'll be good at it."

We weren't thrilled about the untrained part and muttered various things to each other about how we had to give her a chance, but then . . . well, there was always mediation. We would fight the school district to get someone who was trained, if we had to.

We went ahead and gave Dawn Davenport a chance . . . and she wasn't just good, she was incredible. Yes, she started out untrained, but she was so eager to learn how best to help Andrew that we were able to start training her before the school year even began. We started a series of regular meetings at our house with her and the therapists we were already working with, and she quickly learned how to control Andrew's occasional breakdowns and keep him focused. Her instincts were unerring—she always seemed to know just what to do—but whenever she had a question or something new arose, she wrote me a note in the journal that went back and forth to school with Andrew for just that purpose, and we would research the answer. If she encountered a really thorny problem, like when Andrew was having trouble modulating his voice appropriately, we not only consulted our team of experts about what she should do at school, but we also got our speech pathologist and every other therapist working on it at home.

For an unbelievable and wonderful *six* years, Dawn was Andrew's shadow at school, there when he needed her, fading back when he didn't. She helped him connect with other kids, stay focused on his work, learn to control his frustration, and process the teacher's directions. After a few years, she was referring to him as "my boy"—the two of them adored each other—but no matter how much she wanted to guide and protect him, she knew not to hover or get in the way of his interactions with other people. Not surprisingly, she and I went on to become good friends. We're in close touch, so I know she has continued to shadow kids at the same school—we're not the only ones lucky enough to have had her support at a crucial time in our lives.

Because of Dawn's willingness to work as a team member and her openness to training, and thanks to some truly wonderful and dedicated teachers, Andrew's social and academic skills improved dramatically, so that the focused kid who entered second grade was almost unrecognizable from the one who had started kindergarten stimming and laughing to himself.

It wasn't all an easy ride though. At the start of third grade, we received a letter telling us that our school district had decided to transfer any aide who had been with the same student for over a certain amount of time—someone there had decided that aides shouldn't get too attached to their kids—and that Dawn had been reassigned to another student. We were horrified (as was she). Not only was she too good to lose, but we'd all worked hard over the years to make sure our approach to Andrew was unified at school and at home. We'd have to start all that from scratch with someone new. We went to the principal, who was completely on our side (we were very lucky that way). She and we started frantically making phone calls and writing letters and making the case that we'd done too much training and seen too much success to lose what we had.

And, miraculously, by the time school started, we had Dawn back at Andrew's side. Someone at the school said to us, "You guys are so nice, but when you feel like you need to advocate for your kid, you really swing into action." So maybe there is a tiny bit of a Mama Bear in me after all! Most of the credit goes to the principal, though—without her support, I'm not sure we'd have succeeded in getting Dawn back.

Telling the Other Parents

Although Andrew had an aide, he wasn't overtly identified as a special needs kid at school. In fact, the teachers always introduced Dawn as a general classroom aide, rather than as a one-on-one. (The school carried this out so convincingly that one year a parent said to me very seriously, "You've been so lucky—Andrew's managed to get put in the class that Dawn helps out in *every single year.*" I just nodded, but Rob and I laughed a lot about our "good luck" later.) We had many different inclusion specialists over the year, but their sessions with Andrew's classmates were always very general, never specific. They never singled him out publicly as a kid with special needs. He did get pulled out during the early years for adaptive physical education and some language skills work, but we decided at some point that it was more important to have him stay in his classroom than get the extra help. (We had a speech therapist who worked with him regularly at home, and someone who helped him learn some basic athletic skills, like riding a bike and throwing a ball, so we weren't dependent on the school services. Otherwise, we would have continued them.)

In retrospect, I wonder if we made a mistake not talking to the whole class about Andrew when he was still in kindergarten. Back then, he was so obviously different—so weird in his behaviors, so awkward socially—that it might have increased the sympathy of both his classmates and their parents to have known exactly what the situation was. It had certainly helped back in the preschool days.

Over time, I think most people came to know that Andrew had been diagnosed with autism, anyway. For one thing, I told a lot of them. I had already made a habit of being up-front and out there about Andrew's disability, and I saw no reason to stop. People are usually kind, and most families are sympathetic to other people's situations. I learned to be careful, though. If I started talking to someone who seemed narrow-minded or even bigoted in any way, I wouldn't mention it. Nor would I seek them out for future conversations on *any* topic. . . . Life's too short.

And the truth was that anyone who knew anything about autism could have identified Andrew as being on the spectrum those first couple of years in elementary school. So it wasn't like it was any big secret. But telling people formally, in a thoughtful way rather than a random one, might have helped to explain a lot of his oddities, rouse people's sympathy, and enlist their aid. And I do think the kids would have been more understanding.

A friend of mine, whose extremely high-functioning son was diagnosed with autism at the age of five, chose not to tell anyone at his elementary school other than the teachers and administrators. Although she never regretted her choice, she did confide in me that it was difficult sometimes to watch other parents rushing to help another child in the class who had a very clear disability, when those same parents were sometimes cold to her own son's occasionally unusual behavior. The desire to tell them that he had a neurological impairment to gain their sympathy was overwhelming at times, but she resisted it, preferring to keep him "label free."

It's a tough choice. Over time, I've certainly pulled way back these days on discussing Andrew's diagnosis openly. The fewer symptoms of autism he expresses, the less I feel the need to explain anything to other people. But, as I said, it might have helped to have been more open in those early years.

A Successful Run

Andrew had a great six years at that elementary school. It seemed like we had stumbled onto the right formula for making full inclusion work. The luck we had in having a supportive school—a principal who worked with us instead of against us, a truly fantastic aide, and teachers who genuinely loved our son and were willing to go out of their way to help him—was matched by the efforts we had learned to make on his behalf. We did our best to support Dawn by working at home on any issues that cropped up at school and continued to have regular meetings that included her, our therapists, and reports from our regular meetings with Dr. Koegel.

But in this part of California, most public elementary schools end at fifth grade. In the fall of 2002, Rob and I knew we had to start figuring out middle school.

The main problem was that Andrew—as well as he was doing—still had some delays in his social skills. Although he was older than most of the kids in his grade, he seemed younger. Things I loved about him—his gentleness, his kindness, his innocence—set him apart from the other boys, and he was starting to become aware of it. We wondered if we should consider putting him in a special education school.

It was tempting. At a school for kids with special needs, Andrew would be at the top of his class and the top of the heap. Teachers would understand him, and he'd find it easy to make friends. His confidence might well blossom in that atmosphere, whereas it had the potential to be destroyed in a regular middle school. Every adult we knew had suffered psychological torments in middle school—wouldn't that experience be even worse for a kid with autism?

I was slightly reluctant to tell Dr. Koegel what we were thinking. I knew how she felt—that kids with autism do best with full inclusion. Not that Dr. Koegel ever tells people they're wrong. She just gently points them in the right direction. When I told her we were considering the special ed school, she offered to come check it out with us but expressed some concern that Andrew might not grow as much in that environment. Wayne Tashjian, our wonderful behavioral therapist, also said he would prefer to see Andrew in a regular school but left the decision up to us.

With the two experts we trusted the most saying the same thing, it wasn't long before Rob and I realized we were nuts not to continue on the road we'd been taking—after all, we'd seen full inclusion work beautifully for years. Andrew had come such a long way from kindergarten, and it was all because being around the other kids at school had made him want to work hard to be one of the gang. There were so many things he had learned and so many things he still needed to learn—like how to decode sarcasm, read people's expressions, figure out what was cool and what wasn't—things he wouldn't learn from other kids with autism. He had risen to challenge after challenge at his school, and the last thing he needed was for us to *stop* challenging him. He hadn't let us down yet, so why were we lowering our expectations and his opportunities?

Rob and I threw ourselves into checking out "regular" schools—both public and private. Ultimately we preferred the private schools simply because their classes were a lot smaller, and we wanted the better teacher-student ratio, since we felt Andrew was ready to go to school without an aide.

Applying

I decided to stick to full disclosure in our applications. I explained that Andrew had been diagnosed with autism as a preschooler and that he had worked incredibly hard to overcome the worst symptoms of the disability.

Every school thanked us for our honesty. Some of the directors acknowledged some concerns, mostly about whether it would be extra work for their teachers, and we tried to answer them fairly. We said we could promise a lot of support at the home front, and that all we asked from them was to keep information flowing to us, so we could tackle any issues that came up and prime Andrew whenever necessary.

It was a long, difficult process, but one with a happy ending: our first-choice school accepted Andrew as a sixth-grader for the 2003–2004 school year.

Of course, I continued to lie awake at night worrying. Would Andrew do okay without an aide? Were we wrong not to put him at the local public middle school, where a lot of the kids who already knew and accepted him were go-ing? Would the kids at the new school be kind to him, or would they tease him? Would he emerge from middle school with his self-confidence intact? And, fi-nally, how would we ever get through this again in two and a half years, when we'd need to make a decision about high school?

It was hard, but I felt like we'd learned a lot during those difficult preschool days, when it seemed like nothing was working. Now we knew that to make school work we'd have to do our part—monitor what was going on, share infor-mation and interventions with his teachers, prime Andrew when necessary, and tutor or counsel him as the need arose.

We had also learned to trust our incredible kid, who worked harder than anyone else we knew, and who had proven over and over again that he could tackle new challenges with grace, good humor, and a pretty impressive track record.

Ten Years Later

I think the most frustrating thing about having a child with special needs is that you can never be entirely sure you're making all the right choices. I mentioned above how we felt somewhat torn between mainstreaming and special educa-tion and decided that the former would lead to the greatest growth. I still believe that (and the research bears it out). But . . . was it at a cost? As an adult, An-drew has a lot of insecurities and self-doubt. Sometimes I wonder whether he might have had higher self-esteem if he hadn't always felt like a bit of an outsider around typical peers. Maybe he would have made some incredible lifelong friends at a school specifically designed for kids with autism. On the other hand—at what cost to his ability to work hard and meet challenges? Would he still have ended up at a four-year college if we'd made that choice?

Maybe every choice comes with a cost. And, as I said to a friend recently who was dealing with her own children's issues, "We make the best choices we can at any given time with the information we have available to us." There are no "controls" in child rearing. You never know which way a different path might have led.

I have my doubts now about the middle school we chose (it was too small, in the end, and he just never found a good friend there), but we were extremely lucky in our high school, which actually has a program for kids on the autistic spectrum folded into it. Andrew wasn't enrolled in that—he matriculated as a "regular" student—but we knew the support was there if he ever needed it, so we were able to choose the most inclusive environment possible, with a "fallback" situation readily available to us. The best of all possible worlds. Plus it was great that his high school welcomed, nurtured, and supported so many kids on the spectrum, both because it meant there was a wide variety of kids there for Andrew to connect with and because it reflected the school's attitudes toward differences of all kinds, which was and remains welcoming, tolerant, and supportive. (Remember how Dr. Koegel said you can judge a lot about how the school will treat your kid just from talking to the head and seeing whether she views your child as a liability or a welcome addition? Well, the head of our high school made it clear he thinks a good school includes all sorts of different kids. The only kind of student he won't tolerate? A bully.)

A quick aside: We did have one bad teacher at that school. She kept giving Andrew low grades but never sent any of his work back, so we asked to see Andrew's tests. We wanted to go over them and do the error analysis Dr. Koegel suggests in this chapter, so we could figure out why he was struggling in math that year. Would you believe the teacher wouldn't let us have the tests? The only reason we could figure out—from the clues she gave us—was that she was worried we wanted to challenge her grading. But our only interest in the tests was to pinpoint the areas Andrew needed help with, so we could work with him on them at home. She strung us along the whole year, claiming she'd give us back the tests and always "forgetting" to bring them to class or making some other excuse. And Andrew was never able to pull his grade up. Looking back, we should have gotten an administrator involved on that one. I'm not sure why we didn't! We're just not as good at staying on top of everything as we should be, but we did ask her many times for those tests.

Anyway, the good news is that Andrew just finished his junior year at a four-year college on the East Coast. Has college been smooth sailing the entire time? No, but it has been smooth sailing *most* of the time. And he loves it there.

I think about that early session with our very first speech therapist (who was our first therapist of any kind, actually) and how she said, "Sometimes kids like this even go to college!" like it was a long shot and we should have been thrilled she even raised it as a possibility, which devastated us, since we wanted college to be a given. And now here's Andrew today, worrying not about whether or not he'll go to college, but what jobs will be available when he graduates.

So if you're feeling like you'll never even get your kid to settle down and pay attention in preschool, take heart and tell yourself, "If we do the work, anything is possible!" And then reread Dr. Koegel's advice in this chapter and do everything within your power to make school as successful as possible.

Chapter Eight
Family Life:
Fighting Your Way Back to Normalcy

QUESTION: My child wakes up in the middle of the night and can't go back to sleep, no matter what I do. Most days, I'm so tired in the morning that it's hard to be patient with him or my other children. Is this common?

QUESTION: Our family seems to be focused around my child with autism. He goes to all kinds of therapies, and interventionists are coming over to our house at all hours. It makes it impossible for us to have a normal family life, but the therapists tell us that these interventions are critical. Is it always going to be like this?

AS any parent knows, life changes dramatically when a baby is born. But when that child has a disability, life can change in ways you never anticipated. Many of the natural ways we interact with our typical children, ways that help them develop into happy, healthy, intelligent human beings, *don't* work with children with autism. For instance, the more you talk, interact with, and give meaningful experiences to typical children, the more they learn. However, if the child has autism and can't process language correctly or tunes you out, she's not likely to pick up meaningful information—all that talking is just unintelligible background noise. Similarly, many parents try to control their toddlers' tantrums by counseling them to "use their words" instead of whining and crying. But if your child simply isn't learning to communicate verbally, that instruction is useless.

One of the oddly tricky aspects to autism is that children with that disability don't look any different from typically developing kids, so others often don't recognize what a huge challenge the parents have to deal with. I worked with one mother whose in-laws insisted that her child's symptoms of autism were all a result of poor parenting—this despite the fact that the same parents had another perfectly typical child. Another mother told me about a time when her son became so disruptive in public that she had to take him to the car. A stranger followed her out and told her that it wasn't her son who had the problem—it was her. And yet another mother, at her wit's end in the grocery store, with everyone staring at her because her son was "meowing" and licking all the foods, yelled at the top of her lungs, "Haven't any of you ever heard of autism?"

But the worst example I ever heard of the emotional toll that autism can take on your family life was the mother whose husband refused to admit his child had a disability. This caused such tension between them that he told her he was leaving her. She was so angry that she put sleeping pills in his food. When he told her he felt tired all the time, she suggested that he take some vitamins—of course, the vitamins were actually sleeping pills. She took great joy in hearing that he had slept through several important meetings each day. As she gleefully reported, "He left me a complete zombie."

Obviously, this was an unusual situation, but there's no doubt that having a child with autism tends to put families under severe stress. This high level of stress is well researched and well documented (see chapter 1, "Diagnosis," for more about stress and how to manage it). While having a child with special needs can tear a family apart, it can also make it stronger—I've seen many families who have developed a closer and more loving relationship after a child has been diagnosed, families who work together beautifully to deal with the challenges of autism.

Let's make your family one that gets stronger.

There's no question that seemingly simple daily routines can be a challenge with a child with autism. Meals, bedtime, vacations, and even getting a date night with your spouse or significant other can present major challenges. But dealing with these areas uniformly and methodically will help create a more ordinary daily life for your family.

HELPING PICKY EATERS

Lots of kids are picky eaters. Unlike my oldest daughter, who would (and still does) try anything you put in front of her, my youngest has always been picky. If she had her way, she would have lived on bread and chocolate milk in preschool and elementary school. In fact, if we went to a great seafood restaurant, she'd just skip the whole meal, unless they were willing to make her a plate of seafood pasta without the seafood. Just the pasta.

Typical children have a range of eating preferences, and usually parents can put together a balanced meal based on foods they know their kid is willing to eat and can find something acceptable on the menu at any given restaurant. But what about children who simply refuse to eat anything other than two or three very specific foods? The kind you can't take to a restaurant without bringing your own plastic bags of these few foods? The kind who won't eat what the family's eating at home? The kind who make their parents dread dinnertime because they know they're going to wear themselves out begging, coaxing, and demanding that their children try something new, with no real hope of succeeding?

Many children with autism have eating disorders. The most severe case I ever saw was a skinny little wisp of a child who would only drink water and eat one brand of oatmeal. I asked his mother if she had ever tried putting another brand of oatmeal in the same box, and she had, and he had refused to eat it. His pickiness extended to both texture and taste, as he refused to eat the oatmeal if it was too runny or too thick, or if any other food was mixed with it.

Our families have dealt with this kind of picky eating from a behavioral perspective in a number of different ways, although we always recommend checking with your doctor first so she can monitor your child's weight and hydration before starting an intervention program. Here are some solutions.

Serve Only Healthful Foods

Try serving only the foods you want your child to eat. Make it clear to him that he won't get anything other than the choices you're giving him. Although he may spend a meal or two refusing to eat, most will eat when they get hungry enough.

One boy we worked with, Andy, ate only carbohydrates. Even when he went to a fast-food restaurant, he ordered "One hamburger, hold the beef!" Then he proceeded to eat the bun by itself. He also enjoyed French fries and white bread. But that was about it. One day his mother, concerned about his eating habits, simply stopped serving him carbohydrates. After a few fussy meals, he became hungry and tried some chicken—which, to everyone's surprise, he liked! When his choices were narrowed to healthful foods, he began to develop a more well-balanced diet.

Kids can go a few days without food as long as they're hydrated, but again, make sure you coordinate this with a doctor or therapist before you plunge into it. And be prepared for a couple of tough days.

Desensitize Your Child to Food Aversions

We recently published a study showing that many children with autism don't really dislike foods they won't eat, but instead have developed a psychological aversion to them. We tried an intervention where we "desensitized" the children to foods they refused to eat. To do this, we created many tiny steps that involved first getting them used to the sight of the foods, then comfortable touching the food, then able to put their tongues on it. Then we had them actually put the food in their mouths and spit it out. Finally we got them to swallow it. After each step we gave the child a preferred food.

The intervention was done very slowly and systematically so the children didn't get upset, and it worked: by the end, each child was eating dozens of new foods. In fact, many of the children said they liked the new foods and couldn't believe they hadn't tried them before. If you think your child may benefit from this type of program, be sure that you move in very small steps, even if it takes weeks for him to try a new food. If you move too quickly and your child is showing the aversion again, move back to the previous step and develop an intermediary one. Desensitization works when it is carefully planned with very small gradual steps, with success at each step before moving on to the next.

Let Your Child Choose One New Food

I've mentioned before that providing a choice often works to help a child with transitions or unwanted tasks, and that's true when it comes to getting a child to try new foods, too. To do this, we take the child to the grocery store and give him an opportunity to pick one new food—it's completely his choice; it just has to be something he hasn't tried before. The child feels like he has some control over what he's expected to eat, which makes him more open to something new. (One quick note: if your child only eats one type of food—such as carbs—you may want to make that category of food off-limits during the choice.)

This strategy can be very effective, as we discovered when we worked with a high schooler whose parents couldn't travel because he ate such a restricted diet. We took him to the grocery store several times a week where he could pick out his own new foods and then offered him these choices at mealtimes. This led to a rapid increase in his food repertoire. Within a few months his parents were able to travel with him to a foreign country to visit relatives, and they reported that he ate everything that was offered to him—even foods that weren't commonly eaten in the United States.

Use Preferred Food as a Reward (the "First/Then" Approach)

Another method that some families have found to be effective is to provide the desired food only *after* the child has eaten the undesired food.

For example, Liam ate only chips, French fries, and bread. At mealtimes we told him he could have one of his desired foods *only* after he ate one teeny-tiny bite of meat. After reluctantly taking the bite, he was given the whole plate of desired food. Gradually we made the bites bigger and bigger, then we had him eat two bites, and so on, until he was eating a well-balanced diet. The whole process took a few months, and he still has some foods he doesn't like, but he eats dozens of foods now. This is similar to what many parents do with typical children and dessert, giving them their dessert only after they've eaten a healthful meal.

While some people feel you run the risk of making the already desired food even more desirable by using it as a reward, in my experience simply getting the kids to try something new will often lead to a genuine preference for that new food.

Disguise Healthful Food

Some families find it effective to hide or bury healthful food that the child would otherwise avoid within the desired foods. For instance, Gabe ate bread and virtually nothing else. He really wasn't interested in any other foods, although he did drink juice. His mother wanted him to eat some protein, so we began putting small bites of meat inside each bite of bread. The bites were so small at the beginning that he didn't even notice. Gradually she added more and more meat until he was able to eat a regular sandwich. I did something similar with my own child. She wasn't much of a vegetable fan, so I used to grate veggies, like zucchini, into the spaghetti sauce. She never seemed to notice the addition of the vegetables, and she ate it up.

TEACHING GOOD MANNERS

Quite often, children with autism aren't expected to eat meals with the rest of the family. Often it's because they have disruptive behaviors, and family meals are simply more pleasant and easier for the rest of the family without them there. So while everyone else in the family is eating at the dinner table, they sit in front of the TV and just run over and grab something from the table when they feel hungry. This isn't a great setup for family dining, and it makes going to a restaurant impossible.

Remember the golden rule: Expect the same standards of behavior for your child with autism as you would for any child. Running around during mealtimes is not acceptable behavior from anyone.

Getting Your Child to Sit Down to Eat

Start by letting your child know that he can only eat at the table. He can't take his plate of food and sit in front of the TV. And if he leaves the table, he can't take pieces of food with him. The meal is over. Period. You can decide whether to offer food only at the beginning of the meal or, if your child leaves and comes back a half hour later and the food is still on the table, to let him sit down again for another helping. Don't worry about his starving—if he doesn't eat enough, it just means that next time he'll come to the table even hungrier and sit down longer. The idea is that your child has to learn that meals are eaten at the table.

If your child is used to getting a little snack every half hour, and you're not comfortable denying him completely, try to give him just a very tiny amount, so he'll soon be hungry again. It may be a little slower this way, but it's the same idea. You want him to be hungry at the next meal so that he'll sit at the table with you and eat—eating is the natural reward for sitting at the table.

At first, he may stay in his seat only a short while, but you can gradually work this up to longer periods, until he's remaining for the whole meal. This can be done with a timer, or even with the amount of food your child eats, by gradually increasing the number of bites he takes before getting the reward of leaving. You may even want to serve your child very small portions (especially of foods he likes), so that he can use his communication skills to request more helpings. Not only will this reinforce his language, it will also give him an opportunity to interact socially at the table.

Some families find it helpful to have a timer at the table with a treat, such as a cookie or other dessert, placed nearby. If the child remains calmly at the table until the timer goes off, he may then have the treat. Again, the length of time can gradually be increased until the child is able to spend the whole meal with the family.

Regulating the Pace of Eating

Even if she's able to sit down nicely at the table with others, your child may not always pick up on the social cues related to the pace of eating. We often find our children at the school tables at the end of lunch period, still finishing their food long after the rest of the children have gone off to play. This interferes with their social time. The opposite problem can be true, too—if a child eats too quickly, she'll miss out on the social conversation that takes place while everyone's eating together.

Before taking action, you need to assess the situation and figure out why the child is eating slowly or quickly. For example, we worked with a child who ate excessively slowly at school so that she could avoid social interaction on the playground after lunch. Others are simply not paying attention, or "spacing out," and still others are getting some attention from adults for eating slowly—in fact, an adult who's cajoling and prompting the child to eat more quickly can inadvertently provide desired attention and therefore positive reinforcement for the slow eating.

For children who eat too slowly because they're either avoiding what comes after lunch or simply spacing out, you can try putting away their lunch when the other children finish. Pretty soon they'll learn that if they want to fill up, they have to eat more quickly. If a child is eating slowly for attention, make sure she gets the attention only for eating at a faster pace. Talk to her, praise her with "Good job! You finished your carrots!" or give her any other type of attention she desires—but make it contingent on the eating. Alternatively, the school can make sure that lunch will be followed by a favorite activity, so your child is eager to finish and move on. You can do the same thing at home after meals, making sure she has something to look forward to as soon as she's done.

If a child is eating too quickly, you can give her small portions spaced out or teach her to eat smaller bites. This will require a fair amount of adult involvement. Ideally, you can coordinate an eating program across all settings for the most rapid results or, if it's easier, start the intervention at home and carr? it over into the school setting. That is, the parents or a therapist may want work on eating at home, while an aide, special educator, teacher, or peer (old if the child is young) can help at school, with the goal of fading out the intervention as the child's rate of eating improves.

Insisting on Proper Utensil Use

Children with autism often have an unfortunate tendency to prefer using their fingers to utensils for eating. With a little effort, however, you can teach your child to use a fork and spoon correctly.

Start by putting just one bite on your child's plate, and only let her eat that bite if she picks it up with either a fork or a spoon (or, if you need a simpler step before you reach this stage, place the bite on the spoon or fork itself). Make sure that she likes whatever you put on the plate, so she'll want to eat it. She may need a little help at first getting it on the utensil and/or in her mouth, but with enough practice, she'll learn to do it on her own. Once she's eating one bite, add another. Slowly and gradually add to the number of bites she eats with the fork or spoon.

The great thing about eating is that there's a natural reward associated with the task (especially if it's something delicious), so your child will be likely to continue the task of learning to eat properly, even in the initial stages when it's most difficult.

Cutting Down on the Mess

Some of our children have had difficulties staying clean while eating, possibly because they're not socially aware enough to understand the repercussions of being messy. One fifth-grader we worked with had food all over her clothes and face after each meal. Obviously this didn't help her fit in with the other kids. We taught her a couple of strategies to reduce this.

First, we watched her and noticed that when she picked up her finger food, she gripped it with her whole hand rather than with her thumb and pointer finger, or pincers. So, whenever she reached with her whole hand, we prompted her to pick the food up with her pincers. This reduced the surface area that came in contact with the food and got dirty. Next, we reminded ⸀ to wipe her face with her napkin after every few bites. (She was verbal, ⸀ instructions were spoken, but with a less verbal child you may have to ⸀ver the napkin or point to it.) Third, we taught her to use utensils whenⸯ ⸀ppropriate, to keep her hands clean. And, finally, after each meal we ⸀ted her to go to the restroom, look in the mirror, and wash off any reⸯ ⸀ food.

If your child is a messy eater, observe first, figure out some strategies, then incorporate them into the eating routine until they become a habit.

EATING IN RESTAURANTS

Now that your child can sit during meals, keep herself clean, and eat a variety of foods, you're ready to try a restaurant. Don't be discouraged if you encounter some difficulties there. Everything is different at a restaurant. The environment is different, you're surrounded by strangers, you have to wait for your food, and familiar dishes don't always taste the way they do at home.

We recommend you start by finding kid-friendly restaurants that are somewhat noisy and don't have many rules. Fast-food restaurants are great for starters. By ordering the food in advance, you minimize the amount of sitting time. And fast-food restaurants are used to kids and a fair amount of noise.

Work on nice sitting and eating (with your child's favorite foods, of course) the same way you did at home, in this different context, until your child understands what's expected of him. Once your child can sit at one of these less-formal restaurants, it's time to practice at a slightly quieter place where you have to order your food from a waiter but where there are still quite a few families with small children. And remember, *you're not alone*. All parents have to deal with restaurant behavior. I can still remember sitting in a fast-food restaurant when my daughter was young. We were about halfway through our meal when our daughter started to get disruptive. I jumped up, ready to take her out of her high chair and whisk her away, when my husband reminded me that we didn't want to *teach* her to be disruptive at restaurants. So we endured the disruptive behavior (I felt like I wanted to crawl under the table the whole time) until she figured out that behaving badly wasn't the way to make the meal end. It was literally only a few minutes, even though it felt like hours. But kids learn quickly—both good and bad behaviors—so it's important to make sure the reinforcement only follows the appropriate ones. Always remember that what you do in the short run will make a difference in the long run.

But also remember that there's a time and a place for teaching. It's best if you can teach your kids to behave during meals at home before you go to a restaurant, but kids are unpredictable and may act up even if they've been sitting nicely at home. If you're going to wait out a tantrum, be sure it's at a noisy restaurant—it just isn't appropriate to do it at a nice one. If you do find yourself with a crying child in a nice restaurant and need to leave for the sake of the other patrons, it's important that your child have even less fun than she'd have in the situation she was trying to get out of. So, if you need to carry your child out, you can do that, but don't end the meal. Make sure the others stay inside and keep eating, while the disruptive one sits outside the restaurant or in a car with an adult (who doesn't play anything fun with her) until she's calm enough to go back inside and finish. That way, she knows that screaming and crying don't get her out of the meal, but she's also not bothering other people—and she'll definitely learn that screaming is absolutely *not allowed* in a restaurant.

Once your child gets better at the kid-friendly restaurants, you can gradually work your way up to nicer and nicer restaurants until she's comfortable eating anywhere. Don't forget to bring some favorite toys and activities if you're going to expect your child to sit for any lengthy period of time, like when you're waiting for your food or talking after the meal.

TACKLING SLEEP ISSUES

Sleep is critical. It's critical for your child's brain development, and it's critical for successful family functioning. Sleep-deprived adults find it difficult to think clearly, and tired parents argue more with one another.

Unfortunately, it's well documented that children with disabilities are likely to have sleep issues, and many of our families report that their children won't go to bed at night or wake up in the middle of the night. Some parents have told me that they can hear their child during the night for hours on end, engaging in repetitive behaviors such as jumping on the bed or wandering around the room. While a number of books are available that deal exclusively with sleep problems in general, a few strategies seem to be especially helpful with our families.

The very first thing that we recommend families do is to keep a diary of their child's sleep habits—keeping a log often reveals that their child's sleep has a pattern or that he's sleeping at times he shouldn't be. The sleep diary should include the date, what time the child was put to bed at night, what time the child fell asleep, whether the child woke up during the night and for how long, and every single nap during the day.

I like the teachers and families to include any other helpful information, such as what the child was doing when he fell asleep (with some children it always happens during specific activities), what the child did after he was put to bed (did he keep getting up or just lie in bed and hum?), and what he did when he got up in the middle of the night (did he jump on his bed for hours or climb in bed with Mom and Dad?). All this information can be helpful in developing an intervention plan. Make sure the sheets go around with your child at all times, and let everyone who watches your child know to keep an eye out. Sleeping can happen at any time, and we want to know exactly when it does.

Keep Your Child Awake During the Day

Angel was having a terrible time sleeping at night, and after a week of using a sleep diary, his parents figured out why—his teacher reported that he was sleeping for several hours at school each day. Although this had been going on for months, it hadn't occurred to the teacher to tell Angel's parents about his daily naps until she was asked to fill out a formal sleep diary.

Similarly, four-year-old Samantha refused to go to bed until well after midnight each night. A sleep diary revealed that she slept for several hours on the bus each day while riding from her small town to her special education class. Once again, the bus driver hadn't really paid attention to her naps until he was asked to write in the sleep diary. Armed with this information, the family found a school closer to their home, so Samantha no longer had the long rides to school, which cut out those naps and improved her bedtime enormously.

As with Angel and Samantha, if your child is having trouble sleeping at night, it may be because she's getting some sleep during the daytime hours. Keeping a sleep diary should clue you in to this. If this is what's happening, you're going to need to keep your child awake during the day until the sleep cycle is normalized. If your child seems extremely sleepy at any point during the day, you may have to do something active, like taking a walk, playing a lively game, or singing songs. You might also try giving her a favorite sweet snack or gently washing her face with cool water—whatever works. Remember, you're trying to help your child establish good sleep patterns at this point. If she's sleeping during the day, she probably needs that sleep, but you want to channel it toward the nighttime.

If your child is falling asleep on the bus or in the car, it may be necessary to have someone ride with her to keep her occupied so she doesn't sleep. This may include having a one-on-one aide or behavior specialist accompany your child until she no longer sleeps on the bus.

Try Physical Exercise

Years ago we published some studies showing that physical exercise reduced repetitive behaviors and increased on-task behavior in children with autism. The exercise needed to be aerobic, and the effects of the brief jogging periods (twenty to thirty minutes) lasted only a short time so we repeated them throughout the day. We thought that all this physical exercise might have some effect on nighttime sleeping, but the probing we did with parents indicated that it didn't. I'm currently involved with some research being conducted now that suggests timing may make a difference—it looks like the child may sleep better if the exercise is implemented late in the afternoon or early in the evening. This is preliminary, but it may be worth a try, especially since it could be a fun activity for the whole family. But remember: the exercise has to be vigorous, so get on your running shoes! And keep an eye out for future studies that should fill in some more details on the potential effects of exercise on sleep.

Stick to a Bedtime Routine

If your child's sleep problems seem to be mostly about settling down for the night, you have to look closely at how you put him to bed. Most children have difficulties falling asleep, but over time that generally becomes less of a problem *if* there's a bedtime routine and *if* parents stick to the routine. Children with autism are the same. Remember, we always try to reward good behavior, and since bedtime, in and of itself, may not be that rewarding, you should try to provide the child with an opportunity to engage in favorite activities *after* getting in bed. A treasured storybook, an opportunity to listen to some well-loved songs, a chance to have Mom or Dad sing a nursery rhyme, or an opportunity to cuddle with a valued toy can go a long way toward making your child more enthusiastic about bedtime.

If bedtime continues to be a struggle despite these rewards, and your child wants you to lie down with him or demands you rock him, you can do this for a short time, but set a timer or give him some other clear and consistent message that the routine is finished. Then make sure you're firm when the timer ends—leave the room, and don't come back. Only by being firm and consistent will you convince your child to stop calling for you and let himself fall asleep.

Don't Give In

Many parents report that their child gets out of bed and comes into their room in the middle of the night. Consequently, neither the parent nor the child gets a good night's sleep. You can help your child out by teaching him that if he gets up, you will matter-of-factly put him back to bed. You need to do this every time, or he will keep trying to get into bed with you. You're not punishing him. Try not to yell or get mad, no matter how tired you are. But also remember that you don't want to *reward* him for getting out of bed. If you play with him, give him a snack, get back in bed with him, let him come into your bed for even a brief period of time, or interact in any way that's desirable, you will be rewarding him for getting out of bed and waking you up. Your child needs to learn that when it's nighttime, he needs to stay in his room.

There may be times—at two in the morning, for example—when it will seem easier to you to let your child climb into bed with you than to force yourself out of bed to walk him back to his room, but remember that if you give in, you're actually increasing the likelihood he'll continue to wake you up in the future. Look at the long-term goal—that your child stay in bed all night long—and sacrifice a few minutes of comfort for a lifetime of improved sleep for both of you.

Make a Darkness-Versus-Light Rule

Sometimes it's hard for young children to differentiate between the times when they need to stay in bed and when they can get up. They may get confused about why Mommy or Daddy is sometimes annoyed when they appear while at other times happy to give them a good-morning cuddle. One way to help your child make that distinction is by teaching him that when it's dark outside, he needs to stay out of his parents' room. Teach him to look at the window to see if it's light out or dark, and tell him he has to stay in his room if it's still dark but can go into your room if it's light. That way, if you enjoy cuddling in bed in the mornings, you can have that when it's light, but if your child does awaken in the middle of the night, he'll learn not to go into your room and wake you up.

Remember, most kids with autism are good visually. Even if they can't communicate that well, they should be able to learn the difference between light and dark if they get enough practice.

Stick to these rules, and you'll all feel better.

MASTERING TOILET TRAINING

Children with autism generally get toilet trained later than typical children, as their parents already have a lot on their plates. In addition, because of their communication difficulties, it may be more difficult for them to understand the process. But toilet training can be straightforward and easy regardless of a child's developmental or chronological age.

Before starting a toileting program, you should check with your pediatrician. Be aware that most children are ready to be toilet trained when they have the muscle control to hold their urine, indicated by long periods of dry diapers (at least a few hours). If your child's diaper is constantly wet, you'll need to ask your pediatrician if it makes sense to start the training. If she gives you the green light, you're good to go.

Here's how we do it at our clinic.

Use the toilet training data sheet from the appendix in the back of this book to coordinate your child's program. You'll need to make copies of this sheet, so that when you start the program you can write down the location, date, and time, whether your child had an accident (urine or bowel), what happened when he was taken to the toilet (urine, bowel, or nothing), and if he went to the toilet by himself. These sheets will give you enough information to know your child's elimination habits and how the program is going.

The following procedures are adapted from *Toilet Training in Less Than a Day* by Nathan H. Azrin and Richard M. Foxx.

1. Pick a date, at home, when you can get help, if possible. The program is a lot of work for the first few days, and having some extra help is nice, but not necessary.

2. On that chosen day, give your child plenty of liquids all day long. This will ensure that he'll need to urinate and will provide more opportunities for success. Children must make the connection between the sensation of having to urinate and the act of going to the toilet, but it usually happens so infrequently throughout the day that it can be hard to link the two; the excessive liquids can hasten this process by increasing the number of times a child feels that urgent need.

3. Take your child to the toilet every twenty to thirty minutes. Make sure he stays on the toilet long enough to relax his muscles. Feel free to read to him

or entertain him in some other way while he's seated. Personally, if I know the child has had ample liquids I have him sit for longer periods of time or until he urinates. Some researchers suggest that watching a movie or TV may interfere, but I haven't found this to be the case, and sometimes the time goes by faster when your child can watch TV, which is helpful—sitting longer gives more time for opportunities and for muscles to relax.

4. Reward any successes with favorite items.

5. Reward him periodically for dry pants. In the beginning you'll want to check often. As always, you want to increase the odds for success, and frequent checks will help do that. You can check when you take him to the toilet and once or twice in between. Cheer and give him a treat, a hug, or anything else he likes if his pants are dry.

6. If he has an accident, have him practice going from the spot where he had the accident to the toilet, and have him sit on the toilet. Don't punish him and don't scold him. Do this matter-of-factly.

7. Continue to take him to the toilet regularly, be vigilant, and don't miss cues. This is critical in the beginning and until the child starts initiating. Later, you can prompt him to go on his own. Also, make sure that there's coordination in all of his environments. Once you start the toilet training, everyone—babysitters, relatives, school staff, and all the rest—will need to stay on top of this and take him regularly. If the adults in any one setting slip up or allow the child to wear diapers, the whole process will take a lot longer.

Once you've decided to toilet train your child, make sure you stick to it. Don't use diapers anymore, or he may try to hold it until you put the diaper on. Most of the children we work with are completely toilet trained in two to seven days if their caregivers are consistent.

After the first day, you may need to make sure you or whoever your child is with takes him to the bathroom at regular intervals, as it may take a while for him to learn to self-initiate.

The beauty of this program is that many children with autism just don't make the connection that when their bladder feels full, they need to find a toilet, but by giving them lots of liquids, you can help them make the connection and speed up the process.

For nighttime toilet training, remember not to give your child too many liquids after dinner—that's guaranteed to set the odds against him during the night. Also, make sure he goes to the bathroom right before bed. One family I worked with was having a lot of trouble with bed-wetting, but once the parents started rousing their son and bringing him to the bathroom again right before they themselves went to bed, at around eleven at night, the bed-wetting stopped. Their son was so groggy that he always went right back to sleep, which is crucial—don't try that strategy if your child can't go back to sleep easily. And remember, nighttime potty training is different from daytime: some kids get in such a deep sleep that they just don't realize they're wetting the bed. Also, some children dream they're on the toilet! This is where "alarming sheets" or "alarming diapers" (available online) can help. These buzz or alarm at the first drop of moisture. It takes a little effort on the parents' part, but when the alarm wakes up the child (or when the parent hears the alarm and wakes the child), he becomes aware of the need to urinate and can learn to get up to go and not wet the bed. But again, the sleep aspect makes this process very different from training during the daytime—and more challenging.

TAKING FAMILY TRIPS

I can't tell you how many stories I've heard about family trips turning into family disasters. One of our families went to a resort hotel, and their child wouldn't stop jumping on other children in the pool. Pretty soon they were so exhausted and tense from trying to control him that they gave up on the vacation and went home early. Another family's child was so preoccupied with the hotel elevators that he kept sneaking out of their room to ride in them. After a few days of having to call security to track down their son, they decided that they could no longer stay in hotels. One other family's child pulled the hotel's fire alarm three times during the first two days, and the hotel staff gently asked them to leave. Children with autism often don't know how to behave in novel situations, and so much-desired (and much-needed) vacations frequently turn sour.

Traveling with children requires extra preparation. Traveling with children with special needs often requires a *huge* amount of extra preparation, but it's worth it, if it leads to a successful trip.

Before your trip, make sure you've primed your child. Go over the map and talk to him about where you're going, how you'll get there, and how long it will take. (The Street View feature on Google Maps is a great tool for viewing your destination and its surroundings clearly.) If your child's verbal skills are limited, get brochures from the hotel and local attractions and go over the pictures. Make sure you find out ahead of time which restaurants will work for your child and family at your vacation destination. Bring as many of his favorite toys and activities as you can.

In other words, prepare, prepare, prepare. Here are some other suggestions.

Bring or Find Help

Consider bringing with you a regular babysitter or a relative whom you enjoy being around and trust with your child. It may be expensive, but it will give you an extra set of hands and respite at a moment's notice.

If you don't have a babysitter or family member who wants to go on a trip, think about inviting one of your therapists along—many would love the opportunity to go on an all-expenses-paid vacation. Even if none of your therapists can go, one of them might know a coworker with experience who could help you out. An experienced extra adult may be able to avert any potential meltdowns and make the difference between a successful vacation and a disaster.

Another possibility is to arrange for help at your destination—many cities have centers for children with autism, and you may be able to contact a center to get some specialized help while you're on vacation. One of our families recently went to Greece, and we were able to connect them with a therapist we had trained who happened to be living there: it worked out fabulously. So check with the people who work with your child back home to see if any of them might know someone who does similar work at your destination.

Look for Activities Your Child Will Enjoy

Check ahead of time to see if the hotel or community has activities your child enjoys. For example, one of our families stayed at a hotel that had supervised pool activities. Their child loved swimming and was happy paddling around the pool for hours a day, which gave the parents the opportunity to go sightseeing, eat at fancy restaurants, and partake in other adult activities their child wouldn't have enjoyed. Another family whose child loved animals found a local zoo camp that they were able to successfully send her to for the week of their vacation. Making sure your child has activities he likes will ensure that he has a good time and can free you up to have one, too.

Finding fun activities for your child is even more important when you're actively engaged in traveling, on a plane or train or in a car. If your child likes books, bring plenty of them. Some of our parents let their child bring toys they play with repetitively and which the parents normally restrict—that's fine temporarily, if it's the only way you can successfully get through the travel time. Another mother reported that her child loved Play-Doh, so she always threw a bunch of the mini containers into her carry-on bag. He'd sculpt little puppets on the airplane tray table for hours. And don't forget to bring your child's favorite foods and any special stuffed animal or blanket—whatever he enjoys at home.

Remember that most children don't like sitting in one place for very long, so if you're driving, try to plan lots of breaks for your child to get out and run around. If you're on a plane, take lots of walks up and down the aisle. I have found that most airlines will honor a parent's request for the bulkhead, if you're worried that your child might kick the seat in front of her. Heading off any problems in advance is always a good idea.

MANAGING YOUR DAILY LIFE AT HOME

Traveling can be stressful in unusual ways. Daily life can be equally stressful, but it's not confined to certain weeks of the year. You need to take control of your life by making things as easy and pleasant for yourself and your family as possible.

Take Breaks

Parents often feel tremendous stress and guilt when they need to leave their children, even for a short time away. They worry that a babysitter or relative may not understand their child's needs and may not be able to deal with challenging behaviors. Some even choose to stay at home with their child pretty much all the time, getting breaks only when their child is at school or asleep.

First, know that it's important for you to have some time to yourself. You need breaks, evenings out with your spouse or a friend, and ideally even some vacations alone. You're not doing any member of your family a favor by pushing yourself to the edge of exhaustion. You also may be putting your marriage in jeopardy.

We worked with one child whose parents only had nasty things to say about each other and whose marriage seemed on the verge of falling apart. The mom stayed at home with their several children, including a boy of elementary school age with autism, and the dad worked long hours in his law offices. We arranged for one of our clinicians to go to their home for four hours one evening a week, every week. We convinced the dad that he needed to make these evenings special for his overworked wife. So he made dinner reservations at fancy restaurants and got movie or theater tickets. On his own, he would stop by the flower stand and buy her a lovely bouquet of flowers each week. Within a short time, their negative comments greatly decreased, and he even began showing up at meetings and IEPs to support her. Clearly once they spent time having fun alone together, they remembered why they had gotten married to each other in the first place and wanted to make it work again.

To relax and truly have a good time, you need to find someone you're comfortable leaving your child with. Call upon relatives, friends, and therapists to help. Some people trade babysitting with close friends. If you can't find someone with experience to babysit, find a responsible college or high school student and train her—teach her how your child communicates, what your child likes and dislikes, and how to handle the difficult moments. And if something doesn't feel right, find another person.

The bottom line is that your family life will be much happier if you can go out and have fun once in a while, confident that your child is being well taken care of. Put some time and effort into finding the right person, and then you can plan dinner dates, a night away at a hotel, and even a real vacation with your spouse, and enjoy them all thoroughly.

Find a Support Group

Everyone needs support, and people find it in different ways. Some parents find it easy to talk about their concerns in regular meetings with a therapist they trust, while others prefer to confide in family members or their spouses. Others feel the need to talk to a wider group of people who are dealing with a similar issue, and those join support groups.

If you're starting or entering a support group, think hard about what you want from the group, because that will determine what size group will benefit you the most. If you have specific issues that you feel you need to bring up, discuss, and get feedback on, a smaller group may be more helpful—you'll have plenty of chances to jump in and air your concerns. If you want to be somewhat anonymous and focus on more general issues, a larger group may suit your needs. Sometimes larger groups have the resources to bring in speakers and consultants, which you might find helpful. Just remember that if you're in a larger group, you may not have an opportunity to bring up very specific issues about your child's particular situation.

Through our support groups here at the university, we've discovered that it's important that the group remain focused in a productive way on a topic and not devolve into a gripe session—while it's nice to know others share your problems, simply complaining about them tends to make people feel more depressed rather than less so, and the goal of a support group is to help its members feel better. The facilitator needs to direct the group so that they focus on sharing successful techniques, and participants leave with both a positive outlook and new strategies to help their child.

If you yourself are the facilitator of a support group, I suggest you contact each participant individually ahead of time to find out what his needs and expectations are. That way, you can concentrate on the issues that are important to everyone in the group and plan each session's topic to keep things as productive and helpful as possible.

Within the group, you can work together to develop resource lists, culling from each family's list of people they trust and respect, ranging from babysitters to clinicians to advocacy sources. In addition, other group members can attend meetings such as IEPs to provide support if a family needs a friend there. There are also online parent support groups that match people based on similar profiles, rather than geography. If the parents don't live near one another, they can communicate by phone and electronically. Sharing common experiences can be helpful for parents.

Remember: support groups can be useful, but some effort and planning need to go into them to make them worth everyone's time.

Siblings

Before I start, I have to say that most of the siblings of children with autism whom I've met are remarkable people, compassionate, empathetic, and responsible. Maybe this is because they've seen how a family can pull together to handle huge challenges with love and dedication. We've known a number of siblings who have actually gone into the field of disabilities. I had one incredible, intelligent, and hardworking sibling intern for me during the summer when she was in high school, and during that time she wrote an article about what life was like growing up with a sister with autism that was published in the *Journal of Positive Behavioral Interventions*. Now she's a professional in the field of disabilities.

Several years ago, there was a controversy with a school board that wanted to exclude all children with moderate to severe disabilities from regular education classrooms. A number of us went to the school board meeting to support inclusion. At the meeting, one of my favorite friends said that she went because her sister was severely affected by mental retardation, and the only reason her sister is now able to live independently is because she had been included in regular education and community activities throughout her life. This woman's childhood experiences made her a more aware and compassionate adult.

But let's face it. We all know families in which the siblings detest and resent each other. I even have one distant relative who hasn't spoken to anyone in the family for years, and no one can quite figure out what happened to cause her to be so estranged. With families who have children with autism, parents are experiencing severe stress, and that can add to some already complex family dynamics.

While research suggests that, as a whole, the siblings of children with autism don't worry as much or experience the same levels of stress and concern as their parents, life as a sibling of someone with special needs does present its own challenges. Children with autism often have a very full schedule, with therapies and programs that can use up their parents' free time and make it difficult for their siblings to pursue their own extracurricular activities. Further, because children with autism may need regular redirection to engage in typical activities, some parents feel like they aren't able to give their other children as much attention as they'd like. So much energy goes into interventions that there isn't always a lot left over, and sometimes a sibling will admit to feeling ignored.

Most siblings (especially older ones) can recount incidents of vacations cut short or the long-awaited trip to Disney World halted abruptly because of disruptive behavior. Young siblings often feel hurt that the child with autism won't play with them. Some children report that they're embarrassed by their sibling's behavior, such as excessive self-stimulation, when they have friends over, and some teens have reported discomfort when entertaining peers who haven't previously been exposed to children with autism.

Many siblings handle these difficulties well. I remember one close friend I had in high school, Tristam, whose brother had developmental disabilities.

Tristam's brother always sought attention from him when we had parties or were just sitting around his room talking, and Tristam *always* let him hang out with us and gave him all the attention he wanted. I was so impressed by how well he interacted with his brother—I really thought Tristam was extraordinary. But thinking back on it as a professional, I realize there must have been times when Tristam was struggling with feelings that the rest of us couldn't even imagine.

Make It Work for the Whole Family

Developing healthy and strong sibling relationships is a process that takes work in any family. Researchers have found that healthy relationships between children with autism and their siblings, as in any family, don't just happen naturally. They take some effort.

Studies show that feelings can change immensely if siblings are actively included in intervention programs (not to mention that they're usually great assets). Typical kids like attention, and if they can get it from working with their sibling with autism, they will. I've found that siblings are usually enthusiastic helpers and remarkably good at helping with interventions. They provide natural opportunities for communication and social interaction. Just make sure you give them lots of attention for these good deeds, and regularly reward them for being "mini interventionists."

We worked once with a single mother who had five children. To make matters far worse, she had a restraining order against the father, who had beaten her and her children. So the mom was truly on her own with all her children, one of whom had autism. The mother's biggest concern was that she didn't have enough time to work with her son. We discovered that the child's older sister was very interested in helping him, so we taught the son a bunch of board games that both kids enjoyed playing. In the games, we incorporated teaching opportunities, such as learning colors, using communication, and turn taking. The older sister was amazing. She worked with her brother every day and, judging by her enthusiasm, she enjoyed every minute. Each week the little boy showed improvement, largely due to his sister's efforts.

While siblings do make great helpers, it's important not to overlook their own interests. Their role in the family has to be more than just "sibling of the child with special needs"—they're individuals in their own right. Every family who has more than one child struggles with fairness. In my own family, one of my daughters is much more talkative than the other, and when they were younger, we had to make an effort to make sure the less-talkative one always got a chance to put in her two cents. So make an effort to keep things as fair as you can, without sacrificing the interventions that are necessary to your child's progress. Do your best to make sure that your other children aren't missing out on their favorite activities. You may need to recruit some extra help from friends, family members, or a babysitter to make that happen, and your schedule may sometimes seem overwhelming, but being a family means every person counts.

Finally, always be sure you select interventionists who will view the family as teammates and will include you in the determination of target goals—your child needs to learn skills that will help the family function, fit into your lifestyle, and be compatible with your cultural and religious values. For example, a clinician may feel that it's important to work on answering the phone, while the family may feel that toilet training is a much more pressing and immediate goal. Both goals may well be valid, but the family needs to have a say in prioritizing them. Similarly, studies show that families who are required to implement drill-type interventions have greater stress than when less-rigid interventions are incorporated into daily family routines.

How well the family functions as a whole is just as important as how well the child with special needs is doing, and it's your responsibility to work toward both kinds of success.

FACTS

Siblings can be taught to effectively implement intervention procedures.

Learned behaviors are more likely to maintain themselves over time if they are developed with the family.

Parent stress decreases if intervention goals can be incorporated within daily routines.

QUESTION: I'm worried that we're not spending enough time on interventions with my son, but I'm already running on empty. How many hours of intervention does he actually need?

Parents of children with autism frequently ask about how many hours of intervention their child needs each week. The truth of the matter is that they need intervention during all of their waking hours. And if they have a sleep disorder, they need intervention during their sleeping hours, too! That said, an important thing to assess is how often your child is *engaged*. In other words, if your child is engaged in activities that are leading to brain development, he probably doesn't need intervention during that time. But if your child spends hours on end rocking on his rocking horse or watching the same videotape over and over, you want to step in and get him engaged in some learning. Remember that you don't need to run yourself ragged—the goal is to provide opportunities within the ongoing routines of your regular family life, not to alter your life enormously so that it's unbearable.

> **QUESTION:** My husband and I have different styles of interacting with our son. He likes to put demands on him, but I like to give him downtime at home. This is causing a lot of stress in our family. Don't you think he needs downtime after a full day at school?

There's a happy medium here—you can both incorporate teaching activities into your downtime, so that your son can be learning even while you're relaxing. For example, having him request what he'd like for a snack instead of just giving it to him will help his communication, as will having him say "outside" when he wants a break. And having him set the table before a meal will help him learn how to take care of himself independently. The important thing is that you find teaching opportunities within your daily routines, so learning isn't an on-and-off kind of thing.

> **QUESTION:** The therapists for my four-year-old son's in-home program say that it's distracting to have my six-year-old daughter participate, but she wants to so badly and doesn't understand why she's being excluded. Do we really need to keep her away?

Your daughter should be included in the program, especially if she's indicating that she's feeling left out. Perhaps they could begin with some turn-taking games that would help your son's social skills and that she could play with him when the therapists aren't there. Also, they may want to give her specific tasks to do with him. Many siblings of children with autism enjoy these types of interactions so much that they end up working in the field of disabilities. She should be welcomed and encouraged to help if she desires, and, as her competence improves, the therapists can increase her responsibilities.

QUESTION: A student in my class wets his bed at night but is fully toilet trained during the day. His parents have to keep him in diapers at night, but he's getting way too old for this. What should I recommend? They've been making him help change the sheets in the morning and reprimanding him, but he still continues to wet his bed.

Many families whose children have this problem purchase alarming sheets or alarming underwear from a specialty store (discussed above). The child learns to wake up and go to the toilet if he feels the need. But remember to let the family know that in their child's sleepy state, he probably doesn't even realize he's wetting the bed. Getting angry or punishing him won't help. They need to help him understand the connection between needing to go to the bathroom and waking up enough to do it in the toilet. The sheets usually help with this.

QUESTION: How do I get my child to go to the bathroom on his own? He is completely toilet trained—so long as we take him every hour. But it never occurs to him to ask to go.

There are a few ways you can encourage your child's independent toileting. One is to fade your prompting. For example, you may be able to bring him to the door of the bathroom instead of going completely inside with him. Then continue to gradually fade farther back—wait in the hallway a few times, then stop a room away. Gradually you can fade back more and more, until he's going without you.

Some children can also get in the habit of going by themselves if it becomes part of an established daily routine. For example, we worked with a kindergartner who wet his pants daily at school. However, when the staff started having him go just before snack each day, that eventually became part of his routine, and he stopped having accidents.

A MOTHER LOOKS AT FAMILY LIFE

Andrew was an awful infant. I adored him because he was my firstborn, and he was the cutest thing imaginable, with big blue eyes and curly blond hair, but the truth is, he was pretty miserable most of the time. The pediatrician dubbed him a "nervous" baby, which was his way of explaining the fact that the only thing that kept Andrew from crying was nursing him. I nursed him *every hour and a half* for the first six months of his life. For those six months, I got to know the inside of the ladies' room at every restaurant, museum, and department store on the west side of L.A. Not that I always bothered going to the ladies' room—I reached a point where I was so exhausted and indifferent that I would slip him under my shirt and put him on the breast wherever I was. I just wore a lot of oversized T-shirts. Even at night I had to nurse him every couple of hours. For those same six months, my husband slept by himself in what was supposed to have been the baby's room, and I slept with Andrew in a bassinet at my side. He'd wake up several times a night, and I'd nurse him.

He refused to take the bottle for those first six months, so as soon as we finally got him to accept a bit of breast milk from a bottle, I weaned him completely to formula within the week—I was so sick and tired of having him chomp on my breast, I couldn't get him on the bottle fast enough.

Looking back, I realize that even as an infant, Andrew had already staked out the two areas that were going to be difficult for the two of us to deal with together over the years: eating and sleeping.

Sleeping Problems

As far as I could tell, Andrew simply didn't need much sleep. As a baby, he basically didn't sleep at all—or at least it felt that way. He napped between nursing sessions—sometimes—but he never slept longer than a couple of hours. And he never fell asleep on his own.

I remember once going to see someone else's baby a few months after Andrew was born. This other baby was lying happily in a carriage, staring up at the ceiling. While we talked, his eyelids grew heavy until they closed completely, and he was asleep. I was stunned—Andrew had never once fallen asleep without being nursed, rocked, or walked to sleep. I didn't know babies could just drift off to sleep like that!

I would spend my days walking or nursing Andrew to sleep, only to have him wake up again soon after, crying. I didn't have time to do anything but tend to him. The second Rob came home from work, I would shove the baby at him and collapse somewhere. Rob would walk Andrew until about two or three in the morning, and then it would be my turn again. I remember one night Rob came home from work, took Andrew, and said to me, "Go get some sleep," and I said, "I can't, I'm starving—I haven't eaten all day because he wouldn't let me put him down." Rob said, "Well, go eat, then." I burst into tears and sobbed, "I'm too tired to eat and too hungry to sleep!"

A lot of babies aren't great sleepers in the beginning. I know—I have three other kids and none of them slept through the night for months. But eventually (with some effort on our part) they did settle down and start sleeping more. Not Andrew. Even long after we'd stopped feeding him during the night, he continued to need some kind of parental soothing to get back to sleep. I remember going to a hotel when he was probably around two years old, and even there Rob and I took turns pretty much all night long, stepping up and down on a small stairway outside our hotel room, trying desperately to get into a rhythm that would lull the kid back to sleep for a couple more hours.

Not only did Andrew wake up a lot during the night, at five in the morning he'd be up for the day. I'd wrap us up in a blanket, and we'd sit out on our porch swing and watch the sun rise. It would have been nice, if I hadn't been so exhausted I couldn't enjoy anything.

Once Andrew was diagnosed with autism, we found out that sleep problems often came with the disability. All our experts had suggestions, from letting him cry to giving him melatonin every night, but they also admitted that they hadn't yet found any magic cures. We tried letting him cry in his crib (something that worked successfully with our subsequent children), but he never learned to settle himself down. We didn't try the melatonin, though—drugs, even natural ones, make me nervous. I have heard that some parents of kids with autism use it successfully, so maybe I should have tried it.

Eventually Andrew got too big to walk or rock, but he still wanted us nearby whenever he woke up, which was a lot. The one thing that everyone I consulted agreed on was that parents have to be strict and consistent in the middle of the night—not give in to any demands, just insist the kid stay in his own bed. Unfortunately, at two in the morning I was too tired to do anything but whatever would get me back to sleep the fastest, even if it meant letting him get in bed with us. (I think this is often where the gulf between therapists and parents gets widest—in the wee small hours of the night, when you know what you're supposed to do but are just too damn tired to do it.)

I remember Wayne, our behavior therapist, patiently outlining to me how I should make Andrew go back to his room each night when he cried and sit with him there, gradually fading my presence by sitting farther and farther across the room from him, until I was out in the hallway. By doing it gradually, I would get him accustomed to being by himself without triggering any panic.

In the cold light of day, I thought Wayne's plan made sense. But at three in the morning, my mind foggy with sleep and dreams, the last thing I wanted to do was get up to go sit on the cold floor. I just wanted to stay in my own sweet bed, and if that meant Andrew had to crawl in next to me, well, so be it. I always regretted it the next morning, but the next morning seemed far away in the middle of the night.

A mom I knew suggested I put a sleeping bag on the floor in my room and insist Andrew lie down there rather than in our bed (a solution she'd hit upon for her own typically developing child). I went one better—we bought a small chaise longue, and I explained to Andrew that when it was dark outside and the windows looked black, he couldn't talk to me, but he *could* come into my room quietly and settle himself back down on the "lying chair," which was just a few feet away from my bed. It wasn't what the therapists were telling me to do, but it *was* the beginning of Andrew's learning not to need me at night, and more important, it bought me a few more hours of sleep each night.

The "lying chair" solution turned out to be a good intermediary step toward nighttime independence. Without the full reinforcement of sharing our bed, Andrew opted to come in less and less frequently, until he was only coming in on those nights when he had a bad dream.

Unfortunately, he was still waking up painfully early and expecting me to get up with him. I had to go to sleep at nine p.m., hours before Rob (which meant we never got time alone together), just to try to get enough sleep in. This early-morning wake-up call went on for years, but I gradually found some activities Andrew was willing to do alone—he learned to read, for one thing, and he also liked drawing—and I kept reminding him at bedtime that he could do those things when he woke up, and he didn't need to wake me. It was hit-or-miss at first, but eventually he learned that if he *didn't* wake Mom up, he could do whatever he wanted (including self-stimulatory behaviors that I would normally frown upon, like hand puppets), and that freedom gradually became more appealing than my company.

Finally, he wasn't waking me up.

Later On

Years later, Andrew ironically became the only one of my four children who virtually *never* woke me up. Once he figured it all out, he became very self-sufficient. Starting halfway through elementary school, he took over his own bedtime; he didn't even wait for us to tell him he had to go to bed, just brushed his teeth, put on his pajamas, turned out his light, put down his shades, and climbed between the sheets, ready for us to come in and say good night.

Often, though, he would still be awake a couple of hours later when I came in to check on him before going to sleep myself—he'd be in bed, but wide awake. And for years he remained the first one up in the morning, but he'd stay quietly in his room, keeping busy, not waking up anyone else. He rarely ever seemed tired and could stay up late with no repercussions the next day. I found myself wishing I needed as little sleep as he seemed to.

Sleep, Ten Years Later

Well, he sure doesn't get up early anymore. It's possible he wakes up earlier than he lets on, but he doesn't exactly spring out of bed: if Andrew doesn't have a job or internship to get to, he doesn't get out of bed until after eleven, and sometimes not until one or so. Not unless we tell him he has to. Most nights he goes to bed at . . . actually, I have no idea, since it's hours after I do. He's on his own schedule and has been for years. With both my big boys, I made a deal when they were in high school: so long as they got up by themselves and were ready to go when it was time to leave in the morning, I wouldn't bug them about bedtime. For the last three years of high school, Andrew not only got himself up, he drove himself to school, so I didn't have to do a thing in the morning for him other than wave good-bye as he walked out the door. And I don't think he was ever tardy.

Rereading this book really brings home the often incredible gulf between my past and present. Is this independent young adult really the same human being whose inability to sleep destroyed my sanity for so many years? I honestly thought for a while that my child would never fall asleep on his own. Never. It felt like an impossibility. I also thought he would rise with the sun his entire life. And now . . . now I knock at his door at eleven a.m., telling him to get up and get going, and he mumbles sleepily that he's awake—but doesn't actually get up and get going. If he sees the sunrise these days, it's because he's stayed up so late, not because he's woken up so early.

Of course, my ability to sleep was so destroyed by him and his siblings and the years of having fretful infants and anxious toddlers that I rarely sleep through the night anymore, anyway. But that's another story.

Eating

Somewhere between his second and third birthdays, Andrew decided he liked about six foods: bread, cookies, Cheerios, orange juice, pasta, and dairy products like milk and yogurt. That was pretty much it. His diet wasn't unhealthful (I once had a nutritionist check out his weekly intake, and she said it was pretty good), but it sure was narrow.

The very sight of meat made him queasy. If we made him touch his tongue to a piece of beef—and we did on occasion, on the advice of a therapist—he would retch. He was incredibly sensitive to strong odors and foods that were an unappealing color or texture.

A lot of kids are picky eaters, and we knew that, but several of the people who worked with Andrew after he was diagnosed said that kids with autism are especially likely to be picky and that, unlike other kids, they tend to narrow their taste in food even more as time goes by. Wayne even told us a cautionary tale about one teenage boy he knew who would eat only protein bars and milk, and who had grown obese as a result.

Several people suggested that we insist that Andrew eat only what I wanted to serve for dinner—not allow him to have his usual Cheerios and yogurt at almost every meal but put chicken and vegetables in front of him night after night, with no other choices, until he broke down and ate it out of pure hunger. It works, they said. You just have to be firm.

Maybe they were right, but I couldn't go through with it. It wasn't just the part about making my kid starve and be unhappy that bothered me—I had some logistical concerns about the plan. Say you put dinner out, and your kid doesn't eat it; then he asks for milk an hour later. There's nothing wrong with a glass of milk—that's part of a healthful diet. But if you give it to him, then he'll fill up on that, and you've lost ground. On the other hand, it seems arbitrary to say, "No, you can't have milk," when milk is good for you, and you want your kid to drink milk.

I just couldn't figure out a way around that. So we kept giving him the foods he liked, but we would occasionally use the "first/then" approach and insist that he try a teeny-tiny bite of something new before he could have his regular food—hence licking the meat. We hoped he'd have a breakthrough and like something. Although this approach helped, we didn't do it in any organized way; we never worked out an intervention plan for the eating issues, because they never seemed that important compared to things like language acquisition and social skills. You pick your battles when you have a kid with special needs, and since the nutritionist had assured us that his diet wasn't harmful, that wasn't one I cared enough about to fight. I just made sure I never ran out of Cheerios.

A Surprise Benefit

When Andrew was seven, his younger brother Leo was diagnosed with celiac disease, a rare disorder that makes you unable to tolerate any gluten (a protein found in wheat and other grains). Your own immune system basically destroys your intestines in the effort to get rid of the gluten. Four-year-old Leo had stopped growing and was weak and anemic, but once he was diagnosed and put on a gluten-free diet, he grew five inches in one year and became strong and healthy again.

Of course, when Leo went on the gluten-free diet, we pretty much all did. At restaurants, we could each order what we liked, but at home I tried to keep meals gluten free so Leo wouldn't feel left out. This had an interesting effect on Andrew. Since his diet up until then was what you might call "all gluten, all the time," consisting as it did largely of bread, Cheerios, and pasta, at first he was pretty unhappy about the change. We did our best to find decent-tasting substitutes for the foods he missed, but some things just weren't the same (back in those days, gluten-free baked goods weren't nearly as tasty as they are now).

But here's the funny thing: his diet suddenly exploded. The kid who would only eat six things got so bored with the gluten-free diet that he started trying everything—and liking a lot of it. Tamales, enchiladas, sushi, Caesar salad . . . the list went on and on. He still didn't love meat and chicken, but on occasion he'd even eat a hot dog or hamburger.

Ironically and unintentionally, the family's switch to a gluten-free diet forced us to do what Dr. Koegel and a bunch of other therapists had suggested, which was to take away the foods Andrew ate exclusively and make him try new things. Turns out, doing that really works. We just hadn't been able to bring ourselves to do it until going gluten-free forced us to.

Eating, Ten Years Later

So. Not. An. Issue.

Siblings

Years ago, I was talking to a friend of mine who happened to be a speech pathologist. We often talked shop, and she was always very insightful and knowledgeable. We were discussing how well Andrew was doing, and she said to me, "You know, I think a lot of it has to do with how big your family is. There's always so much going on over there—you always have people over, and he always has siblings around. He pretty much *had* to learn to be social."

Of course, when Rob and I decided to have two, three, and then four children, we didn't do it to provide a therapeutic climate for our oldest child. You don't decide to have more kids to service the one you already have. (At least, I hope you don't.) The fact that it worked that way was an unexpected bonus.

There's no doubt that Andrew's little brother Leo was his best therapist from the moment Leo could talk and therefore make demands on him. He assumed his older brother was there to play with him and wouldn't take no for an answer. Even as a preschooler, he seemed to understand that sometimes you had to say Andrew's name more than once to get his attention and that sometimes you even had to say, "Hey, Andrew!" very loudly. Which he did, patiently and comfortably. To him, Andrew's reluctance to play wasn't weird, it was just something he had to get over, because Leo needed a playmate.

As Leo got older and learned all sorts of things, he shared them with both his family and his brother, which helped Andrew out socially. For instance, Leo came home one day in first grade and said that he had to have boxer shorts, because no one else in his class was still wearing tighty-whities. I asked around and discovered he was absolutely right—cool kids wore boxers. I bought him boxers, *and* I bought them for Andrew, who would never have known to ask for them on his own and who therefore ran the risk of looking very uncool in the boys' room. Same thing with socks—Andrew was still wearing crew socks when Leo came home and asked me to get him some ankle-height socks. Sure enough, I looked around and realized that very few boys still wore crew socks. I made Andrew switch over, too.

When Leo started getting sarcastic and talking back, toward the end of his second-grade year, we started hearing the same tone of voice from fourth-grader Andrew. A good thing? Actually, yes. Kids that age get sarcastic sometimes, and up until then Andrew had sounded almost abnormally polite and rehearsed for his age. It wasn't something we could *teach* him ("Can you talk a little less politely to us? Could you be just a little bit rude?"), but his brother was the right person to lead the way. And don't even get me started on how they used to giggle together if the subject of nudity came up.

Because the three younger kids have always liked to throw parties and go on family outings, Andrew's contact with other kids increased over the years, and his social skills were all the better for it. Our house was and remains often crammed with people coming and going—how could anyone not become so-cial in that atmosphere?

Although Leo may have been more socially aware than Andrew, he openly admired his brother for the many things Andrew excelled at: I used to hear Leo bragging to friends about how Andrew knew everything there was to know about the Beatles, how he could list the presidents, or how Andrew was going to start a rock band. (Little brothers take these things at face value.). The summer that Andrew was nine and Leo was seven, they informed me that they only wanted to go to camp if they could go together, and every day they walked onto that field side by side and often hand in hand.

Setting the Tone

Like many other kids with autism, Andrew doesn't have a mean or malicious bone in his body.

I've noticed that in almost all families it's the oldest child who sets the tone and decides whether tormenting siblings or nurturing them will be the household m.o. Because Andrew has always been gentle, kind, and accepting, he created a truly loving household for his younger siblings. The passivity of his early years gave way over time to a basic good-natured acceptance of the responsibilities of an eldest child.

I remember watching one day when Andrew's then four-year-old sister—half his size and weight—thought it would be funny to shove him hard enough to send him stumbling down several stairs. I was furious at her; Andrew just laughed good-naturedly and told me he was all right. He would never in a million years strike back at her. (Although honesty compels me to admit he's not quite so tol-erant of that little sister's mischievousness over a decade later. Fortunately their sparring is only verbal.)

Because Andrew never hit, didn't have to have his own way all the time, and shared his toys without complaining, his younger siblings also found it easy to be good guys. They weren't exactly perfect little angels—there were plenty of battles over meaningless items that two or more children wanted desperately at the same moment—but I honestly think my kids are kinder to each other than most of the siblings I see outside our home. And I give Andrew the credit for a lot of that.

Driving Mr. Andrew

From the age of three until he was seven, Andrew had an incredibly busy sched-ule of therapies and interventions, and, while some of his clinicians came to our house, many of them didn't. That meant someone had to drive him to speech therapy, drive him to occupational therapy, drive him to social skills groups, drive him to—well, you get the idea. That "someone" was sometimes his father, sometimes a babysitter, usually me. It's not that different from life with any busy kid, I guess (some of my friends have kids who are athletes, and they drive them much farther and much more frequently than I ever did Andrew), except that, of course, it *is*.

Andrew was first diagnosed when his brother Leo was a newborn, and I spent the next year or so overwhelmed with the task ahead of me, wading through options and scenarios, trying to find therapists who could help keep him stimulated, challenged, involved, and engaged. When I wasn't doing "autism stuff," I was sunk deep into my own pit of anxiety and exhaustion.

It's not a big stretch to say I was a lousy mother to baby Leo that year.

He survived—we had a wonderful full-time babysitter back then, and his dad filled in whenever he was around, and I certainly loved him and held him a lot—but I wish I could have that year back to enjoy his babyhood, the way I later enjoyed it with his two younger siblings. I wish I had marveled at his every step, adored his every sound, cooed with him for hours on end. I hope I did some of that, but, honestly, that year—the Year of Autism—is all a big painful blur.

For a while I thought my life would always be like that, always be about Andrew and his needs, about planning his schedule and finding his therapists and keeping him engaged. . . .

But he got better and we had more kids and they all got older, and life slowly but surely got much, much more normal.

Making Every Family Member as Important as the Next

I've learned something that I may not have been good enough about when the kids were little—but at least now I can pass my hard-won knowledge on to others—and that's that no child should feel like his sibling's needs are more important than his own (or less important, for that matter). The best kind of family is one where each child feels that if something's important to her, she'll get the time and attention she needs; if something's important to one of her siblings, that sibling will get the same courtesy; and if their two needs should conflict, it'll all be worked out in a fair and balanced manner. It's easy to make your home life revolve around a kid with special needs, but it doesn't help him learn to interact positively with other people, and it's just not fair to your other kids. So schedule your child's therapy but make sure you're present at your other kids' dance recitals, doctor appointments, games, plays, concerts, etc. The goal should be fairness.

No child should feel like his needs matter less to his parents than his sibling's—those needs may be *different*, but they're equally important, and if you make it clear to your kids that your goal is to pay equal attention to every one of them, they'll love you and each other all the more for it.

A Normal Life

I love having four kids. I love having a noisy house filled with children and bugs and friends and junk food and musical instruments and mess everywhere—okay, maybe I don't love the mess so much, but it's a small price to pay for the rest. This is what I wrote ten years ago:

"Andrew is a wonderful, important part of our family. Thanks to him, we all listen to the Beatles, celebrate Presidents' Day, do tons of art projects, and have patience with anyone we meet who's a little quirky. His siblings are equally wonderful and important, and they too have shared their interests and special areas of knowledge with the rest of us. Our lives are no longer about driving Andrew to therapies—we still do some of that, of course, but it's not *about* that. On any given day, we also have to get Franny to a play date, Leo to tennis, Rubin to preschool, and I'm always trying to find time to write. When Leo wanted to go to the bug fair at the Natural History Museum, we all went, even Andrew, who complained that he didn't like insects as much as his brother. Tough. He had to go.

"The point is, we're a family. One of our kids has special needs, one has a rare autoimmune disease, one is an only girl in a family of boys (and recently diagnosed with an even rarer autoimmune disease), and one is the youngest, scrambling to keep up—and none of that makes any one of them more important or less important than the rest. Andrew is a vital part of our family, and so is every other member. Whatever we need to do to make things work for all of us, we'll do."

Ten Years Later

"A normal life"????

What on earth was I thinking when I used those words ten years ago (see subtitle above)?

Maybe I was being funny?

No, to be fair to myself, my point was that no matter what we'd had to deal with (autism, celiac disease, Addison's disease, Hashimoto's disease, anxiety, etc.), we were still a happy, functioning family. Which is as true today as it was back when I wrote that so many years ago.

But . . .

Normal, we're not.

On the other hand, I'm not convinced anyone is. I'm not even convinced anyone should *want* to be. What does "normal" even mean, anyway?

My kids tell me frequently I'm not a normal mother. I'm too honest with them, for one thing—I have no problem answering any questions they might ask, whether they're about sex, genocide, relationships, my own past. . . . We have crazy, funny, ridiculous, possibly horrifying conversations all the time.

For another, I'll do anything to avoid having to drive. Even short drives. I mean, I do it when I have to, but I really hate it. That's just not normal.

For another . . . well, if you've met me and seen the way I dress, you know it's not normal for a mother who lives on the west side of L.A. You might call it "thrift store chic," except without the "chic" part.

My kids seem pretty fond of me, though, and even if they tease me for being strange, they seem content to have a weird mother. And you know what? I love my crazy weird kids right back. Not one of them fits the American ideal that you find in television commercials. They're odd and challenging and wonderful.

I no longer think the word "normal" has any place in a book about child rearing—whether or not your kid has some kind of diagnosis. Our ideas of normal are based on fictional ideals and on what we think other people's lives are like. The truth is, we don't really know what anyone else's life is like, and I truly doubt there's any such thing as "normal" if we dig down deep enough into any family's universe.

If we all accept that and (ideally) embrace it, then we can revel in the good stuff of our lives and deal with the bad stuff and stop worrying about whether we're measuring up to everyone else.

And if we surrender our hopes for normalcy, maybe we'll learn to appreciate the different, the quirky, the weird, the wonderful, the awesome, the bizarre . . . real life, in other words.

Chapter Nine

Self-Management:
Teaching Your Child to Teach Himself

QUESTION: You keep referring to self-management, and I have a vague sense of what it means—clearly it has something to do with teaching your child to monitor and evaluate his own behavior, but I have no idea how to go about actually *doing* it.

WHEN we're very young, we get a lot of help with all aspects of our daily routines and with learning how to talk and socialize and how to control emotions, such as anger and frustration. But over time we gradually become more and more responsible for managing our own lives. We start learning how to take care of our daily needs independently, to evaluate what's appropriate to say to another person—and what might hurt his feelings—and to follow society's written and unwritten rules. We write lists and check them off, and learn to work independently and to control our own behavior. Some people have better self-control than others, but most of us fall into a certain standard range.

Children with autism, perhaps because they tend to be less socially involved throughout their lives, often don't develop enough independence and self-control on their own. So we frequently have to teach them how to self-manage their own behaviors. This isn't to say that self-management is only effective with children with disabilities. In fact, some early research on it focused on college students who smoked cigarettes. The researchers asked the college students to simply write down how many cigarettes they smoked during class. This reduced the smoking. In other words, simply by becoming aware of the behavior, the participants did it less.

It's the same idea for many weight loss programs. Often we don't realize how much we're eating, or how unhealthful the foods are that we're eating, until we start writing down each and every bite that goes into our mouths. Keeping track is a good way to start, and then making a plan and monitoring and rewarding ourselves systematically can really help to change behavior.

Self-management can be especially useful in school settings where you don't want an adult "hovering" over the child. If properly implemented, certain intervention programs can be programmed to occur without needing an adult physically present by using the self-management model. But the program does need to be very systematic and closely monitored to be effective. We'll explain the details in this chapter.

My Own Experience Using Self-Management

I was lucky enough to have known about this strategy when my daughter was in kindergarten. When we had one parent-teacher conference, the teacher told us she was pushing other children and that if she continued to do so, she would be given a "citation." If a kid got three citations, he or she was suspended from school for a day.

(An aside: I always hate how our schools are so punishment oriented. Just think about how many children are suspended or expelled from school who would benefit much more from someone teaching them appropriate behaviors, helping them with their schoolwork, or simply giving them the support they need. When they're given "time out" through suspension or expulsion, they get further behind and spend less time with their peers—neither of which helps them toward future success. Too often the schools don't spend the time to really figure out *why* children are not succeeding . . . but that's another book.)

Back to the pushing. I clearly remembered when it started—it began the prior year when she had imitated a peer in preschool who frequently pushed. When I asked the preschool teacher about it, she said not to worry, that my daughter was just "holding her own" among the boys. So I stopped worrying . . . until kindergarten when it came up again.

Wow. Here we were, her first year of grammar school, and they were already talking about serious behavior consequences. I asked the teacher to try to figure out why the pushing might be happening. The next day the teacher met me at my car and said that my daughter had pushed again. She insisted that it had happened for "no reason at all"; she just randomly pushed. Before I left school, I was able to get a little information out of the teacher, mainly that the pushing only happened in the afternoons and never in the mornings. So I made a plan. First, I had gotten somewhat lax about her bedtime. Since the pushing only happened in the afternoon, I guessed that fatigue might be a variable, so I started putting her to bed a little earlier. Second, I asked *her* why she pushed, and she had a very logical and intelligent reason for each and every push. It was *not* random as her teacher had suggested. Rory cut in front of her friend Emily, so she *had* to push him. Rebecca called Amy "stupid," so she *had* to push her. There were always reasons, even if her teacher was unaware of them.

While it was most certainly necessary to teach her the appropriate substitute behavior (see chapter 3), we couldn't ignore the pushes while we were teaching her to use her words—we had this citation hanging over our heads. So we set up a self-management program. I bought a bag of candy, and every lunchtime I went to school and asked my daughter whether she had pushed anyone that morning. If she hadn't, she got a treat. We did the same thing after school. Once we started the self-management, she never pushed again, and after a week I stopped the lunchtime visits; a week after that we stopped the after-school reward. Our program had worked incredibly quickly.

My daughter and I still talk about those days. She still remembers how much effort it took for her not to push, but how badly she wanted to be able to tell me that she hadn't pushed and to get her special treat.

A few important things to remember here: I started with a short enough time period so that she would experience success. She was only pushing in the afternoon, but I still checked in during the middle of the day, so that she could report on her morning behavior: the fact that it was almost always a positive report at that time of day meant she could get rewarded and instantly feel successful and capable. And finally, ignoring or excusing behavior when it first crops up is a mistake—an effective program can eliminate small problems before they turn into bigger ones.

The Pros and Cons of Self-Management

There are good and bad things about self-management. It's fast and efficient, and can work in all settings, but is especially useful at school, where there's a risk of getting kicked out of a class or some other serious punishment if a behavior doesn't disappear quickly. The bad part is that it doesn't really address the "why" of the problem behavior. And, as we discussed in chapter 3, if we're going to get rid of a behavior problem permanently, the kids *must* learn a replacement behavior. Self-management can buy you time, though, the way it did my daughter. So the first thing you (or the school) need to do is to take some baseline data on the behavior you want to decrease or increase, then you need to figure out *why* the problem behavior is happening so that while you're using self-management you can also work on teaching appropriate replacement behaviors.

Of course, typical children often already have the appropriate behaviors in their repertoires, so for them it's just a matter of making sure the inappropriate ones don't pop up. But for children with communication difficulties, it may take some effort to get the replacement behavior established. First you'll have to figure out if the child has the capability to use a new behavior and just doesn't (sometimes referred to as a "performance deficit") or if he doesn't have the new behavior in his repertoire at all, which means you'll need to teach it from scratch. Nevertheless, self-management still helps while you're teaching and/ or practicing the appropriate replacement behaviors.

Interestingly, when self-management programs first appeared in the literature, they were primarily used with adults of average or above intelligence. There seemed to be a feeling that self-control procedures would be challenging for individuals with disabilities. But, little by little, researchers showed that children could learn to self-manage and that even individuals with mild disabilities could. Our research in the 1980s and early 1990s showed that individuals with more significant disabilities (autism was grouped with those) could also use self-management procedures. In 1990, we were the first to show that self-management could be effectively used in full-inclusion settings to decrease disruptive and inappropriate behaviors, so that students could participate without the need for constant adult supervision. We received federal funding from the National Institute of Mental Health to develop self-management programs for individuals with autism, and over the years I have developed and implemented thousands of them. Based on both research and clinical experience, I can say that children who are over five years old and have some verbal communication can readily learn self-management, although it's possible for younger and less-verbal children to use it, too. Self-management is ideal in settings where a child is expected to respond without constant adult vigilance or where the behavior needs to be changed quickly. We have used self-management techniques to address aggression, on-task responding, self-stimulatory behavior, responding (verbally) to questions, asking questions, taking turns, self-help skills in adolescents and adults, work-readiness, and much more.

Here's how you do it.

How to Implement a Program of Self-Management

1. **DEFINE THE BEHAVIOR YOU WANT TO INCREASE OR DECREASE.** The first thing you want to do is to clearly and specifically define the behavior of

interest. My test when I read my graduate students' reports is whether I can "see" the behavior through the words. If the report says "engages in aggressive behavior," it's not clear to me exactly what's happening, but if it says "hits classmates with a closed fist," then I can "see" what's happening. Similarly, if the report simply notes that the child is "off task," I really don't have a clue what's going on. But if the report says "she's frequently out of her seat, wandering around the classroom and staring into space," I can fully picture that. Always make sure that the target behavior is clearly and carefully defined so that everyone involved is looking at the same thing. If other behaviors pop up later, that's fine, we can address those, too, but at this point we're going to want to monitor whether the specific behavior we're targeting is effectively being increased or decreased when we start our self-management program.

2. **MEASURE THE BEHAVIOR YOU WISH TO CHANGE.** Next we want to get an idea of how often the behavior happens. You'll need to decide if it's more appropriate to measure the length of time the behavior lasts or the number of times it occurs. This is important because some behaviors are more conducive to interval systems (did it happen or not in a minute?), while others are more accurately measured by a frequency count (a tally each time the behavior occurs).

For example, if you want to work on off-task behavior, measure the percentage of time your child stims during a fifteen-minute period. You can mark whether it happens or not every fifteen seconds, every thirty seconds, or every minute, then do the math. Is it 50 percent of the time? One hundred percent of the time? Does it happen more during some activities than during others? On the other hand, you'll want to use a tally system if it's something that has discrete onsets and endings. If you tally the behavior, make sure that the data-recording period is constant. If you're tallying how often a child raises his hand during circle time, and the circle time varies from five to thirty minutes, your data will be meaningless. But if you record how often your child raises his hand every five minutes, then you'll be able to accurately compare the child's behavior during and after intervention.

There are other important things you may want to consider during your data collection. For example, does your child answer questions only after the third time the teacher asks? Does he push other children every time they approach him or only some of the time? In other words, get a good idea of how often and when the behavior is happening (or not happening, if it's something you want to increase). It may be helpful to use the behavior data sheet at the back of this book, especially if you're trying to control a disruptive behavior. Understanding the behavior—when it does and doesn't happen—is crucial in developing intervention plans. Also, as I mentioned above, it helps us understand which behaviors need to be taught and which ones are known but just not being used in all settings. If it's a performance deficit, the appropriate behavior just needs to be prompted in the additional settings; if it's not, you need to teach the behavior.

3. **MAKE A RECORDING FORM FOR YOUR CHILD TO USE.** You'll need to choose a recording device for your child to keep track of the number of times he's performed the desired task. This can simply be a pencil and paper (which works for intervals or tallies), or you can purchase a repeat chronographic alarm (for interval recording), available at sporting goods stores, or a counter (for tallies). You can find all sorts of cool counters online, ranging from mechanical to electronic. Some can be worn on your wrist or even like a ring on your finger. Also, these days most phones have countdown alarms or apps that you can download easily; these can be set for any interval of time, which is very useful if the goal is to have your child spend periods free of the problem behavior. So match the recording device to your measurement. If it's being measured in intervals, you'll need to teach your child to use a form that has time periods—and for that you can use an alarm or countdown feature on a wristwatch or phone or another kind of timer. If it's discrete events, you can use a wrist counter, piece of paper, or other device that can be used to count each time the behavior is used.

4. **TEACH YOUR CHILD HOW TO EVALUATE HIS OR HER OWN BEHAVIOR.** Your child must understand what to record. For example, if you're working on answering questions appropriately, you'll need to have him practice what constitutes both a good response and an inappropriate response. You can model this for your child, or you can teach him to discriminate his own responses by giving him feedback. We worked with one young boy who bit his fingers until they bled—it had started out as nail biting but had gotten worse over time. We taught him to become aware whether his fingers were in his mouth or out of his mouth. We've also taught children to

be aware of "good sitting" (staying in the chair at the desk without jumping up) and "good working" (completing the work). Most children learn to discriminate between the desired behavior and incorrect behavior in one or two sessions, as they're pretty used to people reprimanding them for the latter.

5. TEACH YOUR CHILD HOW TO RECORD RESPONSES. This is called "self-monitoring" and is another important step to the self-management program. One really nice thing about self-management is that it focuses on the positive. Once the child has learned what's expected, we measure the positive behavior during the self-management: we count every time a correct response is made or whenever an interval with appropriate behavior passes.

Even if you're trying to get rid of a negative behavior, you can still focus on the positive. For example, if I'm trying to get rid of a child's hitting, I'm going to reward her for periods *without* hitting, but I'll call it "quiet hands" or "good behavior" to keep the goal positive. Or, if my child doesn't raise his hand in class, I'm going to give him a point every time he answers a question. You want to give your child lots of rewards at first, so make sure you start with short, manageable periods, based on the information that you collected in your baseline.

For example, if your child gets out of his desk approximately every fifteen minutes, you may want to start your self-management intervals at ten minutes. You want him to feel successful by being rewarded for something that's well within his ability, and to do that you need to start with an interval that's shorter than the baseline or with a small number of responses. No one likes to keep trying if most of his attempts are unsuccessful—that's just discouraging—and that's what will happen if your initial expectations are too high. Let your child know what it feels like to succeed and he'll want to keep up the good work.

And sometimes children need different lengths of time for different activities. I recently developed a self-management program for a child with many varied off-task behaviors (staring into space, putting nonedible items in the mouth, such as paper, rocks, and staples, playing with the carpet and items on the desk, spitting saliva and making saliva bubbles, putting his fingers in his mouth, touching and poking peers, and talking out loud). His most challenging time period was circle time, so we started there, with one-minute increments. Prior to the self-management program, we had given him preferential seating right at the front, and the teacher laughed at the way I would slither up on my stomach with his self-management sheet every minute (we hadn't started him on a timer yet) in my efforts to keep from disturbing the class. At any rate, during desk time he spent much more time on task so we were able to start with five-minute increments when he was at his desk. Finally, during computer time he was almost always on task, so there we went for fifteen-minute periods. Within about a month, he was on task almost all day long.

6. **REWARD YOUR CHILD.** Once your child is engaging in the desired behaviors and marking them on the counter or paper, you'll need to reward her. Start with frequent rewards then gradually fade them out. "Fading" simply means to gradually and systematically withdraw the intensive program until it's similar to what would happen naturally. For example, if you've started off rewarding your child for staying in his seat for ten minutes, you can then increase the time to twelve or fifteen minutes. You gradually keep adding minutes until you only need to reward at the end of each day, as with any other child. If your child is marking a box every time she answers a peer's question, you may want to increase it to a few boxes before giving her the reward, and so on. In other words, we want to gradually and systematically fade the reward so that longer periods or more incidents of the desired behavior are required. Interestingly, in all the hundreds of self-management programs we've set up for children with disabilities ranging from mild to severe, we have never had a child complain about the fading of the rewards. In fact, some children even fade their own programs naturally as they begin engaging in the behavior without conscious effort. Remember, rewards have to be meaningful. Small ones can be given for points, and larger ones for big gains. Vary them frequently and check in often to make sure your child still considers them worth working for.

7. **FADE THE SELF-MANAGEMENT.** Eventually you're going to want to have the child responding to all the natural consequences in his everyday environment. At school these usually involve some sort of punishment system (unfortunately). For some reason just about every teacher has been taught how to punish a child to keep their classes in line, but very few have learned that it's just as easy and a lot more fun to keep them behaving by pouring on rewards for good behavior.

Recently I was at a school observing a child in a full-inclusion class. The students were all lined up waiting for their teacher. For some reason she was late, and their behavior got worse and worse. I quietly observed them for a while, until their behavior deteriorated from talking to pushing and yelling, at which point I stepped in and said, "Your teacher is going to be so happy when she sees you all lined up and waiting quietly for her!" A few students immediately shaped up, and I praised them lavishly. Then those kids began shushing the others. Pretty soon, the whole class was once again standing quietly. Kids love the positives.

But an adult isn't always there to provide praise and a pat on the head, so kids have to learn to do the right thing on their own. Which is why, with our kids, we want to fade the self-management program so that the natural contingencies are working. Lengthening the intervals serves as a fading step; as the intervals get longer, the program is being faded. Sometimes I try to get the self-management intervals lengthened to the natural classroom breaks, so that the teacher can do the self-management checking and the aide or support person can completely fade out. Similarly, if the child is tallying points, over time you can up the number of points needed for a reward. You'd think the children would complain about this but they're just fine as you fade. Finally, often the children forget to mark an interval or tally but still engage in the target behavior. This is sort of a natural fading as the behavior becomes more automatic. Additionally, if you use a timer, you won't need an adult to check in on the child—also fading adult support and creating independence. Finally, you can teach the child to self-administer rewards, which helps create complete independence.

Now your child is on the road to evaluating his own behavior and taking another step toward independence. You can send the watch or self-management sheets with him wherever he goes, even if an interventionist isn't there. The beauty of this program is that the children learn to implement the intervention themselves. If self-management is done properly, you should be able to see changes quickly in the chosen behavior. Again, self-management is great for school settings but can also be used at home, in the community, and anywhere else your child goes.

The Last Step

In any intervention program, the last step has to involve active participation by the person whose behavior is being targeted. Every New Year's resolution or behavior change we make depends on our making an effort to do something different, whether it's losing weight, exercising more, spending more time with family, quitting smoking or drinking, or getting out of debt. Sure, we can have people help us with a diet plan or a budget—and I'll admit that I'd probably still leave my shoes outside of my closet if my husband hadn't said a few choice words every time he tripped over them in the middle of the night—but, for a permanent change, we need to take responsibility for ourselves. We have to learn to exercise self-control, but it helps to use a systematic program, such as writing down each and every thing that goes into our mouths or checking off a list every time we complete a task.

The same holds true for individuals with an autism spectrum disorder. In the end, they're going to need to take an active role in their own intervention to be independent. Self-management is a perfect way to help achieve this goal.

SOME EXAMPLES OF SUCCESSFUL SELF-MANAGEMENT PROGRAMS
Ty—Keeping Clean and Groomed

Ty was an eleven-year-old sixth-grade student with autism and visual impairment. His parents had to be at work early, so he was left to fend for himself each morning, which included getting up, getting breakfast, showering, dressing, and being ready for the bus when it arrived. He was extremely bright but attended a special day class for students with mild disabilities (although I thought he should have been fully included).

Anyway, he did a nice job of getting himself up and to school, and presumably getting breakfast, since he never complained of being hungry when he arrived and he reported having a large bowl of his favorite cereal each morning. Unfortunately, hygiene was a different story. He had a "preservation of sameness" issue and each day he wore the same clothes: a filthy T-shirt that smelled of body odor, horribly stinky socks, and light-colored khaki pants that were stained and way too short for him, since he'd been wearing them for at least a year. He never washed his face or cleaned his glasses, and each day his face got dirtier; he often had a large eye crust in the inside corner of each eye.

He was quite brilliant, but few wanted to be near him. He was so filthy, his clothes were so soiled, and he smelled so awful that teachers dreaded his coming near, and peers teased and alienated him. Clearly we had to do something.

Since the school wasn't able to implement a program in his home, and his parents were unable to supervise his morning routine, we decided to develop a self-management program. Of course, for him, the list was long. Appropriate grooming involved a number of tasks including the following: brushing teeth, washing face, washing hands, cleaning nails, using deodorant, cleaning glasses, putting on clean socks, clean shirt, and clean pants, and showering.

To begin, we clearly defined each hygienic behavior (dirt on face, crust in eyes, soiled shirt, previous day's clothes, and so on) and we made a self-monitoring sheet on paper, listing each behavior and the day of the week, with space for his tallies. We discussed rewards with him, and he chose to get reading books from the library for intermediary points and to get special food treats for larger numbers of points.

To start the actual self-management, we decided to put just one item on the sheet: wash his face. We showed him the dirt on his face and the crust in his eyes and told him that if he washed his face and got the sleep out of his eyes, he would get a point. The other agreement we made with him was that if he came to school and hadn't washed his face, he would need to go into the bathroom and wash before going to class.

The first week was hit-or-miss. Sometimes he would have a clean face and have checked a box and other days we had to send him directly into the boys' room after he arrived on the bus. But the second week was better. Much better. He came in almost every day with a clean face, and the one day that he didn't, he got off the bus and announced to us that he had to go to the boys' room to take care of it.

Now that he was succeeding with the face washing, we added a second box. He knew this meant that he had the possibility to earn more points, so he enthusiastically agreed. So we put cleaning his glasses on the sheet. A friend of mine supplied us with a generous pile of the special cloths for cleaning glasses, and we taught our kid to wipe his each morning. Because he was visually impaired he had a tough time being sure they were clean, but we found that counting five good wipes on each side did the trick. Not only did his glasses look cleaner from the outside, I'm sure it was better from the inside looking out, although he had never complained of the dirty glasses bothering him.

As with most self-management programs, if you do the first steps correctly, each additional step is easier. Gradually and systematically, we added on new behaviors, one at a time: brushing teeth, then putting on a clean shirt, then clean pants, and finally clean socks. His parents put out clean clothes the night before, and with the self-management and the possibility of earning points, he no longer dug through the dirty laundry bag in search of the beloved outfit that he had previously worn on a daily basis. And throughout the process, his honesty was incredible. Even days when he looked pretty clean, he reported honestly when he hadn't taken the time to brush his teeth that day or clean his glasses.

The last step was showering (including washing his greasy hair). We were all worried about this step because there really was no way that we could follow through and make sure he had showered before school. So we made a point of offering him a huge reward if he showered independently. We were all over-joyed when he came in the next day with clean hair and an "x" marked in the "shower" box.

His good hygiene continued through the entire school year, and we gradu-ally faded the point system so that he got just a daily check. We also gradually faded the rewards so that they were less frequent—more like he would experi-ence in natural settings.

By the following year, we didn't even need the self-management program. He was no longer teased because he was now a well-groomed, good-looking middle schooler and people could sit near him comfortably. It made a huge difference for him socially.

Sophie—Learning to Stay on Task

Sophie was a first-grader who was a year older than her classmates because her parents had kept her in preschool an extra year, hoping that she would catch up socially. Kindergarten had had its ups and downs, as the one-on-one aide in her full-inclusion classroom had no training in ASD. In fact, several times when the mom was volunteering in the classroom, she noticed the aide catnapping (yes, actually asleep) or chatting on the phone. The saving grace was that So-phie had an amazing teacher who went the extra mile to keep her engaged and on task.

At Sophie's IEP at the end of kindergarten, the team decided that she should engage in self-management so that the aide could be faded. Her main problems were staring into space, reacting negatively when redirected (such as screaming "no" at the aide or teacher or emitting a loud and ear-piercing scream), not following directions, getting out of her seat, and yelling.

When first grade started, the school began to fade the aide without imple-menting a self-management program. Consequently, Sophie's work and be-havior both suffered. Since the parents had documentation of the decline in

Sophie's work, they requested a meeting and showed many examples of assignments that were incomplete or never started. To give you an idea of how completely uninterested she was in doing her work, Sophie had even spelled her own name incorrectly on some of the assignments, despite the fact that she was a gifted speller and had known how to write her name accurately since preschool.

The team agreed to set up a self-management program, but assignments continued to be incomplete or totally ignored. The parents called another meeting and a few problems with the self-management program emerged. First, the school wanted the teacher to check the self-management program every five minutes. Well, with twenty-two other children in the class, it really wasn't possible for Sophie's teacher to monitor it that frequently. But, based on her pre-self-management data, that was where Sophie needed to start. During the beginning of a self-management program an adult needs to be especially watchful to make sure that the child is accurately monitoring—otherwise the child may get rewarded for intervals with inappropriate behavior and consequently not understand what desirable behavior is for that setting.

The second big problem was that Sophie was being given points for "trying." For example, if she yelled out then quickly covered her mouth, the school felt that she had "tried" and self-corrected, so she should be given the point. While I'm all for rewarding trying, this wasn't the time—Sophie was learning that it was okay to yell out at any time as long as she covered her mouth afterward.

The third problem was that Sophie's rewards were connected to the classroom's behavior management system. The classroom system included a clothespin for each child with his or her name on it. One long piece of fabric on the wall had four sections that the clothespin could get clipped to: green if the child had great behavior; yellow if the child needed to remember to behave; red if the child misbehaved again; and white if a kid was having multiple disruptive incidents in one day. Each day the children started on green and if they misbehaved their clothespin would move down the wall. Toward the end of the day, the teacher would try to catch the children being good, so she could then instruct them to move up their clothespins. All the children who were "green" at the end of the day got a stamp on their hand, and the others got a note sent home relaying what color they were and saying that they were going to need to try harder the next day. The problem was that every time the teacher moved her clothespin down, Sophie threw such big fits—tantrums where she'd roll on the floor screaming and crying—that, the teacher confessed, she never used the clothespin system for her. Instead, Sophie got a stamp on her hand no matter how bad her behavior had been that day.

Fourth, the behavior chart was so complex, with so many different behaviors, that I could barely understand it with a Ph.D.; good luck to a first-grader.

Finally—and this happens a lot—the teacher was tallying all of Sophie's points. It really wasn't self-management at all.

So we tweaked a few things. First, we used kid-friendly language and just put "I did my work and had good behavior" on her chart. That's all. Sophie didn't need a list of every appropriate behavior—just the general rules. Next, we had the aide vigilantly watch Sophie and make sure that she was given the proper feedback after she had completed an interval. That way, she clearly understood whether or not she had engaged in the expected behaviors. This was just too much for the teacher to do, which was why Sophie had been getting points for a lot of intervals that didn't have good behavior.

We also implemented a fade plan. Since the teacher wasn't always able to attend to Sophie every five minutes, she rarely had genuinely good intervals because they were, more often than not, excessively long time periods—too long for Sophie to maintain these early attempts at good behavior. Now that the aide was starting with a time period that pretty much guaranteed success (based on our preintervention data), we could begin to fade. We decided that after four successful time intervals we would increase the time period by a minute. After each interval, Sophie was asked how she had done. The aide gave her direct feedback in a short, direct, and matter-of-fact manner: "Yes, I agree, I like the way you behaved so nicely and did your work," or "That's right, you did get out of your seat. Let's try again," or "I saw you staring into space on that one. Let's try again." So Sophie really understood when she was behaving appropriately and when she wasn't.

Within a month, Sophie's work was on grade level, and she was behaving nicely almost all day long. It took some effort and required a period of constant vigilance, but the work paid off. After just a few short weeks, she was fitting right in with the other students, completing her work, and behaving nicely. Implementing a self-management program *correctly* made a world of difference for her.

Kai—Keeping the Conversation Flowing

Kai was a college student with outstanding grades but huge social challenges. He had received interventions for years, confiding in psychotherapists about his difficulties getting along with others and in particular finding a girlfriend. The "talk therapies" were of no help, since the therapists weren't able to pinpoint *why* he had difficulties interacting socially. He was good-looking and sweet, but even when he was able to get a first date, he never got a second one.

We took an initial baseline of his social interaction skills, by putting him with some same-aged peers and simply asking them to engage in conversation. He readily answered questions and attentively listened when peers chatted. However, whenever there was a pause in the conversation, he froze. Dead silence. These extremely awkward pauses made it challenging for others to be around him. Upon analysis, we realized that he never asked questions. He nodded and made great eye contact but never *asked* questions. Even when his conversational partner said something like "I had such an amazing weekend!" which clearly begs a follow-up question, there was just a long silent pause.

So for his program, we combined video modeling with self-management. We had him watch himself on video and gave him feedback on a number of different questions he could ask during those silent pauses. Then came the self-management: we engaged in conversation with him and had him use a wrist counter to note every time he asked a question. Within four sessions he was asking lots of questions and there were no more uncomfortable pauses during the conversation.

It was a simple intervention and so effective that he's had a steady girlfriend ever since. What's more, knowing what to do—what the problem was—boosted his self-confidence and eliminated his social anxiety and depression.

Manny—Learning to Do Household Chores

Manny was an eight-year-old minimally verbal child when we met him. He spent most of his days doing nonproductive activities, like wandering around the house, watching movies, and engaging in repetitive behaviors. His mother was a waitress and had to work most evenings. She reported that she found it very stressful to have to do the chores when she got home at night and had repeatedly asked Manny to help with some of them, like feeding their dog, packing his lunch, and cleaning his room. Manny never pitched in despite her many requests.

We set to work developing a self-management program so that Manny could take on some chores each evening. We used pictures with Velcro on the back: after successfully completing each task, he was taught to take off the picture and put it in an envelope that was taped on the bottom of the cloth board.

The pictures were broken down into very specific individual steps: take out the dog food (indicated by a picture of the food), scoop a cupful into the dish (indicated by a cup being poured into the dish), put the dog food away (indicated by the bag back in the cupboard), and fill up the dog's water dish (you got it—a bowl under the water tap).

We practiced each of the steps, having him self-monitor by removing the picture when he had successfully completed each task.

We had him learn to pack his lunch in the same way. His mom would make a week's worth of his favorite sandwiches on the weekend and store them in the freezer. She would also put small bags of cut-up fruit and vegetables in a refrigerator drawer, and drinks on the shelf. Manny would look at the pictures, get out the designated items, and place each one in that day's lunch bag.

At the end of his chore chart was a picture of a special treat he got to eat for dessert once all the chores were completed. It took Manny a few weeks to learn each chore, but once he had, he had a new lifetime skill. We could mix up the tasks and he would follow the new order of pictures, which assured us that he was truly self-managing and not simply memorizing the work. This greatly helped his mother and hugely reduced her stress.

QUESTION: I would like to teach my child to groom herself using self-management, but she isn't verbal. Can this be done?

Yes, self-management can be accomplished for nonverbal individuals with ASD by using pictures. You can take or download pictures of each activity you'd like your child to complete, such as washing her face, brushing her hair, brushing her teeth, and so on. Place these pictures on a ring, on a cloth board (with Velcro on the back of the pictures), or on the computer. Then you'll need to teach her to engage in the activity and remove or flip the card, or move forward to the next picture, indicating that the task has been completed. Once they're all finished, your child can get a reward.

Using pictures works fabulously to teach a nonverbal child to complete a series of tasks. We have set up picture self-management programs for a number of activities. And if you want to assess whether your child is actually self-managing rather than just memorizing a string of behaviors, try mixing up the cards. If she's actually doing the self-management, she'll do the tasks in the order of the cards, not the order she learned them in.

QUESTION: What do you do if your child insists that she's practicing the desired behavior but you know she isn't? My daughter keeps coming home from school with tons of checks on her self-management chart for good sitting, but the teacher is saying she's still bouncing out of her seat all the time.

Great question! There are a couple of different scenarios that may be happening here. It may be that your daughter is slipping up on the discrimination step—remember that she has to thoroughly understand the difference between the target behavior and the one that you want to eliminate. She may need a bit more practice on discriminating between what constitutes good sitting and what doesn't. You can help her by making it a game and letting her tell *you* when you're sitting properly and when you're not. Keep it fun—we don't want her to think she's being punished. After you've done that a few times, turn it around and have her show you what's appropriate sitting and what isn't, to make sure she completely understands. If she's embarrassed or uncomfortable showing you the inappropriate behavior, don't push it—if she doesn't want to do it, that means she knows what it is.

If you feel like your child already fully understands the discrimination between appropriate and inappropriate sitting, there could be a couple of things going on.

One possibility is that she wants the points so badly she's willing to give herself points even if they aren't earned. Some of the programs we've developed have focused on both accuracy and correct behavior: the child may earn one point for good behavior and one for accurately evaluating the behavior, so even if she doesn't engage in good behavior but accurately reports that she didn't, she still earns a point. And if she reports that her behavior is good, but the adult saw behavior issues, she won't get *any* points—this teaches her to report reliably. If during your discussions you get the feeling she really can accurately evaluate herself, but hasn't been because she wants the points, you may want to add the accuracy column.

Also, sometimes adults aren't vigilant enough and let the children get away with inappropriate behaviors. Consequently, the child may learn—and genuinely believe—that inappropriate behaviors are appropriate. In this case, you'll need to completely start the whole self-management program over again, beginning with intervals that the child can succeed with (based on your data indicating how often the problem behaviors are being exhibited). It's a shame when this happens because implementing a program incorrectly can result in the behaviors becoming no better—or even becoming worse—than when you have no program at all.

> **QUESTION:** I asked the school to set up a self-management program for helping my child pay attention, but when I get the sheets home I can tell that an adult wrote the tallies.

This is one of the most frequent mistakes people make. Even though it is *self*-management (notice I emphasize "self"!), some programs still have an adult make the tallies. It's extremely important that they do it correctly and have the child evaluate and monitor *himself*. Otherwise, it's unlikely that he'll ever become independent and learn to self-control. Similarly, make sure that the adult observing the self-management has the child evaluate without any prompts. For example, if the adult smiles enthusiastically and says, "How did you do?" the child is likely to respond with "Great!" Or if the adult looks upset or angry when asking the child how she did, the child will probably say, "Not so great." It's important that the child learn strategies to self-evaluate his own behavior, which is hugely different from an adult evaluating the behavior.

A MOTHER LOOKS AT SELF-MANAGEMENT

When we went to see Dr. Koegel for the first time, she brought up the idea of self-management for six-year-old Andrew: he was verbal and obedient enough to be a good candidate for it, and she had pinpointed several areas she felt it would work well for. It gives you some insight into my (wimpy, insecure) personality to know that I was embarrassed to admit to her right away that I didn't know what self-management *was*: I felt like a good mother would already know the term. And then, because I hadn't asked right away, I felt it was even more awkward to ask her after she'd used the term a bunch of times. I thought, *Rob probably knows what it is.* So at some point I whispered to him, "What's self-management?" "I don't know!" he whispered back. "I was hoping *you* did."

We eventually bared our souls to Dr. Koegel and admitted our ignorance, and she of course explained it all to us in a way that made it very simple. Which it is. It's also just so practical—almost obvious, once you know how to use it. And it works. I told a relative of mine about it after a teacher said she thought his (typical) daughter had an attention disorder. He wasn't ready to plunge into a diagnosis/medication scenario and wanted to try something less drastic first, so he implemented a self-management program for her. He checked in with her every day after school, and if she could tell him that she had sat nicely and paid attention during classroom time, she got a reward. In less than a week, her classroom habits had changed drastically. Self-management really works.

Technology Is Our Friend

One funny thing—looking back—is how much more rudimentary technology was a short fifteen years ago. None of us had smartphones back then. (Even more amazing is the fact that when I was pregnant with Andrew, who's now twenty-one, Rob actually got a beeper so I could reach him if I went into labor. A *beeper*. It was like the Dark Ages back then.)

Anyway, the first time we met with Dr. Koegel, she suggested we get a wrist golf stroke counter thingamajig. We found one in a department store. It was kind of fun: Andrew wore it on his wrist and could click it every time he did the desired behavior. Of course, now that most people carry phones that have more processing capability than the rocket ship that carried Neil Armstrong to the moon, clickers aren't a necessity (although they still have a satisfying feel). You can keep track of anything on your phone these days. In fact, I wouldn't be surprised if there's a self-management program app that's available by the time this book is published. (And if there isn't—someone should get on that.)

A Way of Life

Andrew so took to the idea of self-management that when he was somewhat older—in middle school or high school—he set up a program for himself without even telling us. My memory's so bad that I can't remember what he was working on, but I *do* remember coming into his room and finding a piece of paper with check marks on it and asking him about it. He explained that he was giving himself a check each time he did whatever it was he was trying to get himself to do more often. (*Why can't I remember anything?*) So when Dr. Koegel says the ultimate goal is for people to learn to monitor their own behavior, she really means it—and it can really happen.

When you think about it, self-management isn't just a tool for behaviorists: it's what we do all the time, whenever we control an inappropriate behavior (*I won't bite my nails in the meeting; I'll wait until I'm alone in my office)* or reward ourselves for a desired one (*I'll order the kale salad for dinner and that way I can have dessert!*). We may have to teach our kids how to get started with this whole concept, and it may have to be pretty structured and supervised for a while, but in the long run, self-management is more a way of life than an intervention program.

And now excuse me—since I've finished this section, I've earned my five minutes of Internet surfing. BRB.

Chapter Ten
Pivotal Response Treatment (PRT):
Improving the Areas that Matter the Most

QUESTION: There are so many things out there that I could do for my child. The stuff you talk about makes sense, but how do I know that it really works? How do I put it all together?

QUESTION: I'm looking for programs for my three-year-old son and I want to make sure that he'll enjoy the program but also learn. One specialist I recently interviewed about an in-home program suggested that my child should be able to do tasks he doesn't like without crying, but so far that goal just seems to be causing him a lot of misery. What should I do?

PRT may be the answer to your question! Read on to see what we mean.

UNDERSTANDING THE ISSUES
Make Life Fun

A couple of important issues underlie all of our teachings. First, and most important, your child *has* to enjoy what he's doing. Think about it. Your child finds social communication challenging. *So* challenging that he tries to avoid it. Making him engage in behaviors he doesn't like is just going to turn him off from more interactions in the future. And that's going to create an even bigger problem than you have now. So everything that we've said about motivation is critical. Your child has to enjoy the teaching. Period.

Also, *you'll* be a lot happier when your child is happy. Don't worry—there'll be plenty of times when your child *has* to engage in nonpreferred activities (school, for instance), but when you're teaching a child, the most important thing is that he's enjoying socializing and learning. And remember, we're still teaching. It's just that we're teaching your child in a way that's fun so he'll want to keep going. Learning to talk, socialize, stay in control, take turns, and everything else is tough for your child, so the least we can do is to make it fun—especially since the research shows that when we make it fun, children with autism learn a whole lot faster, engage in the new behaviors more often on their own, and have a lot less disruptive behavior. What's more important than that?

Be Active

Second, you need to make sure that you're involved in all of the interventions. Parent participation is critical to long-term success. A parent told me once that the private speech therapist she saw twice a week asked her to stay in the waiting room while she worked with her daughter. I recommended that she either insist on sitting in the room or find a new speech therapist. What happens in that room has to be happening all day long. Two hours a week or even two hours a day of talking isn't enough. Your child has to learn to talk all day long, and all procedures need to be coordinated throughout the day.

Another family I consulted with told me that the applied behavior analysis providers reported that their son was "more disruptive" when the parents were present, so they shouldn't attend the sessions. This is so wrong. They should be working as a team, and if the child is more disruptive with one person or another, it's because the procedures aren't coordinated. All good intervention programs should have a parent education component in order to have the best long-term outcomes.

Be a Team

Third, and closely related to parent participation, is the importance of coordination across environments. Years ago we worked with a bunch of older kids who weren't toilet trained despite many years of effort. Most were nonverbal (this was before we used the motivational procedures described in detail below) and had been wearing diapers for six or seven years or more. What we found was that when we coordinated the procedures across all settings, the children learned to urinate in the toilet within a matter of weeks. Simply coordinating all the environments with the same procedures made all the difference. This is true of every behavior. As I mentioned above, my nephew started saying words only after everyone in the family used a coordinated approach. If someone isn't keeping up with the program, the child may never fully learn the desired behavior.

Include, Include, Include

Fourth—and I know I've mentioned this over and over already, but it's so important that I'll do it again—make sure your child is participating in natural environments. This means with typical peers as often as possible. And while it may be tempting to leave your child at home with a relative or babysitter when you run errands or go shopping, it will be better in the long run for your child to learn how to behave in those settings.

For example, one family I worked with never took their son to the grocery store because he became fixated with the electric doors and would go in and out of them repeatedly. When the parents tried to get him into the store he'd throw a huge fit, so they stopped taking him. But obviously if he never went, he'd never learn to behave appropriately there. So instead of not letting him go shopping, we designed a program: after they purchased their items, he got to roll a die and whatever he landed on was the number of times he could go in and out the door. He enjoyed the game, and the family counted down together, so to others it just looked like a fun family activity. Further, since they had all agreed on the number ahead of time, once they had counted down he left the doors without a tantrum.

So, regardless of the activity—sports, school, grocery shopping, after-school or mommy and me programs—it's important that your child learn how to navigate these activities appropriately and to enjoy them, and she'll be gaining all the new neural connections in the brain that get made when we're exposed to novelty.

Target Pivotal Areas

Finally, but no less important, remember to focus on "pivotal behaviors."

Pivotal Response Treatment (PRT) got its start in the past when the effective therapies in the field were slow and laborious. The kids learned and progressed, but we had to teach every single target behavior individually, one child at a time. We were always in a race against time because we wanted our children to catch up, but teaching every behavior one at a time took hours and hours of daily drills—and even with that kind of intense work, many children never caught up.

One day my husband was thinking out loud (a habit of his that most of the time is interesting because he's really intelligent, but sometimes can be a bit annoying) and said, "It's too bad the kids just aren't motivated to learn. It doesn't look like they're having fun and about the only thing they seem motivated to do is to get out of the session." Now remember, this was back many decades ago, when teaching meant we drilled them for hours on end (which unfortunately many people still do even though this is a really outdated practice). So we got on this mission to try to find ways that would "motivate" the children.

At first our data came in slowly. A finding here and there. We found bits and pieces through our research: for instance, we discovered that offering kids a choice of the toys or materials we used was helpful, that varying the task made them more interested, and so on. All the things we've discussed in this book.

Initially we were targeting communication because we had a lot of kids who just weren't learning to talk with the old structured, drill-type methods. It just wasn't fun and the kids didn't even try to talk. Eventually we put all the pieces together—giving children choices, varying tasks, rewarding attempts, using maintenance tasks, and tying in to natural rewards—and found that kids who had never talked before were saying their first words. At that time, the general statistics in the field were suggesting that even with the best intervention programs only about 50 percent of children with autism would ever learn to talk and the remaining 50 percent would remain nonverbal for life. But when we combined these motivational components into a package, about 90 percent of the children under five were talking—a huge improvement over the previous 50 percent. And the kids were having fun. The intervention was fun so they tried to talk. And almost all did learn how to talk with these new methods.

We first published the findings in an article entitled "The Natural Language Paradigm" because the teaching looked so different from the previous drill-type sessions and appeared so natural—the way typical kids learn language. But shortly thereafter, we realized that the motivational procedures worked with many more behaviors than communication, so we renamed it "Pivotal Response Treatment" (also discussed in the literature as "Pivotal Response Teaching" or "Pivotal Response Training"). Essentially, the behaviors we focus on teaching are "pivotal" in generating widespread positive changes in lots of untreated areas. More bang for your buck. And that's critical when we're in a race against time to get the children caught up.

What Is PRT?

Pivotal Response Treatment is a type of applied behavior analysis, and ABA, in turn, is a field of psychology that uses specific techniques to make socially significant changes in behaviors. It's vital that these behaviors be objectively measured—we'll talk more about that later.

In ABA, we focus on changing behaviors rather than discussing them. Many people come to us saying that they've spent years in therapy "discussing" why they couldn't make friends or why they felt anxious. Instead of these discussions—which often don't translate to better skills out in the world—we observe the individual, develop some concrete goals, and practice those goals in increasingly more challenging settings until the individual can use them in natural settings without support.

For example, many individuals with ASD have difficulty with social conversation and over time feel anxious about being with peers and meeting new people. In this situation, instead of discussing why there might be a problem, we would observe them with peers and try to figure out what's going on that makes them unsuccessful. Are they asking enough questions? Are they looking the other person in the eye? Are they using the right body language for the situation? Are they giving compliments? Are they being too "honest" in a way that comes across as critical? Are they adding too much detail during conversations? And so on.

Once we've figured out which specific areas would benefit from intervention, we make a systematic plan and get to work implementing it.

This isn't to say that we don't consider people's feelings and thoughts. We welcome communication and appreciate it when our clients open up to us, but we've learned from experience that it's far more helpful to figure out a behavioral solution to what often appears to be an emotional problem. For example, some people with autism develop depression because they don't have friends. So they may come in complaining of depression, but making friends is really the core issue, and once we've figured out how to help the person with that, the depression goes away. So you can see that we really try to focus on concrete behaviors that will make an important difference in a person's life.

Terminology

Now that you know the roots of PRT, let's talk a bit about terminology. Sorry if this is a little boring but it will be helpful to our overall discussion.

First, there's a "trial" (which is why you'll sometimes hear people refer to the intervention as "discrete trial training," or DTT). A trial has an A-B-C format. The A stands for *antecedent*, which is like an opportunity or an instruction. Next is B, a *behavior*—essentially the child's response to the antecedent. And C refers to the *consequence* for this response.

An example:

A (antecedent): Mom holds up a cookie and says "cookie."

B (behavior): Child makes an attempt at the word and says "coo."

C (consequence): Mom gives the child a cookie.

In this trial, the child gets a reward as a consequence for making an attempt at a word. This increases the likelihood that he'll try to say the word in the future to get a cookie.

Let's take another example:

A: Mom holds up a cookie and says "cookie."

B: Child cries.

C: Mom gives the child a cookie.

In this example the child is rewarded for crying—and has just learned that if he cries, he's likely to get a cookie. He may try crying to get a cookie in the future. On the other hand, if the consequence had been *not* receiving a cookie, the child would eventually learn that crying isn't a good way to get a cookie.

Putting It into Action

Now that you know what a trial is, you can see how easy it is to observe someone and make sure that each trial is done correctly—i.e., that rewards are given for the desired behaviors and not the undesired ones. Also, you want to make sure that there are enough trials throughout the day so that the child learns quickly. As I mention later, there's some research to suggest that in many school programs the children only get about two trials an hour for communication. This is by far too few. We want them to get a few every *minute* throughout much of the day. Your child will need lots of trials with the motivational procedures if she's going to succeed quickly.

At times, you may also want to look closely at what happens just before the antecedents (also known as "setting events," "establishing operations," or "motivating operations"). Sometimes you're doing everything the way you have been, but your child just isn't responding the same way to the same antecedent you've already used over and over again. For example, you may be used to shaking your keys to get your child to respond with "ride." This may have worked a hundred times, then one day your child has a huge tantrum when you do it. You can't really figure out what happened because it's the same thing you've been doing for weeks and it has been working all that time. Usually this is related to the strength of the reward, which can influence the child's response to the antecedent.

Put simply, sometimes things happen that change how rewarding something is to your child. For example, if she's full, a cookie may not be appealing, so if you're trying to get her to say "cookie," she might not be interested. Or if she's feeling sick or tired she may not be interested in active play. When things just aren't as rewarding, you may not see the same responses that you did on other days. In such cases, you'll need to change things around. If the child is sick or not feeling well, you may need to incorporate more maintenance tasks or let her take a break. If she's full, she won't be interested in food activities, so make a different plan.

But be sure not to reward this behavior if your child just doesn't feel like doing a task that day. I sometimes like the children to say, "I don't want to play that game right now, but thanks for asking" (or some part of that sentence) so they learn that they need to respond verbally even if it's to get out of a social activity. Some children get inadvertently rewarded for sick behavior and guess what? Yes, they get sick more often! Even if they aren't really sick. So be careful on this one, but do make sure to pay attention to real issues that may change how your child responds to you.

As you can see, the basic principles of ABA are important, but the motivational components *must* be incorporated into the intervention. If the motivational procedures aren't incorporated, you'll probably have an unhappy child who cries when the therapists drive up or who refuses to go to school every day.

Is There Research to Back PRT?

Yes. A ton. If you've been looking up information about autism, you've probably seen terms like "evidence based," "empirically validated," "scientifically documented," and "data based" over and over again. These are just fancy terms to let you know that an approach or technique is backed by well-controlled studies that have been published in accepted journals. And why is this so important? It's important because there are so many treatments for autism these days. Just google "autism" and thousands of things will come up. And you know what? Most of them don't work. Over the years I've seen things pop up that are not only expensive but totally ineffective. Many of these programs won't help your child and some are even harmful. There aren't any miracle cures and if someone promises you one, grab your wallet and run as fast as you can!

There are, however, many organizations and authors who have published reviews of interventions that work, and PRT is a method that's well established in the literature as being effective. Our laboratories have conducted over two hundred studies that have been published, and the procedures have been replicated in other labs both within the United States and abroad. These studies are carefully designed and reviewed by a number of other researchers before they're published. And it isn't easy to get an article accepted for publication. We first have to run the study using a scientific design that assures that there's no experimenter bias and that the results aren't just a chance occurrence. Then we have to write it up for publication. After that, it's reviewed by two or three professionals who are already well established in the field for their work in the same area. They can accept the article, accept it with revisions, or reject it.

Even when an article is accepted, the reviewers almost always have some recommendations for improving it or for explaining something more clearly. All revisions have to be completed before the article goes back to them for a second review. Then it goes into the queue of articles to be published in an upcoming edition—only, before it comes out in print, it has to be copyedited and rechecked by the authors. Phew! As you can see, the whole process can literally take years. But it's worth it, because the process assures us that the procedures really work and that they won't be a huge waste of your child's time.

So you can see why it's so frustrating when an approach that really doesn't have any data to back it up gets picked up on the news or by a popular TV show. Many reporters have no idea how to evaluate whether a procedure is scientifically based—I guess they just don't teach that in journalism school. In fact, it's pretty common for reporters to look for a different slant on things and want to report on something really outrageous or unusual to get people talking or interested. But it can do a real disservice to those who need to know which approaches are scientifically proven to be effective and which ones aren't.

In fact, recently I did a segment for a well-respected cable channel, and the first reporter I met with said that he wanted to find the cure for autism on air. He thought that if they did an MRI or some other type of medical imaging, they would find the cause of autism. Well, I felt obligated to mention that some of the best researchers in the country have been working on that very same thing for many decades now and still haven't found the cause, so it was fairly unlikely that they would find it in a few weeks of filming!

Anyway, my point is: be sure to look for scientific validity in any technique that interests you—PRT definitely has loads of it.

PIVOTAL AREAS
How Do You Know If a Behavior Is Pivotal?

When we teach a pivotal behavior, we see a lot of improvements in other areas. Let's take motivation, for example. This was the first pivotal area we discovered. But what happens when we incorporate the motivational procedures into the intervention? Well, the child responds more frequently and doesn't try to avoid or escape the teaching situation by engaging in disruptive or off-task behavior. Also, the child shows higher levels of happiness, interest, and enthusiasm.

You might wonder how we measure happiness, interest, and enthusiasm. Well, we videotape the children in the learning sessions, then we have observers review the tapes and rate the children's reactions on a scale from 1 to 6. For example, on the happiness scale, a score of 1 or 2 means that the child is showing a low level of happiness: the child may be crying, pouting, throwing a tantrum, or appear to be sad, angry, frustrated, or simply not enjoying herself. A score of 6 means that the child is smiling, laughing appropriately, and acting like she's enjoying herself.

When we're scoring interest, if the child looks bored, uninvolved, uninterested, or reluctant to continue the activity; if he yawns or avoids or even tries to escape the activity; or if he looks around distractedly or responds super slowly, his level of interest would get a score of a 1 or 2. However, if the child attends readily and willingly to the task and is alert and involved, it would get a 5 or 6.

Enthusiasm would be scored low if the child tries to leave the room, throws tantrums, kicks, screams, throws material around the room, cries, pushes the assignment away, or refuses to engage in the task. In contrast, if the child attends to the task quickly, laughs or smiles while working on the task, predominantly watches the clinician and engages with materials intently, performs extra behaviors related to the task, and shows other related creative behaviors—well, that would be considered high enthusiasm and would be given the highest score, a 6.

With this system, we get a good, detailed feel for the child's overall engagement. Remember, we want happy, interested, and enthusiastic learners. When we love what we're doing, we do more of it, and if we hate what we're doing, there's little chance we'll seek it out if we don't have to. And when it comes to things like communication and learning, a lot of that *has* to be child motivated. We don't want our kids only to talk when they have to or are forced to by an unrelenting adult. We want them to enthusiastically engage with adults and to initiate interactions on their own. And when the motivational components of PRT are incorporated into the intervention, we get kids who are scoring 5s and 6s. If you do it right, they're happy and enthusiastic. This is so important for the long haul.

Through our research and work, we've discovered a number of different pivotal areas, which we have discussed throughout this book. Here's an overview of them.

Motivation

Motivation is critical. For children with autism, communication is challenging, socialization is tough, and activities that typically developing kids like are often overwhelming. And these difficulties can overlap into self-help areas—it's hard to toilet train a child who has a language delay and can't fully understand what the goal of it all is. Similarly, it's not easy to explain to a child how to get dressed or how to get each foot in the correct shoe or how to put on a shirt so the tag lies in the back when she has a small vocabulary. So much is difficult for your child and sometimes she probably wants to just give up and stop trying. That's why it's so critical to target the child's motivation. Everything changes when we target motivation, and every child—typical, with autism, or with any other type of disability—should have an education that includes motivational teaching procedures.

Just think how much more fun doing a scavenger hunt is than getting drilled on text passages. Or think how many people have no trouble whatsoever doubling or tripling recipes but hate multiplying. In fact, I remember being a kid and making brownies with my sisters. One of them accidently put a quarter of a cup of baking powder in the brownies rather than a quarter of a teaspoon. I still remember that disaster decades later because it was a crash course on measurement (after we'd ruined a whole pan of brownies). Similarly, many kids can add up their own allowance when they're in preschool—long before they start learning the decimal system.

It's so easy to teach fractions to itty-bitty kids by just asking if they want a half, a quarter, or a twenty-third of a cookie. Most go for the larger number, certain that it will be larger. But when you start cutting that cookie into twenty-three pieces and they get the smallest little morsel, they learn in one trial that a smaller denominator means a larger piece!

These motivational components can be incorporated into all the other pivotal areas. Motivation is just one of those things at the top of the list for any child's program. From now on think, "Am I motivating my child?" before, during, and after every activity. There are a few behaviors that need extrinsic rewards to get the child started, but not many, and those generally involve very complex behaviors. For the most part, the motivational components we discussed can and should be a part of everything you do from here on out.

So remember, for children with autism, all the activities have to be motivational: we want them to love the activities, to participate enthusiastically, to learn and to catch up. This isn't a luxury—it's a necessity. It will take some creative thinking and rethinking to keep every activity motivational, but soon it will become second nature, and you'll be wondering why all teachers for all kids don't use motivational strategies.

Initiations

Another pivotal area is initiations. Most kids with autism just don't initiate much, and questions are almost nonexistent. I'm not sure why they can answer questions but don't ask many (if any). In chapter 2 we told you how to teach question asking, but we may not have emphasized how important that is.

When we looked at long-term outcomes of children we'd worked with who had since become adults or adolescents, we found that the ones who initiated interactions when they were little had much better outcomes than the ones who didn't. The initiations may have been bringing a toy to their parent, showing their parent something, or going up to another person and labeling an item—any type of social interaction that *they* initiated. In contrast, the children who played by themselves and never exhibited any social initiations had poorer long-term outcomes. What's more, when observers rated the children's tapes on a "normalcy" scale, they gave the children who didn't initiate interactions very low ratings—indicating that they appeared to have a significant disability. On the other hand, the children who were initiating interactions received very high scores from naïve observers on the normalcy scale.

This research emphasizes how important it is for kids to learn to initiate. Initiations, like questions, round out a child's language so that her repertoire includes more than just requests and protestations, which makes her appear much more appropriate. Questions are social by nature, and they also give the child an opportunity to engage in an interaction that will increase subsequent learning opportunities. This is why we started our long line of research to figure out the best ways to motivate the children to use initiations.

We recently published a study showing that if the children with autism spectrum disorder don't learn how to initiate a social activity at school recess and lunch periods, they'll probably end up being alone during those times. Even children who were able to be quite social when an adult facilitated the play didn't interact on the days an adult wasn't there, if they hadn't been taught to initiate the activity. So whenever you can, teach initiations.

Teach your child to ask all the questions a typical child would ask and to respond with a question during conversation—and keep the interaction rewarding for her. In chapter 2 we discussed how to teach a whole variety of questions starting with "What's that?" which is the first question typical language developers use. But we also want to teach question asking and initiations in other contexts. For example, when you say, "I ate something delicious today," your child should learn to respond with "What did you eat?" Then you can tell her that you ate a cookie—and go get one for her as a natural reward!

You can also teach your child to initiate his favorite activities. If he likes to slide, have him ask a friend, "Go slide?" or "Do you want to slide?" before he gets the natural reward of sliding. If you tie asking questions to natural rewards and use the motivational components we discussed above, your child will enjoy asking questions and initiating activities. And we know that if the activity is fun and kids get something rewarding from it, they'll do it more often—which is what we want.

Self-Management

We have a longer discussion of the use of self-management in the previous chapter, but I wanted to mention it here as well, because it's an important component of PRT.

Whether we like it or not, we have had to learn how to take responsibility for our own actions and behaviors. When we were little, all the responsibility was on our parents: they took care of us, taught us to walk and talk, and provided a nurturing environment. But gradually they also taught us to take responsibility for ourselves. We learned how to take care of ourselves—to get dressed and groomed, to get up on time, to show up at school or work—and to take responsibility for the mistakes we make. We learned to abide by the law and to live within the social norms that our society dictates. We gradually became more independent and stopped needing others to guide our behavior; we became less likely to get into trouble and have problems related to a lack of self-control.

Now, most of us don't have some innate ability to self-manage and self-control all of our behaviors: we all have some areas that we have to actively decide to self-control, whether it's watching what we eat, counting the drinks we consume at a party so we don't have to suffer the next day, making a shopping list, checking off tasks at work, writing New Year resolutions, and so on. Targeting behaviors and developing our own self-management programs help us become better people. We sometimes even get feedback from our friends and family about behaviors that we need to self-control, and self-management is a perfect way to improve them. In fact, I've developed lots of self-management programs for typical children and adults, ranging from learning to be positive with one's children to not arguing at faculty meetings (one I developed for my husband that worked spectacularly). So self-management is part of all our lives, whether we call it that or not.

Many individuals with autism need extra support to learn how to manage their own behaviors, but once they gain the ability to self-manage and self-control their behavior and actions, we see a lot of positive changes. Most important, when individuals with ASD learn to self-manage they can take responsibility for their own behaviors.

Because individuals with ASD find socialization challenging, they may need some support in learning how to self-control some behaviors and how to increase other behaviors with self-management, to help them in social situations.

There are several steps that an individual needs to take when starting a self-management program. A child must first learn to discriminate between the desired and undesired behaviors. That sometimes takes a while. Then the child must keep track of his own success, by noting the number of times or the length of time he has successfully done the desired behavior. When he has been successful for a previously agreed-upon number of times or length of time, he needs to have this achievement acknowledged with a reward, which can be given by another person or self-administered.

Learning to self-manage is important for independence. But the programs need to be carefully and systematically implemented.

Unfortunately, self-management programs often aren't implemented correctly. I'm consulting with a school district now, and the staff wanted me to observe a child for whom they had begun a self-management program for off-task behavior. The child was fully included in an elementary school classroom but wasn't completing his work. When I went to observe this so-called self-management program, I found that the school had decided to start with five-minute intervals based on the length of time the staff determined he could engage appropriately during class. His self-management sheet had a whole list of vague behaviors, and the teacher marked a tally on his sheet whenever she had a chance, which usually was every fifteen or twenty minutes, at best.

There were many things wrong with the program, and I bet you've caught some of them already. First, it wasn't self-management at all if the teacher was marking the tallies. Second, the child had a lengthy list of behaviors that he needed to decrease at school, including staring into space (off task), putting objects in his mouth (everything from rocks to staples), sucking on his fingers and shirt, playing with items at inappropriate times (the carpet, pencils, scissors), and so on. While he was able to get a fair number of points during preferred activities, like computer and math, he had nonstop inappropriate behaviors throughout activities that were highly verbal, such as circle time. When I asked him, even after a minute, whether he was working hard and had good behavior he *always* said yes—clearly he couldn't accurately discriminate between appropriate and inappropriate behavior.

Because the teacher couldn't watch him closely with twenty-four other students in her classroom, he ended up getting random points even if he was off task during most of the interval, so he was getting reinforced for undesired behaviors. What's more, he often got a class reward at the end of the day, even if he had thrown dirt at another child, yelled, cried, fidgeted, and spaced out for a good part of the day, so he was learning that all that stuff was perfectly fine to do at school.

It wasn't the teacher's fault—it simply wasn't humanly possible for her to stay on top of the program—but he was getting away with a ton of stuff. So we went back to square one. We shortened the intervals during the more challenging times, taught him to discriminate what was appropriate versus inappropriate, greatly simplified the self-management sheet (I couldn't even figure out the original one, because it had so many target behaviors, so we changed it to say "Did my work and had good behavior"), and had *him* evaluate his own behavior and mark his own points.

We had a special education aide watch the student for a few weeks to make sure he was doing it accurately and that the program was being implemented consistently, but in just a few weeks he was on his own, behaving beautifully and working to his capacity. Just tweaking the program a bit proved to be successful, and now that he wasn't spacing out, fidgeting, and engaging in all the other off-task behaviors, our guy began to interact more with his peers and complete his work.

You can see from this example how self-management can be "pivotal." Once it was implemented correctly, he went from an average of five minutes on task to good behavior for most of the day (more than most of his classmates) and work completion on all of his assignments. And learning how to manage and control his own behaviors was a lifetime skill. Altogether, we made a small time investment for a great long-term outcome.

Please read chapter 9 for a more detailed discussion of self-management and instructions for setting up a self-management program.

Multiple Cues

Responsiveness to multiple cues is an area that some children need focused intervention programs for and others don't. In the old days, most children responded to a single cue and put too much emphasis on it (for example, a bend in the corner of a flash card—from then on, they'd recognize the card from the bend and ignore the other, more meaningful cues), but now that we use motivational strategies, fewer children have this problem. If a child isn't responding to multiple cues, learning is almost impossible, as is functioning independently in everyday environments. You can usually tell if a child is responding to multiple cues by giving her a somewhat complex instruction, like "Go put on your blue T-shirt." If your child comes back with a T-shirt on, but it isn't blue, she may not be responding to multiple cues. Similarly, if a teacher asks the child, "Take out your book and a pencil, and turn to page eight," and the child simply takes out her book and sits there, it may be that she isn't responding to multiple cues. I have had many teachers tell me that a child is "noncompliant" because of situations like this, and I've had to set them straight: if a child were truly noncompliant, she probably wouldn't respond to *any* of the instructions, but the fact that she takes out his book suggests that she simply isn't responding to all of the cues, not that she's being noncompliant.

You can see why this behavior is pivotal—so much of everyday life requires us to respond to many cues at the same time. By the preschool years, most children can respond to several cues, and if a child with autism is only responding to one (which may or may not be the relevant one) she's at quite a disadvantage. Many typical children have some difficulty with attention, such as distinguishing the letter "b" from the letter "d," but these struggles can be significant for children on the autism spectrum.

For example, on occasion you'll meet a child with autism who can only recognize someone if that person is wearing certain glasses or a certain outfit—looking the way he did the day they were introduced. When the person doesn't have the glasses on or is wearing a different outfit, the child doesn't recognize him. This is called "overselective attention": the child is attending to a single, irrelevant cue. All children have some areas of overselectivity, which is why they all make mistakes with some letters (like "b" and "d") or call every animal with four legs a "doggie" or any man they see "Daddy." But quite quickly they learn to respond to all the different cues, so that a big animal with spots isn't a "doggie" but a "cow"—even though it *does* have four legs like a doggie.

Overselective attention used to be a huge problem for children with autism, but we noticed over the years that, as we began incorporating the motivational components, many tuned in so much more that they were able to attend to multiple cues without the need for specialized interventions. But if your child is demonstrating overselective attention, you can work on this: it's quite straightforward and simply involves making sure that the child responds to all of an object's aspects, and providing a positive and natural reinforcer when he does.

Here are some examples: I just had a family use balls to help teach multiple cues. Their middle schooler loves to rock in the family's swinging chair and throw balls to his mom, so instead of just using one ball, we got big balls and small balls of different colors. Before he could play this activity he loved, he had to pick a ball, and his mom would specify exactly which one, like "Throw me the big yellow ball." So you see, he had to distinguish both size and color, attending to two cues instead of just one.

Similarly, another child was super addicted to chocolate milk and requested it at every meal, so his parents got all kinds of different-colored straws and cut half of them short. He had to respond to both the color cue and the length before he could take a drink of his favorite beverage, thereby learning multiple cues at the same time.

Finally, one other family used different sizes and colors of bowls to serve their child's snack in. When he requested a snack, the family would say, "Okay, give me the big green bowl," and he got the snack in the bowl as soon as he picked the correct one. Sometimes they'd turn it around to work on expressive language, by asking him which bowl he wanted and waiting for him to respond with both color and size before giving him the snack in that bowl.

You can gradually work up the number of cues the child responds to while continuing to give him natural rewards.

Be careful: a lot of people make a mistake when teaching multiple cues. They'll say something like, "Get your green pencil" and think it's a multiple cue because it has both the color and the item. But this isn't teaching the child to respond to multiple cues—you *must* have other colors and other items available so the child has to listen to the choices. In this case, assuming the child likes to color, you would want to get a pile of different-colored pencils and different-colored markers. Now, when you ask the child, "Get the green pencil," she has to discriminate both the color and the item (green vs. other colors and pencil vs. markers). You see? Now she's really learning how to respond to multiple cues.

But remember, first the child has to learn to respond to single cues. If he doesn't know his colors or many labels, you'll want to teach that before you expect him to put it all together.

As I said before, your child may not need any special intervention for multiple cues, but if you're noticing that he just isn't getting some things even though he's really trying, you might want to test out whether he's able to respond to multiple cues, and if not, gradually and systematically increase the number of cues he responds to.

Joint Attention

Another area you may have heard of is joint attention, which seems to be related to responding to multiple cues. At a young age, children begin to share their focus between another person and objects. Before most toddlers are a year old, they'll look back and forth between an adult and an object. They also look at what you're pointing at and even what you're looking at.

These types of sharing attention are often not seen, or they happen at low levels, with children on the autism spectrum. Many have hypothesized that this lack of social orienting can interfere with development by depriving them of important social stimulation that's necessary for social and intellectual progress. Fortunately, research has shown that when motivational components are incorporated into the intervention, children with autism begin to develop joint attention without any specialized interventions—it just naturally increases. Again, lots of good things happen when a child is motivated.

Empathy

Empathy is an area that we believe is pivotal but it's been less well researched. Many people believe that individuals with autism can't understand someone else's feelings or put themselves in another person's shoes. And there are tons of studies that show that people with ASD do have more difficulty understanding how another person may feel in a given situation. But I'm not completely convinced they *can't*. It's a bit more complicated than that.

To start, here are some of the problems with the tests that show that people on the spectrum can't see things from the perspective of another person. First, kids with autism are often not that involved socially, so they may not have the opportunities to learn how to "read" other people. For example, they may not learn that if someone is sitting alone looking sad, he may have just had a bad experience. If they haven't been part of a friend group, they may not have learned that if someone says, "My mom got mad at me because I broke her vase," you should probably say something like "Oh, I'm sorry, I know how that feels—would it help if you apologized?" And second, showing an empathetic response requires a lot of language, and for kids with language delays, it might be a formidable task to put together all those concepts and words. It's a lot! I've never seen a goal to address this on any child's IEP or behavioral program, but I'm convinced that many kids *do* feel empathy, they just don't know how to express it.

For example, we were working with a little guy in the clinic recently, and I wanted to test whether he needed some intervention for empathy, so I had his dad pretend that he had bumped his foot and it really hurt. The dad faked a collision with the chair and grabbed his foot while saying "Ouch!" The son turned quickly and looked at his dad with deep concern. His expression said it all. He cared. But he didn't say a word. So for that little guy all we would need to do would be to teach him to put words to the feeling of concern and to say "Are you okay, Dad?" or "You okay?" Not rocket science.

You can teach children, adolescents, and adults to express empathy for others. We've also found that if the situation is related in some way to their restricted interests, they come much more easily. For example, my daughter was working with a young adult recently and confided to him that she's scared stiff when she has to fly on a plane because she's afraid that the engine will malfunction. His restricted interest happens to be airplanes, and he responded that most of the large airplanes have multiple engines, so she really shouldn't worry because it's quite unlikely that all of the engines would go out at the same time. Another college student we worked with appeared not to show any empathy during our probes until someone mentioned that her grandmother had died recently. He responded that she must feel sad, because he remembered feeling sad when his own grandmother died. So some personal experience with a topic may make a big difference. And that's important to know when people make these broad generalizations about people with ASD lacking empathy.

Let's step back and take a broader look at the many different levels of empathy. Most guys don't learn to be as empathetic as girls, right? Many women can chat for hours when a friend needs support, while the majority of guys just kind of brush it off or get to the bottom line. In fact, there's research showing that females often prefer discussing a problem to taking some kind of action. But tell your husband about your issue, and he's instantly on the phone trying to solve it—whether you want him to or not! It's just how we're socialized.

Now let's think about how we teach children with autism who have language delays. We start with requests, right? And this is the right way to do it because we want them to be able to get a natural reward. They can usually learn to make these requests, but they aren't necessarily learning how to vocalize their emotions. As I mentioned earlier in this book, when my nephew was little, I realized that he could say "I want juice" and "I want cookie" but he had no idea what "I'm thirsty" and "I'm hungry" meant. So we started teaching him to say those emotion words before he requested a specific drink or food. In a similar way we taught him other emotion words using fun activities, such as "I'm scared" when we played his favorite game where I carried him around the house to find his mom who was hiding and then jumped out. Having his mom pop out was a natural reward for him expressing the emotion.

Remember all those things that typical kids kind of pick up on their own, but that we have to teach kids with ASD? A child with social communication difficulties isn't likely to use words that show compassion and sympathy toward others without being taught. Knowing if someone is feeling empathy toward others is not a directly observable thing, so it's just a theory that this is difficult for them. But if no one taught you how to read, you would be illiterate, right? And if no one teaches a child with autism empathetic responses, they may not learn them. We're finding that not only can we can teach empathetic responses, but they also seem to open up a whole new area of other positive behaviors, especially in regard to social communication, suggesting that this may be another pivotal area.

TRACKING PROGRESS

Now let's talk about something important. Really important. We need to make sure your child is improving with a given intervention program, and we can only do this by collecting data.

I know the word "data" often scares people off. And some people will even say that "not everything can be measured." But some programs just don't work well with some kids, and we need to know that—even really good programs that work with other children may not be a good match for your child, and the only way you can make sure that a program is working is to collect some data on it.

We talked in other chapters about how important it is to take a baseline, but it's also important to collect data while the intervention is being implemented. That way, if it isn't working, we can tweak it a bit to make it work.

Another good reason to take data? People get lazy. Right after a team meeting or an IEP, people may be all fired up and eager to provide a lot of opportunities or trials. But a few months later they may lose some of that energy and get a little lax. Monitoring progress is a good way to make sure no one's slacking and your child is still getting what he deserves. This is true at home, too. Sometimes a child gets too much downtime at home and taking data across settings can help elucidate where things aren't working.

But how much data is too much data? It's true that people can accumulate huge files full of papers that no one ever looks at—this has been a problem with some of our grant research, when we took extensive measures. But in real life, we need to be practical. If your child is learning tons of new words every day, perhaps once a week is enough to collect data. However, if your child is struggling to learn each and every word, data on every response may be helpful to see what he's saying, when he's saying it, and where. Perhaps the data show us that he's saying lots of words at home but only a few each day at school: this can be helpful to determine where he may need additional intervention. For example, you may want to collect data on how quickly he responds after a prompt is provided, how many times he says a word spontaneously, the number of words he says in a given time period (such as ten minutes) and the different words he says, and whether he's using other behaviors to communicate (grabbing items, disruptive behavior, etc.). This way we understand the child's behavior and can carefully look at any changes. Be practical but be observant. It isn't enough to just collect data yearly right before the annual IEP (and, believe me, I see this all the time). Data need to be collected regularly if we're going to get a good idea of how your child is progressing. And if someone can't take data on a behavior, it shouldn't be included as a target. Everything can be measured.

IMPORTANT THINGS TO BE AWARE OF WHEN IMPLEMENTING A PRT PROGRAM
Heading Off Comorbidity Issues

"Comorbid" is just a fancy word psychologists use to describe a secondary disorder that occurs alongside a primary one. For many individuals with autism, comorbid disabilities can develop—usually in adolescence. The most common ones are depression and anxiety. But before you start to worry about yet another thing, let's talk about how to head these off before they take root.

We talked earlier about studies that have shown that people with ASD want to have friends and be socially active but find it challenging. Well, later on they may develop depression out of feelings of social isolation. Or they may feel anxiety about challenging social situations.

You want to head off potential future depression and anxiety by making sure your child has a rich and active social life. Schools are an ideal place to teach socialization, but—believe it or not—I *still* see IEPs that don't include a single social goal, and I still see kids who aren't socializing at all but who the school insists have met all their social goals. Now, some schools are attentive to kids' social needs and have excellent programs, but many are simply not addressing socialization the way they need to. One thing I'll never understand is why a school will have carefully defined goals for reading and math and can tell you if a child is flunking those areas, but that same child can be spending all of his time isolated in the corner of the playground and it never even comes up at a parent-teacher conference or IEP. Especially if the child has autism—so long as he isn't bothering anyone, no one questions the social isolation.

Anyway, the point here is to coordinate social skills support across every environment to ensure that your child is capable of making and keeping friends and navigating through ever more challenging social situations. It's the best way to avoid future comorbid issues and will make for a happier and more successful child in every way.

Strengths

For the rest of my career I'm going to focus on the strengths of the people I'm working with. It's hard to do sometimes, because to get services we often have to point out all the weaknesses a child has. If kids don't score below a certain percentile on standardized tests, they can't get services at school, and if they aren't pretty significantly affected, they can't get insurance or state coverage—in fact, many third-party payers only fund kids who have aggression or self-injury. These requirements force us to nitpick and focus on every single little negative behavior and overlook all the positive ones. But that's for a specific reason, and in your daily life it's vitally important that everyone recognize the special strengths your child has.

Whenever you meet with a professional, make sure he tells you all that your child's been accomplishing. If he's telling you that your child has a problem, also ask about the times when he didn't have that problem and about his successes. If you're a professional yourself, remember to phrase things positively. For example, don't say, "He's three years behind in his language and speaks at the three-year-old level." Say, rather, "He has a good vocabulary and can combine words to make short sentences, so we have a lot to work with."

If your child has special strengths, make sure everyone knows them. I've had kids who were experts on a topic—and the school never even knew. These strengths can be used for social activities or to impress classmates in a structured way. I recently worked with a child who found handwriting aversive and difficult and flunked every spelling test, but after the school started letting him use a computer to type the spelling words, he got 100 percent right on every test.

Every child has strengths and weaknesses, and many children with autism spectrum disorder have great strengths that the world needs to know about. Focusing on strengths and not weaknesses will make a big difference for your child in the long run. And while we're talking about it, there's some research—very new research—that shows that parents who focus on the positive do a much better job working with their child. "Focusing on the positive" includes noticing and rewarding the child for every little thing he or she does well and appreciating your own successes as a parent. Make sure you have confidence in yourself. Don't be too hard on yourself: realize that you know how to deal with your child's behaviors, then be consistent and do the work! Remember that parenting is under your control and the more you think, "I can do this," the more likely you are, indeed, to do it.

As all parents know, it's easy to doubt ourselves. I sometimes lie awake at night and think of all the things I could have done or could do better as a mom. Certainly no one's perfect—but we don't have to be. In fact, we consider "fidelity of implementation" (that is, success in consistency at sticking to the program we've created) achieved when a parent meets 80 percent of our criteria—that's because it's almost impossible to score 100 percent on the procedures, even for a highly trained professional. So give yourself a pat on the back for reading this book, learning the strategies that are effective for helping your child, and implementing them in a consistent manner. Your child is lucky to have you! And doesn't that thought inspire you to keep moving forward?

Brain Functioning

A major Yale University study has recently revealed the impact of our Pivotal Response Treatment on brain activity in children with autism spectrum disorder. Specific areas of the brain, known to be structurally different in children with autism, were measured through functional magnetic resonance imaging (fMRI). This was an important study and quite challenging because the children had to be desensitized ahead of time to be able to tolerate lying still long enough for the measures to be collected. And the researchers had to be assured that the children would respond under these noisy and somewhat claustrophobic conditions. To that end, we used favorite videos to help the children relax and rewarded them for their responses.

Following the initial fMRIs, PRT therapy was provided, which targeted pivotal areas of development, including motivation, social initiation, and responsivity, in order to improve social and language functioning.

In addition to the expected (and already researched) positive behavioral changes, fMRI measures showed that after Pivotal Response Treatment, the brain activity of children with autism more closely resembled that of typically developing children. This compelling finding reveals that PRT goes beyond behavior modification to alter the physiology of the brain, offering a biological explanation for observed behavioral gains. This significant breakthrough in autism treatment research is likely the first of many studies that will explore the benefits of PRT on brain function and development in children with autism.

The Future

As a rule, interventions aren't developed overnight. It would be great if there were some breakthrough that resulted in a complete cure of all the symptoms of autism that bring challenges into peoples' lives. And having been in the field for a long time now, I've seen a number of these sorts of claims. But those supposed breakthroughs tend to disappear as quickly as they appear. Some so-called interventions that weren't well researched have even been harmful to children and families. A parent once told me that if someone promised her a miracle cure for autism, she would grab her purse and run away as fast as she could.

This is why research needs to continue. One of the beauties of working at a university is that we can have lofty goals. Our goal is to cure the aspects of autism that cause someone with ASD difficulties. But to do that, more effective interventions need to be developed that build upon what we already know. If the intervention looks completely different a few decades from now, that's good, so long as it's better than what we have now and is helping more people with ASD reach their potential and goals. I hope in my lifetime that I work my way out of a job!

It will take a team effort to continue to build upon what we know and to find ways to improve the areas that still trouble individuals with ASD, their families, and friends. We aren't supporting families the way we should. We need future research on how we can provide the right kind of support to reduce families' stress. We need to figure out how communities can come together so that a family's circle of friends doesn't dwindle when their child is diagnosed with autism but instead expands to support them more fully. We need research on how to provide long-term care and support for individuals with autism throughout their lives, so parents feel that our society embraces the many gifts that people with ASD have to offer. And we need more inclusion. It still shocks me how often I go to meetings where a child is being kicked out of an after-school program or the school is threatening to place the child in a more restrictive setting.

I'm sorry that we, as a society, haven't supported the families so that these issues don't have to trouble them. We still have a long way to go. Change is slow and sometimes difficult, but with increasing numbers of individuals being diagnosed with autism, these issues can't be swept under the carpet any longer. These are real problems that need good research to find good answers.

Parenting isn't easy, and parents of children with autism deserve awards for learning all the special and individualized techniques that help their child learn and grow. They need a special pat on the back for dealing with their child's communication difficulties and with the people who attempt to exclude them from the natural settings they're entitled to be part of; they should be commended for attending extra meetings, for learning what works for their child, for going out of their way to train teachers, babysitters, aides, and relatives. They should be getting their praises sung from the highest rooftops. It's because of the parents' strong advocacy that things have improved immensely from the days when children with autism were considered "uneducable" and almost all children with autism were institutionalized by adolescence, to now, when all are educated and many are included. It's a long road and there are miles to go, but tremendous changes have occurred as a result of parents' efforts, hard work, and perseverance.

FAQ

QUESTION: My four-year-old child has been in a structured program for years. He gets very upset when the therapists come to our home. Can anything be done?

If your child is upset when the therapists arrive, it usually means that they aren't incorporating motivational components. As we mentioned earlier, disruptive behaviors occur at far greater levels when the therapeutic approaches don't include motivational components. So have your therapists make a concerted effort to find out what your child enjoys and use a little creativity to get those important goals incorporated into the intervention.

Also make sure your child is getting a natural reward. Too often I see children who are getting treats when they're not a part of the activity. For example, just yesterday a mom called me in tears because her child was running around the classroom and wouldn't complete his math. It turned out that the math was just a set of boring problems. I suggested she get some pretzels out (his favorite) and have him add and subtract them. Voilà! He did all the problems super fast when the intrinsic motivation was there.

Although PRT often seems like fun and playing, it takes some thought and effort to make sure the target goals are being implemented systematically and that motivational components are incorporated. It's much easier to just hold up a flash card or give the child a preprinted worksheet, but children learn slowly that way and they don't like the intervention. We want enthusiastic and active learners and to get that, motivational components must be incorporated.

> **QUESTION:** My school regularly calls me to pick up my child because he's being disruptive. It's really stressful. Does this seem right?

There are several problems with this scenario. First and foremost, children with autism often act out because they want to get out of a task that doesn't seem fun or to avoid a task that's difficult. If you pick your child up from school, you've helped accomplish this goal! Whether the challenge is social or academic, your child most likely will have reduced demands at home. So you see what's happening: your child is inadvertently getting rewarded for the disruptive behavior. The way he sees it is pretty much this way: "The task is hard—I act up—Mom picks me up and I don't have to do that difficult math" or "I don't want to socialize—I throw dirt in another child's face—I get sent home and don't have to socialize."

The same is true for time-outs at school, too, which can be very rewarding for a child trying to escape a difficult or uninteresting activity. Their use should be discouraged for kids on the autism spectrum.

The school needs to look at why the behavior problem is happening. Nine times out of ten, the instruction or social lesson isn't being provided in an interesting way, so the child is bored or would prefer to get out of it and therefore acts up. Motivational components need to be incorporated into all activities, and that might mean making a fun snack with a friend so there's a natural reward, or reading sentences that will end with a desired item or activity. Make sure that the activities are motivating. Then also make sure that the school is teaching the child replacement behaviors for the disruptive ones, like teaching the child to say "This is hard, I need help" when she's struggling, or "I don't want to play on the slide, but do you want to swing with me?" Finally, the special education staff should have training in how to implement a positive behavior support plan: ask them what they're planning to do to make sure the behavior doesn't happen in the future. And make sure they have a bunch of ideas.

There are so many effective ways to reduce behavior problems. If your school staff can't come up with a list, or at least several strategies, they need more training.

QUESTION: The school says my child is interacting with other children, but they have her at her own table with an aide at lunch. Whenever I visit she's just with the aide. What can be done?

It sounds like your school needs to put more effort into making sure that your child interacts with other children. It may be helpful to collect some data. Then call a meeting and tell the school that you've been there on several specific dates and that your child interacted with peers zero percent of the time (or whatever the low number is) and that you want to increase the quality and quantity of the interactions. Ideally, you would put these goals on the IEP—then the staff is obligated to work on them—but if you don't want to wait until your annual IEP, the school may be able to start working on the socialization sooner.

It isn't uncommon for aides to be untrained and unaware that they need to be doing more to help the socialization. This week I was consulting at a school to develop a self-management program for a fully included child. The school also had a self-contained (i.e., segregated) special education autism class, and the two aides from the classroom spent the entire recess and lunch periods chatting with each other while the children with autism played alone. It broke my heart when one child came up to me four times to ask if I wanted to play tag with him. But without training, supervision, and data collection requirements, many aides don't have the skills or awareness to be able to implement a good intervention program. Many aides themselves report that they feel under-trained and underskilled. But our research suggests that it doesn't take much effort to improve aides' training. It sounds like you need to make that happen at your school.

QUESTION: Everyone tells me that my child is doing so well because he's in preschool and can use full sentences, but the only thing he says is "I want [some food or object], please." I'm happy about this, but it doesn't seem like it's enough. Any suggestions?

Teaching a child to request is a wonderful way to start an intervention program for expressive communication. You can use child-chosen items and there's a natural reward involved in the learning activity. That was a great starting point, and your child can now use verbal communication to express himself in this way. But, as we discussed above, if your son is going to be communicatively competent and have the chance of a better long-term outcome, someone will need to teach him other communicative functions. You can start with simple questions, such as "What's that?" and "Where is it?"

It's critical that your child learn to use communication for more than requests, and questions are a good place to start, but make sure you include the motivational components while you teach those questions. Your child will learn them faster and will enjoy the intervention, and if it's enjoyable you're likely to notice him using the questions on his own—the end goal for everything we teach. Please refer back to chapter 2 for a longer discussion of teaching language and chapter 5 for one on increasing social interactions.

> **QUESTION:** I'm trying to teach my son his first word, but he just isn't interested in anything. Nothing seems rewarding or motivating. How can I use the PRT motivational components when nothing motivates him?

Most children have something they like—an activity, a toy, or a special food. But if you can't seem to find anything your child is motivated enough to talk for, and your child simply keeps trying to avoid or escape the teaching situation, you can start by having the child say something like "bye" to end the session. Then let him stop right away. If you make him do anything else after he says "bye"—for example, if you make him clean up or you redirect him to another activity—then the reward will be too delayed and he probably won't say it again. If we're starting with a child who only wants to get out of the session, we prompt the child to say "bye" or "done," or even just to make a verbal attempt at one of those words, which then offers the natural reward of ending the session. Then we let the child leave immediately—no adult chatting.

Interestingly, once the children learn that their communication can have that much power, they stick around a bit longer. Later on, once "bye" comes easily, we can have the children say "open" to open the door, and "off" to turn off the lights, and so on, all leading to the natural reward of leaving. So, even if it seems like your child doesn't have any activities he likes, you can still use a different type of reward to teach him to communicate.

A MOTHER LOOKS AT PRT

To be honest, I wasn't even going to write a section at the end of this chapter (which we added for the revised, updated edition). After all, PRT is essentially a term for professionals—it even *sounds* clinical. Dr. Koegel's scientific studies and research are what's important in any discussion of it; what can a mom add to it?

But then I realized that, like everything Dr. Koegel discusses in this book, PRT isn't just a term that people can throw around to sound knowledgeable: it's an active, alive, meaningful part of how we helped Andrew grow and blossom into the outgoing young man he is today.

The Pointing Game

The best way I can illustrate this is with a truly wonderful memory of one of our early visits to the Koegels' autism clinic. We arrived that day with a couple of specific questions for Dr. Koegel, one of which was how we could get Andrew to look at something when we pointed to it. He was already over nine at this point—I know, because we had brought all four kids to the appointment and our youngest is almost nine years younger than Andrew—but he still didn't get the concept of pointing. If I said, "Your book is over there," and pointed at a table, he would look at my finger, not at the table—and often at neither.

I didn't know enough at that point to use the phrase "joint attention," but I'm sure Dr. Koegel instantly had those words in her head. I did know enough (because of my three other kids) to be aware that typical children love to point things out to their parents and expect parents to point things out to them. In fact, most of my memories of Franny's early years were of carrying her in my arms while she sucked on a pacifier and pointed imperiously at everything she wanted to show me or wanted me to get for her.

And meanwhile nine-year-old Andrew didn't understand that when he asked where his backpack was and I pointed to it, I was answering his question.

Dr. Koegel thought for a while—she's the most thoughtful person in the world—and then nodded and said, "Okay, here's what we're going to do. . . ."

She told us all to leave the room for five minutes, then she called us back in and said to the kids, "I've hidden M&M's all around the room. I'm going to point to where they're hidden and you can take turns finding them—and eating them." The kids were thrilled. They were going to get to eat candy? Talk about motivation!

Leo and Franny were all over this game. The second Dr. Koegel pointed at a hidden spot, they were racing over to find the M&M's and eat them. Andrew was a little slower at first, but he figured it out pretty quickly: between the candy rewards and the fact that his siblings were modeling the behavior for him, he suddenly understood that when someone pointed at something, you weren't supposed to look directly at the pointing finger, but instead follow an imaginary line in the air to an object. Pretty soon all three kids were flying around the room, laughing and begging for another turn and getting all sugared up.

I'm not exaggerating when I say that from that day on, we could point things out to Andrew and he knew where to look.

It sounds kind of miraculous, but the truth is that this little game simply incorporated the most basic and brilliant tenets of the Koegels' PRT approach: there was a natural reinforcer (the candy), there was fun (it was a game), there was inclusion (the other kids loved playing it, too, and still remember how exciting it was to find those M&M's), and it was something we could easily incorporate into our own daily life—even though we played it in the office, it was the easiest game in the world to do at home, and if we needed to work more on that skill, we could set it up in an instant, or even just make sure we covered up and then pointed to any of Andrew's favorite foods (or his beloved orange juice), telling him it was a game and he had to find it.

Finally, and most importantly, this one activity successfully focused on improving Andrew's joint attention skills . . . which made him more responsive and more social all across the board. Now when peers and teachers pointed to something, he'd know where to look, just like everyone else.

Fifteen minutes in Dr. Koegel's office did all that. No wonder she was (and remains) my hero.

Empathy

Dr. Koegel has already discussed above how she doesn't feel that kids with ASD necessarily lack empathy, even though many professionals claim they do; she believes it's more likely that they lack the skill to express it than the feeling itself. And I just want to say how deeply I agree with her.

It's sort of a parallel situation to the way people used to say that kids with autism had low IQs. The truth seems to be that, for the most part, they just don't have the social or language skills or the motivation to do well on IQ tests, which is a very different thing. I truly believe much of the same is true with the idea of empathy—that people are looking at an inability to *express* empathy and calling it a *lack* of empathy, when it's something quite different.

CONCLUSION
Another Angle on Andrew

YOU'VE now read this book and gotten an idea of Andrew from Claire's perspective, but I thought the clinician angle might also be interesting.

Andrew was a preschooler when I first met him. Like so many children with autism, Andrew was beautiful. He had stunning big blue eyes surrounded by long dark eyelashes, and his head was completely topped with thick, brown, exquisite curls. Behind Andrew was his mother—petite, slim, attractive, and unpretentious—and his tall, friendly father. Rob, Andrew's dad, got down on the floor and played with Andrew while I talked with Claire.

I still vividly remember our conversation. Claire was really worried about Andrew's hand puppets—he spent hours on end pretending his fingers were little individual characters, talking away to each other. And she was right to be concerned—the hand puppets were stigmatizing and asocial.

But at the time I was more worried about what Andrew *wasn't* doing than what he *was* doing. Clearly, he was able to answer questions (although sometimes I had to ask a few times) with short sentences and clear articulation, but he wasn't asking any questions or initiating any interactions. Thanks to a great team of clinicians, and dedicated parents, he was progressing nicely and steadily for a child with autism. However, we had just finished some research suggesting that if children don't initiate interactions, such as asking questions and using questions to keep a conversation going, they still tend to have significant symptoms of autism when they're older. And there Andrew was, a well-behaved little boy who just sat there until someone asked him a question. He'd usually answer with a slightly mechanical response that sounded like it had been practiced over and over again. He lacked spontaneity, he wasn't attentive, and to be quite honest, he was a pretty lousy conversationalist.

During the next hour, I outlined several areas that I felt would improve Andrew's symptoms. Now that you've read the book, you can probably figure out why I gave Claire the following recommendations, but let me explain a bit.

1. **USE A FUNCTIONAL ANALYSIS FOR ANY PROBLEM OR INAPPROPRIATE BEHAVIORS.** Because I only saw Andrew for a brief period of time, I wasn't sure if his inappropriate behaviors, even the hand puppets, had a function. Was he bored? Was he avoiding tasks? Was he trying to get attention? Claire and Rob had a pretty good intuitive feel as to why he engaged in some of his inappropriate behaviors, but not all. I wanted them to be thinking about when these behaviors were occurring, with whom, what happened before, what happened after, and most important, *why*, on a regular basis.

2. **USE SELF-MANAGEMENT TO INCREASE APPROPRIATE BEHAVIOR DURING FREE TIME.** During most of his free time, Andrew was driven to engage in repetitive and asocial behaviors, whether it was swinging on his swing set for extended periods or endlessly talking to himself. Instead of focusing on simply distracting him from favorite repetitive activities, I wanted them to prompt him to engage in appropriate play and then reward him when he did.

3. **MAKE SURE HE'S ATTENDING BEFORE GIVING INSTRUCTIONS.** During our initial visit Andrew tended to tune out and not respond to others. However, when we got Andrew's attention, simply by calling his name or gently tapping him, he almost always responded. This would be a simple way to increase his responsiveness and decrease his parents' frustration.

4. **INCREASE QUESTIONS AND OTHER CHILD INITIATIONS.** As I said before, I was worried that Andrew wasn't going to make it if all of his interactions were one-sided. In short, you will always look like you have autism if you never initiate any social interactions. Andrew didn't ask even one question during the visit. Not to me, his parents, or anyone, for that matter. This was directly related to my next concern.

5. **TEACH HIM TO "REFLECT BACK" AND ASK QUESTIONS RATHER THAN ONLY TALK ABOUT HIS OWN INTERESTS.** Although Andrew could talk about a few topics that interested him, he really took no interest in others. I probed a few times, saying things like "I have something for you," then waiting. Andrew sat there silently. "I had a great lunch today." Again, Andrew sat there silently. And so on. It was clear that we had to teach him how to listen to another person and then reflect back and make comments

about what they just said. Otherwise, he would never be able to keep a conversation going.

6. **WORK ON PAST TENSE.** As I said before, Andrew was pretty good at answering direct questions and labeling things, but he had difficulty discussing the past. If you asked him what he did yesterday, he could get the message across that he went to school, but he said "I go to school," instead of "I *went* to school." This was one remaining language delay that still lingered to interfere with his social interactions.

7. **KEEP AN EYE ON RESPONSIVENESS AND RATE OF RESPONDING.** Andrew still seemed to have difficulty responding on a regular basis, but I felt that with everything else, he might just improve in this area without a special program.

8. **GIVE HIM FEEDBACK WHEN HE'S ENGAGING IN SELF-STIM.** One thing that struck me when I first met the LaZebniks was how well their children behaved. Each one, no matter what age, was perfect. They played nicely with their toys and with each other, they cleaned up everything they played with, and never once did any of them have a behavior problem. But I could tell that this was no accident. Rob and Claire were constantly guiding their children, praising them for their good behavior, and when one accidentally played too roughly or improperly with a toy, they would, in their kind and gentle manner, remind him or her not to do that. But with Andrew and his stim, it was different. If he engaged in repetitive behaviors, like the hand puppets, they were afraid to say anything. Andrew's language was pretty good, and his comprehension was up there, so I asked Claire if they had ever thought of simply telling Andrew that things like the puppet talk looked silly when he did them in public. Claire said that, as much as she worried about the puppets, she had never thought about plainly telling him that it looked funny when he did that. She said it was interesting that she had never thought of telling him, because she was perfectly willing to tell her other children not to pick their noses or engage in some other childhood habit in public. So she did, and that was the beginning of Andrew's learning when and where he could stim. I also was pretty sure that we'd see less and less stim as Andrew started initiating more and engaging in more meaningful conversations, but I also felt that he wasn't fully aware that the stim was an inappropriate thing to do and I thought he might actually appreciate the feedback.

This was our first of many meetings, and over the years I have come to love this family. I've been impressed not only by the way they've wholeheartedly tackled every problem and symptom of Andrew's autism, but also by the respect Claire and Rob have for each other. Whenever I talk to Rob, he has something really complimentary to say about Claire, and Claire's always saying something flattering and loving about Rob. I know some of the early years were difficult, and that the stress of Andrew's diagnosis affected their marriage to the point where they had to get some couples therapy. So it hasn't always been easy for them. But they've faced every obstacle as a devoted and loving team, supporting one another. And if there is a problem that seems to be affecting their family, their marriage, or Andrew, they tackle it. Furthermore, since we started this book, Claire and I have had at least daily phone conversations and sometimes multiple daily phone conversations, and she is completely incredible in the way she can multitask—keeping four kids happy while talking on the phone and writing all at the same time. I'm not really sure how she does it, but she does it well.

ANDREW TODAY

Years ago I attended a party celebrating Claire's first published novel. All four of the LaZebnik children were at the party, and all four were signing autographs, since their names were in the dedication. At the party, Rob gave the warmest and funniest toast I have ever heard. At the end of his toast, Rob mentioned that Claire was currently working on a nonfiction book with me. Immediately after the toast, a guest at the party ran up to me to ask what the new book was about. When I replied, "It's about autism," she looked completely shocked and amazed and said, "How does Claire know anything about autism?" I thought she was going to go into cardiac arrest when I told her that Claire was writing about one of her sons who has autism. She thought for a while, and after an uncomfortable silence she looked at me, puzzled, and said, "Is it Leo?"

Today Andrew is an accomplished artist attending an East Coast college. I see him a few times a year and he's friendly and outgoing. He has roommates and a group of friends. I remember how hard it was for Claire and Rob at times, like when they had to fight for aide support at school and make sure the aide was adequately trained, but it paid off in the long run. Andrew is such a great guy and has already made such great contributions to the world with his warm and friendly personality, unconditional friendship to many, and awesome art creations. Transforming the finger puppets to drawing paid off! He's sweet and talented. You couldn't ask for a nicer guy. I could see why the friend had trouble guessing which kid. Andrew's symptoms are now so mild that he seems like he's within the typical range.

IS ANDREW CURED?

A few weeks ago we had a consultant, another autism researcher from a major university, come to our center. When I was driving him from his hotel to our center, he said, "Have you ever cured a kid?" I told him that I never use the word "cure," since we don't even know what autism really is, but if he meant, do we have any kids who don't have any symptoms of autism anymore, yes, we do, lots of them. Then I asked, "How about you?" and he replied, "Yes, we do, too."

But what does it mean not to have any symptoms? If I met Andrew today, in a context outside the clinic, I wouldn't pick him out as a kid with autism. He does ask questions and take an interest in other people. He can carry on a conversation, and if there's a pause he'll ask a question or make an interesting comment. And, he's *super* sweet. I don't think he has a mean bone in his body. He is always thoughtful and positive. Since we don't know the cause or cure for autism, I guess I can just say that he's overcome it.

WHAT DOES THE FUTURE HOLD?

No one can read the future—not for any child, and especially not for a child with autism. I often lie awake at night worrying about the kids I work with. I worry when they aren't making the progress I want them to make or when the progress is just too slow. (I wish I didn't lie awake worrying, since it affects my work the next day, but I just can't help it.) I must admit, I did stress about Andrew a bit when he was little, but now I don't worry about him at all. He doesn't cause me any sleepless nights.

Of course, I know Rob and Claire still worry about him more than they do their other kids. But now that he's an adult, he dates and goes out with friends and is a great conversationalist, and I'm guessing that he'll find a wife who adores all the remarkable things he has to offer. If someone didn't know about all he and his family had to overcome, they'd guess he's just a typical outgoing adult.

WHAT ABOUT THE OTHER CHILDREN?

We're not there yet. While just about all children improve with behavioral interventions, just how much and how quickly they'll improve varies considerably. There are still lots of unknowns with children with autism, and although researchers are working on finding more effective interventions, we can't really rest until all the children are doing as well as Andrew. More federal funding needs to be allocated for research on behavioral interventions, so that families whose children have autism can find solutions to dealing with their symptoms on a day-to-day basis. This research benefits everyone—the procedures that work with children with autism also work with their peers, and logically so. All kids have communication problems, difficulties in certain social situations, behavior problems, and so on—it's just where you are on the continuum.

The bottom line is, if we continue to refine and improve interventions based on scientific research, then one day maybe all children with autism will improve to the extent that Andrew and so many others have.

APPENDIX

BEHAVIOR DATA SHEET

DATE:

NAME:

BEHAVIORS

TIME						
PLACE						

NOTES

BEFORE:
Told to do something
Change in activity
Moved
Alone
Interrupted
Told "No"

AFTER:
Given attention
Given something
Lost something
Removed from area
Ignored
Punished
Request withdrawn

WHY:
Get out of...
Transition
To obtain...
Attention
Avoid (person/place)
Other: Specify

From *Understanding Why Problem Behaviors Occur: A Guide for Assisting Parents in Assessing Causes of Behavior and Designing Treatment Plans,* by W. D. Frea, L.K. Koegel, and R. L. Koegel (1994).

TOILET TRAINING DATA SHEET

U = URINE   B = BOWEL   N = NOTHING   SI = SELF-INITIATION

Place	Date	Time	Accident-u/b	Taken to toilet u-b-n	SI-u/b

From *Toilet Training for Children with Severe Handicaps: A Field Manual for Coordinating Training Procedures Across Multiple Community Settings*, by G. Dunlap, R. L. Koegel, and L. K. Koegel (1989).

RESOURCES

WE hope that by now you've read this book thoroughly and that it has helped you with practical and tested procedures for setting in place a coordinated program of interventions for your child, with the help and guidance of professionals in your area.

Along the way, questions and issues may come up that will send you searching for more information. In addition, new and improved findings are regularly discovered that will continue to help your child. We've therefore put together a short list of resources that we feel will be valuable as a next step for parents and educators. We encourage you to keep reading and questioning. The more you know, the greater an asset you will be to your child.

FURTHER INFORMATION ON OUR WORK

There have been estimates that it takes about ten years from the time a research finding is made until it gets into everyday practice. Feel free to contact us at our Web site (www.autismprthelp.com) for the latest research and treatment findings, grant projects, training projects, and other information. You may also find information about our autism research and training center and the techniques we use when you search "Pivotal Response Treatment," "Pivotal Response Training," or "Pivotal Response Teaching" on the Internet. "Pivotal Response" is the name given to our work because our research is focused on pivotal behaviors. When the child is taught pivotal behaviors, such as motivated responding, self-management, initiations, empathetic responses, and responsivity to multiple cues, we see lots of positive changes in other areas. Getting these freebies is what it's all about: our goal is to speed up the habilitation process so our children can overcome their symptoms as quickly and efficiently as possible.

ADDITIONAL BOOKS

Educating Children with Autism by the National Research Council (Washington, DC: National Academy Press, 2001)

Our first suggestion is the National Research Council's book that reviews many procedures and presents ten comprehensive programs. The book is helpful because it was put together by a committee that consisted of well-respected researchers in the area of autism. Catherine Lord, who is well known for her work in developing diagnostic tools for autism, chaired the committee. The book includes a comprehensive review of the literature and summarizes it so that parents and practitioners can get a feel for what is going on in science today. It also reviews ten comprehensive programs (including ours, listed under "Pivotal Response Training") and, based on the research, provides important treatment suggestions, such as starting intervention early, providing lots of treatment hours for your child, coordinating programs with families, and so on.

The PRT Pocket Guide: Pivotal Response Treatment for Autism Spectrum Disorders, by Robert L. Koegel and Lynn Kern Koegel (Baltimore, MD: Paul H. Brookes, 2012)

The pocket guide will give you more information on Pivotal Response Treatment and the techniques discussed in this book.

Teaching Children with Autism: Strategies for Initiating Positive Interactions and Improving Learning Opportunities, by Robert L. Koegel and Lynn Kern Koegel (Baltimore, MD: Paul H. Brookes, 1995)

This book also discusses PRT but is a bit more academic. It has lots of references and more data than *The PRT Pocket Guide,* above.

Sleep Better!: A Guide to Improving Sleep for Children with Special Needs, by V. Mark Durand (Baltimore, MD: Paul H. Brookes, 1998)

If your child is still having trouble sleeping, Durand has a whole book on suggestions for dealing with sleep difficulties.

The Everyday Advocate: Standing Up for Your Child with Autism, by Areva Martin (New York: New American Library, 2010)

This book has helpful suggestions for getting services and advocating successfully for your child. Martin has a child with autism and understands what parents go through.

MANUALS

If you would like more information on some of the specific intervention procedures described in this book, in an easy-to-read format with self-quiz questions, you may want to check out our manuals, available at our Web site (www.autismprthelp.com).

Using Pivotal Response Treatment to Teach First Words to Children with Autism (2011), by Lynn Kern Koegel

Pivotal Response Treatment: Using Motivation as a Pivotal Response (2011), by Lynn Kern Koegel

Teaching the Pivotal Behavior of Initiations to Children with Autism (2011), by Lynn Kern Koegel

Pivotal Response Treatment: Improving Socialization in Individuals with Autism (2012), by Lynn Kern Koegel

How to Teach Self-Management to People with Severe Disabilities: A Training Manual (1992), by Robert L. Koegel, Lynn Kern Koegel, and Deborah Rumore Parks

Increasing Success in School Through Priming: A Training Manual (1992), by Laura D. Wilde, Lynn Kern Koegel, and Robert L. Koegel

Toilet Training for Children with Severe Handicaps: A Field Manual for Coordinating Training Procedures Across Multiple Community Settings (1989), by Glen Dunlap, Robert L. Koegel, and Lynn Kern Koegel

Understanding Why Problem Behaviors Occur: A Guide for Assisting Parents in Assessing Causes of Behavior and Designing Treatment Plans (1994), by William Frea, Lynn Kern Koegel, and Robert L. Koegel

JOURNALS

Again, because of dedicated researchers, lots of new information is accumulating daily, and you will find many of the newest discoveries in journals. There are many to choose from, and most, like the following ones, offer practical solutions. They present recent research and developments in the field, so you may find it helpful to subscribe to more than one.

Focus on Autism and Other Developmental Disabilities
    Subscriptions and articles through: PRO-ED, 8700 Shoal Creek Blvd., Austin, TX 78757-6897, or its Web site: www.proedinc.com

Journal of Autism and Developmental Disorders
    Subscriptions and articles through: http://link.springer.com/journal/10803

Journal of Positive Behavior Interventions
    Subscriptions and articles through: PRO-ED, 8700 Shoal Creek Blvd., Austin, TX 78757-6897, or its Web site: www.proedinc.com

ORGANIZATIONS

The following national organizations hold regular conferences where you can hear about the latest discoveries long before they are published and applied to everyday practice. In addition, most of these organizations have newsletters or journals with current information and helpful resources. They can also help you to find support groups and professionals in your area. Most of the organizations are also strong advocates for families of children with autism and other disabilities and regularly advocate to state and national government agencies.

Association for Behavior Analysis International (ABAI) (www.abainternational.org). This organization has smaller conferences in almost every state, so check for your local one if the international one is too far to travel to.

Association for Positive Behavior Support (APBS) (www.APBS.org)

Autism Society (www.autism-society.org). This organization has local chapters in many cities.

Autism Speaks (www.autismspeaks.org). Autism Speaks doesn't hold conferences but it does have a lot of great resources.

TASH (www.tash.org). Formerly the Association for Persons with Severe Handicaps, "Tash" also has many state chapters that have state conferences.

Also check out our annual PRT conference at the University of California in Santa Barbara, California (www.education.ucsb.edu/autism).

INDEX